# WORLD PRICES AND DEVELOPMENT

In memory of Dudley Seers

who made this book possible, and who contributed so much by his academic excellence and his personal warmth which made work on it enjoyable.

# World Prices and Development

edited by

Stephany <u>Griffith-Jones</u>
and
Charles Harvey

Gower

Published by
Gower Publishing Company Limited,
Gower House,
Croft Road,
Aldershot,
Hants GU11 3HR,
England

Gower Publishing Company,
Old Post Road,
Brookfield,
Vermont 05036,
U.S.A.

British Library Cataloguing in Publication Data

World prices and development.
  1. Developing countries—Economic conditions
  2. Prices—Developing countries
  I. Griffith-Jones, Stephany    II. Harvey, Charles, *1937–*
  338.5 2 091724    HC59.7

ISBN  0–566–00890–4

ISBN  0–566–00891–2 Pbk

Typeset in Great Britain by
Guildford Graphics Limited, Petworth, West Sussex.
Printed and bound in Great Britain by
Biddles Ltd, Guildford, Surrey.

# Contents

# Foreword

For several years there has been an increasing awareness among the world's development aid institutions of the effect of inflation on the efforts of Third World countries striving for economic and social development. The Kuwait Fund for Arab Economic Development, established in 1961, first recognised the problem during the second half of the 1960s, when the emerging inflationary trends and their adverse consequences for economic developments of the poorer nations became apparent. This early recognition emanated from a close understanding of the detrimental effects of inflation on resource allocation and income distribution in those countries, which were exacerbated by their lack of appropriate corrective measures and policy instruments to cope with what was a rapidly intensifying problem. As a consequence, the capital funds directed by the development aid institutions to the financing of development projects and programmes were being continually eroded. All these factors contributed to an increasing realisation of the need for a deep and comprehensive investigation of this far-reaching and seemingly intractable problem.

Although inflation is by no means a solely recent phenomenon, the speed with which modern inflation has been transmitted internationally and the rate at which its impact on developing countries has escalated have given added cause for concern. The increased intensity of inflation and the structural changes taking place in many Third World countries seem to have facilitated the speed of imported inflation to the developing world in general. Their increased demand for industrial goods, foodstuffs and energy, at the same time as they face much higher interest rates, have underlined the urgency of the need to understand the process by which imported inflation is transmitted. It is vital to know its effects on the development process, and also to assess the efficiency of the consequent adjustment policies adopted by various countries. Since the late 1970s, many of these countries have been facing deteriorating terms of trade, worsening balance of payments, and rapidly escalating indebtedness. The critical situation in which such countries have found themselves transcends the more usual problems of resource allocation, as the problems caused have struck at the very roots of their prospects for long-term growth and development. The urgency of a thorough investigation into the basic problem has been compounded by these more recent events.

In view of the importance of the study, it was felt that an independent institution of internationally-recognised competence and with long experience of development issues should be entrusted with its execution. The Institute of Development Studies at the University of Sussex was a natural and appropriate choice. In turn, the Institute adopted similar criteria in their choice of specialists to assist in the studies of individual countries which constitute a central part of the overall investigation.

Given the varying economic conditions prevailing among Third World countries and the need to make a comparative evaluation of their various adjustment policies, a group of eleven countries was selected to provide as wide a coverage as possible. Countries at different stages of development, with dissimilar resource endowment, diverse social and economic systems and different balances of trade in food, energy and capital goods were identified for close study and analysis. Apart from a short review of the previous economic development of each, emphasis was placed on investigating the extent of imported inflation, its impact on development efforts, and the nature of adjustment policies adopted to alleviate its distortive effects. In each study particular attention was paid to the assessment of success achieved by the adjustment policies adopted. Despite the wide diversity of the economic and social conditions among developing countries, it was hoped that it would at least be possible to draw some general conclusions that would prove of use to policy makers and others concerned with development issues.

At various stages of the study, IDS initiated a series of workshops and informal meetings to exchange views and to discuss experience. In addition to IDS staff, those attending included individuals responsible for country studies, invited participants, and ourselves. These exchanges of view contributed to a better understanding of the various issues relating to each country study and made it possible to develop a common sense of appreciation of the overall problems associated with imported inflation, the main phenomenon under investigation. The success of these joint exchanges became immediately apparent. The extensive body of knowledge already available to IDS, the first-hand familiarity with their detailed subjects of the individuals undertaking the country studies, and the practical experience of the representatives of the sponsoring agencies all combined to make each meeting a valuable contribution to the overall study and to the improved understanding of each participant. The coordination of the work of individual contributors afforded by such meetings is evident, and the support which they gave to each contributor has significantly enhanced the quality and therefore the usefulness of the study and its final outcome.

M.W. Khouja

A-K.T. Sadik

# Acknowledgements

We wish to express our thanks to the many people and institutions which have co-operated on this research programme and book. We owe a very special debt of gratitude to the late Dudley Seers who contributed so much to make this project possible, and who enriched so much the work of all those involved in it.

We are extremely grateful to the Kuwait Fund for Arab Economic Development and The OPEC Fund for International Development, not only for contributing significantly to financing this research but also for making an important academic input into the programme. We also wish to thank the Leverhulme Trust for financing the Brazil and Argentina case studies and CENDES in Venezuela for self-financing its case study.

We would like to express our appreciation to the outside participants in our workshop. Dr M. Khoudja, Mr D. J. Ordoobadi, Professor G. Ranis, Dr A. Sadik, and Mrs F. Stewart for giving us their valuable time and comments; we were also very grateful to all authors of the case studies for attending this workshop, thus contributing more broadly to the project. We especially wish to thank our colleague Reg Green, for contributing so very generously with his time and insights to the final manuscript.

The opinions contained in this book are the sole responsibility of the individual authors under whose names they appear, and do not necessarily reflect the opinion of their institutions or the funding agencies.

Marion Huxley, Joan Thomas, Danielle Hodges, Pat Lacey and Sue Kirwan diligently helped type and prepare the final manuscript.

Stephany Griffith-Jones

Charles Harvey

# The Contributors

**Marta Bekerman** Institute of Development Studies, University of Sussex, 1982/83; currently CENDES, Buenos Aires, Argentina.

**Reginald Herbold Green** Institute of Development Studies, University of Sussex.

**Stephany Griffith-Jones** Institute of Development Studies, University of Sussex.

**Ricardo Hausmann** CENDES, Caracas, Venezuela.

**Charles Harvey** Institute of Development Studies, University of Sussex.

**In June Kim** Department of International Economics, Seoul National University, Korea.

**D.J.M. Kamari** Director of Economic Research and Policy, Bank of Tanzania.

**G. Kurukulasuriya** Marga Institute, Sri Lanka.

**G. Marquez** CENDES , Caracas, Venezuela.

**Philip Mishalani** Institute of Development Studies, University of Sussex.

**Peter Sadler** Planning Economic Industrial Development Advisers (Wales).

**Dudley Seers** Institute of Development Studies, University of Sussex.

# 1 Introduction

*Stephany Griffith-Jones*[1]

> 'to recommend thrift to the poor is both grotesque and insulting.
> It is like advising a man who is starving to eat less.'
>
> *Oscar Wilde (1890)*

The impact of imported inflation and other major changes in the
international environment on individual national economies has become
of increasing significance, particularly during the 1970s and early 1980s
when very large changes occurred in international prices, in the
volumes and direction of international trade and in the magnitude and
composition of international financial flows.

Much of the debate and research on the policy response to changes in
the international environment has until now been focused on short-
term adjustment.[2] Implicit in such an analysis is the assumption that
financial equilibria (both of internal variables such as inflation and
external variables such as the current account of the balance of
payments) are a pre-condition for healthy development. As a consequence, the restoration of balance once disturbed (for example by
external events) is considered to have priority over all other objectives.
The impact of different forms of short-term adjustment on growth and
particularly on development has often been neglected in such analysis.
Furthermore, the emphasis on short-term adjustment also implies the
assumption that the international environment has remained – in terms
of conditions and stability – as easy to adjust to as during the brief
disruptions of the 1950s and 1960s, disregarding the more profound and
drastic recent changes in the international economy.

This project attempts to redress the balance, by laying particular stress, in its evaluation of countries' policy responses on changes in the international environment, to the long-term implications for those countries' growth and development.

The need for an approach which stresses the link between adjustment and development was becoming even more evident in the late 1970s. Chenery (1979) wrote:

The conventional separation between stabilisation and development, or short-term and long-term policies, has become increasingly inappropriate to the international economic problems of this decade (the seventies), in which the adjustment policies of individual countries must be assessed over periods of five to ten years and are heavily dependent on actions by other countries.

In a similar vein, a major UNCTAD/UNDP study directed by S. Dell and R. Lawrence (1980) emphasised

the importance, at both national and international levels, of placing the adjustment process in the broader context of long-term development strategies and needs. A period of adjustment should be nothing more than an episode in a long-run process, and it is therefore indispensable that the categorical imperatives of the short-run should not be allowed to dominate and perhaps even overwhelm the requirements of the long-run.

In particular, this research programme is concerned with the impact of rises in import prices on national economies. In this respect we will attempt to evaluate not only the short-term impact of such changes and of policy responses, but also the changes carried out in development strategies and the impact of both on long-term development.

Furthermore, the short-term view of adjustment usually tends to over-emphasise financial variables of a macro-economic nature, neglecting to a large extent the study of necessary physical changes in the patterns of production, investment, consumption and trade. This research programme attempts to analyse countries' policy responses to imported inflation related to particular key sectors, especially the energy and food sectors. Although the decisive importance of sectoral considerations in adjustment has been stressed by some authors (particularly Dell and Lawrence 1980) there has been very limited research on countries' sectoral responses to changes in the international environment and their links with overall macro economic adjustment. We hope that our project makes an initial contribution to work in this field and may perhaps encourage further much-needed research in it. We would like here to emphasise the particularly valuable contribution of the late Professor Dudley Seers, who throughout his involvement in the project insisted on the importance of sectoral considerations.

A further element which we have attempted to introduce into our analysis in a greater depth than it is examined in most existing studies on adjustment is the interaction between political and economic elements. In examining individual country experiences it seems essential to evaluate to what extent political factors have placed a 'constraint' on the options open for adjustment. At the same time, it is necessary to evaluate – from the positive side – to what extent the existence (or absence) of certain political forces may in some countries imply the avoidance of extreme adjustment measures (for example, drastic curtailment of real wages) which though 'desirable' from a short-term adjustment or financial point of view may be detrimental to large sectors of the population and/or to the country's growth and development prospects. This latter statement by no means implies an underestimation of the crucial significance of short-term and financial variables for the viability of long-term development.

In fact, in dealing with adjustment policies it is often difficult to establish where scientific economics ends and political preference begins. In this respect our approach did *not* begin with an explicit hypothesis about an 'optimum' short or long-term adjustment policy, e.g. in aspects such as 'optimum' speed and depth of 'opening up' of economies. The main reason is that following writers such as Diaz-Alejandro (1979), we believed that 'judgements about the speed of adjustment in different markets and evaluation of the social costs of alternative dynamic patterns are still based mostly on hunches and sketchy evidence'. As a consequence, we believed a certain level of eclecticism was inevitably required, as well as an explicit statement of political preferences where those preferences have an impact on the conclusions reached. In this respect, we would like to make explicit the high priority we have tried to place on variables such as a more egalitarian income distribution and a greater level of national autonomy in policy-making. However, we have tried not to underestimate – as some 'structuralist' or 'Marxist' authors may do – the crucial significance of financial variables and a minimum of financial equilibrium, not only for the sustainment of economic growth but also for achieving targets such as increasing national autonomy (a clear discussion of the relationship between both can be found in Seers' Preface to Griffith-Jones, 1981).

A final caveat should perhaps be made here about political preferences in our analysis. Although the authors of the different country studies worked to a common previously agreed outline, their political preferences were not uniform or necessarily close to those of the editors of this volume. The criteria for choosing the authors were academic · excellence and knowledge of the country to be analysed (often their own) and *not* acceptance of certain political or ideological assumptions.

In our analysis we have assumed that uniform models and even criteria of evaluation applied to all countries have a real but limited explanatory value, even though comparisons and some 'lesson-extraction' can be valuable, if very carefully carried out and if differences as well as potential similarities between country experiences are equally stressed. However, such comparisons are not a substitute for contextual analysis nor for formulating specific analytical and policy hypotheses for any individual country.

In this respect we would like particularly to emphasise the need to examine the specific structural features of each economy (such as its size, its previous experience and level of industrialisation, the structure of its trade, the degree of its 'openness' and the availability of technical skills and infrastructure). We believe that it is such features, together with an understanding of political and social forces in the country, which determine countries' differential ability to adjust to changes in the international environment.

Furthermore, the need to adjust at all in the short-term to unfavourable changes in the international environment (and if so how far and how fast) is determined not only by the size of those changes (or 'shocks', as it became fashionable to call them in the 1970s due to their large magnitude) but by the availability of additional external finance. Particularly in the 1970s (but also in other decades), access to foreign financial flows was clearly unequal for different categories of countries. Some countries, such as the industrialised ones and the so-called middle-income developing countries, had unprecedented access to large private international credits which practically allowed them (for a few years at least) to reject any idea that a deficit on their current account would have to be solved mainly through recession; other countries had large access to official flows due, for example, to 'geo-political' reasons. Such an option of postponing adjustment to the current account deficit through large net inflows of foreign finance was clearly not feasible for a number of the poorer developing countries without 'geo-political' importance, who had very limited access to such foreign exchange resources.

It would therefore seem necessary to be particularly careful about overall comparisons and generalisations on policy responses of completely different countries. Relevant comparisons of countries with relatively similar economic structures and levels of development seem much more feasible, even though consideration still needs to be given to political and cultural differences.

In a similar vein, it seems important not to extrapolate mechanically conclusions which may be valid for one period (e.g. the mid-1970s) to other periods in which the international environment is quite different (e.g. early 1980s). As Lewis (1980) has pointed out, development theory (and to a certain extent policy) has clearly lagged behind world trade trends. In the 1950s and early 1960s (when world trade had a very dynamic growth) the dominant development economic theories (e.g. two-gap model, structural inflation) were influenced by the poor performance of the previous inter-war period and would have made more sense had world trade been stagnant. Only in the late 1960s was the rapid growth of world trade clearly perceived and the emphasis placed on export-led development strategies. During the 1970s, the growth rate of world trade practically halved (in the early 1980s it was further reduced and in 1982 was even negative); nobody knows whether this deterioration is temporary or permanent. Many economists (particularly more orthodox ones) have, however, continued to advocate policies such as export-led growth, which may have been for some countries extremely successful in earlier periods but whose potential for growth is under substantial doubt unless and until world trade recovers the rapid growth which it had after the Second World War. Similarly, theories, policy analysis and policy-making during the 1970s assumed (particularly but not only in more orthodox circles) almost as a *permanent* feature of the world economy, the existence of large net transfers of private financial credits to certain developing countries. As has become particularly clear since late 1982 (and as should have been clear to anybody who had examined the history of private flows to developing countries during the last century), this was in fact a very bold and simplistic assumption. In this respect perhaps the most fundamental critique of perceptions that stress as 'optimum' for developing countries those policies which maximise 'opening up' of the economy, both in trade and capital flows, is that they pretend to be permanent or ahistorical; they are in fact much more relevant in times of rapid growth of world trade and large sustained net financial flows to those countries, which occur only during certain discreet periods in economic history and are perhaps more the exception than the rule. Because we believe that an understanding of changes in the international environment plays such an important role in defining appropriate policies and strategies, we have devoted an important section of our research programme (and this book) to this aspect.

It seems worth emphasising that just as it is incorrect to extrapolate the past booming conditions of world trade and financial flows, it would also seem incorrect to project the gloomy performance of the world economy in the early 1980s into the future and extract policy prescriptions largely from such a projection. Perhaps the main lesson from recent violent fluctuations in the world economy is the need to design adjustment and development strategies which imply a maximum of potential flexibility, given high levels of uncertainty and variability in almost all economic variables which are internationally determined (prices of commodities and of industrial goods, levels of international interest rate, level and composition of world trade and world financial flows).

The situation in the early 1980s seems to have become particularly difficult for all categories of developing countries. Practically all of them (with very few exceptions such as India) have seen their rates of growth slow down, grind to a halt or even decline absolutely during the early 1980s; this is in sharp contrast with the mid-1970s when some developing countries not only grew at a faster rate than the industrialised ones, but were also able to sustain or even increase their growth rate in spite of a deteriorating international environment.

This generalised deterioration in developing countries' performance in the early 1980s seems to be the result of three closely inter-linked phenomena, which we will attempt to describe briefly here and explore in further detail in the case studies which will follow and in the concluding chapter.

The first is the very negative evolution of the international economy and particularly the longer recession of industrialised countries from 1979 through 1982/83. This seems to explain the sharp contrast between the development of the different groups of non-oil exporting countries' current account external balances in the early 1980s and in the mid-1970s. In 1976–77 there was a marked narrowing of aggregate current account imbalances in the different groups of non-oil exporting countries, followed in 1978 by the re-emergence of something like the pre-1974 world structure of current account balances, with the industrial countries again becoming the main net suppliers of goods and services to the rest of the world. As the recession was short in the mid-1970s, those countries with access to credits could relatively easily ride it out by borrowing. In contrast, in 1982 the recorded current balances of industrial countries were still in deficit, while the aggregate deficits of non-oil exporting developing countries were larger in proportion to world exports than in 1976–77. This seems to have been largely due to the widespread adoption of strong anti-inflationary policies after 1979 in the industrial countries (as reduction of inflation became the main target of industrial countries' economic policies) which depressed their demand for much longer than in the mid-1970s and led to significantly higher nominal interest rates in their currencies. This implied that real interest rates increased from very low or even negative levels in the mid-1970s to very high levels since 1979 (as nominal interest rates rose sharply and as inflation slowed down). As a result, developing countries

(and particularly oil-importing ones) were simultaneously burdened by
a decline in demand for their exports (reflected in slower growth or even
decline in the volume of these exports) and by considerably higher
service payments on foreign debt; the Bank for International Settlements
(1983) estimates that non-OPEC developing countries' net interest
payments on their external debt almost quadrupled from $11 billion to
$43.5 billion between 1978 and 1982. The simultaneous occurrence of
recession, low world trade growth and high real interest rates in the
early 1980s seems a particularly negative combination which is unique
in economic history.

The second problem was that certain characteristics of the development countries' 'response' to their large deficits during the mid-1970s
have made the problem more serious in the early 1980s. This is clearly
the case with the growth of the 'debt overhang', which would have been
a serious problem (though probably a more manageable one) even
without the long recession in the early 1980s. In particular, the rapidly
growing indebtedness of some developing countries – at the high and
fluctuating interest rates and relatively short maturities which
characterise private bank lending to LDCs – was unsustainable *unless*
very rapid export growth could be maintained and interest rates
remained very low or negative. In other countries (especially the poorer
ones) the 'margins for adjustment' were also dramatically reduced as
the proportion of non-essential consumption goods in total imports
was reduced or as foreign exchange reserves (including access to low
conditionality IMF facilities) were run down. One could argue that in
the mid-1970s the easy adjustment had been done (the term easy is used
in a similar way here as in the distinction between 'easy' and 'difficult'
import substitution); in the early 1980s the only evident short-run
option for adjustment in most developing countries was the undesirable
one of restricting growth or, even worse, causing a decline in total
production.

A third related problem in the early 1980s was that a number of
mitigating factors which in the mid-1970s had helped to protect
developing countries' real GNP growth in the face of a harsh external
environment characterised by low industrial country growth rates and
high global inflation, *were no longer at work – or worked to a far smaller
extent* when industrial countries' growth rates again declined in the
early 1980s. We are referring in particular to factors such as increased
migrants' remittances (both from industrial countries and from oil
exporting ones), increased availability of external finance to developing
countries (both from private and official sources) and to an increased
share of their exports being channelled to other developing countries
(particularly, but not only, oil-exporting ones). All these factors which

helped to sustain developing countries' growth in the mid-1970s while industrial countries' growth declined (Goldstein and Khan 1982) were operating far more weakly in the early 1980s, as slower growth spread to the oil exporting developing countries, as already accumulated debts (and other elements discussed in the next chapter) led to declining net financial flows to developing countries, at very high interest rates, and as overall slower growth in developing countries (including the oil-exporting ones) restricted the possibility of rapid intra-developing countries' trade growth.

The fact that the world recession in the early 1980s has harmed so deeply both industrial countries and practically all groups of developing countries would seem to imply a joint world interest in economic recovery. If, however, the industrial countries' governments continue to give first priority to other objectives (and in particular to that of reducing inflation in their countries still further) it may be necessary for different groups of developing countries' governments (oil exporters and oil importers, food exporters and food importers, low and middle-income countries) to explore jointly mechanisms to boost their national and their collective growth prospects, because they share common interests in growth and development which differ significantly from the current perceived interests of industrial countries' governments. As we will discuss in more depth in the next chapter, it may become increasingly urgent for developing countries' governments to attempt to provide their own growth engine rather than waiting for the industrial countries to provide them with such an engine; instead of – 'collective self-reliance' may become increasingly a practical necessity and not merely an attractive ideological option.

After this brief Introduction, the rest of the book will be divided into three parts. The first part (chapter 2) will review in some detail changes in the world economy after the Second World War, with special emphasis on the period 1971–81. It will first examine the changing performance of the industrial economies since 1945. Then it will analyse world trends in international prices for the same period, with particular emphasis on the prices of foodstuffs, energy and capital goods. Finally, it will review the evolution of financial flows to different categories of developing countries during that period, and draw some conclusions for the 1980s from the previous analysis.

The second part of the book will examine both short-term and long-term policies, through which different countries adjusted to changes in the international environment, with special reference to the impact of imported inflation. Although mention will be made to the historical background, the period analysed will be that of 1971–81.

As the point of entrance for the country analysis is the impact of imported inflation on national policies and on countries' growth and development, we have classified countries according to the way their structures of production are linked to the world economy via their trading patterns.

We have gone further than the simple division fashionable in the 1970s between developing countries which are oil exporters and those which are oil importers, by highlighting three categories of goods traded: cereals, oil and capital goods, (as well as looking at other primary commodities and other manufactures). In each of the categories defined, we have chosen to examine in-depth at least one country's experience.

We have distinguished the following categories of countries:

(a) Countries that are net importers of oil and capital goods and export other primary products:
   (i) cereals importers: Tanzania, Sri Lanka
   (ii) self-sufficient in cereals: Malawi.

(b) Countries that are net importers of oil, capital goods and cereals, but export other manufactured goods and (increasingly) some capital goods: Brazil, Ireland and Korea.

(c) Countries that are self-sufficient in oil and export cereals, but import capital goods: Argentina.

(d) Countries that are net exporters of oil, but import cereals and capital goods:
   (i) small population, so-called capital surplus oil exporters: Kuwait
   (ii) large population: Venezuela
   (iii) net oil exporters, but exporters of other products: Tunisia.

(e) Countries that import oil, cereals and capital goods, and export (minor amounts of) other commodities and manufactures: Jordan.[3]

These categories are only a starting point. During the 1970s, the structure of trade was modified very significantly for some of these countries, and their ability to change, especially in developing an export trade in manufactured goods, was an important part of their response to changes in international prices and other transformations in the international environment.

The analysis of each of the country case studies follows a commonly agreed outline. In the first section, the international determinants of the country's economic developments and policies are examined. In examining the impact of imported inflation, the approach has tried to be much broader than much of the recent conventional literature which focused almost exclusively on the price of oil as a key element in explaining imported inflation.

A first important point to stress is that imported inflation may be caused by the rise in the price of one or several different types of goods. As discussed above, in our analysis we are focusing mainly on the following categories: cereals, oil and capital goods (other primary commodities and other industrial products are residual categories). The importance of price rises in different categories in helping to explain imported inflation varies through time and for different countries.

Second, imported inflation refers not only to rises in the prices of imported goods but also of services. Included in 'services' could be international lending; an important element of imported inflation would be the increase in interest rates.

Third, the concept of imported inflation (that is inflation originating in factors external to a country's economy) should not be limited only to the impact of rises in import prices. Indeed, rises in export prices – if unaccompanied by increases in import prices – may lead to an accumulation of foreign exchange reserves which may cause an important expansion in the money supply. More importantly, particularly in the 1970s, a significant external element in explaining inflation in many developing countries has been the rapid increase in capital inflows. As Bhalla (1981) and others have shown, one of the major mechanisms for the international transmission of inflation during the 1970s was the large growth of foreign exchange reserves, reflecting increased inflows of capital into specific developing countries, which led to unusually high increases in the domestic money supply. Another similar element not mentioned in the literature is the impact in some countries of rapid increases of workers' remittances from abroad (see, for example, the Jordan case study in this volume).

There are two other mechanisms forgotten in the existing literature through which imported inflation may be reflected in national inflation. First, as a result of forced reductions of imports (caused by imported inflation accompanied by a consequent deterioration in the terms of trade) prices may go up nationally because of supply restrictions; this will probably imply an increase in the profit mark-up on cost. Furthermore, supply restrictions will result in cost-push inflation because the lower number of units produced will result in higher fixed costs on each unit (e.g. depreciation, basic wage bill, debt service). Second, if imported inflation is accompanied by a serious deterioration of the terms of trade which leads to a large current account deficit that cannot be externally financed, rapid and forced import substitution and/or export promotion may be feasible (if at all), particularly in less diversified economies, only at a marginal cost which is significantly higher than the average cost of production in that sector. As a result, indirect inflationary pressures may arise from imported inflation, which again would not be examined in a conventional analysis.

After looking at the impact of imported inflation and other changes in the international environment on the domestic economy, each case study analyses the policies pursued by the government to adjust to its impact, with reference to the political and social reasons that led to the choice of the adjustment alternative actually pursued. Two types of national policies are distinguished: macroeconomic ones and micro-economic ones.

In the discussion on macroeconomic policies, focus is placed in each case study on the extent to which such policies basically implied a postponement of adjustment (via reduction of foreign exchange reserves and/or increase of international debt) or actual current adjustment; a further distinction is then made between adjustment based mainly on changes in expenditure levels (basically demand management via monetary, fiscal and/or incomes policies) or based mainly on expenditure switching (via policies affecting the country's international trade flows, through import substitution and/or export promotion). Then, goverment policies applied in the food, energy and capital goods sectors, as a result of increases in imported prices, will be discussed in the subsequent section on microeconomic and sectoral policies.

The impact of the changes in the international environment and of national policies will then be examined at three levels for each country study:

(a) *macroeconomic variables,* which will stress both the financial (inflation and balance of payments) and real variables (rate and composition of growth).

(b) *pattern of development,* which will examine the long-term effects on employment, distribution of real income and consumption of the changes discussed above; in particular an attempt is made in the different case studies to examine the impact (if any) of changing *relative* international prices on the patterns of production technology and on consumption structures. The question will be examined to what extent governments adopted (often perforce) less energy-intensive and foreign-exchange intensive development strategies which might in the long-term stimulate employment and reduce dualism as well as external dependence.

(c) *possible political implications,* which will briefly analyse implications at a national level of the changes previously studied.

In the third and final part of the book, conclusions (where possible) are extracted about similarities and differences which emerge from the country case studies. An assessment will be made of how much the problems and opportunities facing the countries studied can be generalised. Finally, implications will be drawn for suggested policy conclusion both at a national and at an international level. Due to the nature of our research programme, much more emphasis will be placed on national policy conclusions. However, as so many countries faced similar constraints due to the characteristics of the international environment there is inevitably need to refer to desirable international changes and policies which would lead to a more favourable environment for national short and long-term adjustment policies.

## Notes and references

1   The discussion of the research framework for this project was carried out with a number of colleagues. Doubtlessly a major contribution was made by the late Dudley Seers; valuable comments have also been made by Reg Green and Charles Harvey.

2   A good example of such research focused practically exclusively on short-responses can be found in B. Balassa, A. Bargony and A. Richards (1981).

3   Jordan's case is an unusual one. It has a very large 'structural' trade deficit, financed mainly by workers' remittances and official aid (see Chapter 13).

## Bibliography

Balassa, B., Bargony, A. and Richards, A. (1981) *The Balance of Payments Effects on External Shocks and of Policy Responses to These Shocks in Non-OPEC Developing Countries*. Paris, OECD Development Centre Studies.

Bank for International Settlements (1983) *Annual Report*. Basle.

Bhalla, S.S. (1981) 'The transmission of inflation into developing economies' in W. Cline *et al. World Inflation and the Developing Economies*. Washington, DC, The Brooking Institution.

Chenery, H. (1979) 'Comments' on A. Krueger's paper, at Brookings Conference on Economic Stabilisation Policies in Less Developed Countries. October 25, Washington DC.

Dell, S. and Lawrence, R. (1980) *The Balance of Payments Adjustment Process in Developing Countries*. Oxford, Pergamon Press.

Diaz-Alejandro, C.F. (1979) 'Southern cone stabilisation plans'. Paper presented at Brookings Conference on Economic Stabilisation Policies in Less Developed Countries, October 25, Washington, DC.

Goldstein, M. and Khan, M.S. (1982) *Effects of Slowdown in Industrial Countries on Growth in Non-Oil Developing Countries*. International Monetary Fund Occasional Paper no.12, Washington, DC. August.

Lewis, W.A. (1980) 'The slowing down of the engine of growth'. *American Economic Review* vol 70, no. 4, September.

Seers, D. (1981) 'Preface' in S. Griffith-Jones. *The Role of Finance in the Transition to Socialism*. London, Frances Pinter (Publishers).

# 2 Impact of World Prices on Development: The International Environment

*Stephany Griffith-Jones*[1]

## Introduction

This chapter will analyse the impact which changes in international prices have had on development in different categories of countries since the Second World War. Particular emphasis will be placed on the period 1971–81. This should provide the international framework for the country chapters, which focus on national development policies. The changing evolution of international prices, as well as other important international factors such as the availability of international finance, define constraints, risks and opportunities for national growth and development.

We will examine first the evolution of the industrial economies since the Second World War. Particular emphasis will be placed on the difference in the performance of the OECD countries in the 1950s and 1960s (which was very impressive) compared with the stagflation of the 1970s, and the impact which this differential performance had on the so-called developing countries. Second, we will examine the evolution of international prices, for the same period, with particular emphasis on the prices of foodstuffs, energy and capital goods. Third, we will examine the evolution of international financial flows to different categories of developing countries: their influence on how countries have adjusted (or not) to changes in international prices, and their impact on world inflation.

The concept of the 'international environment' has undergone changes with the passage of time.[2] After the Second World War, major developed market economies (and particularly the United States) felt that their own national development and policies conditioned to an important extent world economic developments; in their case, the distinction between internal and external conditions was somewhat blurred. Industrial countries' governments placed the emphasis on liberalising trade and finance; the system was based increasingly on open and non-discriminatory trade, free currency convertibility, international provision of credit facilities for short-term balance of payments adjustments and the encouragement of international private capital flows. The post-war system was remarkably successful, until the late 1960s, in supporting the attainment of high levels of employment and growth in the developed market economies, as well as a rapid expansion in world trade and production. However, as we shall discuss below, although increased liberalisation and the nature of the Bretton Woods system contributed to this rapid growth, other specific measures and conditions in the post-war period (less stressed in the conventional literature) played a very fundamental role.

From the early 1970s the system's performance was much less successful, *even for the developed economies*. Furthermore, the original post-war system has been increasingly replaced by a series of multilateral arrangements which, even though reflecting the liberal objectives of Bretton Woods, gave a prominent role to negotiations as a means of resolving problems.

As a result, the international environment is no longer perceived by developed countries' governments as the reflection of a system tending towards a full employment equilibrium path, but to a certain extent as the outcome of negotiations. National policies are no longer viewed – as in the post-war period – according to their consistency with the rules of a well functioning system, but rather according to their impact on other economies (e.g. recent debates among industrialised countries on US interest-rate policies and on the level of the US exchange rate). Furthermore, it is increasingly accepted that the management of the system requires the participation of a much greater number of countries than in the past, as their national policies have growing influence on the world economy in the spheres of production, trade and finance. The participation in the management of the world economy of developing countries' governments in general – and particularly of certain categories amongst them, e.g. 'newly-industrialised countries' (NICs) and large oil exporters – has begun to be accepted by OECD countries' governments.

The developing countries' governments have always perceived that the development of their economies was critically dependent on the international environment. In the 1950s and 1960s, they did not question the ability of OECD countries to obtain full employment and sustained growth in their economies. Therefore, they emphasised other factors, such as commodity agreements to stabilise their export earnings, higher compensatory balance of payments finance, and increases in official aid.

Their attitude changed in the 1970s. The slow progress of negotiations concerning measures in favour of developing countries within the framework of the existing system led to widespread disillusion concerning the prospects of a reformist strategy. Also the view gained ground that the external environment, even when favourable, was by no means neutral to the kind of domestic development that it rendered feasible. The real turning point was when it became widely realised that full employment in the OECD economies and rapid growth of world trade could no longer be taken for granted. If the system did not guarantee high rates of growth it seemed much less attractive. Governments saw it increasingly as the reflection of negotiations, whose outcome they should attempt to influence. Furthermore, groups of developing countries' governments began to take collective action such as fixing international prices of their commodities, instead of accepting passively what the 'international market' dictated.

## CHANGES IN THE INTERNATIONAL ENVIRONMENT FOR DEVELOPING COUNTRIES 1948–1981

### Evolution of the developed countries

The experience of the 1950s and 1960s in industrialised countries was so positive, as regards a growth path with high employment, low inflation and impressive productivity advances, that the conventional wisdom increasingly accepted such a favourable record as part of the normal course of events, provided that governments followed appropriate demand-management policies and adhered to the rules of the game underpinning the international economic system. As a result, to most observers 'the problems of the pre-war world had been banished to the pages of history as deplorable monuments to an earlier age of economic and political ignorance!'[3]

This favourable record of growth and high employment in industrial countries and particularly, the accompanying growth of world trade, was unprecedented. As can be seen in Table 2.1, the average annual growth rate in the volume of world trade during the period 1948–71 was spectacular: it *was far higher than the growth rates of any previous period for which statistics are available.*

## Table 2.1 Growth of world trade 1820–1980

| *Average annual percentage rates of growth* | |
|---|---|
| 1820–1840 | 2.7 |
| 1840–1870 | 5.5 |
| 1870–1890 | 2.2 |
| 1890–1913 | 3.7 |
| 1913–1938 | 0.4 |
| 1938–1948 | – |
| 1948–1971 | 7.3 |
| 1971–1980 | 5.8 |

*Source:* UNCTAD, *Trade and Development Report,* 1981.

The rapid growth of world trade in 1948–71 was very closely linked to the favourable performance of the industrial countries during that period. Growth rates for industrial production in the main West European countries (UK, Germany and France) were the highest for this century and the evolution of Japanese industrial production followed a similar pattern. Only the US economy experienced slower growth in 1948–71 than in the 1938–48 period.

Indeed, exports of manufactured goods from the main industrial countries were the fastest growing item in world trade, increasing by 770 per cent in the period 1950–71, as compared with 598 per cent for all their exports and only 281 per cent for exports of other countries.[4]

Table 2.1 shows that the international economy does not move along a continuous growth path: it has had long periods of prosperity (like 1840–1870 and 1948–1971) and long period of relative stagnation (for example, 1913–1938). So it seems wrong to extrapolate past trends of growth in estimating future growth. In particular, it was incorrect in the late 1960s to project continued high growth rates for world trade; equally, it would be dangerous today to use the poor performance of world trade in recent years as an estimate for future developments.

Liberal principles of trade and currency convertibility, centred around the Bretton Woods institutions and the General Agreement on Tariffs and Trade (GATT), are often credited for the sustained growth in the post-war period. In particular, the relaxation of quantitative restrictions and the Dillon and Kennedy Rounds of negotiated tariff reductions had a large impact in the 1950s and 1960s. Because the biggest tariff reductions had already been made, the effect of the Tokyo Round in the 1970s must have been much less. While these factors (as well as the fixed exchange rate system established at Bretton Woods and the role of the dollar as reserve currency) undoubtedly contributed to post-war expansion, it is often insufficiently stressed in the conventional literature that there was a specific set of post-war features which also played a fundamental role.

Thus, a combination of enlightenment and self-interest led the US to help finance and support the reconstruction of Western Europe, mainly via the Marshall Plan. Net US government flows to Europe during 1946–51, mostly grants, were extremely large. The increasing regional economic integration of Western Europe, culminating in the establishment of the EEC, made it possible for industrial production in, and trade between, those countries to expand more rapidly.

Undoubtedly, another set of factors which contributed to sustained non-inflationary growth were the conditions in key markets, particularly those of labour, foodstuffs and energy. In most industrial countries, the expansion of the labour force was adequate to sustain high levels of economic activity. In addition, there were large migratory flows to several industrial countries. Consequently, wage settlements were not substantially out of line with productivity gains.

Conditions in the markets for foodstuffs were also favourable to growth in the industrial countries. As can be seen from Figure 2.1, the market price index for cereals was remarkably stable in the 1950s and 1960s. The real price of cereals, particularly in relation to manu-factures, clearly declined during the period 1955–69. Furthermore, the nominal price index for cereals in 1969 was *lower* than that of 1955. Many countries had succeeded in substantially increasing productivity and agricultural output; more importantly, the existence of large grain stocks in the US, resulting from policies of farm support, helped to maintain relatively stable and low prices.

The price of energy (and in particular oil) also declined in real terms during the 1960s (again see Figure 2.1). This implied that the price of petroleum declined in real terms, particularly in relation to manu-factures. Extraction of oil at very low marginal cost led to a low price, un-related to the long-term scarcity of the resouce. The cheap price and abundance of oil facilitated the rapid growth of industrial production in OECD countries; however, it led to the adoption of highly energy-intensive technologies and consumption patterns.

Another factor was the diffusion of new technologies on a world-wide scale. Some analysts see in the initial productivity differentials between OECD countries after the Second World War and the subsequent 'catching up' by the Japanese and West Europeans one of the main impulses for growth. This interpretation stresses that there was a backlog of innovations whose feasibility and profitability the US had demonstrated by 1950, but whose utilisation had been delayed in Europe and Japan by the two world wars and the Great Depression.

## Figure 2.1

### World market price indices for cereals, petroleum and manufactures, 1955–1970 (1963=100)

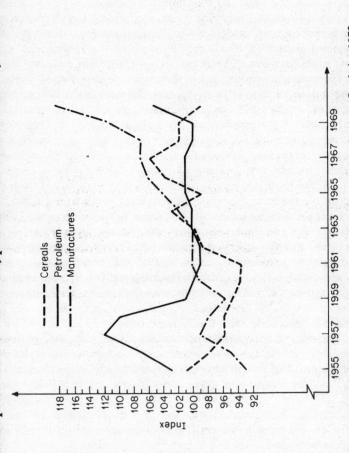

*Source:* UNCTAD, *Handbook of International Trade and Development Statistics, 1972.*

However, many analysts[5] also stress that the differentials in long-term productivity growth (between the US and the rest of the industrial countries) went well beyond a mere 'catching up' and in fact became one of the critical imbalances leading to the problems of the 1970s.

One of the most striking characteristics of the post-war world political economy was that the US emerged – even more than before – as the preponderant power. The differentials in productivity levels in 1950 of the US vis-à-vis Western Europe and Japan were very substantial (see Table 2.2). Particularly striking is the fact that Japanese productivity amounted in 1950 to only 8 per cent of US productivity. From 1950 to 1970, all other OECD countries (except Britain) grew faster than the US, with the Japanese growth rate almost triple the American one. The high growth of GDP reflected higher rates of investment in plant and equipment, and higher growth in productivity, than in the US.

Differential growth rates of productivity and the declining rate of profit seem to be the two main factors which increasingly undermined the possibility of sustained growth in the industrial countries. The effects of the large differential in productivity growth and its impact on a gradually deteriorating US trade position was initially obscured by the

**Table 2.2 Selected indicators of development and structural change of large developed market-economy countries: 1950–70**

| | Index of relative productivity levels (1950: US=100) | Annual average compound growth rate of: | | |
|---|---|---|---|---|
| | | GDP | Manufacturing productivity[a] | Agriculture productivity[b] | Gross fixed capital formation[c] |
| US | 100 | 3.5 | 2.8 | 5.1 | 4.1 |
| UK | 52 | 2.7 | 3.5 | 3.9 | 6.7 |
| France | 42 | 5.1 | 6.1 | 5.3 | 7.4 |
| FDR | 39 | 6.2 | 6.8 | 5.6 | 8.0 |
| Italy | 22 | 5.6 | 7.1 | 5.9 | 7.0 |
| Japan | 8 | 9.4 | 9.8 | 6.1 | 19.7 |

*Source:* UNCTAD, *Trade and Development Report*, 1981.

*Notes:*
(a) Output per man hour in US, France, Federal Republic of Germany; output per employed person in all others. Growth rates cover the period 1959–1970 for France, 1958–1970 for UK and Italy, and 1956–70 for all others.
(b) Value-added per person employed in agriculture (1950–1970).
(c) Excluding residential construction except for Federal Republic of Germany and Japan; growth rates cover the period 1953–1970, except for France (1958–1970).

special status of the dollar as the main reserve currency. However, this special role for the dollar carried in itself a crucial contradiction, often called the Triffin dilemma.[6] This contradiction accentuated world economic problems in the early 1970s. Briefly, the Triffin dilemma was that if the US continued to run a large balance of payments deficit it would provide additional international liquidity. However, the dollar would be increasingly weakened, as US foreign liabilities would inevitably come to exceed by far its ability to convert dollars into gold upon demand and would bring about a 'dollar crisis'. If the US deflated or pursued other measures to reduce this deficit, the dollar would be strengthened but the growth of the US economy and that of the rest of the world would be constrained by insufficient growth of international liquidity (as world reserves would be inadequately increased by gold production at US$35 an ounce).

Clearly, until the late 1960s the US followed the first alternative. Combined with the trend of lower productivity growth (see Table 2.2) this implied that the American trade surplus gradually dwindled away. The US recorded its first trade deficit this century in 1971. Thus in 1971 a trade deficit was added to the very large deficit on capital account which had characterised the US balance of payments since the 1950s – and which reflected mainly large US military expenditure, foreign aid and foreign investment.

The consequent large increase in world monetary reserves must have contributed to some extent to the acceleration of world inflation which began in the late 1960s and continued in the 1970s – even if only by accommodating cost increases and allowing them to be reflected in higher prices (we are not arguing here that the expansion of world money supply mechanically 'caused' an increase in world inflation).

The acceleration of inflation during the 1960s was almost entirely in industrial countries; inflation in non-oil developing countries was much the same at the end as at the beginning of the 1960s.

The collapse of fixed exchange rates and the devaluation of the US dollar in the early 1970s did not produce a long term solution to US current account deficits; but it began a period of exchange rate instability which created great difficulties for developing countries.

Furthermore, as is shown in Table 2.3, the 'recycling' exports of US capital increased even faster in the 1970s than in the 1960s, continuing to fuel the growth of world monetary reserves and world inflation. The average yearly increase of 10.4 per cent in world consumer prices during the 1970s was more than double the rate (4.2 per cent) of the 1960s and triple the 3.5 per cent of the 1950s. *The sustained rise in inflation extended to all areas.* Inflation became a much more global phenomenon. At the end of the 1960s slightly over *one-third* of countries had rates of

**Table 2.3 The US balance of payments: 1960–1979**

| | | *1960–69* | *1970–79* |
|---|---|---|---|
| | | | (US$ billion) |
| A. | US *current account*[a] | +51 | +28 |
| | 1. net earning on past investments | +49 | +150 |
| | 2. other | −2 | −122 |
| B. | 'Recycling': exports of US capital | *94* | *374* |
| | 1. monetary reserves | −5 | 1 |
| | 2. bank claims | 8 | 138 |
| | 3. foreign aid | 35 | 56 |
| | 4. other | 57 | 179 |
| |    i) direct investment | 43 | 124 |
| |    ii) foreign securities | 10 | 34 |
| |    iii) other | 4 | 21 |

*Source:* R. Triffin, 'The contribution of gold and the dollar to the international monetary disorder of the 1970s', paper presented at the North-South Round Table, SID Conference at IDS, Sussex, June 1980. Based on US *Survey of Current Business Statistics*.
    In the original table presented by Triffin, the sum of A and B is equal to the Recorded Debt Increase of the US Treasury, Banks and others, as well as to Statistical Discrepancy.

*Note:* (a) Refers to goods, services and remittances.

increase in consumer prices in excess of 5 per cent; by 1979 this proportion reached *83 per cent*.

Not only did the unequal development of the US and other industrial economies lead to serious financial and economic problems: the decisive shift from the mono-polar situation amongst developed market economies after the war to the multi-polar conditions of today also implied that decision-making on the management of the world economy became increasingly difficult.

A second trend which seemed to be crucial in undermining growth in industrial countries was the decline in corporate profitability. Economists with very different viewpoints (ranging from neo-classical analysts in international financial institutions such as the IMF and the BIS to Marxist academics) stress the problem of the declining rate of profit since the late 1960s in the industrial countries, and coincide to a great extent on its main causes.[7]

**Table 2.4 Share of operating surplus in GDP: major industrial economies 1963, 1970 and 1980**

(per cent)

|          | 1963 | 1970 | 1980 |
|----------|------|------|------|
| USA      | 22.9 | 18.3 | 17.0 |
| Japan    | 37.5 | 38.0 | 25.0 |
| Germany  | 27.6 | 25.5 | 21.4 |
| France   | 29.1 | 27.6 | 20.5 |
| UK       | 20.3 | 17.9 | 14.0 |
| Italy    | 34.7 | 33.9 | 28.4 |
| Canada   | 24.3 | 20.1 | 23.8 |

*Source: OECD National Accounts 1963–1980*, Vol. 2, Paris, 1982.

A number of factors contributed to the decline in corporate profitability: an increase in labour's share of income; an increase in government expenditure as a proportion of GDP and therefore of taxation; and a deterioration in industrial countries' terms of trade as food and energy prices increased.[8] As a result, there was a sharp fall in the share of profits in GDP in all the major industrial countries, except Canada (see Table 2.4). This in turn helped to reduce investment, already depressed by declining prospects for output growth.

Because of this decline in the rate of profit and in the rate of investment (as well as other factors), by the late 1960s and very early 1970s growth in the industrial countries was already slowing down. Slower growth emerged temporarily first in the US and the UK. In the US industrial production declined by 3.6 per cent in 1970 and grew by a mere 2.0 per cent in 1971; in the UK, industrial production grew by only one per cent in 1970 and was stagnant in 1971.

Since the early 1970s the conditions of two key markets, foodstuffs and energy, changed rather drastically. This implied a deterioration in the terms of trade for some industrial countries which led to a further decline in the rate of profit in them. (However, particularly in the case of the US, the rise in the price of foodstuffs improved the terms of trade: that country is a large net exporter of food in general, and grain in particular).

In the case of foodstuffs (and particularly cereals) the low international prices of the 1960s had encouraged many developing countries to shift away from their production. This shift was reinforced by the policies pursued by many of these countries' governments which discriminated against agriculture in prices, allocation of funds and technological capacity.

As in the case of foodstuffs, internationally low prices for oil encouraged demand to run ahead of supply during the 1960s. The relation between known world reserves and the level of world consumption of oil deteriorated. Low prices for oil led to an increase in the share of petroleum consumption in total primary energy and encouraged countries to rely increasingly on imports. The sharp increase in oil prices in the early and late 1970s had a rarely recognised long-term positive effect: it exercised pressure for crucial energy saving and development of new supplies. However, it also had a negative short and medium-term impact on profits, inflation and growth in industrial countries. (For a more detailed discussion of the food and fuel markets, see pp. 29–34 below.)

Growth rates in *all* the major industrial countries declined substantially after 1970. The decline was sharper for some of the high growth economies, e.g. Japan and the Federal Republic of Germany, and smaller for the United States, starting from a slower rate of growth (see Table 2.5).

A second trend that emerged after 1970 was that growth (however low) was no longer the norm, as total production fell quite significantly at least once in practically all the major industrial countries. In the UK and the US total production fell during three of the ten years after 1970. This contrasts sharply with the record in the much longer 1948–70

**Table 2.5 Growth of output in major industrial economies, 1948–70 and 1970–80**

|  |  | (per cent) |
| --- | --- | --- |
|  | *1948–70* | *1970–80* |
| USA | 3.7 | 3.2 |
| UK | 2.9 | 1.8 |
| France | 5.3 | 3.6 |
| Germany | 5.3 | 2.7 |
| Canada | 5.0 | 3.9 |
| Italy | 5.3 | 3.0 |
| Japan | 9.8 | 4.6 |

*Source:* IFS computer tapes and yearbooks.

*Note:* 1. GDP at 1975 factor prices for UK, France, Italy; GNP at 1975 factor prices for the others.
2. Growth rates computed by fitting a trend line by least squares method.
3. First column: France 1950–70, Germany 1953–70, Italy 1960–70, Japan 1952–70.

period, where only two very slight declines were registered for the major industrial countries.

So far, we have focused more on the 'real' sector of the economy. However, many of the factors discussed above, such as significant growth of world monetary reserves, larger increases in earnings than in productivity, and increases in the prices of foodstuffs and energy, were amongst the main factors leading to the rapid acceleration in inflation which occurred after the late 1960s. This systematically higher rate of inflation (which has prevailed throughout the world economy) has since the late 1960s (and particularly the early 1970s) become an important feature of industrial countries, as well as for the whole world.[9]

In the industrial countries, the medium-term strategy adopted to combat stagflation was since the 1970s increasingly based on the assumption that effective control of inflation was a prerequisite for the attainment of higher levels of economic activity.[10] The extreme priority given to the fight against inflation, and the use mainly of monetary policy, has increased since 1979.[11]

Many analysts would argue that the increasingly restrictive monetarist policies, pursued particularly by the US and the UK, were intended not only to reduce inflation as is claimed, but to increase the rate of profit and thus the rate of investment.[12] Whatever their motivation, the main impact of recent macro-economic policies in industrial countries has been a further deterioration in the evolution of their total and industrial output. Even though there are important underlying structural causes for slow growth in the industrial countries (several of them outlined above), the acute recession of the early 1980s was to a great extent consciously accentuated by government policies in several industrial countries. There is a basic contradiction in such policies. Tight macro-economic policies may lead to an increase in the *share* of profit (as the recession reduces real costs of inputs and labour) but may also imply a decline in the *level* of profit and more importantly in levels of output, as wages are not just an element of cost, but a causal determinant of demand (furthermore the recession discourages entrepreneurs from investing, which further depresses demand).

Higher growth in industrial countries is *probably feasible in the near future if more expansionary policies are pursued*, particularly as there is so much idle capacity, unemployment, and a glut of scarce resources such as oil. Whether it *will* occur will depend to a large extent on decisions taken by governments in industrial countries. A more expansionary policy faces, however, the problem of increasing the *rate* of profit or finding other mechanisms to ensure a more rapid growth of investment. Given this and other dilemmas it seems quite probable that the industrial countries will not grow at such high rates as they did in the twenty-five years after Bretton Woods, particularly while the underlying structural problems which constrain their growth have not been clearly dealt with.

## Trends in international markets

In this section we will examine the main trends in international markets. First, we will describe briefly the evolution of markets for industrial and primary products. In discussing the latter we will focus much more on the markets for food and energy.

It is interesting that trade in the 1930s did not respond fully to the exceptionally rapid growth of output in the years of recovery from the depression. This was clearly connected with the restrictive international trading policies then in operation. The reverse applies to the period since the mid 1950s, in which trade has been stimulated by some relaxation of quantitative restrictions, the creation of the EEC, EFTA and other limited free-trading areas, as well as the Dillon and Kennedy Rounds of tariff reductions. The Kennedy Round reduced the average duty on manufactures by about 35 per cent of its base level over a period of four years, with the biggest cuts, 50 per cent of the base level, falling on machinery and equipment. *Very high rates (many of them prohibitive or almost prohibitive) were largely eliminated during the Kennedy Round*, thus reducing the dispersion of tariff rates in all participating countries.

The reductions achieved during the Tokyo multinational trade negotiations were much smaller, partly because there was much less scope as most of the large tariffs had already been reduced. The resulting expansionary impact of the Tokyo Round on world trade seems to have been much smaller.

It is important to note that even after these two rounds of multi-national trade negotiations, the duties and other restrictions on the imports of manufactured goods from developing countries are still relatively high. The average nominal and effective rates of protection on manufactures are higher on industrial imports from developing countries than on imports from other industrialised countries.

It is useful to stress that *during the fifteen years preceding the world recession of the mid 1970s, the rate of expansion in production, and still more in trade, of manufactures was without parallel over a period of comparable length for at least a hundred years; during this period, per capita world output of manufactures doubled and world trade in manufactures trebled in volume.*

The larger relative expansion in the volume of trade in manufactures in the post-war period appears to have been linked to slower growth in the demand for primary products than for manufactured goods. The shift occurring after 1945 was much sharper than previously. In the industrial countries, demand growth shifted to sectors (such as engineering and chemical industries) whose raw material content per unit of output – with the exception of energy – was lower than in the traditional industrial sectors. Thus, between 1959 and 1977 world output in metal and chemical products expanded at almost double the rate of that in textiles and clothing. Furthermore, synthetic substitutes for several primary products were developed; and the industrialisation of many primary-producing countries led them to increase their demand for imported capital equipment and semi-finished manufactures.

Demand for fuel followed a different path from that of other primary commodities, with very high growth rates for the 30 years after the Second World War. The World Bank[13] estimated that world commercial energy consumption between 1950 and 1974 grew at an average annual rate of 5.0 per cent. World oil demand grew particulary fast: in the period 1950–60 by 8.1 per cent per annum and in 1960–70 by 8.3 per cent per annum.

Production of crude oil was increasing very fast in the post-war period, doubling between 1950 and 1960, and doubling again to 2,000 million tons by 1968.[14] By the beginning of the 1970s, the rise of proven world oil reserves began to slow down and was no longer able to keep up with the rapid rate of increase in production. Concern began to spread that such a rapid rate of growth in consumption and production of oil might not be sustainable in the future, as oil was an exhaustible resource. The volume of international trade in crude oil and oil products increased during the 1960s at an annual rate of 11 per cent.[15] The growth of world trade in fuels grew at a much slower rate during the seventies – the total increase during those ten years was a mere 29 per cent;[16] this reflected a much slower growth of the demand for oil and gas.

World production of food, in contrast, is estimated to have risen by only 2.5 per cent per annum in the 1961/65–1976/80 period.[17] This result may seem satisfactory at a global level, as world population growth has slowed down somewhat and per capita food supplies increased at a global level. However, the big increase in per capita food consumption in the developed countries was primarily due to the higher consumption of animal products. Fifty per cent of world production of cereals is now used for animal feed; about 80 per cent of the calorific content of cereals is lost during the transformation of the vegetable energy into animal calories.

There are two further important problems with the evolution of food production in the post-war period. On the one hand, *there remains a group of developing countries where food production has not kept up with population growth, and where other sectors of the economy have also shown poor performances.* As a result food consumption has been declining. The picture is most grim for the low-income countries of Sub-Saharan Africa, where foodgrain consumption per capita has been declining in the last two decades. This decline accelerated in the 1970s. On the other hand, at a global level, the world's ability to grow enough food for its population has often been questioned; each successive food crisis has accentuated such concerns. The 1973 food crisis, reinforced by crop failure in the USSR, coincided with a period of drought in the Sub-Saharan region. As a result, supply could not meet world demand, and the market disequilibrium, as well as other factors, brought about a large increase in real grain prices.

Relative changes in prices can be traced in Table 2.6 and Figure 2.2,

**Table 2.6 Price indices for internationally traded goods, 1957–1981**

(1970=100)

| Year | Primary commodities (excluding crude petroleum): | | | | | Crude petroleum | Manufactures[c] |
|---|---|---|---|---|---|---|---|
| | Total[a] | Food[b] | Tropical beverages | Metals | Agricultural raw materials | | |
| 1950 | 97.2 | 88.2 | — | 55.4 | 175.0 | — | 69.0 |
| 1955 | 107.2 | 94.5 | 116.8 | 84.7 | 154.4 | 132.2 | 79.2 |
| 1957 | 99.2 | 91.8 | 110.6 | 75.7 | 132.8 | 143.8 | 83.5 |
| 1958 | 90.3 | 85.3 | 109.9 | 70.4 | 110.8 | 141.3 | 83.2 |
| 1960 | 89.0 | 84.3 | 86.4 | 69.7 | 128.3 | 115.7 | 83.5 |
| 1962 | 83.8 | 83.2 | 79.4 | 67.9 | 114.6 | 109.1 | 85.2 |
| 1964 | 95.1 | 95.7 | 89.3 | 83.0 | 117.3 | 102.5 | 87.0 |
| 1966 | 96.2 | 88.9 | 84.4 | 98.2 | 116.6 | 102.5 | 90.6 |
| 1968 | 89.4 | 87.8 | 85.3 | 86.2 | 103.4 | 100.0 | 90.8 |
| 1970 | 100.0 | 100.0 | 100.0 | 100.0 | 100.0 | 100.0 | 100.0 |
| 1971 | 94.3 | 102.0 | 92.3 | 84.6 | 99.5 | 127.3 | 105.6 |
| 1972 | 107.5 | 116.8 | 101.0 | 86.6 | 130.1 | 146.3 | 114.8 |
| 1973 | 165.6 | 179.8 | 124.6 | 127.1 | 233.2 | 208.3 | 135.2 |
| 1974 | 211.5 | 288.0 | 148.8 | 158.8 | 224.9 | 752.1 | 164.8 |
| 1975 | 173.4 | 226.8 | 143.1 | 128.0 | 180.5 | 826.5 | 185.2 |
| 1976 | 195.3 | 185.0 | 274.3 | 135.7 | 224.2 | 887.6 | 185.2 |
| 1977 | 237.7 | 178.2 | 475.0 | 145.7 | 231.4 | 956.2 | 201.6 |
| 1978 | 226.6 | 203.2 | 344.6 | 153.8 | 248.9 | 979.3 | 231.5 |
| 1979 | 263.8 | 231.8 | 364.7 | 199.6 | 303.6 | 1308.3 | 264.8 |
| 1980 | 289.4 | 310.7 | 320.2 | 220.9 | 316.1 | 2209.9 | 387.0 |
| 1981 | 247.0 | 268.0 | 249.0 | 191.0 | 285.2 | 2505.8 | 272.5 |

*Source:* IMF, *International Financial Statistics* (various issues); UNCTAD, *Handbook of International Trade and Development Statistics* (various issues).

*Notes:*
(a) The period 1950–1956 includes petroleum.
(b) The period 1950–1956 includes tropical beverages.
(c) Unit value index of manufactured goods exported from the developed market-economy countries.

**Figure 2.2**
**Commodity prices and terms of trade[a], 1950–1982**
**(1972=100)**

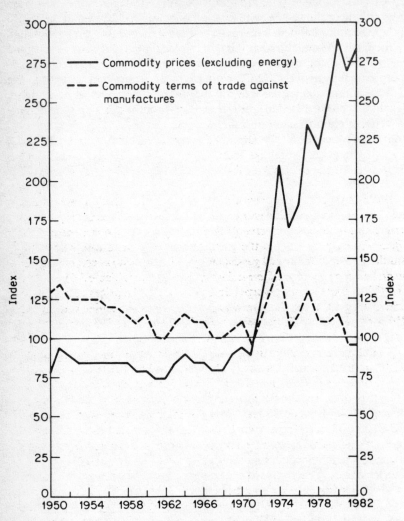

*Source:* UNCTAD secretariat calculations, based on UNCTAD commodity
price index (1960–1980), United Nations price and unit value indices
(*Monthly Bulletin of Statistics*) and UNCTAD spot price forecasts.

[a] Excluding mineral fuels.

remembering that in the base year (1950) commodity prices were high because of the Korean War. The terms of trade between primary commodities (excluding oil) and manufactured goods declined in the 1950s, and to a lesser extent in the 1960s. In the 1970s they increased at first, only to decline again, with further declines to 1982. Prices of manufactured goods used here are a reasonable proxy for capital goods' prices, particularly for the 1970s, as the item machinery and transport equipment (SITC 7) increased at approximately the same pace as other manufactured goods in the 1970–79 period.

After increasing in the late 1970s, prices of primary commodities (excluding oil) declined in *nominal terms* from 1980 onwards, mainly as a result of the recession in industrial countries. As a result of these trends, in March 1982 the UNCTAD combined index of the prices of non-oil primary commodities deflated by the unit value of manufactured exports from the developed market economies *reached its lowest level since 1960*.

It is interesting to stress within our analysis of primary commodities two key sectors, food and energy. As can be seen in Figure 2.1, *prices of cereal and of petroleum actually declined in nominal terms during the fifties*. During the 1960s, the price of food rose at a rate somewhat similar to that of industrial goods; petroleum prices, however, continued to *decline even in nominal terms during the sixties* (see Table 2.6). During the 1970s, these trends changed dramatically, as the prices of both food and energy shot up; the rise was particularly spectacular during the 1972–74 period, when the price of food increased by 150 per cent and that of petroleum grew by around 400 per cent.

The temporary decline in the terms of trade between industrial goods and primary commodities, occurring particularly in the 1972–74 period, *was a sharp reversal of post-1950 trends*. Several factors acted simultaneously to determine the rapid increase in primary commodity prices during 1972–74. Since the late 1960s, inflation had been accelerating in the industrial countries; from 1971, violent fluctuations in exchange rates became increasingly common. These conditions encouraged speculative buying of commodities at a time when demand was strong. Furthermore, a synchronised expansion of aggregate demand occurred in all the major OECD countries in 1972–74, as their governments simultaneously pursued inflationary policies. Such synchronisation has been rare since the Second World War, occurring only in certain specific periods, like the early 1950s, 1958–59 and 1971–75; during the rest of the time it was the largest economy, the United States, which provided the global aggregate with its principal fluctuations, as national cyclical movements of other industrial countries tended to offset each other.[18]

The rapid expansion in the demand for primary commodities

coincided with reduced growth in the supply of most commodities, as well as depletion of their inventories. At the beginning of 1972, stocks as a percentage of trend production were lower than their 1965–70 averages across a wide spectrum of storable commodities, ranging from grains, oilseeds and fats to beverages and industrial raw materials. At the same time, worldwide markets for meats and fish were becoming tighter, as marine stocks were depleted and beef herds were in a building phase of their production cycle. In the case of metals, processing capacity was in short supply. Therefore, the normal mechanisms for buffering sudden disturbances were lacking in important markets. At the same time, production shortfalls occurred for many agricultural commodities. Although world agricultural production fell only 2 per cent below trend in 1973, this was the largest shortfall since 1957.

The evolution of world demand and supply plays an important role in explaining the large magnitude of price commodity variations in the 1970s. However, in the markets for food and energy – whose price fluctuations are particularly important for a study of imported inflation – institutional factors seem to predominate, with governments widely involved in the price-setting process. As a result, sharp changes in price behaviour in these two markets during the 1970s can be attributed far more to changes in institutional factors than to changes in global demand and supply.

The evolution of world grain prices during the 1970s must be seen against the background of substantial changes in the structure of the world grain market. First, between 1947 and 1968 world grain prices were essentially controlled by governments under an international wheat agreement. Big reserves were built up, as the US and Canadian governments bought up grain to support national prices for their farmers. As a result of this agreement, grain prices were controlled within a very narrow band. The wheat agreement broke down in 1968 and the exporting countries reduced their stocks through restrictions on production. World acreage devoted to wheat production was reduced by 8 per cent between the 1968–69 and 1970–71 marketing years and stocks were reduced by 35 per cent. The reduction in reserves was the result of conscious government policies that, while maintaining a floor price, eliminated the ceiling on world markets. Second, important changes occurred in the Soviet relationship with the grain markets. During the 1960s, when production of Soviet grain declined, the Soviet government either curtailed domestic consumption (e.g. in 1964) or used up the carry-over from the previous year's good harvest (e.g. 1966). In 1973, however, imports covered *75 per cent of the supply shortage*. In some of the later years net Soviet imports continued to be very large.[19] The emergence of the Soviet Union during the 1970s as a consistent net importer with wide year-to-year fluctuations, combined with the *previous* decision of the large exporting countries to reduce their reserve positions, represented a major shift in the structure of the grain market.

The imbalance between world supply and demand of grain was largely covered by increasing reliance on US exports after 1973. This did not reflect above-trend US production levels; the surge of US exports was initially met by a depletion of US reserves and later by a sharp fall in domestic consumption. US consumption of grain fell by 23 per cent in 1975 and remained 10 to 15 per cent below trend at the end of the decade; this reduction was much larger than in other industrial countries. The difference in the response of consumption to world market prices seems to be explained largely by government policies that prevented the rise in price from being reflected in the price paid by consumers. Thus, the EEC reduced the variable import levy on wheat from $55 a ton in 1972 to $0.39 a ton in 1975, as world wheat prices rose by $100 a ton. In Japan, prices and marketing of grain are controlled by the government; during 1973–75 the Japanese government stabilised consumer prices by not raising the resale price in line with higher world prices. The US had a greater capacity than other industrial countries to reduce grain consumption, because of the importance of grains for animal feed. As a result of higher feed-grain prices, demand for feed declined; this led to a decline in the US animal herd.

As with the market for grain, the oil market suffered great structural transformations during the last twenty years which had a very significant influence on the path of international prices. The most fundamental change was a transformation in the property rights of the oil industry, together with OPEC's successful intervention in the market. Particularly since the late 1960s, there was an increasing tendency for developing countries' governments to control their natural resources and intervene in markets with a view to obtaining higher export prices. In some cases – wool and rubber for example – this intervention has taken the form of support buying; in others – e.g. copper, tea – export quotas have been fixed under formal or informal arrangements between producing countries. Though significant in some cases, the impact of such intervention has been on the whole unspectacular. The outstanding exception is the case of oil.

In the case of petroleum, the increasing role which producing countries' governments assumed was complemented by a situation in which the price of oil had been declining in the last twenty years (in real and nominal terms) to levels clearly inconsistent with its scarcity rent as an exhaustible asset.

As is well known, in the immediate post-war period, seven major oil companies dominated all aspects of the exploration, production, refining, transportation, distribution and marketing of petroleum. Their ability to present a united front, combined with the global diversification of supplies, allowed them to determine prices; the concession agreements obtained from host countries gave them virtual sovereignty over the fields they discovered and developed. The oil companies' strength was dramatically shown in 1959 and 1960, when they unilaterally lowered the posted prices that formed the basis of taxation for profits. This event contributed to the formation of OPEC as oil-producing governments reacted to this decision.

In the 1960s, the members of OPEC were able to obtain several concessions: they prevented further cuts in posted prices, separated royalty payments from tax payments and regained control of unexploited territories. However, the price of oil continued to decline in both nominal and real terms. The power of OPEC was still limited, partly because the oil companies had excessive productive capacity and could replace curtailed supplies from one country by increases elsewhere.

However, in the early 1970s some long-run trends, reinforced by short-term circumstances, set the stage for a reversal of power in which OPEC could play a leading role. Largely as a result of extremely low and ever declining prices, world consumption of oil was growing dramatically, as oil-intensive technologies (for example in domestic heating) became widespread and as production of goods with high oil intensity (e.g. large cars) grew rapidly. In the US during the 1960s consumption had been growing faster than domestic production and new discoveries. Domestic reserves were equal to 13 years' supply in 1960, but by 1970 they were equal to only nine years. The shortfall was filled by a rise in US petroleum import demand. The growth in dependence on foreign oil was even larger in energy-poor Western Europe and Japan. The share of oil imports in total energy consumption in Japan and the OECD countries of Europe had grown from 10 per cent and 35.9 per cent, respectively, in 1960 to 57.9 per cent and 77.8 per cent in 1970.[20]

By 1970, many smaller, less geographically-diversified independent companies, which were more vulnerable to actions taken by individual countries, had entered the market. This was particularly important in Libya, where a small independent company depended on this one country for a high proportion of its revenue. A favourable agreement reached between this company and the Libyan government in 1970 spread to other companies (who had few inexpensive alternatives at the time). Since the companies' agreements with many oil-producing countries contained a 'most favoured nation' clause, committing them to extend favourable conditions granted from one country to others, the companies were forced into making similar deals with other OPEC members.

More importantly, members of OPEC also increased formal participation in oil-producing affiliates, either through outright nationalisation
(e.g. Libya, Iraq and Algeria) or through 'participation agreements' to
increase host-country equity (e.g. Saudi Arabia). *As a result, in 1971 and
1972, the ownership of a large proportion of the world's oil reserves
changed hands.*

In 1973, the new ability of OPEC to influence prices could be more
easily exercised, as the oil market was tight due to the synchronised
global expansion in the industrial countries discussed above. Thus, in
the US, demand for oil products increased by 7.4 per cent in 1972 and
5.7 per cent in 1973, while domestic oil production declined; imports of
oil rose from 3.9 million barrels a day in 1971 to 6.3 million in 1973. So
although the cutbacks in production by the Arab oil producers as a
result of the October war created an ideal situation for large price rises,
an increase in oil prices had been imminent even before the war began.

After the large 1973 rise in the price of oil, the growth in oil
consumption declined significantly, from 7.2 per cent in 1968–73 to 3.2
per cent in 1973–79.[21] The largest decline in growth occurred in
Western Europe, possibly because the rise in international oil prices was
allowed to feed through to the internal market.

After declining in real terms during the 1974–78 period, the price of
oil again increased rather dramatically in 1979, mainly as a result of
disruption in Iranian supplies during and after the revolution in that
country. It is interesting that in 1979 (as in 1974) production was
practically equal to the volume produced the year before. Although the
failure of supply to grow with demand clearly exerted upward pressure
on prices, the size of the scarcity experienced was largely the result of
panic buying by consumers. Particularly, in 1979 upward pressure on
prices continued, even when levels of production were recovering,
because of factors such as expectations of further price increases and
anticipation of further production interruptions. As these fears eased,
and as the world recession became deeper and more widespread,
downward pressure was exerted on the price.

It can be concluded that changes of a structural nature in the market
were very important factors in determining the price of oil. The rapid
change in property rights of the oil industry and the extremely rapid
growth of international demand during the 1950s and 1960s set the
stage for large price variations. The stage of the international business
cycle, as well as specific political developments, only catalysed these
long-term trends.

It is interesting to note that in the 1970s economists have passed
through three phases in their thinking about the optimal price of oil.[22]
At first, static micro-theory predicted that the price should equal the

marginal cost for marginal supplies, which was particularly low for Middle Eastern producers with very large crude oil reserves. This analysis obviously confused marginal cost of extraction with marginal cost of production, ignoring the fact that oil was an exhaustible asset. Later analysis incorporated the fact that oil reserves were limited and that profit-maximising producer nations would foresee exhaustion. Finally, Johany[23] combined capital theory and property-rights theory to explain the sharp increase in crude oil prices. In response to increasing fears of nationalisation the oil companies shifted production from the future to the present, causing real prices to decline. The host countries' governments, with no threat to their property rights and – for the capital-surplus countries – with a low opportunity cost for their financial surpluses, had a much lower discount rate than the oil companies; so they reduced output growth and raised prices.

Whether or not there is a long term secular decline in the terms of trade of primary commodities against manufacturers (the well-known Prebisch-Singer thesis),[24] there is little doubt that they declined for 30 years from 1950 with only a brief reversal in the 1970s.[25] In response to this, and taking advantage of the strong growth of world trade in manufactured goods, *the share of manufactures in developing countries' total exports has increased significantly in the last 15 years (from 14.9 per cent in 1965 to 20.5 per cent in 1979).* As a result, developing countries' share in world exports of manufactures rose from 5 per cent in 1965 to about 9 per cent in 1979. The share of machinery and transport equipment in the LDCs' total exports, though still relatively low (5.4 per cent in 1979) was significantly higher than in 1965 (1.1 per cent). The share of primary commodities, especially of food and beverages, has correspondingly declined.

The growing importance of manufactures in developing countries' exports was dominated by a few fast growing countries – Argentina, Brazil, Republic of Korea, Singapore, Uruguay, Yugoslavia and Hong Kong – which accounted for 62 per cent of such exports in 1977. Although labour-intensive products, such as clothing and electronics, were the bulk of these products, these countries have also started to penetrate the markets of more advanced capital intensive industries such as shipbuilding, machinery and basic chemicals.

As can be seen from Table 2.7, there are marked differences in the trade performance of different groups of developing countries. The volume of exports from the fast-growing exporters of manufactures, including Argentina, Brazil and Korea, *grew at about 12 per cent in the 1970s, more than twice the 5.8 per cent rate of the 1960s.* In contrast, the least developed countries saw their export volume *decline at an annual*

**Table 2.7 Foreign trade indicators for developing countries**
(Annual percentage rates of change)

| | Export volume | Purchasing import volume | Purchasing power of exports | Terms of trade |
|---|---|---|---|---|
| All developing countries | | | | |
| 1960–1970 | 6.4 | 5.4 | 6.2 | −0.2 |
| 1970–1980 | 3.1 | 7.3 | 10.0 | 6.8 |
| Major oil exporters | | | | |
| 1960–1970 | 8.6 | 4.7 | 7.2 | −1.3 |
| 1970–1980 | −1.4 | 14.3 | 17.9 | 19.6 |
| Non-oil exporting developing countries | | | | |
| 1960–1970 | 5.1 | 5.6 | 5.7 | 0.6 |
| 1970–1980 | 7.6 | 4.8 | 4.5 | −2.9 |
| Fast growing exporters of manufactures | | | | |
| 1960–1970 | 5.8 | 6.9 | 7.0 | −1.1 |
| 1970–1980 | 11.8 | 7.1 | 8.2 | −3.2 |
| Least-developed countries | | | | |
| 1960–1970 | 4.4 | 5.5 | 3.6 | −0.8 |
| 1970–1980 | −0.4 | 1.5 | −2.2 | −1.8 |

*Source:* UNCTAD, *Trade and Development Report,* 1981.

*rate of 0.4 per cent in the 1970s.* As their terms of trade also deteriorated, the *purchasing power of their exports deteriorated at an annual rate of 2.2 per cent.*

The fast growing exporters of manufactures increased their share of world exports from 3.9 per cent in 1960 to 4.9 per cent in 1980. Their flexible response played an important role, for example when they reacted to protectionism in industrial countries by product diversification and shifting of their exports to other countries.

The share of developing countries' exports in world exports, having decreased steadily from 31 per cent in 1950 to less than 18 per cent in 1972, turned around and grew to 28.1 per cent in 1980. One reason for the increase was the rise in the price of oil, which was mainly exported by developing countries. A second reason was the slowdown in the economic growth and trade of developed countries. *A third important reason was the growth of developing countries' trade with other third world countries.* During the 1970s, the share of intra-developing countries trade increased from *20.9 per cent in 1970 to 24.7 per cent in 1979*. If fuel is excluded, the rise of the share of intra-developing country trade is even greater, from 19.9 per cent in 1970 to 30.1 per cent in 1979, (see Table 2.8). This was a new and important phenomenon.

An important reason for it was that developing countries as a group grew faster in the 1970s (5.6 per cent a year) than all of the major industrial countries (including Japan). So developing countries provided each other with more dynamic markets for each other's products, and moved as a result towards greater collective self-reliance and less dependence on the growth of developed countries. However, the growth of intra-LDC trade was greatest in fuel and raw materials, rather than in manufactures; geographically, the big growth areas were West Asia and Latin America as importers of LDC products, and West, South and South East Asia (and to a lesser extent Latin America) as suppliers. The fall in the price of oil, the debt crisis in much of Latin America, and the fact that a low proportion of intra-LDC trade in the seventies was in manufactured goods, may make it much more difficult for intra-LDC trade to continue growing as fast as it did in the seventies.

## International financial flows to developing countries, 1950–1980

During each of the decades since the Second World War a different type of financial flow played a major or more dynamic role in transmitting foreign exchange to developing countries. Even though partly responding to the needs and pressures of the Third World, the main motivation for these flows was that they were perceived as serving best the interests of the agents carrying them out. In the 1950s, foreign investors pursuing greater profits and other corporate aims provided the main source of finance. During the 1960s, official aid agencies played the most dynamic role as, in that decade, aid was perceived to be

**Table 2.8 Significance of intra-developing countries' trade, 1960–79**

| | | | | | (Percentages) |
|---|---|---|---|---|---|
| | *1960* | *1965* | *1970* | *1975* | *1979* |
| All product categories | 22.3 | 20.9 | 20.3 | 23.4 | 24.7 |
| All product categories, excluding fuel | 19.3 | 19.7 | 19.9 | 27.2 | 30.1 |

*Source:* Data based on Table 17, UNCTAD, *Trade and Development Report*, 1981.

in the interests of industrial countries' governments. During the 1970s, the most dynamic component of capital flows to developing countries was private bank credit, as at the time it was in the multinational banks' perceived interest to expand their lending to several developing countries. One of the most problematic aspects in the world economy of the 1980s seems to be the lack of a new actor willing and able to play this dynamic role. The actors who played this role in former decades (e.g. multinational banks, official aid agencies) are very unwilling to continue to do so to the same extent as in the past. In each decade after the Second World War the flows were mainly initiated by US institutions or enterprises; subsequently the process became 'transnationalised' or internationalised as institutions or enterprises from other countries increased their share.

*The 1950s and foreign direct investment*
As the Second World War came to an end, two developments had an important influence on the future nature of international financial flows: the creation of the Bretton Woods institutions and the great weight of the US in the world economy.

The attempt at control of the world monetary system by the recently created official international institutions was not accompanied in practice at the time by large financial flows from them, particularly to the so-called developing countries. The main feature of international capital movements after the Second World War was *the large outflow of funds from the United States*. Even though it basically dominated the two Bretton Woods institutions (the IMF and the World Bank), the United States preferred to channel its financial flows to other countries mainly on a bilateral basis; and there was increasing emphasis, particularly in the United States, on private foreign investment.

The basic dynamism for the dominant financial flows came therefore from large multinational corporations, mainly seeking more profitable investment opportunities abroad. Profitable opportunities to invest in the Third World (and particularly in Latin America) arose mainly because of the deliberate import-substitution policies those countries were pursuing. Direct investment predominated; international credit markets had not yet recovered from the Great Depression and the War.

In 1950 approximately half of US foreign direct investment was in the so-called developing countries, of which over 40 per cent went to Latin America. The share going to developing countries systematically declined between 1950 and 1979 mainly because the share of investment going to Latin America was falling. During the same period, the share invested in industrial countries, particularly Western Europe, increased systematically.[26]

*The 1960s and official aid*
Towards the end of the 1950s, American attitudes towards official aid began to change rapidly: 'Its [the increase in aid] *motivation was unashamedly political.* Americans believed that contributing to the economic and social development of the uncommitted nations would lead to the growth of societies sympathetic to their way of life'.[27] As different American authors (both radical and liberal) themselves agree, the Cuban revolution in 1959 marked a significant turning point in US attitudes towards aid to Latin America in particular and to developing countries in general. This had a determining influence on the very large magnitude of the US aid programme in the 1960s. The Kennedy administration believed that economic development and social reform, spurred by North American aid, could blunt the appeal of radicalism.[28]

It is interesting that, as in the early 1960s, Third World governments were again pressing for increased aid in the late 1970s and early 1980s. International big business – particularly the big banks – tends to support such initiatives. However, in contrast with the 1960s, the industrial countries' governments (and particularly the US government) *do not* at present perceive a large increase in aid as serving their interests.

*Net official flows became, during the 1960s, the main source of net financial flows to developing countries*, although the importance of official flows – and particularly of ODA – declined somewhat from the mid-1960s.[29] As in the case of foreign direct investment, the major initiative for official flows came first from the US. Over 60 per cent of net total bilateral flows to developing countries in the first half of the 1960s (1960–66) came from the US. During the 1960s, other industrial countries began to play an increasingly important role in aid flows, partly because of American persuasion to share the financial burden and partly because of those countries' own perceived interests. While the share of official bilateral US flows to developing countries declined from the late 1960s, ODA from Japan, Canada, Australia and the Scandinavian countries increased their share substantially. By the mid-1970s, even in Latin America, US net bilateral official flows were increasingly surpassed by those of the rest of the industrial countries.[30]

*The 1970s and private multinational banks*
A major feature of the world economy in the 1970s was increased imbalances in international payments and in financing capable of sustaining them. The composition and nature of financial flows also changed very substantially.

A first major trend was that oil-importing countries' current account deficits increased more than threefold in real terms during the period 1970–80. So that such high deficits could be sustained, the total external

**Table 2.9 Oil-importing developing countries' current account deficits, 1970–80**

|  | 1970 | 1973 | 1975 | 1978 | 1980 |
|---|---|---|---|---|---|
| A. *Current account deficit* | *billions of 1978 dollars* | | | | |
| a) all oil-importing developing countries | 18.5 | 11.6 | 49.8 | 25.5 | 58.0 |
| b) low income oil-importing developing countries | 3.6 | 4.9 | 7.0 | 5.1 | 9.1 |
| c) middle income oil-importing developing countries | 14.9 | 6.7 | 42.8 | 20.4 | 48.9 |
| B. *Current account deficit* | *per cent of GNP* | | | | |
| a) all | 2.4 | n.a. | n.a. | n.a. | 4.9 |
| b) low-income | 1.9 | 2.4 | 3.9 | 2.6 | 4.5 |
| c) middle-income | 2.6 | 1.0 | 5.5 | 2.3 | 5.0 |

*Source:* Based on World Bank, *World Development Report 1981*.

flows to deficit developing countries were dramatically increased, at an annual rate of growth of 9.0 per cent in real terms during 1970–80 (see Table 2.9).

The rapid growth of deficits in the current accounts of oil-importing developing countries was mainly caused by the sharp deterioration of their terms of trade and slower growth in industrial countries. A third factor, rarely mentioned in the literature, is that gross domestic capital formation outstripped gross domestic savings: the ratio of foreign savings to GDP increased from 1.6 per cent in the 1960s to 3.0 per cent in the 1970s. The increase of foreign savings was higher in the least developed countries (from 1.2 per cent to 6.4 per cent of GDP) because an increase in gross domestic capital formation was actually accompanied by a decline in gross domestic savings.

A second important trend was that credit flows to deficit developing countries became increasingly 'privatised'. Private medium and long-term credits which represented only 37 per cent of total net capital flows to the Third World in 1970 are estimated to have increased to *50 per cent* of those flows by 1980, as they grew at an average annual real rate of about 20 per cent (see Table 2.10).

Equity finance – which until the early 1970s was the main source of *private* financial flows to the Third World – grew slower than other

**Table 2.10  Oil-importing developing countries: Financing of current deficits, 1970–80**

| | Level ($ billion, current prices) | | Annual percentage growth (constant prices) |
|---|---|---|---|
| | 1970 | 1980 | 1970–80 |
| *Current account balance* | −8.6 | −69.6 | 12.1 |
| *Financed by:* | | | |
| 1.  Net capital flows | 9.1 | 55.3 | 9.0 |
|    a)  total aid (grants & concessional loans) | 3.1 | 16.3 | 7.5 |
|    b)  medium and long-term borrowing | 4.3 | 33.4 | 16.6 |
|       official export credits | 0.5 | 2.6 | 7.2 |
|       multilateral | 0.5 | 3.2 | 9.4 |
|       private | 3.4 | 27.5 | 19.7 |
|    c)  private direct investment | 1.7 | 5.6 | 2.7 |
| 2.  Change in reserves and short-term borrowing | 0.5 | 14.3 | |

*Source:* World Bank, *World Development Report 1981*, Table 5-3.

forms of external capital during the 1970s, and therefore declined rapidly in importance, from about 20 per cent of financing in 1970 to 10 per cent in 1980. With the expansion of commercial bank lending, the financing of foreign direct investment in developing countries itself changed, as the financing needs of transnational companies were covered increasingly from sources other than parent companies, such as borrowing from local banks or the euro-currency markets.

Rapid expansion of private bank lending to deficit Third World countries during the 1970s by no means implied a deliberate initiative by multinational banks to help solve developing countries' problems. The main motivation of the private multinational banks was the search for profitable outlets for their rapidly growing deposits, in the context of very low corporate credit demand in the industrial countries.[31]

In contrast, the International Monetary Fund made an almost negligible contribution. In the period 1973–80, net use of Fund credit plus short-term borrowing by monetary authorities amounted to a mere 3.1 per cent of current account deficits of oil importing developing countries.[32] Limited net IMF lending during the 1970s was caused both by developing countries' reluctance to borrow from the Fund (mainly because of the stringent conditionality attached to their upper credit tranche loans) and by the slow increase in the resources available to the Fund, as quotas rose very slowly.

The large volume of private lending helped *some* developing countries sustain or even increase levels of economic activity. Furthermore, it helped to sustain economic activity in the developed countries, by maintaining demand from the Third World for their exports. But the claim of some observers[33] that recycling from surplus to deficit countries via the market mechanism was extremely satisfactory during the 1970s, and could be largely relied on to carry out the same task in the 1980s, is clearly incorrect.

Private banks clearly preferred lending to countries with relatively high per capita income, as well as to those whose recent growth record was more impressive. Poor countries (both in income levels and/or natural resources) were not considered to be sufficiently 'creditworthy' to attract significant flows. As a result, private bank lending was extremely concentrated among the upper and middle income developing countries. Low income countries are estimated to have obtained *only* *2.6 per cent* of total net lending to oil importing developing countries in the period 1972–80.[34] So the swing to private flows worsened the distribution of access to external finance among developing countries.

A second problem is that the conditions of the private loans are fully commercial. Compared with official loans, maturities are shorter. Of greater importance is that the cost of borrowing privately has been higher. Perhaps even more problematic is that the interest rate on much of private lending is variable, changing every three to six months as interest rates in the main industrial countries change, especially those of the US. This variability adds an important element of uncertainty to borrowers' attempts to predict and plan their balance of payments flows.

The risks involved in borrowing with floating interest costs were much greater in the 1970s than previously: the yearly average for deposit rates varied between 5.5 per cent and 16.5 per cent between 1970 and 1981, with monthly averages varying even more, from 4.9 per cent (May 1972) to 19.9 per cent (March 1980). The actual cost of borrowing was between two and four percentage points above deposit rates, when margins and other costs were included (the actual difference depending on the creditworthiness and bargaining power of the borrower).[35] The effect of an increasing proportion of such debt in total borrowing, and the resulting higher rates of interest and shorter maturities, was to increase sharply the cost of interest and total debt service as a proportion of total debt and of exports. Furthermore, the proportion of gross borrowing actually available for buying imports and increasing reserves, the net transfer, fell sharply – from 50 per cent in 1975–76 to 22 per cent in 1980. In fact, at the average debt terms available to Latin America in 1981, *gross lending would have had to double after six years and quadruple after ten years, merely to sustain a constant level of net transfer.*

Another problematic effect of large private bank lending is its impact on the country's autonomy in policy-making. Initially, a government or an enterprise has much greater freedom to use funds in the case of private loans than with aid. However, this greater degree of freedom is severely restricted if the country faces a difficult balance of payments situation. In fact initial excessive private bank lending seems – in the medium term – to reinforce, instead of weaken, dependence on IMF conditionality. If a country has a serious external disequilibrium, renegotiations of loans or even new private credits becomes conditional on an agreement with the Fund. This trend has become widespread since 1982.

Another increasingly problematic aspect of private bank lending to the Third World is its potentially negative impact on the stability of the international financial system. Debt crises and reschedulings became particularly widespread from late 1982, as a result mainly of the vast amount of debt already accumulated by developing countries, of the prolonged recession in the industrial countries and of private banks' unwillingness to continue lending (in both gross and, particularly, net terms) at the previous high levels. It was estimated (in the February 1983 issue of Morgan Guaranty's *World Financial Markets*) that the debt of the 25 countries who were then in arrears, in the process of re-scheduling, or had already rescheduled portions of their debt, was equal to *nearly half the total debt* which LDCs and East European countries then owed to commercial banks. As the debts owed by some of the largest borrowers often exceed the total assets of their lenders (particularly in the case of several of the largest US banks) fears have been expressed that an explicit default by one of the large borrowers could threaten these banks' survival, with serious danger of such bankruptcies spreading.

It is more likely that the fear of such defaults will continue to discourage private banks from lending to developing countries, particularly at times when these countries are in serious balance of payments difficulties; the growth of net international bank credit is estimated to have declined from about 20 per cent in 1981 to 10 per cent in 1982, to about 5 per cent (annualised) in January–July 1983.[36] As a result, transfers became negative in certain regions during the early 1980s. For example, there was a negative net transfer of capital flows amounting to US$15 billion from Latin America during 1982.[37] As a result of such trends in their external financial flows, many developing countries were forced to reduce significantly their current account deficits, a process carried out to a large extent by deflation, implying lower growth or in many cases actual decline of GDP. The option of increasing exports was much more difficult than in the 1970s: the value of world trade in 1982 was actually declining.

In fact a large proportion of the net private bank lending to developing countries which has occurred since late 1982 has been reluctant or even involuntary. In particular, the 'packages' of rescheduling put together in late 1982 for the large debtors (which usually included large new private credits) implied a large degree of direct pressure applied on private banks by official institutions, particularly by the IMF and the major industrial countries' central banks. The degree of pressure thus exerted seems to have no historical precedent and may in the medium-term increase private banks' reluctance to lend to developing countries.

A number of proposals have been made to deal with the problems of the 'private debt overhang' and a number of measures have been suggested to sustain net private financial flows to developing countries, particularly – but not only – in times of distress, including an explicit international lender of last resort and far stricter private bank supervision by central banks.[38] It seems, however, unlikely that such measures will be taken by industrial countries' governments, unless the threat to the stability of their financial institutions becomes even larger.

*Official flows in the 1970s*
Even though official flows to developing countries during the 1970s increased less than the total capital flows to the Third World, they did grow significantly. Within official flows, 'multilateral loans' was the item which grew most rapidly during the 1970s (by 9.4 per cent a year in real terms: see Table 2.10).

The evolution of official flows was much more satisfactory in the first half of the 1970s, when aid grew quite rapidly, largely as a result of the sharp increase in OPEC aid (see Table 2.11). OPEC aid rose to US$4.9 billion in 1975 – 27 per cent of total aid and 2.94 per cent of OPEC GNP, as compared with OECD aid which reached only 0.34 per cent of OECD GNP in 1975. In the first half of the 1970s, official development assistance received by low income countries increased significantly, growing in real terms by 60 per cent between 1973 and 1975. In the second half of the 1970s, with inflation more rapid, official flows grew more slowly. Of particular concern was that *in the case of low-income oil importers, official flows actually declined in real terms*. This is particularly

**Table 2.11 Financial flows to developing countries, 1970 to 1980**

($ billion)

|  | *1970* | *1975* | *1980* |
|---|---|---|---|
| *Concessional* | 8.1 | 19.3 | 36.4 |
| Bilateral |  |  |  |
|     DAC countries | 5.7 | 9.8 | 18.0 |
|     OPEC | 0.4 | 4.9 | 8.3 |
|     Other (mostly CMEA) | 1.0 | 0.8 | 2.3 |
| Multilateral | 1.1 | 3.8 | 7.7 |
| *Non-concessional* | 10.9 | 34.3 | 59.3 |
| *Total* | 19.0 | 53.7 | 95.7 |

*Source: DAC Annual Review, 1982.*

serious, since low-income countries rely to such an extent on concessional flows to meet their increased deficits; in 1979 ODA was 81 per cent of total finance for the low-income countries, while representing only 42 per cent for middle-income countries, and 2 per cent for NICs.[39]

It should be pointed out that comparisons such as those made above of the flows coming from industrial and OPEC countries are subject to at least three major, though non-quantifiable, qualifications.[40] First, the development assistance flows of OPEC are based on a temporary surplus derived from a depletable natural resource, as compared with those of OECD countries, which are overwhelmingly derived from their renewable sources of wealth. Even in the short-term, the size of this financial surplus may fluctuate significantly as the price of oil is subject to large variations. As a result, it is likely that OPEC ODA will necessarily fluctuate in the same direction as the price of oil. Second, OPEC flows to other developing countries are essentially untied, differing in this respect from the bilateral flows of several OECD donors, whose real benefit to the recipient is reduced to the extent that they are tied to procurement in the donor country. Third, most of the aid provided by the OECD countries is recycled back to those countries as a group – even if those flows are untied – as imports of capital goods, services, certain foodstuffs; the majority of OPEC aid is *not* recycled to OPEC countries, except for oil imports.

A final important feature of international financial flows during the 1970s was that (as shown in Table 2.12) *during several years OPEC countries replaced the industrial countries as the main source of funds to the rest of the world* (and therefore to the developing countries). This is a new phenomenon, on which insufficient emphasis seems to have been placed. The Bank for International Settlements estimates[41] that *over half* of the sources for total net bank lending to countries *outside* the Group of Ten and Switzerland during 1974–80 came from OPEC net deposits, with large annual variations. Net deposits by OPEC countries to the banks were however negative in certain years.

In private lending – as well as in other capital flows – there was an *asynchrony in the 1970s between the rapidly increasing importance of funds originating in OPEC countries and the continual dominance of industrial country institutions for channelling those funds.* The main reason seems to have been that initially the new surplus countries lacked financial markets or enough 'know-how' to enable them to lend the surplus directly to deficit countries as the major surplus countries (i.e. UK in the nineteenth century, the US in the twentieth century) had in the past. The late 1970s and, particularly, the early 1980s saw a very important increase in the growth of OPEC controlled financial institutions; an example of this was the rapidly growing importance of Arab bank-led syndication of Euro-currency credits.

## Table 2.12 The pattern of global capital flows[a]

|  | | | | | ($ billion) |
| --- | --- | --- | --- | --- | --- |
|  | *1967–73*[b] | *1974–77*[b] | *1978* | *1979* | *1980* |
| Group of Ten Countries and Switzerland | −8¼ | −¾ | −19½ | 23½ | 51½ |
| Smaller developed countries | 1½ | 17¾ | 10½ | 12 | 22 |
| Non-oil developing countries | 6 | 21 | 22½ | 36 | 51 |
| Oil-exporting countries | −1¼ | −38 | −4½ | −68 | −116 |

*Source:* A. Lamfalussy, 'Changing attitudes towards capital movements', BIS 1981; based on OECD and IMF data.

*Notes:*
    (a) Minus signs indicate capital export.
    (b) Annual averages.

*Conclusions on financial flows to developing countries*

From our previous analysis, it can be seen that the key problem for different developing countries is whether a sufficiently high and appropriate level of financial flows can be channelled to them, so that they can incur deficits high enough to sustain or increase their rates of growth.

In this sense, the experience of the 1970s was not as satisfactory as has been claimed. In fact, it could be argued that insufficient transfer of funds from surplus to deficit countries was a very important factor in explaining lower growth, and in particular in the low-income oil-importing developing countries.[42] *These countries were forced in many cases to adjust via restraining growth.* Their terms of trade worsened, the markets for their exports declined as a result of the recession in the industrial countries, and their access to international finance was limited (it represented a declining proportion of total flows to LDCs, falling from 18 per cent to 12 per cent between 1973 and 1980).

Although other factors, such as domestic economic policies, also play a large role, there is important evidence that, during the mid-1970s, those countries that were able to maintain higher rates of growth of imports (often largely as a result of increased borrowing) were on average able to sustain higher growth of GDP and of domestic investment (see Table 2.13).

This suggests that the short and medium term prospects for developing countries would be less dismal[43] if the flow of finance to them, particularly in the form of balance of payments support, could be

**Table 2.13  Import  capacity  and  economic  performance  of non-oil developing countries**

(per cent)

| | Annual increase in GDP | | Annual increase in investment | |
|---|---|---|---|---|
| | *1965–73* | *1973–76* | *1965–73* | *1973–76* |
| Thirty countries with sustained or improved growth of import capacity | 4.3 | 5.3 | 6.1 | 15.3 |
| Forty countries with diminished growth of import capacity | 4.9 | 2.9 | 5.3 | 4.3 |

*Source:* S. Dell and R. Lawrence, 1980, *The Balance of Payments Adjustment Process in Developing Countries,* New York, Pergamon Press.

increased. Even if countries decide to increase their *national* savings and seek to rely more on South–South co-operation, the necessary structural changes require financing. Yet there seems to be no set of international institutions ready to play a dynamic role in providing such finance; indeed existing sources of finance appear most unwilling to supply more than the minimum required to prevent financial disaster, in contrast to the dynamic role which they have played at various times in the past. This may lead in particular years and for particular countries or areas to substantial net transfers of foreign financial flows from developing countries to industrialised ones, with very negative consequences for the growth of those countries, and the world economy.

The relatively unsatisfactory recycling record of the 1970s, the existing high level of indebtedness, the widespread debt crises of the early 1980s, as well as the very insufficient dynamism to be expected from existing financial institutions and mechanisms, make urgent the need for major changes in the international and monetary system.

## Final comments and some conclusions for the 1980s

Three important characteristics seemed to emerge in the 1970s, with implications for the 1980s. First, the benefits obtained from international trade and finance were very unequally distributed *amongst* developing countries. The least developed countries suffered from a decline in their export volume and in their terms of trade. On the other hand, the fast growing exporters of manufactures had a spectacular increase in the purchasing power of their exports, as the rapid increase in export volumes more than offset the deterioration in their terms of trade. Similarly, in international finance the low-income countries obtained a decreasing share of net flows to the Third World.

Second, developing countries sustained their growth better than industrial countries in the 1970s. But as the international environment deteriorated in the early 1980s, growth in developing countries declined dramatically.

Third, the developing countries provided increasing dynamism for each other's growth: intra-developing country trade grew much more rapidly than other Third World trade; and the share of external finance flowing to deficit developing countries from other Third World countries increased quite substantially.

Despite the beginning of recovery by industrial countries in 1983, the unprecedented growth rates experienced by OECD countries during the 25 years after the Second World War are unlikely to recur in the near future. Furthermore, at the end of the 1970s industrial countries reacted to growing inflation in their economies mainly by restricting demand, with strong emphasis on monetary policy. The impact on their performance was very negative. The impact on developing countries was also very harmful. Their terms of trade export volume declined, as before at a time of slower growth in industrial economies. But to this was added the dramatic increase in real interest rates. Stringent fiscal policies applied by industrial countries' governments were also reflected in their restrictive attitudes towards aid to the Third World.

More expansionary policies in industrial countries (both internally and in their attitude towards international growth, i.e. through aid flows) would naturally improve the international environment for developing countries. However, it does not seem probable that counter-cyclical policies alone would be able to move industrial countries back to the growth path characteristic of the 1950s and 1960s, nor does it seem likely that attitudes towards financial flows will change substantially amongst industrial countries' governments and banks.

If developing countries were to base their development prospects on the evolution of the international environment as determined mainly by the industrial countries, those prospects would be rather bleak. Whatever their differences, developing countries' governments seem to share a common perception that low growth rates would have politically and socially unacceptable effects for their populations. The common interest in growth of both oil exporters and oil importers differs substantially from the currently perceived interests of industrial countries.

Oil-importing developing countries require higher levels of external finance so that they can sustain higher growth levels to allow for more acceptable levels of consumption, investment and employment; and higher growth in these countries, by boosting their demand for oil, would clearly be in the short and medium-term interests of oil exporters. Thus, both oil exporters' and oil importers' governments have a common interest in supporting higher levels of world demand and higher growth levels than those perceived as 'optimum' by industrial countries' governments.

In these circumstances, developing countries may want to play a more active role in the world economy, instead of waiting for the industrial countries to provide them with an engine of growth, and to introduce necessary institutional reforms. Relatively more 'collective self-reliance' may become, increasingly, not an attractive ideological option but a practical necessity. Unless and until the performance and attitudes of industrial countries' governments change rather dramatically, the alternative to important intra-Third World initiatives in trade and finance may be stagnation or even declining output in many developing countries, as well as increasing international financial problems both for them and their creditors.

Together with greater collective Third World efforts to improve the international environment, it seems essential for individual developing countries' governments (as well as 'development experts') to review their policy recommendations in the light of recent changes in the international environment. One area, which seems to have received insufficient attention, is the impact in the 1970s of large changes in *relative international prices* on policy, in particular technologies and consumption patterns (many of which were not fully perceived or implemented at the time prices changed). Similarly, the sharp rise and variability in international nominal and real interest rates will have important effects on the rate of investment and choice of technologies (both relating to capital-intensity and foreign-exchange intensity of technologies).

Another crucial area for developing country policy-makers to review in the new international environment is the extent to which integration into the world economy – through 'opening up' to trade and finance – is a far less attractive option at present, even for the larger, middle-income developing countries which seemed to pursue such strategies rather successfully in the 1970s.

**Notes and references**

1  I am very grateful to several of my IDS colleagues for very valuable comments on a previous draft; in particular, I benefited from comments by Manfred Bienefeld, Philip Daniel, Charles Harvey and the late Dudley Seers. I also received very useful comments from the participants of the Imported Inflation Workshop held at IDS, and in particular from Dr. M. Khouja, D.J. Ordoobadi, Professor G. Ranis, Dr. A. Sadik and F. Stewart.

2  A valuable discussion of this concept can be found in UNCTAD, *Trade and Development Report*, 1981, TD/B/863, 31 July 1981.

3  Tinbergen, J. *Shaping the World Economy*, Twentieth Century Fund, New York, 1962.

4  Based on data in Batchelor, R.A. *et al. Industrialisation and the Basis for Trade*, the National Institute of Economic and Social Research, Cambridge University Press, 1980, p. 19.

5  See, for example, Bienefeld, M. 'The international context for national development strategies: Constraints and opportunities in a changing world' in Godfrey, M. and Bienefeld, M. *The Struggle for Development: National Strategies in an International Context*, Wiley, 1982.

6  This term was initially used in 1961 in Altman, O. 'Professor Triffin on international liquidity and the role of the Fund', *IMF Staff Papers*, 8, May 1961, pp. 151–191. For a more recent review of the problem see Triffin, R. 'Gold and the Dollar Crisis: Yesterday and Tomorrow', *Princeton Essays in International Finance*, No. 132, December 1978. As is well known, Triffin and others advocated alternative mechanisms for creating international liquidity, so as to overcome this dilemma. These alternative measures (i.e. creation of SDRs) were adopted to a very limited extent in the late sixties.

7   In 1970 about one third of countries had inflation of consumer prices above 5 per cent a year; by 1979 this proportion reached 83 per cent.

8   See, in particular, the excellent Bank for International Settlements, *Fifty-first Annual Report*, 15 June 1981 for a representative view of international financial institutions, and Rowthorn, R. *Capitalism, Conflict and Inflation*, Lawrence and Wishart Ltd., 1980, particularly the chapter on 'Late Capitalism' for a Marxist interpretation.

9   For shares of labour in income see BIS *Fifty-first Annual Report*, p. 41; for government spending as a percentage of GDP, ibid., p. 24.

10   See, for example, OECD Communiqué on meeting of Council at the Ministerial level in June 1976 (*Activities of OECD in 1976. Report by the Secretary General*), Paris, 1977.

11   See IMF *Annual Report 1981*, Washington D.C., p. 3.

12   For a recent discussion, see *IDS Bulletin*, 'Monetarism and the Third World', January 1982, particularly Preface and article by John Wells. See also the OECD *Economic Outlook*, December 1981, p. 7, which stated that an important aim of tight monetary policies was to protect profit margins by ensuring that inflationary wage settlements could not be financed.

13   World Bank, *Energy in the Developing Countries*, 1980, Washington D.C., p. 21.

14   Odell, P. *Oil and World Power*, Penguin Books, 1981.

15   Batchelor. *et al. Industrialisation and the Basis for Trade*.

16   World Bank, *World Development Report 1981*.

17   UNCTAD, *Trade and Development Report 1981*, Annex, Table A13.

18   See Bosworth, B.P. and Lawrence, R.Z. *Commodity Prices and the New Inflation*, The Brookings Institution, 1982, especially chapter 4.

19   For data, see Bosworth and Lawrence, *Commodity Prices and the New Inflation*.

20   de Carnoy, Guy *Energy for Europe: Economic and Political Implications*, American Enterprise Institute for Public Policy Research, 1977.

21   American Petroleum Institute, *Basic Petroleum Data*, API Washington D.C., 1979.

22   For interesting analyses, see Mead, W.J. 'An economic analysis of crude oil price behaviour in the 1970s', Johany, A.D. 'OPEC and the price of oil: Cartelisation or alteration of property rights' and El Serafy, S. 'The oil price revolution of 1973–74', articles in Rasaei El Mallakh (ed.) *OPEC: Twenty Years and Beyond*, Westview/Croom Helm, 1982; and Nordhaus, W.D. 'The Allocation of Energy Resources', *Brookings Papers on Economic Activity*, no. 3, 1973, pp. 529–576.

23   See works cited in n.22 and Johany, A.D. 'OPEC is not a Cartel: A property rights explanation of the rise in crude oil prices', Ph.D. dissertation, University of California, Santa Barbara, 1978.

24   Prebisch, R. 'The economic development of Latin America and its principal problems', *Economic Bulletin for Latin America*, 1962, vol. 7, pp. 1–22. Singer, H. (1950) 'The distribution of gains between investing and borrowing countries', *American Economic Review*, Papers and Proceedings (May), vol. 40, pp. 473–485.

25   Spraos, J. 'The statistical debate on the net barter terms of trade between primary commodities and manufactures', *Economic Journal*, vol. 90, no. 357.

26 Data from *Survey of Current Business*, February 1981, US Department of Commerce.

27 Prout, C. 'Finance for developing countries: An essay', in Strange, S. *International Monetary Relations*, vol. 2 of Schonfield, A. (ed.) *International Economic Relations of the Western World*, Oxford University Press, 1976.

28 For a more detailed discussion of US aid to Latin America, see, for example, Griffith-Jones, S. 'The Alliance for Progress: An attempt at interpretation', *Development and Change*, vol. 10, no. 3, July 1979.

29 OECD, DAC, *Development Assistance, 1971 Review*.

30 Inter-American Development Bank, *Economic and Social Progress in Latin America*, 1979 Report.

31 For a much more detailed description, see, for example, Griffith-Jones, S. 'The growth of multinational banking, the Euro-currency market and their effects on developing countries', *Journal of Development Studies*, January 1980.

32 Sengupta A. and Stewart, F. *Framework for International Cooperation*, Frances Pinter, 1982 (based on IMF data).

33 For example, the British Foreign and Commonwealth Office stated in July 1980 that, 'The Government believes . . . the international capital market can continue to play the primary role in recycling'. See *The Brandt Commission Report*. Memorandum proposed by the FCO for the Overseas declarations of Ronald Reagan at IMF Bank Annual Meeting in September 1981.

34 OECD *Development Cooperation Review 1981*, Table V-6.

35 For a detailed account of the cost of variable interest rate borrowing and how to make comparisons with other types of loan, see Harvey, C. *Analysis of Project Finance in Developing Countries*, Heinemann, 1983, pp. 115–131.

36 *Economic Review*, Morgan Grenfell, August 1983, based on BIS data.

37 Net total capital inflows reached approximately US$19 billion, net repayment of profits and interests reached approximately US$34 billion. *Economic Commission for Latin America (ECLA) News*, January 1983.

38 Lipton, M. and Griffith-Jones, S. 'International lender of last resort, are changes required?', *Study on the International Financial and Trading System*, Commonwealth Secretariat, London; also forthcoming as *Midland Bank Occasional Paper No 1*.

39 OECD, *Development Cooperation, 1981 Review*, Table IV-2.

40 Most of these points are clearly brought out in an UNCTAD Secretariat Report on a *General Review of OPEC Aid*, UN Document TD/B/C.7/31; for a useful summary of this report, see OPEC Fund for International Development, *Occasional Paper No. 6. The UNCTAD Report in OPEC Aid: A Summary*, 1979.

41 BIS, *1981 Annual Report*.

42 This point is clearly argued in Sengupta and Stewart, *Framework for International Cooperation*.

43 For growth projections, see *World Development Report 1983*.

# 3 Imported Inflation, Global Price Changes and Economic Crises in Tanzania, 1970–1982

*Reginald Herbold Green* with *D.J.M. Kamori*[1]

'In the present economic order we have two rights – to sell cheap and to buy dear'.

*President J.K. Nyerere*

'A world without growth and without rules is harder on poor countries than on the rich'.

*Commissioner Edgard Pisani*

## Introduction

*Tanzania: A structural overview*

Tanzania is a relatively large (900,000 square miles), moderate population (20 million) low GDP (in 1981 $200 per capita, national $4,000 million) country. It is by UN definitions among the 'least developed' and 'most severely affected'. Over 1961–1971 and 1971–1979 it achieved moderate rates of growth: about 4.5 per cent per annum for real GDP and 3.5 per cent for agricultural output (above the 2.75–3 per cent population growth) – a performance above the 'least developed' and Sub-Saharan African averages but below its own goal of 6 per cent.[2]

The economy was until 1973 structurally very open with exports plus imports exceeding 50 per cent of GDP. By 1981 the ratio had fallen to about 35 per cent but more because of relative price changes and stagnation of exports than because of reduced external structural dependence. However, the makeup of imports had shifted between 1961 and 1981 from domination by final consumer goods to about 50 per cent capital goods, 33 per cent intermediate (of which two-thirds was petroleum) and 18 per cent consumer goods (of which almost three-fifths was food).[3]

Tanzania has no domestic oil source. Electric power is basically hydro and household consumption basically wood. Historically it has usually been a net staple food (cereals) importer; albeit beverages (coffee, tea) and speciality foods (cashew, cardamom) dominate exports.

Inflation in Tanzania through 1979 paralleled global trends – 1979 price levels were 151 (to a 1975 base) versus the world average of 152 (albeit the rate of increase over 1971–75 was higher, and over 1976–79 lower).[4] During 1980–82 there have been unprecedented (25–33 per cent) annual cost of living increases;[5] this inflation has been linked to import strangulation of production which has not merely reduced the availability of goods but caused the government to run a recurrent deficit by eroding the indirect tax base.

## And a political-economic sketch

The public productive sector is dominant in large and medium scale activity – except road transport and construction. Through import/export, wholesaling, financial and agricultural marketing dominance it has substantial leverage over retail trade and perhaps two-thirds of marketed peasant production which comprise two-thirds of exports and half of domestic food.[6] Its performance has been uneven. Finance and distribution performance is above average, manufacturing mixed and agricultural production and marketing (except coffee) below average. The sectoral total for public enterprise operating surpluses peaked at about 6 per cent of GDP in the early 1970s (and again in 1977) but then fell to near zero.[7] The negligible net surplus sectorally is made up of cross-cancelling enterprise surpluses and losses of about 4 per cent of GDP.

Domestic economic integration has been stressed, with substantial progress but major gaps – in capital goods (except construction materials), fuel and (in bad weather years) staple food.[8] By increasing the ratio of machinery and transport equipment to investment and GDP, the structural integration strategy has raised absolute import requirements and achieved only slow declines in the ratio of imports to GDP.

Reduction of inequality of income distribution and of access to basic services (health, education, water) have had sustained emphasis since 1967 with substantial results.[9] The ratio of the top 1 per cent to the bottom 20 per cent of public sector employees' pre-tax incomes was about 5 to 1 in 1980. Literacy has been raised to 70–75 per cent, access to water to over 50 per cent and life expectancy to 51 (from about 35 at independence).

The basic planning approach has been a managed market one, via price incentives and disincentives together with a large public enterprise sector. Since 1971 foreign exchange and bank credit budgeting have also been central to economic management. Physical balance planning is very limited in coverage and compulsory production or delivery systems unknown. Fiscally Tanzania has traditionally followed a high tax, balanced recurrent budget policy. The first recurrent budget deficit, which came in 1978–79, was linked to the war with Uganda.

Until 1980 there was no overall export strategy – positive or negative. Fragmentary product (e.g. tea) and sectoral (e.g. pre-export processing) strategies existed but received relatively low policy or resource priority.[10]

## International determinants: 1970–82

*Toward an export impasse*
Exports are dominated by eight primary products – in descending order coffee, cotton, cloves, diamonds, sisal, cashew nuts, tea and tobacco plus sisal twine and cashew kernels. With the exception of cashew nuts and diamonds these products have been characterised by low global consumption growth and by real price patterns ranging from secular through moderate decline, to trendless radical instability. They account for 75–80 per cent of total exports, which in 1981 totalled about $500 million (a nominal record and a recovery to about 90 per cent of the 1966 volume peak). However, volume and value have since declined by about 30 per cent.[11]

Manufactured goods exports – excluding residual oil – have been as high as 16 per cent of exports in 1979 but declined to under 10 per cent in 1981. In the case of processing (leather, cashew kernels, sisal twine), supply constraints at the imported spares/chemicals level, shortages of raw materials and – in the case of sisal twine – European cartel nontariff barriers were dominant. In other cases the devastating impact of import constraints on manufacturing affected several producers (e.g. tyres, batteries, aluminium circles) as did lack of foreign exchange or the availability of reciprocal tradeables from previous external purchasers (e.g. textiles).

The lack of a coherent export strategy until 1980–81 and the global (and consequent national) terms of trade shifts against several exports have led to a slow decline in export volume since the mid-1960s. Declines in both volume and receipts have been exacerbated by losses totalling perhaps $175 million in 1981: about a quarter from faulty 1975–80 pricing (especially for cashews), another quarter from delays in payment for crops and a half from import constraints on fertiliser, pesticides, transport and processing equipment.

*Imports: Price explosion, quantity implosion*
Superimposed on the 1961–81 trend towards dominance of capital and

intermediate goods imports have been sharp price changes and a cereals import pattern related to taste changes (to wheat and rice), drought (1973–74, 1979–82) and inadequate storage (600,000 tonnes food loss over 1976–80, i.e. two years drought-level imports).

Petroleum prices rose more than tenfold during 1974–81 while quantity fell about 7 per cent. Share in imports rose from 6 per cent (netting out transit trade) to 22 per cent. Over 1973–76 however a massive increase in grain imports (paralleled by a trebling of unit cost) had a greater impact on external balance than did petroleum prices. This was not repeated in 1979–81. Import quantities were significantly lower and there was no grain price explosion so that 1981 total food imports were nearly 10 per cent of all imports versus 3.5 per cent in 1970 and 22 per cent in 1974.[12]

No reliable terms of trade data exist. Because of transport costs and differential price increases – related to commercial arrears – Tanzania's unit costs of manufactured imports have risen faster than global averages. Rough estimates based on partial data suggest 1981 gross barter terms of trade were about 50 to a 1977 base or 55 to a 1972 one (1976 was about 65 to a 1972 base).[13] This means that at 1977 relative prices, 1981 exports would have covered over 100 per cent of actual imports as opposed to just over 50 per cent at 1981 prices.

*External finance: Costs and limits on access*
Tanzania has never had substantial access to normal commercial credit. Over 1978–82 it used about $250 million of supplier export credits and ran up $300–350 million commercial arrears (by 1982 including $50–75 million delayed government debt service) in attempts to sustain investment and import levels respectively. External grants and soft (or semi-soft, e.g. World Bank) loans have been a major source of foreign exchange. In 1973 they were about Sh1,200 million (35 per cent of imports), in 1977 Sh1,800 million (30 per cent of imports) and in 1981 Sh3,500 million (37 per cent of imports). Divided by average import prices 1981 aid in real import capacity terms was perhaps as high as 1973 or about 25 per cent lower on a real per capita basis.[14] The 1981 total of grants, soft loans and import support was about $20 per capita.

Therefore, external finance could not cushion the 1973–82 fall in earned import capacity. Aid was stagnant in import capacity terms while indiscriminately used export credits and accumulation of arrears only postponed the import constraints' impact on investment and production briefly, at a high cost in terms of still greater constriction in 1981 and 1982.

## National macro-economic policies

*1970–72: A prelude*[15]

In 1970–72 Tanzania faced its first post-independence foreign exchange crisis. Gradual declines from late 1969 culminated in a massive fall in the second half of 1971. The causes were fairly readily identifiable: excess domestic credit formation (to enterprises), capital flight to Kenya (following nationalisation of rented buildings), a shift in State Trading Corporation (STC) buying policy from 180-day external commercial credit to f.o.b. financed by domestic overdraft, and STC stock control and ordering weaknesses.

The measures taken included detailed foreign exchange budgeting and allocation, commercial bank-credit allocation (to major enterprises and the government), exchange control on transactions with Kenya and Uganda and a restructuring (decentralisation) of STC. By the end of the first quarter of 1972 reserves were on the rise and continued to climb reaching record levels in the final quarter of 1973.

Over the same period, concern with imported inflation – and especially its magnification in the distributive system – led to the creation of a prices management commission. Its approach was efficient production cost plus a proportion of assets or net worth combined with fairly tight restrictions on gross distributive margins. This strategy was moderately successful until 1978 but has since been largely swamped by the extreme scarcities and falling capacity utilisation ratios of 1979–82.

*The 1974–76 emergency programme*[16]

In early 1974 the government realised that – despite high reserves – it faced a crisis from quadrupled oil prices and massive grain imports consequent on the impact of the 1973 (and projected 1974) drought on harvests. The choices debated were a classic demand reduction approach and a 'produce/invest out of trouble' strategy calling for substantial bridging finance. The latter was adopted – largely because the political climate was favourable to it but partly because it was technically better presented (largely by the Ministry of Finance). The policy package adopted in the second quarter of 1974 included: near immediate adjustment of domestic prices to imported fuel, fertiliser and oil price rises and increases of 50 per cent in grower prices and 40 per cent in the minimum wage (tailing down to 6 per cent on upper salaries); protecting real income of peasant food growers (via grower prices), minimum wage earners, drought hit areas (by 'famine' relief); sustaining enterprise surpluses (by price increases) and recurrent budget balance (by tax increases – including on petroleum products – and a 1974/75 freeze on recurrent expenditure). It also aimed at maintenance of real investment levels; consumption cuts; and production promotion centred on food (grower prices and input subsidies), consumer and intermediate goods manufacturing to reduce the ratio of imports to GDP and, in theory, export development. The other main measures taken included tightening foreign exchange and bank-credit allocation and mobilising bridging finance (e.g. IMF – SDRs, oil facility, first credit tranche) and interim (e.g. bilateral grants, IBRD programme loan) to cover the anticipated 1974–76 bulge in the trade deficit.

This policy was in a sense demand management via demand switching to protect low income groups and to maintain investment and basic services. Over 1974–76 the strategy was pursued – with distinct lags in the completion of projects in manufacturing and rather low attention to the export component. It was largely successful. After a poor 1974, growth returned to over 5 per cent a year, manufacturing returned to fairly rapid expansion, a record total in marketed crops was recorded, reserves rose. What was not fully noted was how heavily this depended on the 1976–77 beverage price boom (which sent coffee to 20-year record real peaks) while, in volume terms, export stagnation/slow decline had not been reversed.

### 1977–78: The typhoon's eye

With reserve levels climbing to five months imports at their late 1977 peak and the recurrent budget (which on normal accounting had remained just in the black) returning to healthy surplus, a certain laxity in respect to external and internal balance emerged. Foreign exchange budgeting was greatly relaxed (including for non-essential consumer goods) under World Bank/IMF pressure[17] and bank-credit formation controls fell into disuse. The overall rate of expansion in domestic credit formation was low, masking a disquieting increase in respect to grain marketing, which in fact represented losses not inventories. The 1977–78 and 1978–79 recurrent budgets were optimistic, creative or lax depending on point of view.

With the collapse of the coffee boom and the rise in imports, reserves melted away in 1978 and the recurrent budget moved towards deficit. An imminent crisis (the response to which was already delayed relative to 1974's action time frame) exploded into an immediate one – and attention was distracted from its resolution – by the war which followed Uganda's invasion of Tanzania's Kagera region in the last quarter of 1978.[18]

### Tactical sorties and strategic retreats: 1979–81

Over the period 1979–81 no effective adjustment strategy comparable in relevance, operationality or results to 1974–76 was achieved. Until mid-1979 the demands of the war prevented proper estimation of (or single-minded attention to) the requirements of adjustment, while belief that the 1979 poor harvest, 1979–80 oil price rise and the industrial economy stagnation would be reversed as quickly as 1973–74 problems, hid the true magnitude and urgency of the rapidly opening external gap. By the time a full scale attempt to reduce government expenditure was possible in late 1979, the recurrent budget deficit had exploded to 10 per cent of GDP and the revenue base (dominated by sales tax on domestic manufacturers) was being eroded by import constraints.

Compared to 1974 there were fewer consumer goods imports to cut so that reductions were delayed; they came after a buildup of suppliers' credits and arrears had mortgaged the future and had rapid negative results on manufacturing, agriculture, transport and exports. Initial efforts to maintain investment (queried in 1980 and reversed in 1981) were both foredoomed and inappropriate given the length and depth of the terms of trade decline, the much lower starting level of real per capita aid (at least 35 per cent below 1973 in 1977) and the lack of low conditionality IMF facilities. Similarly while the real prices of food and selected export crops were raised, attempts to protect the real minimum wage in 1980 and 1981 proved unsustainable given continued bad weather and the 40 per cent 1978–81 fall in real manufactured goods production. Weaknesses (from deferred maintenance and total loss of physical and financial control by several agricultural marketing corporations) which had built up from 1973 (and not been fully attended to in the 1977–78 period of relaxed resource constraints) were brutally exposed by the new pressures and diverted attention to desperate – and none too successful – patchworks. Tanzania's adjustment proposals were not seen as credible by the IMF and World Bank, leading to long delays in negotiation (which eroded the underlying position long enough to make the proposals obsolete) or to incomplete and fudged packages which had no chance of success (e.g. the 1980 IMF programme, hit especially by the failure of the World Bank's expected Structural Adjustment Programme Credit to materialise,[19] despite being budgeted for in the IMF projections).

Thus by 1982 Tanzania – despite ruthless cutbacks which had won some time in 1980 – faced a far more severe crisis than in either late 1974 or late 1979. While an export strategy had been agreed in principle in 1980 and articulated to some purpose in 1981, its production side was severely handicapped by lack of foreign exchange to cover requisite transport, raw materials, spares, agricultural supplies and replacement inputs, while its payoff was also limited because of the impact of global recession on primary export prices and regional markets' ability to pay for manufactured goods.

## 1982 – A thing of shreds and patches

1982 saw rapid further retrenchment in real basic and defence recurrent expenditure, in wages and salaries (no increases in the face of 25–30 per cent cost of living increases), in real imports (which became an exercise in desperate juggling) and in new capacity-creating investment – all of which continued through 1983. However, with declines in real import capacity and continued erosion of the revenue base and the financial position of export marketing and transport corporations, this merely averted instant collapse. Real GDP fell by about 2 per cent in 1981 and 3 per cent in 1982 (the first falls since independence with the possible exception of 1979), and ability to plan ahead was sapped by the day-to-day demands of the very crises which made it essential.

External negotiations marked time – partly because Tanzanian formulations remained relatively imperfect, partly because the Structural Adjustment Programme produced by an independent Tanzania Advisory Group remained remarkably unarticulated[20] (and remarkably inadequate at regaining budgetary balance), and partly because bilateral donors waited on the Bank and Fund (who were not in fact agreed on some key issues). Equally basic, nobody (in Tanzania or elsewhere) could envisage a viable solution not involving substantial ($300–500 million a year for three years) added import capacity and medium term real export level increases, nor any practicable approach to achieving the first increase (or without it the second).

## National micro-economic policies

### Fiscal prudence and frustration

Fiscal policy was conservative in intent. A recurrent budget breakeven in poor years, and a surplus in good years, was sought until 1980 (and until 1978/79 was achieved) and a ceiling on bank borrowing for the capital budget (on balance, though not annually, achieved over 1972–78) was set. Taxation included relatively high and progressive income taxes which yielded 30 per cent of revenue in the early 1980s. As taxes in foreign trade declined (to 10–15 per cent in early 1980s), sales tax on domestic manufactures became dominant (13.5 per cent in 1972/73 and 35–40 per cent in early 1980s). This pattern worked well so long as manufacturing was not constrained by raw material and spares import strangulation. In 1974–76 substantial rate increases and modest quantitative growth made ex-post sales tax revenue buoyant. It proved disastrous over 1979–82, when the volume of manufactures fell by more than 40 per cent, wiping out most of the nominal and more than all the real rate and price increases in sales tax revenue.

Total annual recurrent expenditure has been relatively constant at about 20 per cent of GDP since the end of the 1960s; it may have increased slightly in 1981/82 and 1982/83 when increases in parastatal reconstruction finance, to repay past deficits initially covered by bank borrowing as well as phasing out continuing losses, offset defence cuts and basic cuts in services.[21] Capital expenditure rose fairly steadily from 7.5 per cent of GDP at the end of the 1960s to 15 per cent at the end of the 1970s but has since been cut to 10 per cent of GDP. Bank borrowing varied sharply as a share of financing requirement – 38 per cent 1969/70, 1 per cent 1972/73, 28 per cent 1975/76, negative in 1976/77, 19 per cent 1977/78 (all capital budget related) but rising to over 40 per cent on a sustained basis from 1978/79.

### Credit budgeting and fiscal weakness
Bank credit allocations by major enterprise (or enterprise group) was begun in 1970–72 and intensified over 1974–76. It more or less lapsed over 1976–79 prior to severe reintroduction over 1979/82. It was based on estimates of output, cash flow and prices partly disaggregated to enterprise level; but it was relatively weak for agricultural marketing bodies because their borrowings were sharply influenced by harvest volumes which forced less precise limits and allowed passing off of losses as increases in stocks.

While government bank borrowing targets were not always held, they influenced actual spending; and until the war undershooting was almost as common as overshooting. Since then both the delay in bringing military spending and agricultural marketing losses down and the collapse of revenue meant consistent overshooting of up to 50 per cent until 1981/82.

### Agricultural policy – The weaknesses of external technocracy
Agricultural pricing and management was relatively weak until 1975 but price co-ordination had maintained plausible relative prices. Over 1974–75 sharp increases were made in grain prices to protect peasant incomes and provide incentives. Similarly, taking one year with another, marketing authorities had net surpluses. Over 1975–81 price setting, parastatal supervision and related areas were delegated to what was *de facto* an autonomous, expatriate staffed parallel bureaucracy – the Marketing Development Bureau.[22] The results were damaging in respect to relative prices (which severely reduced cashew nut production and led to unmanageable coarse grain and cassava surpluses). More particularly, deterioration of marketing parastatal (except coffee) performance included failure to pay on time, collapse of accounting systems and in some cases of physical control and large, unknown deficits ($200–250 million or 8 per cent of GDP in the staple food case).

These were exacerbated by the failure to achieve an inter-year storage policy so that 600,000 tonnes of 1976–78 surpluses were spoilt, deteriorated into poultry feed or dumped abroad and were thus unavailable to meet 1979–82 maize import demand. Relative prices were restored to some semblance of order over 1980–82 for all officially marketed crops taken together, but less so for exports relative to domestic food crops which then stood above 1972/73 in real terms. But collapse in the terms of trade and the overvaluation of the shilling resulting from rapid 1980–82 inflation[23] left export crop production incentives far lower than optimal and created a Treasury subsidy burden of up to 15 per cent of recurrent revenue to cover marketing authority losses. Restoring order to parastatal physical and financial systems and creating a workable storage system had barely begun by the end of 1982.[24]

## Incomes, equity and the shrinking pie

Incomes policy centred on grower prices (raised about in line with the cost of living over 1974–82 but not uniformly for all crops), wages (which fell perhaps 40 per cent in real terms over 1973–82) and salaries (which fell by about two-thirds in real terms over 1973–82). In 1969, 1972 and 1974 minimum wage increases to offset cost of living increases were made while in the last year all wages and salaries were raised statutorily – tapering from 42 per cent at the bottom to 6 per cent at the top. A minor minimum wage increase in 1975 was followed by a long gap until 1980 and 1981 when there were 25 per cent increases (broadly offsetting those years' cost of living rises) with a partial repeat of the 1974 exercise in 1981 including 15–25 per cent wage and salary increases. In 1982 no increases were seen as practicable despite an anticipated rise of more than 30 per cent in the cost of living.

The results of the incomes policy have included reduced intra-urban and urban–rural inequality.[25] However, since 1978 this has been within an 'all boats sink lower' context of allocating sacrifices to spare the weakest, not of dividing increases.

## Price management under pressure

Price management, as noted earlier, has been on an 'efficient operating-cost plus' basis at major product and firm level. The Prices Commission has taken a highly sceptical view of asserted costs, especially in distribution, but have granted increases they believed adequate to sustain profits of efficient enterprises on an annual or semi-annual basis. Over 1973–78 it did hold the inflation of domestic manufacturing and distribution costs below the average cost of living increase and did not result in massive 'parallel marketing' or enterprise losses (the latter is not entirely surprising, as investible surplus was one of the targets the Price Commission was bound to seek to increase). Since 1979 cost-push inflation from falls in capacity utilisation and similarly caused physical shortages have radically reduced the Commission's ability to ascertain realistic cost projections (with resultant falls in enterprise surpluses), to hold down price increases or to avert widespread 'parallel marketing'.

*Fuel pricing and production*
Fuel policy has involved petroleum pricing (taxation), allocation, alternative commercial fuel development and afforestation/woodlot programmes. Fuel prices (petroleum products and electricity) rose about 360 per cent and petroleum products alone about 425 per cent from 1972 to mid-1981 compared to about 300 per cent for the overall cost of living. From late 1981 onwards premium gasoline prices have exceed $1 per litre with gas oil and kerosene at $0.40 to 0.45.

All direct import cost increases were passed on to users. There were at no point any fuel subsidies and both the petroleum refining/distributing companies and the national electric power company showed rising pre-tax profits in real as well as nominal terms through 1981 despite a volume decline in the case of petroleum products.[26]

Similarly, government surplus from petroleum (here defined as taxation on products plus the profits of the state importing/wholesaling firm substituted for the majors in 1976) rose by 350 per cent (slightly above the cost of living index) although it declined somewhat as a share of final price and fell from about 75 per cent of petroleum import cost in 1972 to under 45 per cent in 1981. Within this total taxes (the only source of government surplus in 1972) fell to less than the pre-tax profits of the Tanzanian Petroleum Development Corporation (TPDC), or from 75 per cent to 20 per cent of import cost, and declined in real terms.[27] Petroleum pricing policy was designed to: avoid subsidisation and enterprise losses; ensure an adequate TPDC cash flow; and limit increases in the cost of rural transport and of low income-group lighting.

As a result tax increases were limited after 1974 and the relative prices of kerosene and gasoil were lowered (i.e. they rose less) compared to gasoline.

From 1981 physical allocation by region and to key users was instituted with rather uneven but fairly visible effect. Gasoline rationing in Dar es Salaam – while possibly useful as a demonstrable burden imposed on the elite like the 1974 limitation on Sunday driving – had limited impact on volume or distribution of users. By late 1983 petrol and gas oil shortages were endemic, especially in the Lake regions.

Hydroelectric capacity was increased substantially over 1972–81 allowing elimination of thermal plant generation on the national grid. In

1980 extension of the grid was begun (with a tentative 1986 completion date) to allow substitution for thermal plant at the main southern and lake towns. Exploration for oil from 1969 on has yet to discover any although major programmes are in hand. It has discovered gas which should by the late 1980s add 40 per cent to 1982 export value through manufacture of urea and ammonia. Coal development has to date made little progress and – except for small or isolated processing plants – is probably less economic than hydro or gas development.

The dominant fuel for household use and tobacco curing is wood. There is little trade-off with oil but an urgent need to develop more secure and accessible supplies, to reduce the inordinate share of women's and girls' time spent 'wooding', to halt desertification in certain districts and to avert the collapse of the rapaciously wood-intensive tobacco sector. Since the mid-1970s the forestry division has – apparently with increasing success – placed major emphasis on tree planting both for ecological purposes and (especially in the case of village woodlots) for direct household fuel supply.[28] However, replanting is still not equivalent to cutting particularly in tobacco growing areas and near major cities.

## Impact of international and policy changes

*Price changes: Importation and accommodation*
Until mid-1979 domestic price changes were largely in response to global price movements both in extent and timing. Because Tanzanian imports were intensive in grain at the time its price exploded and petroleum use could not readily be compressed except by multiplied output reductions, the overall increase was slightly more rapid than average and more concentrated in 1974–75.

Domestic policy was relatively accommodationist – i.e. real grower prices and real minimum wages were substantially protected, though not fully in the latter case or uniformly in the former. However, in respect to manufactured goods, distributive margins, public utilities and salaries price increases were deliberately held below the average cost of living or import price increase.

Since 1979 the impact has been different. The initial inflationary impact came from war costs – recurrent budget deficits and disruption of transport. Its continuation relates to the cumulative impact of importing industrial recession as cost-push (and revenue-base erosion) inflation. A 50 per cent fall in the terms of trade over 1977–82 led to a 40–45 per cent decline during 1977–81 in earned import capacity, despite a (small) export volume increase. There was a further 30 per cent fall in 1982 as transport, processing and input bottlenecks more than wiped out export-production promotion efforts.

*Balance of payments – A receding historic memory*
Over 1974–77 balance of payments management was responsive to and able to manage very large swings in the trade deficit. In part this related to their being substantially reversed (in real terms) by 1977. An additional factor was the 1974–75 availability of substantial IMF low-conditionality resources to bridge the gap before other aid commitments (which in practice basically offset the rapid decline in Chinese transfers) became effective. But equally critical was the possibility of cutting consumer goods and maintenance imports sharply with little immediate impact on production.

*Per contra* 1978 was a rake's progress. Imports (especially of consumer goods) were substantially liberalised in 1977 precisely as the terms of trade turned sour. An imprudently high projected use of reserves was exceeded and corrective action delayed. The war with Uganda thus caught Tanzania with a precarious and rapidly deteriorating reserve position.[29]

Over 1979–82 the combined impact of external shocks – war, sluggish and relatively tightly tied real resource transfers, drought and falling terms of trade – would have made balance of payments management very difficult even under 1973 conditions. In fact the starting point was much worse: neither owned reserves nor low conditionality IMF facilities were available to buy time. The deferred maintenance backlog, which had only partially been cleared, made spares and related imports cuts much more damaging to production. There were few consumer goods left to cut. The unselective use of supplier credit in 1979–81, to sustain investment related imports for low priority projects, heavily mortgaged 1981 and subsequent export earnings. By late 1982, to speak of a balance of payments was a misnomer and foreign exchange allocation in practice was collapsing into *ad hoc* juggling to cover particular shipments on a day to day basis.

*Exchange rate adjustment: from responsiveness to deadlock*
Tanzania has not viewed the exchange rate as a major positive tool for causing desired results. Until 1979, however, it viewed exchange rate changes (several small devaluations and one mini-revaluation) as a necessary minor part of adjusting to changed global price relationships (e.g. to avoid absolute decreases in grower prices).

From 1979 on a proto-policy of small, frequent adjustments (25 per cent in 5 half-yearly changes was canvassed in 1979 and 40 per cent in five or six in 1981–82)[30] was blocked by two factors. First, it was argued that it would complicate inflation control and – perhaps – protection of low income groups. Second, and more critical, it collided head on with IMF advice for 'jumbo' devaluations (25–30 per cent canvassed in 1979 and 60–70 per cent in 1981–82) which made the mini-adjustment strategy seem useless in gaining an agreed IMF programme and aroused an equally fundamentalist response on the part of some Tanzanian leaders of opposing any devaluation at all.

As a result the only exchange rate change from mid-1979 through to the end of 1982 was a 13 per cent adjustment (devaluation) in March 1982 which really only corrected the 1980–81 accidental revaluation flowing from a dollar-dominated currency basket adopted in 1979 (and not changed until 1982). Even that was delayed nine months because of the domestic reaction to the IMF's stance which led to a deadlock on negotiating a programme throughout 1981 and 1982. Over 1982–83 the increase in overvaluation's impact on the budget (via subsidies to export crop authorities) and the need to achieve a credible position for negotiating with sources of external finance, resulted in an increasingly firm and clear commitment to phased devaluation, beginning with 20 per cent in June 1983.

If one accepts the World Bank's view that there was limited overvaluation in 1980[31] – and by implication very little in 1979 – then one arrives at a plausible range of rates for mid-1983 of 16 to 22 shillings to the dollar versus an actual rate of 12.4. It is believed that Tanzanian strategy is to move by several steps to a point within this range by the end of 1984, and to adjust in small steps subsequently on the basis of relative inflation rates.

*Economic growth: Recovery and collapse*
The initial impact of the 1974 Emergency Programme – and more importantly of the 1973–74 drought – was to cause GDP growth to decline to about 2 per cent (and agricultural output to fall 2 per cent) in 1974. Thereafter, growth rapidly recovered to almost 6 per cent in 1977 (with agricultural growth over the 1975–78 period also averaging about 6 per cent). GDP stagnated or fell in 1979, recovered in 1980, and fell throughout 1981–83. Real agricultural output declined from 1980 onwards. This was largely weather related, but was exacerbated by input and transport shortages caused by import constraints.[32]

The pattern is fairly typical of sub-Saharan African economies – a manageable crisis in 1974–75 and a larger, unmanageable one beginning in 1979. The onset of the crisis (and the 1980 declines in manufacturing output and in crop production) are explicable in terms of unwise use of reserves in 1978, war in 1978–79 and drought from 1979. Its continuation and unmanageability stem primarily from sustained importation of industrial-economy recession, which prevented growth of exports and therefore import capacity. By 1983/84 the situation had deteriorated so badly that OECD recovery, even if including a beverage price boom, could no longer be expected to turn the situation around. Outside agriculture (and in part even there) the basic problem was not one of available capacity, nor even of technical and managerial personnel to utilise it, but of the 20–25 per cent direct import component needed to operate and maintain it.

*Development pattern impact – Adjustment or distortion?*
Because 1974–76 was seen as a stochastic shock – albeit with some permanent price shifts in favour of oil, grain and manufactures – its impact was to reinforce rather than reverse sectoral priorities. Integration of the industrial sector[33] and self-sufficiency in grain were seen as demonstrably correct – as was increased emphasis on hydrocarbon exploration. While, in principle, more emphasis was to be placed on export expansion (especially by pre-export processing and buildup of selected manufactured goods sales in regional markets) this was *de facto* largely deferred over 1974–76 and lost sight of over 1977–78, when the external account position seemed less worrisome and there was a relaxation from tight macro-management of 1974–76. Substantial export processing capacity was created but inadequately supplied, managed and marketed.

The 1979–82 crisis appears to be having a more complex result. This is partly because it is perceived as semi-permanent and partly because (short of finding liquid hydrocarbons) no set of sectoral-balance changes appears both practicable and adequate.

Increased relative resource allocations have been made to agriculture and supporting services (the only sector to show a volume increase in imports over 1979/80–1982/83) and to projects/inputs directly relevant to boosting exports and/or saving actual current imports. However, reallocation is crippled by rapidly falling total import capacity – a higher share of a shrinking cake has often meant an absolute decline. In respect of energy (hydroelectric generation and transmission, hydrocarbon exploration and gas-based export development) and part of forestry (pulp and paper mill, wood supply) the reallocation of imports to date appears just adequate to allow progress towards higher production and exports. Elsewhere it seems to have crippled industry, health, water and education without being adequate to restore agricultural or primary export growth.

*Morale, morality, political viability*
Morale was shaken in 1975 but the 1974 programme was broadly accepted as a bold and necessary response to external crisis, and as equitable in allocation of burdens. Over 1976–78 morale recovered sharply as success became apparent (admittedly apparent not real in

1978). Over 1979 it was sustained because the liberation of Uganda produced a temporary euphoria. Recollection of 1974–76 sustained morale in 1980 but it has manifestly deteriorated as the record of unsuccess has lengthened. There is for the first time substantial doubt as to the government's ability to cope, hardly surprising with national command over resources per capita one-third down on 1978.

Morality also suffered over 1975–76, partially recovered over 1977–78 and worsened radically over 1979–82. However, this is in relative terms and in a particular context. Very few major decisions or contracts are influenced by bribery. Private and public corruption and profiteering are both rhetorically and actually seen as evil and as exceptions; they are attacked to some effect, albeit somewhat frenetically and episodically. 'Parallel marketing' is tolerated where need based (e.g. the peasant paddy crop and minor overcharges at retail) but deeply hated in cases of full scale 'entrepreneurs of adversity'. The pressure that the upward trend of scarcities and the downward trend of wage, salary and small business real incomes put on future evolution of morality is alarming.

Tanzania's government still seems to have a broad base of support (in the sense of popular acceptance of its objectives). This is consistent with a decline in morale for two reasons. First, no potential alternative ruling coalition exists. There are vocal critics, pro-capitalist as well as left-wing, but they lack the necessary institutional and sub-class bases to be credible alternatives. Second, the experience of Tanzania's neighbours with widely varied capitalist strategies – and in Mozambique a socialist strategy distinctly less pro-rural and open than Tanzania's – strongly suggests to the leadership and to many workers, peasants and even officials and managers that domestic strategy mistakes cannot be the basic cause of the crisis.

This similarity in basic problems, given the disparity in political-economic strategies and division of costs, suggests to many Tanzanians that the basic causes of the economic crises are indeed external and therefore not in themselves strong reasons for querying official goals and strategies or even seeking a wholesale change in leadership (of which there has been a fairly high turnover through normal elections and appointment procedures). Predicting the effect of the continuing crisis in this respect is risky. Acceptance of sincerity without success is presumably not infinite – Tanzanians expect results from the state. On the other hand unless a credible alternative strategy and political coalition emerge, criticism is likely – as at present – to be of failures and alterations of degree and emphasis within, rather than alternatives to, the present political-economic paradigm of the state and party.

## Outlook and general reflections

### Through a glass grimly

It is extremely difficult to make any reasoned projections for the Tanzanian economy. Any which offer a prospect of stabilisation and recovery require one or more highly optimistic assumptions about import capacity. Any which take as given present (and reasonably projectable) earned import capacity and resource transfers point to continued decline. At some not terribly distant point this would result in a collapse into Ghanaian or Zairois conditions which are not really comparable to – or analysable in the same terms and categories as – normally (even if badly functioning) economies.

Prospects for existing exports are bleak. Quota limits in the case of coffee, and demand and cartel limits in the case of sisal and twine, preclude major gains in earned import capacity. Tobacco faces a fuel threat to viability and poor price prospects. Cotton also faces ecological barriers to even sustained output as do cloves. The diamond mine is nearing exhaustion. Rebuilding cashew picking/collection (and in the medium term replanting) requires uncertain quantities of time, of disease control and of transport rehabilitation; restoring real price levels to growers has at best stemmed further declines. No major terms of trade recovery can be expected.[34] Greater efficiency in allocation of resources to support export production and marketing and to clear bottlenecks might raise earned import capacity 2–4 per cent a year over 1983–90 (barely offsetting the rise in debt service).

New exports in sight for the late 1980s – paper and ammonia/urea – should raise total exports by 30–45 per cent but over their first decade will have very substantial capital repayment obligations. They might allow a modest import growth were present levels adequate (as opposed to 20–30 per cent below minimum for efficient operation), arrears negligible (in fact they are $500 million) and the export cover of imports 75 per cent (vs 50 per cent at present). As it is they are a necessary part of any answer, but far from the whole of it.

Major aid increases are unlikely – partly because overall ODA in real terms simply will not grow rapidly over 1983–90. Reallocation of 75 per cent (versus about 30 per cent now) of ODA to maintenance and capacity utilisation support might provide a basis for stabilisation, by allowing import shifts to spares and intermediate goods, with recovery in the late 1980s as the new exports came on stream.

However, such transfers seem dependent on a Tanzania/IMF Agreement (also necessary if arrears are to be reduced this side of 1990). The main obstacle is the Tanzania government's belief (backed by at least two independent analyses) that a 60–70 per cent one-off devaluation and 50 per cent interest rates – as proposed by the IMF – would catapult inflation from the 25 to 30 per cent range to over 100 per cent, make subsequent reduction almost impossible and greatly weaken economic management capability by diversion of attention and increase in uncertainty. *Per contra* Fund Missions have viewed Tanzania's approach of gradual devaluation as not worth negotiating about. As a result neither approach is acted on and others delay their decisions while real economic decline and capacity erosion continue.[35] Had no proposals for maxi-devaluations been made by the IMF, the actual exchange rate would probably have depreciated by more than it did in 1981, 1982 and 1983.

### Tanzania in perspective – Some tentative generalisations

The impact of imported inflation on Third World and fringe industrial economies over 1970–82 has varied significantly as have the constraints on their responses. To generalise from Tanzania to the Republic of Korea or to Kuwait would be otiose. However, several elements of Tanzania's experience do seem relevant to the low income, economically small countries with exports dominated by primary products and lacking assured domestic fuel and/or basic food supplies – e.g. Malawi and Sri Lanka within this study and to a majority of Sub-Saharan African and least-developed economies.

These economies exhibit a variant of the *Giffen (inferior) good paradox*. When the real prices of their exports decline they are unable to switch resources to alternative exports. Beyond a finite point they cannot reduce real imports without economic collapse. As a result they are virtually forced to ignore market price signals and normal allocational efficiency criteria and seek to raise exports of precisely those products for which the world market prices signal relatively less production. If a significant number of countries succeed in raising physical exports, the ensuing acceleration of real price erosion actually reduces their collective real export earnings and those of most individual countries. This certainly has been the 1976–81 record in coffee, with value stabilisation and recovery achieved in 1982–83 because International Coffee Association quotas reduced exports.

*Industrial-economy deflation* can be – and is – *imported as cost-push and 'parallel-market' inflation*. This is true because industrial-economy deflation and stagnation result in low growth of global trade in primary products and in worsening terms of trade. Resulting declines in real import capacity force cuts in capacity utilisation, infrastructure maintenance (e.g. transport, water, power) and in agricultural sector inputs (e.g. fertiliser, pesticides, implements). All tend to raise unit costs (often dramatically) and to create acute physical shortages, making profiteering and 'parallel marketing' (whether technically illegal or not) inevitable. In the case of Tanzania, imported inflation resulting from the export of depression by industrial economies over 1979–82 has apparently (if not readily quantifiably) been more sustained and intense than imported inflation of the more standard type over 1973–75, partly because the period of importing depression has been substantially longer.

At present, use of *short term commercial credit* (including unselective acceptance of supplier export credit and commercial arrears), especially at high interest rates, is analogous – for these economies – to the use of heroin to cure depression, *a quick fix at the price of worsening the underlying problem*. While bolstering import capacity for two or three years, it reduces medium-term import capacity unless: terms of trade recover; sustained, rapid quantitative growth of exports despite declining real unit value is possible; or commercial short-term borrowing can not only be rolled over but rolled up to cover repayment of principal and interest and a steadily rising net inflow. None of these is very plausible and when the merry-go-round stops the impasse is worse than if the import cuts had been made sooner.

Structural change toward greater national economic integration *produces paradoxical results* unless real earned import capacity can, at the least, be sustained. The initial impact of such change is to increase import requirements absolutely (e.g. in plant and machinery) and to shift them from final consumer to intermediate and capital goods. If successful in raising output and increasing intersectoral linkages (as Tanzanian industrial policy was through 1978) this too raises absolute import requirements because the volume growth more than offsets the decline in import content per unit for many years. If a prolonged fall in real export earnings comes while such a process of structural change is in its early stages the results are traumatic. Very few imports can be sacrificed without an impact on domestic production – a situation unlike that of a pure 'plantation' economy basically importing final consumer goods. But because of remaining production gaps it is not possible, in general, to reallocate domestic resources to substitute for intermediate-goods imports. The resultant cost of import cuts is a *multiplier negative impact* on domestic value added (over three in Tanzanian manufacturing) and on domestic goods availability (up to 10 at retail prices in respect to manufactured goods in Tanzania: i.e. three times value added in manufacturing, two to six times indirect and profits tax, two to three times transport and distribution costs and margins). The impact is thus more acute in respect both to output and inflation if substantial, but incomplete, initial steps towards national integration have been taken prior to an import-capacity collapse than for either a flexible industrial or semi-industrial economy *or* a pure 'plantation' economy. A substantially integrated economy has some immunity to trade shocks while in a 'plantation' economy there is no multiplier impact of import cuts on domestic production.

External imbalance *gap closing* by standard methods appears *impracticable within the national structure constraints and the present world economic outlook.* The crisis has undermined the possibility of export growth (e.g. Malawi), resulted in massive growth in output and investment being paralleled by real per capita consumption falls as well as worsening external gaps and inflation (e.g. Sri Lanka)[36] and/or blocked continuation of systematic reduction of import dependence (e.g. Tanzania). The World Bank prescription[37] of temporary reversion toward a 'plantation economy' (i.e. primary export growth led recovery) and sharp increases in real concessionary transfers appears technically and politically unattainable (quite apart from any judgement on its desirability).[38] The UNCTAD Integrated Commodities Programme increasingly appears to be neither integrated, an operational programme nor of much use to commodity producers or commodity export dependent economies.

*Domestic inefficiency compounds* the impact of external shocks but is also a nearly *inevitable consequence* of such shocks. Both markets and analytically based allocation management work less well under conditions of rapid change and substantial uncertainty. The sudden escalation of the need for day-to-day crisis management reduces (for the private enterprise and peasant sector as well as for the public sector) the ability not simply to undertake medium-term strategic planning but even to stand back to see what immediate allocational and semi-structural changes would increase the efficiency with which existing (reduced) resources were applied.[39] There is a built-in tendency to seek to do a little less of everything in about the same way, no matter how inappropriate (*vide* Malawian plantation concentration; Sri Lankan fixation with large-scale capital and energy-intensive water works; Tanzania's 1970– 81 deferral of developing an export strategy to sustain – as opposed to an import control strategy to reduce – basic import requirements).

*Domestic political constraints vary* widely but are *never absent.* In Tanzania, policies overtly causing major reductions in minimum wages and real peasant incomes cannot be adopted by the present leadership because of its base, its commitments and its psychology.

## Notes

1 Professor Green has served frequently as adviser to Tanzania since 1964 while Mr. Kamori is Director of Economic Research and Policy at the Bank of Tanzania. Both wish to stress that the analysis and conclusions of this

study are their personal responsibility and are not necessarily those of the Tanzanian authorities and that Professor Green alone prepared and is responsible for the final text.

2 Basic data can be found in the Statistical Annexes to World Bank 1981, 1982, 1983 and in Tanzania *Economic Surveys*.

3 Adapted from Bank of Tanzania *Annual Reports* supplemented by Trade Statistics detailed printouts.

4 See Table 14.10 (Chapter 14 below) for global data. Bank of Tanzania *Annual Reports*.

5 The Tanzania National Cost of Living Index is computed from prices of sample purchases of items in the index (not officially set prices). This method would slightly overstate prices, in comparison to those paid by a real shopper using his own money, but the relative underweighting of rural areas would have the reverse impact. The IMF – on no stated reasoning – asserts the COL Index understates price increases. ILO, 1982 after detailed examination suggested that it overstated.

6 Agricultural quantity data are weak. The estimates for marketed share of food are based on a formula assuming 5 per cent – vs 13–15 per cent actual – urban population and no rural food sales. About 35 per cent of households have basically non-agricultural incomes and on balance use somewhat higher proportions of high-value foods, while peasants do, in fact, buy some food. A 50–50 division between subsistence (household self-provisioning) and marketed food is a plausible working hypothesis.

7 Unpublished national accounts working data and unofficial estimates from Treasury enterprise data. See also *Economic Surveys*.

8 See Bienefeld, Coulson, Green in Fransman, 1981.

9 See ILO, 1982 and 1977.

10 See Green, Rwegesira, Van Arkadie, 1981 for a fuller explanation of the reasons for this strategic gap.

11 Preliminary 1982 and first half of 1983 data from Bank of Tanzania.

12 *Economic Survey* data supplemented by Bank of Tanzania detailed foreign exchange allocation and use records.

13 A new national series is being constructed by the Bank of Tanzania. The 35 per cent 1972–76 fall is an UNCTAD estimate. The 50 per cent 1977–81 fall is a semi-official Treasury one based on rough estimation from actual prices received and paid for main products traded. It corresponds roughly to Ugandan estimates. The much lower falls shown by World Bank and UNCTAD series are based on industrial economy import and export prices used as proxies but these seem to understate how rapidly prices actually paid by Tanzania have risen and overstate actual growth of unit receipts on exports.

14 Most 1973 aid was from China so that OECD aid shows a much more positive trend.

15 For a fuller account and detailed sources, see Green, Rwegasira, Van Arkadie, 1981.

16 Green, Rwegasira, Van Arkadie, 1981.

17 See Payer, 1983. Why Tanzania agreed is less clear as it was not then using either an IMF facility or a Bank programme loan.

18 See Green, Rwegasira, Van Arkadie, 1981.

19  See 1981 *Budget Speech* of Minister for Finance.
20  Based on Interim Report of TAG and 1982 Tanzania Structural Adjustment Programme 'Bluebook' and implementation checklist.
21  Data from Bank of Tanzania, *20 Year Economic Survey 1961–81,* in press.
22  For a fuller account see Payer, 1983. There was very little political pressure on MDB as to specific prices – indeed almost all of its proposals were rubber-stamped until 1981 and the changes then were to higher average *consumer* prices for grain and producer prices for cashew nuts.
23  From 1980 on Tanzania's inflation rate (in cost-of-living terms) has been above the African average or that for developing countries as a whole, albeit far from being in the top tier in either context.
24  Over 1980–82 a step-by-step clawback of power from MDB took place culminating in a new Minister and a Tanzanian Agricultural Policy Study forming the basis for the 1983 Agricultural Policy Statement.
25  See ILO, 1977 and 1982 for detailed review and analysis of data.
26  Largely based on TPDC *Annual Reports* and unpublished Ministry of Water and Energy and sales tax revenue breakdown data.
27  This was partially reversed over 1982–83 especially for premium gasoline, both to raise revenue and to deter consumption.
28  Largely from unpublished national energy survey materials and scattered Forestry Division reports.
29  See Green, Rwegasira, Van Arkadie, 1981.
30  See Green in Williamson, 1983.
31  World Bank, 1983, p. 62.
32  1982 and 1983 Budget Speeches, *Economic Surveys.*
33  See Bienefeld and Green in Fransman, 1981.
34  See World Bank, 1983, pp. 7–13, 30.
35  A result which Williamson points out (1983, p. 652) reflects little credit on the Fund, the Bank or Tanzania.
36  See World Bank, 1982, p. 28.
37  World Bank, 1981.
38  See Amoaka and Please, 1983 for a partial admission of this with respect to rapid increases in earnings from primary product exports.
39  For example, in Tanzania rough calculations of ratios of import allocations to metres of cloth produced for sub-sectors within textiles shows a tendency to allocate in favour of firms with low ratios of output to imports (mostly in the private sector). Further analysis by the Ministry of Industries has identified and corrected several more cases. In the absence of crisis management, this analysis would probably have become routinised much earlier.

## Bibliography

Allison, C. and Green, R.H. (editors) *Accelerated development in Sub-Saharan Africa: what agendas for action?* IDS (Sussex) Bulletin, 14–1, January 1983.
Amoaka, K.Y. and Please, S. (1983) *The World Bank's report on accelerated development in Sub-Saharan Africa: a critique of some of the criticism.* Society for International Development (Kenya) Nairobi, conference paper, in press Journal of African Studies 1984/85.
Bank of Tanzania (1967–81) *Annual Reports.* Bank of Tanzania, Dar es Salaam.

Bank of Tanzania (1984) *Tanzania: Twenty Years of Independence (1961–1981) – A Review of Political and Economic Performance*, Bank of Tanzania, Dar es Salaam.

Fransman, Martin (1981) (editor) *Industry and accumulation in Africa* Heinemann, especially chapters by Bienefeld, M.A., Coulson, A. and Green, R.H.

Government of Tanzania (1960–61 to 1982–83) *Economic Surveys* (formerly *Background to the Budget*) Government Printer, Dar es Salaam.

Government of Tanzania (1960–61 to 1982–83) *Budget Speeches* Government Printer, Dar es Salaam.

Government of Tanzania (1983) *Political-economic adjustment and IMF conditionality: Tanzania 1974–81* in John Williamson (editor) *IMF conditionality* Institute for International Economics, Washington D.C.

Government of Tanzania (1976) *Aspects of the world monetary and resource transfer system in 1974: a view from the extreme periphery in* Helleiner, G.K. (editor) *A world divided: the less developed countries in the international economy* Cambridge University Press.

Green, R.H., Rwegasira, D. and Van Arkadie, B. (1981) *Economic shocks and national policy making: Tanzania in the 1970's* Institute of Social Studies, The Hague, Research Report no. 8.

Green, R.H. and Singer H.W. (1984) *Sub-Saharan Africa in depression: the impact on the welfare of children in* Jolly, A.R. and Cornia, G.A. (editors) *The impact of world recession on children.* World Development, March 1984.

ILO (1977) *Towards self-reliance: development, employment and equity issues in Tanzania.* JASPA, Addis Ababa.

ILO (1982) *Basic needs in danger: a basic needs oriented development strategy for Tanzania.* JASPA, Addis Ababa.

Payer, C. (1983) *Tanzania and the World Bank* Chr. Michelsen Institute, Development Research and Action Programme Working Papers A285.

Tanzania Petroleum Development Corporation (1979–80 to 1981–82) *Annual Reports.* TPDC, Dar es Salaam.

Williamson, John (1983) *IMF Conditionality.* Institute for International Economics, Washington D.C.

World Bank (1981, 1982, 1983) *World Development Reports.* Washington D.C.

World Bank (1981) *Accelerated development in Sub-Saharan Africa: an agenda for action.* Washington D.C.

There is an appendix to Chapter 3 beginning on p. 351.

# 4 The Impact of Imported Inflation on National Development: Sri Lanka

*G. Kurukulasuriya*

## The general characteristics of the economy

Sri Lanka is an island of 66,000 sq.km. with a population in 1981 of 14.8 million; the growth rate of population fell from 2.4 per cent in the 1950s to 1.8 per cent in the 1970s. The World Bank's *World Development Report 1982* gave the *per capita* GNP in 1980 as US$270. The island is classified among the Low Income Countries and ranked as the 21st in the list from the bottom up. This report gave the average annual growth rate of GNP *per capita* 1960–80 as 2.4 per cent, about twice the rate for all low income countries. The average annual rate of inflation 1960–70 was 1.8 per cent and in 1970–80 was 12.6 per cent. The growth of GDP was 4.6 per cent per year in 1960–70 and 4.1 per cent per year in 1970–80. The annual growth rate of energy consumption 1960–80 has been estimated at 3.8 per cent; and energy consumption per head (kilograms of coal equivalent) was 110 in 1960 and 135 in 1979. However, 60 per cent of the energy consumption is from firewood, 28 per cent from oil and about 12 per cent from hydroelectricity. Oil goes into critically important sectors of the economy and kerosene is used throughout the country for lighting.

The same World Bank report observes that the value of merchandise exports grew at an average rate of 4.7 per cent from 1960–70, but fell at an average rate of 2.4 per cent from 1970–80. The

## Table 4.1 Foreign trade indicators

|  | 1952 | 1960 | 1970 | 1975 | 1981 |
|---|---|---|---|---|---|
| A. *Share of selected commodities in total imports* | | | | | |
| 1. Food, Drink & Tobacco of which | 46.3 | 39.0 | 46.2 | 48.0 | 13.9* |
| 1.1 Rice | 19.3 | 12.3 | 13.7 | 20.2 | 2.8 |
| 1.2 Flour | 7.1 | 3.3 | 11.2 | 19.1 | 0.1* |
| 1.3 Sugar | 4.9 | 4.0 | 7.3 | 4.7 | 8.0 |
| 2. Petroleum products | 7.7 | 6.2 | 2.5 | 16.6 | 24.5 |
| 3. Fertilisers | 1.8 | 3.0 | 3.5 | 4.0 | 3.4 |
| B. *Total foreign trade* | | | | | |
| 1. Value of imports CIF Rs.bn | 1.7 | 2.0 | 2.3 | 5.2 | 35.3 |
| 2. Value of exports FOB Rs.bn | 1.5 | 1.8 | 2.0 | 4.0 | 20.6 |
| 3. Imports + exports as % of GDP at constant factor cost prices | | 62 | 37 | 42 | 72 |
| C. *Breakdown of imports by end-use* | | | | | |
| 1. Import of consumer goods as % of total imports (value) | | | 56 | 51 | 26 |
| 2. Import of intermediate goods as % of total imports | | | 20 | 36 | 51 |
| 3. Import of investment goods as % of total imports | | | 24 | 12 | 23 |
| D. *External assets* (Rs.m., year end) | 837 | 458 | 367 | 834 | 9,222 |

*Source:* Central Bank of Ceylon, *Annual Reports.*

*Note:* In 1981 the import of whole wheat for flour milling was classified elsewhere under 'intermediate goods'. In 1980 the import of flour as a percentage of total imports was 5.4 per cent.

See Table 4.4 for exchange rates. On 16 November 1977 the rate moved from $ = Rs.8.59 to $ = Rs.15.97.

terms of trade (1975 = 100) is rated by the World Bank at 203 in 1960 and 93 in 1980. However, because of the post-war socially oriented policies, the country enjoys both a high adult literacy rate of 85 per cent (1977) and a high expectation of life at birth of 66 years (1980).

The import and export dependency of the economy is seen in the pattern of trade relations presented in Tables 4.1 to 4.4. External price changes of critical items (regardless of the presence or not of inflation in the exporter's country) affect the economy both directly,

**Table 4.2 Major exports as percentage of total exports**

|  | 1952 | 1960 | 1970 | 1975 | 1981 |
|---|---|---|---|---|---|
| *Tea* | 48 | 60 | 55 | 49 | 31 |
| *Rubber* | 25 | 21 | 22 | 17 | 14 |
| *Three major coconut products* | 15 | 10 | 12 | 10 | 7 |
| *Major exports* | 88 | 91 | 89 | 76 | 52 |

*Source:* Central Bank of Ceylon, *Annual Reports and Review of the Economy.*

*Note:* In 1975 the export value of *petroleum products* was 9.9 per cent of the value of total exports. In 1981 it was 16.4 per cent. In 1981 the export of 'textiles and garments' constituted 16.4 per cent of total exports, minor agricultural products 6.3 per cent and gems 3.1 per cent.

**Table 4.3 Composition of the Colombo Town workers' cost of living index**

| *Weightage given in items as at 1982* | | | |
|---|---|---|---|
| *By type of items* | | *By trade characteristics* | |
| Food | 61.9 | Domestically produced items (1968:51%) | 60.0 |
| Clothing | 9.4 | Imported goods (1968:44%) | 35.0 |
| Fuel & light | 4.3 | Goods mainly exported (eg tea, coconuts) | 5.0 |
| Rent | 5.7 | | |
| Miscellaneous | 18.7 | | |

*Source:* Central Bank of Ceylon, *Annual Reports.*

*Note:* The more affluent are more import dependent.

## Table 4.4 Export volumes and export earnings

(US dollars)

| Year | Tea | | Rubber | | Three major coconut products | |
|------|-----------|---------------|-----------|---------------|---------------|---------------|
| | *vol. m.lbs* | *value $m.* | *vol. m.lbs* | *value $m.* | *vol. m.lbs* | *value $m.* |
| 1950 | 298 | 158 | 265 | 85 | 1030 | 52 | 328 |
| 1955 | 362 | 251 | 222 | 74 | 1531 | 47 | 408 |
| 1960 | 410 | 230 | 235 | 79 | 976 | 39 | 385 |
| 1965 | 495 | 254 | 267 | 64 | 1270 | 58 | 410 |
| 1970 | 460 | 188 | 354 | 74 | 874 | 40 | 342 |
| 1975 | 468 | 251 | 354 | 85 | 845 | 52 | 515 |
| 1980 | 407 | 345 | 266 | 145 | 700 | 69 | 983 |

*Source:* Central Bank of Ceylon, *Annual Report,* 1970, Table 1–6 for series from 1947 to 1970; other *Annual Reports* and *Bulletins* of Central Bank.

*Exchange Rates (US$):* 1947–49 = Rs.3.32 (devalued in Sept. 1949); 1950–1967 = Rs.4.76 (devalued in Nov. 1967); 1968 = Rs.5.95; *End-1976* = Rs.6.39; *End-1975* = Rs.7.71; *End-1976* = Rs.8.86; *Nov. 15 1977* = Rs.8.59; *Nov. 16 1977* = Rs.15.97; *End-Dec. 1980* = Rs.17.98; *End-1981* = Rs.20.53; End-Sept. 1982 = Rs.20.97; Feb. 1983 = Rs.22.95.

and also indirectly through a rise in the value of inputs in domestic production. The income elasticity of demand for Sri Lanka's exports is low, but essential import items have an inelastic demand.

The country's dependence on external trade may be measured by the value of imports plus the value of exports, taken together as a percentage of the GDP at current factor cost prices. This was 62 per cent in 1960, 37 per cent in 1970 and 42 per cent in 1975. It rose rapidly with the 'liberalisation' of the economy in 1977 and was 72 per cent in 1981. With the liberalisation and the expanded development and investment programme, the value of consumer goods as a percentage of total imports fell. The percentage represented by intermediate goods rose rapidly. The share of capital goods also recovered rapidly from the low level of 1975.

Table 4.4 shows the drop in export volumes of major commodities in the 1970s. The volume of rubber exports is not greater than in 1950, and the volume of exports of coconut products has fallen 32 per cent since

1950. Only tea exports have grown since 1950, but there has been no volume growth since 1960. This failure of traditional exports to grow has greatly exacerbated the problem of rising import prices.

Both money wages and the cost of living have been kept under control in Sri Lanka through a number of policies. Minimum wages (established by law and enforced) are linked to allowances which vary with changes in the Cost of Living Index. The country has free medical and hospital services, and free education including university education. Essential foods (and infant milk food) have been subsidised, rationed under import control, and at certain times (including the present) sold at legally enforced retail prices. Kerosene was subsidised and, after 1971 when the Government Oil Refinery was established, the prices were kept particularly low. The reduction of subsidies began with the 'liberalisation' policy of the new government in 1977. Free health and educational services continue in operation and the new government has supplied all school children up to Grade IX with free text books.

Maintaining welfare programmes remains a budgetary strain in times of economic stagnation because the elasticity of revenues does not match fluctuations in export prices or domestic economic changes. About 40 per cent of the GDP is generated today by the government or government-controlled corporations. The government's revenue was 24.3 per cent of GDP in 1964/65, rose to 28.9 per cent in 1978 and was 20.7 per cent in 1981. As a matter of general policy the government has protected the low-income classes by sustaining the level of government outlays and economic demand through credit creation (and running down external assets) in bad years.

Policy measures have often been a package deal to meet both 'internal shocks' (such as the harvest failures of 1965 and 1975, the insurgency of 1971, the land reforms of 1972 and 1975) and 'external shocks' (such as sharp fluctuations in imported food prices, changes in oil prices, freight rates, the continued rise in prices of capital goods). Sri Lanka did not enjoy what the President of the World Bank (in his address of 6 September 1982 to the Board of Governors) referred to as 'more than 25 years of unprecedented development progress'.

However, in the last decade three things helped to steady the economy: export of petroleum products after the establishment of the government oil refinery in 1971, the continued expansion of tourism, and the rapid growth of migrant workers' transfers after 1975. Forty per cent of the petroleum products from the refinery are exported. The value of these exports rose from Rs. 134.4 million in 1973 to Rs. 3,375 million (SDR 149 million) in 1981, amounting to 16.4 per cent of total exports of SDR 908 million. Petroleum product exports were 44 per cent of crude oil imports, by value, in 1981. In addition, other industrial exports had risen to 18 per cent of total exports in 1981, (SDR 162 million) also helping to offset the decline of the traditional exports. The balance of payments figure under 'travel' was Rs. 49 million in 1973. It rose to Rs. 1,541 million in 1981. Net private transfers, which amounted to Rs. 2 million in 1973, rose to Rs. 3,918 million in 1981.

There have also been limitations in the scope for using domestic monetary policy as an instrument to cope with external price changes. In times of boom, domestic money supply gets expanded by the monetisation of the net increase in banking assets. In slump periods there is an externally caused contraction in money supply which is often modified by the government's domestic credit creation.

The banking structure itself has certain limitations. After the war the British exchange banks dominated the scene both in holding deposits and financing foreign trade. In 1960 there were 28 Sri Lankan bank offices, which held 45 per cent of the island's bank deposits; 17 foreign bank offices held 55 per cent of the deposits. By 1975 there were 449 Sri Lankan bank offices holding 85 per cent of the deposits, 4 British bank offices holding 11 per cent of the deposits and 4 Indian and Pakistan bank offices holding 3 per cent of the deposits.

Because of the uneven accrual of profits and deposits in an export boom, the reserve ratio instrument of credit control was used very cautiously. The ratios now are 14 per cent of demand deposits and 6 per cent of time and savings deposits. The rates at which the Central Bank accommodated commercial banks to overcome temporary liquidity problems (the Bank Rate) was used as a policy instrument from 1960 onwards. This rate which was 4 per cent in 1960 went up to 5 per cent in 1965, 6.5 per cent in 1970, 10 per cent in 1977, 12 per cent in 1980 and 14 per cent in 1981. There was a ceiling set by the Central Bank for accommodation at these rates. Above the ceiling, borrowing meant paying a graduated penal rate going from 20 per cent to 30 per cent. Interest rates as a whole rose sharply in 1977 and continued to remain high. In 1981 the money situation was tight. The call money rates which stood at 11½–13 per cent in January 1981 moved to 19¼–23 per cent by end-June 1981. Ceilings were also imposed on commercial banks' expansion of credit to the private sector. The resort to open market operations has generally been small, as the Central Bank's portfolio was small.

After the 'liberalisation' of 1977, foreign banks were invited to open branches in Sri Lanka and the response was good. Banks were encouraged to enter off-shore banking through Special Foreign Currency Banking Units. Furthermore a Credit Plan has been formulated by the Central Bank to make the best use of the capacity to expand credit. In this plan priority is given to agriculture, industry, tourism and exports.

In financing the external resources gap during the 1950s there was no recourse to suppliers' credit, international bank borrowings or IMF drawings. These began to appear in the 1960s and after.

As noted in the overview of Sri Lanka in the World Bank's *World Development Report 1982*, the major strain on the economy had been the continuous decline in the terms of trade: 'Sri Lanka adjusted by raising investment; but in the face of declining capital inflows, this necessitated consumption constraint. Thus while the volume of production rose in the 1960s, *per capita* consumption fell markedly'. In the 1970s investment grew even faster, but *per capita* consumption was held in constraint, because of further deterioration in the terms of trade.

## Economic responses and adjustment to external price changes: 1960s

The growth of the island's population over the decade of the 1960s remained high, ranging from 2.5 per cent to 2.2 per cent per annum. The growth of the economy in terms of 1959 constant prices was 3.9 per cent between 1960 and 1967. For 1960–69 it was 4.5 per cent because of a growth of 8.2 per cent in 1968 and 5.7 per cent in 1969, after the devaluation of the rupee in 1967 and certain policy changes that accompanied it.

The Freedom Party (SLFP) governed the country from 1960 to 1965. It followed a set of economic management policies which were difficult but appropriate in the face of difficult external circumstances. An attempt to reduce the rice subsidy in 1962 cost the Minister of Finance his portfolio. The SLFP Government was more inward looking and protectionist in its attempt to promote import substitution and limit external dependence, as well as protect the standard of living. Management of the economy and of farming resources was attempted and structures built for the purpose. The new government of 1965 (the United National Party – UNP) could not change course in 1965 and 1966, which were bad years. The changes towards a more open economy came in 1967–70.

However, over the decade there was no effective adjustment of the economy through structural changes. For 1960, tea, rubber and coconut products accounted for 90.5 per cent of the value of domestic exports. In 1970 the figure was 89 per cent. In 1960 the value of imports of 'food and drink' amounted to 39 per cent of the value of total imports. In 1970 the figure was 46.2 per cent. The value of imports of rice, flour and sugar was 19.6 per cent of import value in 1960. In 1970 the figure was 32.2 per cent. It was only in the second half of the 1970s that changes occurred.

The decade of the 1960s showed three phases of change and adjustment: 1960–64, 1965–67 and 1967–70. During 1960–64, in consequence of adverse terms of trade and stagnant revenues, the government resorted to deficit financing and domestic credit creation to sustain mass demand. Consumption levels were protected through subsidies, price control and rationing of scarce essentials. The 1960s saw the imposition of import controls. In 1963 a Foreign Exchange Budget was formulated. In 1965 all food imports except those directly imported by the Government Food Commissioner (mainly rice, flour and sugar) came under import control. In 1966 all merchandise imports came under the purview of the Foreign Exchange Budget, classified as Essentials, Semi-essentials and Luxuries. In 1965/66 commodity aid was fitted into this budget. By 1965/67 as much as 60 per cent in value terms of the island's merchandise imports were handled directly by government or through government-controlled corporations. All other imports were subjected to licencing and quotas.

In 1963 the world's sugar prices shot up and in 1965 bad weather caused a 29.5 per cent drop in the paddy harvest and a drop in coconut production of 10.6 per cent. This kind of internal shock was a setback to both liberalisation and expansion of investment. The UNP Government had to act cautiously because the year 1965 began with a level of external assets at only 15.4 per cent of the total value of imports in 1964.

The SLFP government (1960–64) had kept down both the cost of living and foreign borrowing. Between 1960 and 1967 changes in the Cost of Living Index were negligible but many items of middle class consumption were scarce and costly. The Index (1952 = 100) rose from 103.5 in 1960 to 112.2 in 1965. It went up to 138.7 in 1970.

The year 1966 was the worst year for external earnings since 1957. Labour unrest and bad weather contributed to it. The terms of trade fell by 13.1 per cent and 1967 saw a further drop, of 9.4 per cent. The devaluation of sterling by 14 per cent was followed by a devaluation of the rupee by 20 per cent on 22 November 1967. Wage levels were raised by a small 'devaluation allowance'. In December 1967 the rice ration was reduced from two measures (4 lbs) to one measure per week per person and one measure per person was given free. This was for all, regardless of the income level. Meanwhile the prices for all imported goods rose and also those of imported production inputs.

The index number (1967 = 100) for export volume was 103 in 1968 and export price 117; import volume index moved to 101 but import price went to 126. The import price index for 'Food and Drink' went up to 132. The COL Index which had an annual rise of 0.95 per cent in the seven years 1960–67 had an average rise of 5.35 per cent in the four years 1967–70.

The drive for food production and import substitution was pushed further. There was a marked rise in the output of non-export agricultural products. Paddy production which was 43 million bushels in 1960 went up to 77 million bushels by 1970 and later to 106 million bushels in 1981. The exchange rate was still considered to be unrealistic. The government instituted a dual exchange rate in May 1968 with the Foreign Exchange Entitlement Certificate (FEEC) scheme which covered all imports and exchanges (including invisibles) other than the three major traditional exports (tea, rubber and three major coconut products), Food Commissioner's imports, drugs and books. Under this scheme importers had to pay a premium of 65 per cent for the scheduled imports and non-traditional exports earnings received a bonus of 65 per cent in rupee cost. This move was accompanied by a liberalising of import licensing giving a stimulus to the import of capital goods and raw materials which were in short supply. The terms of trade and the trade balance continued to be adverse but economic growth was stimulated.

Under the relatively more open economy after 1967 there was a marked rise in the growth of GNP, as already noted. But the public debt and the cost of living rose faster, and the level of external assets dropped. The out-turn is given in the following table.

**Table 4.5 Movement of selected indicators, 1960–1970**

(Indices: 1967 = 100)

|  | 1960 | 1965 | 1970 |
|---|---|---|---|
| Import price index | 83 | 100 | 140 |
| Import volume index | 133 | 86 | 102 |
| Export price index | 122 | 113 | 118 |
| Export volume index | 87 | 115 | 102 |
| Terms of trade | 148 | 112 | 84 |
| Total external assets (Rs. million) | 457.7 | 407.6 | 366.6 |
| Net external debt (Rs. million) | 222.8 | 446.6 | 1,550.9 |
| Cost of Living Index | 103.5 | 112.5 | 138.2 |

*Source:* Central Bank of Ceylon, *Annual Reports.*

The main battle in the 1960s was that of contending with the economy's structural limitations, in the face of volatile and adverse external circumstances, combining growth and employment with a measure of economic independence. These problems continued into the 1970s when the SLFP again came into power and attempted to manage the economy in a difficult external situation.

In financing the external resources gap there was from 1968 a sharp rise in short term credits. For the first time the country resorted to suppliers' credits (Rs. 176 million and Rs. 85 million in 1969 and in 1970) and also, for the first time, to foreign bank borrowings which amounted to Rs. 227 million in 1969 and Rs. 123 million in 1970. This was a change which was destined to continue.

## 1970s: Responses to external price changes

The industrialised countries continued to experience domestic price rises. The seven major OECD countries ran into double digit inflation (or nearly) by the eve of the quadrupling of oil prices in 1974. The 1970s also saw the world food crisis and the all-time high sugar prices of 1973/74. The sharp recession of 1974/75 affected Sri Lanka adversely with a further downward trend in the terms of trade. A new pattern of adjustment to global conditions began only in 1977 with the change of government.

Exchange rate variations also troubled the economy. The rupee had been linked to the US dollar from November 1971. When the UK decided to float the pound sterling the Sri Lanka rupee was re-linked to the pound sterling from 10 July 1972 at the existing parity rate of £ = Rs. 15.60. The dollar was Rs. 6.39 by the end of 1972. On 15 November 1977 the dual exchange rate and the FEEC (exchange tax/bonus) system was abolished. The dollar became Rs. 15.97 and the pound sterling Rs. 29.00. The currency was allowed to float and rates were announced by the Central Bank. The depreciation is outlined in Table 4.6.

## Table 4.6 Exchange rates

|          | £ Sterling | US$        |
| -------- | ---------- | ---------- |
| end-1979 | Rs. 34.53  | Rs. 15.43  |
| end-1980 | 42.66      | 17.98      |
| end-1981 | 39.66      | 20.53      |
| end-1982 | 35.19      | 20.83      |

A quick overview of the decade is given in Table 4.7 and the different phases described thereafter.

*Phase I – 1971–1973*
The growth of the GNP at constant 1959 prices was only 0.09 per cent in 1971, the year of the insurgency. It was 2.6 per cent in 1972 and 3.5 per cent in 1973. The paddy harvests were also poor in these years.

The year 1972 saw the land reforms in which all lands other than

# Table 4.7 Selected indicators of change, 1970–81

|  | 1970 | 1973 | 1974 | 1975 | 1980 | 1981 |
|---|---|---|---|---|---|---|
| **A.** *Trade indices (1978 = 100)* | | | | | | |
| Export value index (all exports) | 19 | 24 | 25 | 32 | 119 | 132 |
| Export volume index (all exports) | 107 | 103 | 89 | 107 | 99 | 102 |
| Export price index (all exports) | 17 | 20 | 31 | 29 | 126 | 129 |
| Import value index (all imports) | 18 | 18 | 28 | 34 | 205 | 208 |
| Import volume index (all imports) | 77 | 60 | 42 | 52 | 140 | 145 |
| Import price index (all imports) | 16 | 24 | 42 | 49 | 217 | 282 |
| Import price index (investment goods) | 31 | 29 | 43 | 43 | 160 | 149 |
| Import volume index (investment goods) | 54 | 39 | 23 | 45 | 172 | 293 |
| Terms of trade index | 106 | 82 | 72 | 58 | 58 | 46 |
| **B.** *Balance of payments (Rs.m)* | | | | | | |
| Balance on current account | −350 | −161 | −907 | −772 | −10912 | −8343 |
| Private transfers (net) | −5 | 2 | −2 | 19 | 2260 | 3918 |
| Travel (Tourism) | 1 | 49 | 86 | 111 | 1081 | 1541 |
| **C.** *Cost of Living Index (1952 = 100)* | | | | | | |
| Colombo Town. All items | 138 | 165 | 186 | 198 | 318 | 375 |
| Food only (weight 61.9) | 137 | 165 | 190 | 204 | 340 | 400 |
| Fuel & light (weight 4.3) | 136 | 164 | 221 | 237 | 564 | 768 |
| **D.** *Interest rates (year end)* | | | | | | |
| Treasury Bill rate | | 5 | 5 | 5 | 13 | 13 |
| Central Bank advances (bank rate) | | 6½ | 6½ | 6½ | 12 | 14 |
| Commercial bank lending against government securities | | 6½-9½ | 7-10 | 7½-11 | 15-28 | 15-28 |
| **E.** *Savings and investment (Rs.bn)* | | | | | | |
| 1 GDP at market prices | 13.7 | 18.4 | 23.8 | 26.6 | 66.5 | 85.4 |
| 2 Net import of goods and non-factor services | 0.4 | 0.2 | 1.8 | 2.0 | 15.0 | 14.4 |
| 3 Investment | 2.6 | 2.5 | 3.7 | 4.1 | 22.5 | 24.9 |
| 4 Domestic savings (3-2) | 2.2 | 2.3 | 2.0 | 2.2 | 7.4 | 10.5 |
| 5 Domestic savings as a percentage of GDP | 15.8 | 12.5 | 8.2 | 8.1 | 11.2 | 12.3 |

*Source:* Central Bank of Ceylon: *Review of the Economy,* 1979, Appendix Table 5; 1980, Appendix Table 5 and Table 11; *Annual Report,* 1981, Tables 7 and 8.

those owned by companies were brought under regulations limiting private ownership to 50 acres (and in the case of paddy land to 25 acres) held between parents and children under eighteen years of age. In 1975 all land came under land reform and special state-controlled bodies were vested with the company owned land.

By 1973 the government oil refinery was providing refined products locally and also exporting at the going market prices 40 per cent of the output. The value of imported petroleum products (mainly crude) amounted to 11 per cent of the total import value. Domestic petrol prices had already been raised, to increase government revenue. In August 1973 domestic petrol prices rose 14.5 per cent, kerosene by 45.6 per cent, auto diesel by 28 per cent and industrial diesel by 36.8 per cent above the price at the end of 1972. Price increases in January 1974 were therefore smaller than would otherwise have been the case. Domestic petrol prices virtually doubled and the retail price of kerosene was raised by 87.5 per cent. A five-day working week was adopted in order to reduce transport costs.

The cost of food imports rose sharply in 1973/74, though consumers were protected by subsidies and controls. The percentage changes in the Cost of Living Index (1952 = 100) in the years 1971–73 were 2.7 per cent, 6.4 per cent and 9.7 per cent respectively. The import price index for 'Food and Drink' (1967 = 100) was 143 in 1971. In 1973 it was 233.

In 1971–73 the external resources gap was financed with the help of grants, project and commodity aid, and long term loans. There was also a sharp rise in trade credits, suppliers' credits and some short term credits. Interest rates however remained low.

*Phase II – 1974–1976*
The GNP at constant prices rose by 3.4 per cent and 3.6 per cent and 3.0 per cent respectively in the years 1974/76. In 1974 the value of imports of petroleum products became 20 per cent of import value from a low of 3 per cent in 1970. Proceeds from the sale of bunkers and naptha rose to 16.4 per cent of the value of total exports. Freight rates however, rose: because of the variations in the rupee value of dollars there was another charge, i.e., a 'currency adjustment factor' in freight rates.

Despite the recession abroad the tourist trade expanded. There were 77,888 arrivals in 1973. By 1976 it was 118,971 and it grew to over 370,000 by 1981. Employment opportunities in the Middle East rose rapidly. Private transfers (migrants' transfers) net, rose from Rs. 2 million in 1973 to Rs. 19 million in 1975 and Rs. 1,541 million by 1981 (see Table 4.7).

During 1974–1976 there was a rise in the value of gem exports and of **a number of non-traditional exports.**

The rise in prices of imports was met by cutting down import volumes (see Table 4.7) although after several years of import and exchange controls the volumes imported were small. The drop in imports of investment goods retarded the growth of employment. The trend in the Cost of Living is given in Table 4.7 but many items of middle-class consumption were scarce and a black market developed.

Besides the rise in retail fuel prices (already mentioned) general retail prices rose a little because of transport costs. Wage rates moved up. The index number (1952 = 100) of nominal wage rates for 'Wages Boards Trade' (covering export trades, transport and manufacturing) rose from 169.9 in 1973 to 212.5 in 1974. The real wage rate index rose from 102.7 to 114.3. Wages of government servants also rose but their real wage rate index only moved from 108.8 in 1973 to 109.2 in 1974.

The year 1975 saw a severe harvest failure. The import price index also moved up again and the terms of trade index fell from 72 to 58. Price controls and rationing of essential food continued to operate.

In 1976 the economic situation eased somewhat. Food import prices too eased, but petroleum products took 25 per cent of the value of total imports. The price index of investment goods continued to rise. However the terms of trade index at 58 in 1975 moved up to 75 in 1976 and 102 in 1977 after which it began a downward trend.

In 1976 the balance of trade deficit, which was Rs. 1,263 million and Rs. 1,421 million in 1974 and 1975 respectively, came down to Rs. 710 million. The balance of payments deficit was financed without difficulty because long term commodity and project aid and soft loans amounting in value to Rs. 943 million were received during the year. The 'basic balance' (i.e. the current account of the balance of payments after adjustment for inflow of long term capital) showed a surplus in 1976 of Rs. 665 million as against a deficit of Rs. 159 million in 1975. External assets increased by Rs. 568 million during the year 1976 and amounted to 25.8 per cent of the total value of imports in 1976. The debt service ratio (i.e. service payments expressed as a percentage of the value of the exports of goods and non-factor services) came down to 20.1 per cent as against 22.9 per cent in 1975.

*Phase III – 1977 and after*
By 1976, despite the improvement in the international situation, the economy showed the severe strain of excessive management and controls from 1970 onwards. In July 1977 the people voted the United National Party (UNP) once again into office, with an unprecedented majority. The new government set out to free the economy. The previous government had re-valued the rupee in March 1977 by 20 per cent. The new government reversed this by a pegged downward crawl.

Through three separate devalued adjustments the rupee was brought back to the pre-revaluation level. In November 1977 the government abolished the FEEC system – the dual exchange rate. The rupee (on a unified exchange rate) was put at Rs.16 to the US dollar and allowed to float. By the end of the year the buying and selling rates of the dollar had settled at Rs. 15.33 and Rs. 15.59.

Import liberalisation was combined with exchange rate depreciation. A greater use was made of the price mechanism for the allocation of resources and controls began to be dismantled. An agreement with the IMF provided a standby credit of SDR 93 million. The existing food subsidy was replaced by one which gave a subsidy only to families earning less than Rs. 300 per month. In the case of the sugar ration, only the children of such families under the age of 12 were eligible. There began a stage by stage upward movement of the retail prices of flour, fertiliser, petroleum, milk, transport, postal and electricity charges, in the months that followed. Interest rates were raised all round.

To buffer the price rise, an across-the-board wage increase of 25 per cent subject to a ceiling of Rs. 50 per month was put into effect. The government internal purchase price of paddy from farmers was raised from Rs. 38 to Rs. 40 per bushel. Export promotion was pursued, backed by the establishment of an Export Promotion Zone and tax benefits. Foreign investors and foreign banks were invited and given safeguards for their capital and remittance of profits. The response of foreign aid became substantial, in particular to back the major capital works of the Mahaweli multi-purpose River Valley Project.

The economy responded with rising investment for replacement of obsolescent equipment, new capital works and an elimination of excess capacity. A spurt in new employment opportunities occurred and by 1980 the unemployment level fell, from 24 per cent in 1973 to 15 per cent. The rate of growth of the economy rose from 3.0 per cent in 1976 to 4.4 per cent in 1977, 8.2 per cent in 1978, 6.2 per cent in 1979 and 5.6 per cent in 1980. By 1980 the main spurt was over and in 1981 the growth rate was 4.2 per cent though at a higher level of general performance.

A disconcerting feature, however, was the rising rupee commitment of the government which was met by credit creation at home as well as by expanding the public debt.

The value of Treasury Bills outstanding was Rs. 2.5 billion in 1977, but it rose to Rs. 13.9 billion in 1981. In 1977 the external public debt more than doubled, mainly for extending capital works: but, because of more favourable terms and grant components the debt service ratio fell from 20.1 per cent to 16.9 per cent and kept falling to 12.4 per cent in 1980. If we exclude the commitments to the IMF it was only 7.5 per cent in 1980 and 6.8 per cent in 1981. However, these figures may be misleadingly low, because of an increased use of short term trade credit, as explained below. By 1981 the net domestic public debt rose from Rs. 11.8 billion to Rs. 29.5 billion (up 86.8 per cent). The broad money supply (i.e. including savings deposit held by the public) rose from Rs. 8.7 billion to Rs. 24.4 billion in 1981 (up 180.4 per cent), creating a high potential for volatile movements in domestic prices and also of import pressures.

In financing the external resources gap, IMF transactions plus stand-by aid and compensatory finance provided Rs. 1,870 million in 1977 and Rs. 1,512 million in 1978. In 1979, 1980 and 1981 there was heavy use of IMF resources, trade credit, suppliers' credits and some short term credits.

After 1977 there was a general lifting of interest rates. The Treasury Bill rate rose from 9 per cent in 1977 to 13 per cent in 1981. The Central Bank rate for advances against government securities rose from 10 per cent to 14 per cent. Loans and overdrafts by banks against government securities rose from 12.5–18 per cent to 15–28 per cent.

Many causes contributed to keep the debt service ratio down despite the rise in the external public debt. (The total outstanding debt was of SDR 623 million in 1975 and rose to SDR 1,154.6 million in 1980). A major cause was the higher earnings on 'merchandise exports and services' which totalled SDR 530.7 million (Rs. 4,477.6 million at the prevailing rate of exchange) in 1975 and rose to SDR 1,037 million (Rs. 22,316.3 million) in 1980. A cause of the fall in the debt service ratio in 1980 was the re-emergence of credits of a very short term nature which were not included in the public debt figures. A further reason was that the official long-term debt contracted in the recent past was on more concessional terms, with long grace periods.

Two other features may be noted: (a) remissions of public debt by certain creditors (particularly the UK) and (b) alterations in the rupee liability because of changes in the exchange rate. Table 4.8 indicates the change.

From 1978 onwards (with the higher rupee price for imports following the new rate of exchange), the cost of living moved up by double digits each year. A cost push also contributed to it. In 1979 the government abolished the old subsidy scheme and issued food stamps to the value of the ration for which each family was entitled. The value of the stamp issue for each entitled person has remained the same up to now, but with the elimination of subsidies prices have moved upwards. Table 4.9 shows how prices moved up in 1979/80 for certain items.

Prices were brought into line with open market prices. Besides the disengagement from the subsidies and the government 'administered' prices of essentials, there was also the general upward trend in

**Table 4.8 Foreign assistance 1977–1981**

(Rs. million)

|  | 1977 | 1978 | 1979 | 1980 | 1981 (provisional) |
|---|---|---|---|---|---|
| Gross receipts | 1,314.7 | 3,716.6 | 2,878.4 | 4,115.8 | 5,486.7 |
| Repayments | 434.0 | 501.4 | 499.2 | 599.8 | 606.6 |
| Net receipts | 880.7 | 3,215.3 | 2,379.2 | 3,516.0 | 4,880.1 |
| Change in liability due to exchange rate variations | 4,745.1 | 773.0 | −316.6 | 2,921.3 | 2,162.6 |
| Liability as at end of period[a] | 10,593 | 14,582.3 | 15,840.7 | 22,276.8 | 29,172.1 |

*Source:* Central Bank of Ceylon, *Review of the Economy*, 1981, p. 250.

*Note:*    [a]Adjusted to include to Rs. 0.3 million, Rs. 0.5 million, Rs. 804.4 million, Rs. 1.3 and Rs. 147.5 million being written off balances in 1977, 1978, 1979, 1980 and 1981 respectively.

wholesale prices covering the totality of national consumption. The general upward movement of wages and salaries, of employment (and earners per household), and migrants' inward transfers helped to soften the impact of price rises and sustain consumption levels.

The new government of 1977 had moved up fuel prices but retained the subsidy on kerosene. In the 1974 fuel crisis the five day week had been introduced and transport fares raised. In the 1979 rise in fuel prices, the price of all grades of fuel moved up. Kerosene, which was only Rs. 4.40 a gallon, went up to Rs. 9.50 in 1979 and Rs. 12 in 1980. A

**Table 4.9 Selected retail price changes, 1979–1980**

|  | 1979 | 1980 |
|---|---|---|
| Rice (measure) | 3.86 | 5.17 |
| Wheat flour (lb) | 1.21 | 2.23 |
| Bread | 1.09 | 1.94 |
| Pulses | 4.20 | 5.68 |
| Sugar | 3.00 | 5.53 |
| Fresh milk (bot) | 1.87 | 2.00 |
| Milk powder (lb) | 6.85 | 9.64 |
| Kerosene (gallon) | 5.88 | 14.22 |

greater interest has grown up in forest conservation, growing of fuel wood, bio-gas, use of windmills and the possibilities of using solar energy. These changes took place in a general context of rising incomes but income distribution took a turn for the worse in this growth of prosperity after 1977. Preliminary data of a survey by the Central Bank is presented in Table 4.10.

**Table 4.10 Income distribution, 1953–78**

|  | 1953 | 1963 | 1973 | 1978 |
|---|---|---|---|---|
| Mean income (Rs. monthly) | 108 | 134 | 228 | 574 |
| Median income (Rs. monthly) | 68 | 83 | 180 | 352 |
| Percentage of total income received by: |  |  |  |  |
| Lowest 10 per cent | 1.5 | 1.2 | 1.8 | 1.5 |
| Lowest 40 per cent | 13.0 | 12.0 | 15.1 | 12.3 |
| Highest 10 per cent | 42.5 | 39.5 | 30.0 | 39.0 |
| Gini coefficient | 0.50 | 0.49 | 0.41 | 0.49 |

*Source:* Central Bank of Ceylon, *Annual Report*, 1979.

In 1981 the budget deficit was brought down to about 15 per cent of GDP. Inflation which was at about 26 per cent in 1980 came down to 18 per cent. A new and more stable economic situation appeared to have arrived but the drop in the new terms of trade index (1978 = 100) from 58 in 1980 to 46 in 1981 was a cause for concern. The new policy aimed at generating a higher level of domestic savings and investment *as well as a higher level of foreign exchange earning in order to liquidate the external debt.* The magnitude of the adverse value effect of the terms of trade was estimated by the Central Bank at Rs. 284.7 million in 1978, Rs. 835.1 million in 1979, Rs. 1,205.8 million in 1980 and Rs. 1,406.2 million in 1981. If the adverse terms of trade effects do not persist, the prospect for the 1980s is favourable. At present (1983) the term of office of the UNP Government has been extended by a referendum. Pragmatic policies in the context of an 'open economy' should continue in effect.

The Annual Report of the Central Bank for 1982 (issued in May 1983) showed that the GNP increased by 4.9 per cent in 1982 as against 4.1 per cent in 1981. The *per capita* GNP was put at US $284. The terms of trade showed a further drop. However, the rate of inflation was brought down to single digit level. *Inward* migrants' transfers reached a record level of Rs. 5,789 million as against Rs. 4,430 million in 1981. In financing the foreign exchange gap, commercial credits rose relative to concessional aid. Direct investment continued to rise. The disconcerting feature was a 14 per cent growth in imports as against a disappointing 3.4 per cent growth in exports. The expansion and development process remained dependent on access to external resources.

# 5 Malawi

*Charles Harvey*[1]

## Structure of the economy[2]

Malawi, formerly Nyasaland, has an estimated population of 6.3 million, with GNP per capita of $200. The population is estimated to be growing at 2.9 per cent a year. The proportion of the population living in urban areas has grown from 4 per cent in 1960 to 10 per cent in 1980; Malawi's population is therefore considerably more rural and less urbanised than the average for Sub-Saharan Africa (21 per cent) or than the average for other low income countries in the world (17 per cent). As might be expected, therefore, the share of agriculture in Malawi's GNP (43 per cent) is higher than the average for Sub-Saharan Africa (32 per cent), and the share of industry is lower (20 per cent against an average of 32 per cent).

Exports amounted to 22 per cent of GDP in 1980; and exports and imports together were 55 per cent of GDP. But although Malawi has a very open economy by world standards (exports are only 11 per cent of GDP for all low income countries), the country's economy is no more open than the average for Sub-Saharan Africa, despite the relatively small size of the population.

Malawi has no domestic supply of oil or coal, which must therefore all be imported. The country does, however, have some hydroelectricity potential, some of which has already been developed. Petroleum imports as a proportion of total commercial energy consumption, at 59 per cent, are therefore slightly below the average for Sub-Saharan Africa (65 per cent). Furthermore, petroleum imports were only 6 per cent of total imports in 1960 and had risen to only 13 per cent by 1980. These low figures must be a result of the country's relatively low level of industrialisation and also, to some extent, of the relatively high population density (49 persons per square kilometre as compared with 16 for Sub-Saharan Africa). However, Malawi is land-locked and therefore exceptionally vulnerable to increases in the cost of energy-intensive overland transport from the ports to the country's borders; such increases would not show up in petroleum imports but in the c.i.f. cost of all imports.

Malawi has been broadly self-sufficient in basic foodstuffs. Only 5 per cent of total imports were of food in 1978, and production of maize (the basic food of the majority of the population) has been adequate for local consumption in normal years, with imports in bad years and exports in good ones. However, there is some evidence that this was no longer true from the late 1970s. A five-year moving average, calculated in order to smooth out the year-to-year distortions caused by changes in the weather, shows that the trend of net exports became negative sometime between 1975 and 1978, and became steadily more negative thereafter.[3]

Manufactured goods dominate the country's imports. Machinery and transport equipment accounted for 37 per cent of total merchandise imports in 1978, and other manufactured goods for a further 44 per cent, both figures being slightly above the average for low-income countries in Sub-Saharan Africa. Only 4 per cent of exports are of manufactured goods, mainly processed agricultural goods. The main commodity exports are shown in Table 5.1.

In general Malawi has diversified its export structure. Sugar exports have been developed from almost nothing to 15 per cent of the total.

## Table 5.1 Structure of Malawi's exports, 1970 and 1980

|  | Value (million Kwacha) | | Percentage shares | |
|  | 1971 | 1980 | 1971 | 1980 |
|---|---|---|---|---|
| Tobacco | 22.1 | 105.1 | 37.3 | 43.9 |
| Tea | 11.9 | 29.8 | 20.1 | 12.5 |
| Sugar | 0.3 | 36.3 | 0.5 | 15.2 |
| Groundnuts | 5.9 | 15.9 | 9.9 | 6.6 |
| Re-exports | 9.7 | 13.8 | 16.4 | 5.8 |
| Other | 9.4 | 38.3 | 15.9 | 16.0 |
| Total | 59.3 | 239.2 | 100.0 | 100.0 |

Furthermore, although the share of tobacco has actually gone up, from 37 per cent to 44 per cent, slightly increasing Malawi's already considerable dependence on this crop, tobacco is in fact a very heterogeneous commodity. Different varieties of tobacco have different short-term and secular price trends, and Malawi's tobacco industry has diversified since 1970 by producing large flue-cured and burley crops, in addition to the traditional dark-fired crop.

Concerning policy, Malawi has maintained a relatively market-oriented economy. This is not to say that the government has not intervened. Certain government policies have had a major influence on the way in which the economy has developed since independence, notably in favouring estate agriculture over smallholders by means of agricultural pricing, credit and labour availability. But there has been relatively little use of import controls (which were used to protect local industry but not to reduce total imports for balance of payments purposes) or of foreign exchange controls; and price control has been mainly confined to producer prices for smallholder agricultural goods, with only a handful of retail prices being controlled (albeit including such key consumer items as maize and sugar).

## Impact of international events 1964–1978

Malawi became independent in 1964, having led the fight to break up and escape from the Federation of Rhodesia and Nyasaland. The Federation had been opposed from its origins by Africans and remained unpopular throughout its 10-year life (1953–63), despite the fact that one of the features of the Federation was a net subsidy to the Nyasaland Government from the other two territories. At the time of independence, therefore, the government had to seek a grant-in-aid from Britain to balance the current budget, and was wholly dependent on external finance for development spending. Nevertheless, real GDP is estimated officially to have grown by more than 5 per cent a year from 1964 to 1970,[4] and the government's current budget was balanced without grants-in-aid from 1971/2 onwards. This process was helped by some improvement in the country's external terms of trade, which increased by 15 per cent from 1967 to 1970 (see Table 5.2 below – no figures are available prior to 1967).

In the period 1970 to 1973 growth continued even more strongly, at more than 7 per cent a year, despite declines in the terms of trade in 1972 and 1973. Exports increased at a rapid rate and the foreign exchange reserves more than doubled, from 3.5 to nearly 6 months' worth of imports. Consumer prices increased much faster than previously in 1970 and 1971 (9.5 per cent and 8.2 per cent), but the rate of increase fell in the next two years to rates below those in the rest of the world (3.6 per cent and 5.0 per cent compared with 5.8 per cent and 9.6 per cent). So it turned out that just prior to the first big increase in world inflation in general, and in oil and manufactured goods prices in particular,[5] Malawi's economy was in a relatively strong position.

In the period 1973 to 1975 the index for the unit value of imports rose by 64 per cent (it rose by 35 per cent in 1974 alone), and the total cost of imports rose by 95 per cent, from K99m. in 1973 to K193m. in 1975. However, the export unit value index rose by 49 per cent and the value of exports by 53 per cent, so that the trade deficit rose by only K60m. This turned out to be manageable, because of a small improvement in the invisible balance and an increased inflow of long term capital, including some modest drawings on IMF facilities. As a result, the gross official foreign exchange reserves were virtually unchanged over the two years in Kwacha terms (they fell slightly in US dollar terms as the Kwacha was devalued by a small amount in 1975). Net foreign assets of the banking system fell by K30m. but remained positive; the debt service ratio increased hardly at all, from 7.4 per cent to 7.7 per cent. Meanwhile, real GDP continued to grow at between 6 per cent and 7 per cent per annum. So Malawi managed to get through this first period of increased world inflation and world recession with very little damage to the economy: some additional short and medium-term debt was taken on, and the domestic inflation rate rose from 5 per cent in 1973 to 15.5 per cent in each of 1974 and 1975, but strong export prices and adequate access to credit enabled rapid growth to be maintained.

In the period 1975–78 real GDP continued to grow rapidly, although the first signs of trouble appeared in 1978. In that year, export receipts fell sharply, the first fall since 1968. Both the volume and the unit value of exports decreased, and this, combined with an exceptionally large rise in import volume, caused a large increase in the current account deficit. However, long-term capital inflows were nearly enough to cover the deficit[6] and the foreign exchange reserves fell by only K15m. Over the three year period, the reserves actually rose slightly, mainly because of a large increase in capital inflows. Put slightly differently, some large additional imports for major capital projects were mainly covered by long-term borrowing. The year 1978 could easily have been just a temporary deviation from trend and thus manageable without serious disruption in the economy's progress. However, it was followed by a series of bad years as developments in the international economy became increasingly and sustainedly adverse, pushing Malawi into quite severe debt problems and not only halting growth, but appearing to extinguish most of the sources of the economic growth that occurred in the 1970s, as explained below.

Malawi's policies to cope with this much more severe set of problems, and the question as to whether the nature of the growth that took place in the 1970s was appropriate for the country's long term development, are discussed in the next two sections.

## Macroeconomic adjustment 1979–81

As can be seen in Table 5.2, Malawi's terms of trade were only mildly unfavourable during most of the 1970s. Up to and including 1978, the index was only 17½ per cent below the peak year of 1971. In particular, it fell only 10 per cent from 1973 to 1975.

**Table 5.2 Malawi's barter terms of trade, 1967–80**

(1970 = 100)

| 1967 | 87 | 1972 | 93 | 1977 | 94 |
|------|-----|------|----|------|----|
| 1968 | 90 | 1973 | 90 | 1978 | 84 |
| 1969 | 93 | 1974 | 84 | 1979 | 67 |
| 1970 | 100 | 1975 | 81 | 1980 | 57 |
| 1971 | 102 | 1976 | 79 | 1981 | 57 |

*Source:* Reserve Bank of Malawi, *Financial and Economic Review*, no. 3, 1981; *Economic Report*, 1982.

*Note:* The weights in the export index were not changed during the period shown, and fail therefore to allow for changes in the structure of exports. As a result, the impact on Malawi was not as severe as suggested by the figures in the table. Rough estimates suggest that the terms of trade may have fallen by only 30 per cent from 1970 to 1980, instead of the 43 per cent shown in the table.

In 1979, 1980 and 1981 however, there was a drastic worsening of the terms of trade. Import prices rose by 54 per cent in two years (from the fourth quarter of 1978 to the fourth quarter of 1980) and export prices, which in 1974 and 1975 had more or less kept pace with import prices, did not rise at all in 1979 and 1980.

More or less at the same time as this large loss of real income from the movement of external prices, the government embarked on a very large increase in its own spending. After increases averaging only 11 per cent p.a. in the previous four years, total government spending rose by 48 per cent in 1978, and by an average of 22 per cent in the next three years. Some part of this was because of disruptions in international transport routes in 1979, which led to very expensive short term expedients, including the air-freighting of fuel into the country. But a significant part was also caused by increased spending by the government on a number of large infrastructural investments whose contribution to output, in the short and medium term, is bound to be very small in relation to their cost: the new international airport at Lilongwe, the tarred road to the North, the building of the new capital city, the extension of the railway to the Zambian border at Mchinji (still some 400 miles from the Zambian railway network); and increased spending on the military and on purely prestige projects.[7] Some of the apparently more productive investment was in agricultural estates, mainly in capital intensive flue-cured tobacco, using a lot of imported machinery, fertiliser and energy. Many of these estates were inefficiently run and experienced large deficits.

The current account worsened by K92m. in 1978, but only some K19m. of this can be attributed to the terms of trade; similarly, the terms of trade only account for some K40m. of the further worsening of the current account in 1979. Meanwhile, total government spending rose by K66m. in 1978, and another K50m. in 1979 – huge increases on the 1977 figure of K136m.

As can be seen from Table 5.3, there was a slight recovery in the current account in 1980: some exports which had been held up by

### Table 5.3 Current account of Malawi's balance of payments, 1978–80

(million Kwacha)

|                   | 1977 | 1978 | 1979 | 1980 | 1981 |
|-------------------|------|------|------|------|------|
| Balance of trade  | +15  | −69  | −72  | −39  | +12  |
| Invisibles        | −79  | −79  | −133 | −139 | −157 |
| Current account   | −57  | −148 | −205 | −178 | −145 |

*Source:*  Reserve Bank of Malawi, *Financial and Economic Review,* vol. 13, no. 2, 1982; *Economic Report,* 1982.

transport difficulties finally left the country which contributed to a 26 per cent rise in the value of exports; a series of measures to restrain domestic demand introduced in August 1979 resulted in imports rising by only 9 per cent in money value, so that there was a fall in volume; and the balance on invisible trade improved slightly. This improvement continued in 1981: exports increased, imports actually fell in money terms by 10 per cent indicating a fall in real terms of as much as 20%, and this was only partly offset by higher debt service payments. The fall in imports in 1981 was even more remarkable in that government spending continued to rise in that year, by K60m. (20 per cent).

It is normal for Malawi to run a current account deficit, financed by the foreign transfers and capital flows that accrue each year, mainly to the government. Nevertheless, the deficit increased from an average of K68m. in 1975–77 to an average of K169m. in 1978–1981. The average additional amount to be financed each year, at just over K100m., was more than twice the official foreign exchange reserves, which averaged about K50m. from 1974–1977. There could be no question, therefore, of financing the increase in deficits out of the reserves.

Some of the finance came from an increase in net transfers to the government which tripled from K18m. in 1977 to K54m. in 1980. This represents a considerable response to Malawi's externally-induced difficulties.[8] In addition, the government borrowed increasing amounts from the IMF under various headings (in 1979 and 1980), public enterprises doubled their foreign borrowing (in 1980) and the government slightly increased its other long term borrowing, including some eurodollar finance.

These long term sources of finance were not enough, however, and short-term foreign borrowing increased sharply, especially in 1979, when net inflows were K52m. compared with net inflows of between K10m. and K20m. in 1978 and 1980.[9] Such large-scale short term borrowing could be very damaging if it had indeed to be repaid quickly. For the time being it was rolled over successfully, in that the large borrowing of 1979 was followed up by further net inflows in 1980, 1981 and 1982. So long as net inflows do not turn into net outflows, short-term borrowing is in some respects little different from long-term borrowing. However it does increase Malawi's vulnerability to a change in foreign lenders' views of the country's creditworthiness and to changes in international interest rates, which would affect the cost of all short-term credit quite quickly. Long-term finance is only gradually affected by changed interest rates, as new borrowing replaces old, with the exception of eurocurrency finance. Although Malawi has increased its variable interest rate eurocurrency borrowing, it remains a relatively small proportion of the total – about 20 per cent of all arranged credits, including undisbursed, at the end of 1979; only a further K11.5m. of eurocredits was arranged in 1980.[10]

As noted already, Malawi was in a relatively strong position to borrow in 1979 because external debt had been kept within manageable limits during the 1970s. External public debt outstanding grew from K120m. in 1970 to K423m. in 1979, but the 1979 figure was a smaller proportion of GNP (at 33 per cent) than the 1970 figure (39 per cent). Because there was a rise in the proportion of commercial borrowing, with higher interest rates and shorter repayment periods, the debt service position was not quite so favourable: debt service rose slightly as a percentage of

GNP (1.8 per cent to 2.1 per cent) and as a percentage of exports of goods and services (from 7 per cent to 9.4 per cent).

The real cost of commercial borrowing also increased quite sharply, moving from negative real interest rates in the mid-1970s to positive real interest rates thereafter, with quite exceptionally high rates in 1981. For example, eurodollar deposit rates rose as high as 19 per cent in 1981, which implied that eurodollar borrowing could have cost as much as 22 per cent or 23 per cent when financial margins and other costs are included. Industrial country inflation averaged 10 per cent in 1981, so that some loans were costing as much as 12 per cent or 13 per cent in real terms. Furthermore, the calculation of 'real' rates of interest implies that the rate of inflation used in the calculation applies to the income of the borrower who is thus able to make interest and capital payments out of increased earnings in devalued monetary units. If, however, the borrower's income does not rise with the general level of inflation then the real cost of borrowing is even higher. Put slightly differently, a country in Malawi's position facing declining terms of trade, must somehow increase export volume (and borrowing) not just to pay the higher cost of imports but also to pay higher interest on external debt, an item not included in the conventional terms of trade calculation. In 1982, central government external debt service commitments were estimated to be K63m., and public corporations owed a further K21m. Total public sector debt service, at K84m., resulted in a debt service ratio of 29 per cent on the basis of the official export forecast for 1982 (in the 1982 *Economic Report*). Thus the debt service ratio rose from 9 per cent to 29 per cent in just three years.

The impact of a switch from mostly soft loans, to a roughly equal mix of soft and hard loans is shown in Table 5.4. Between 1978 and 1981, Malawi's external debt increased by K264m., approximately half of which was in the form of hard loans with market rates of interest and relatively short repayment periods (less than 10 years and in some cases as little as 5 years). Previously, only a very small part (about 6 per cent) of external borrowing had been on commercial terms. There was also some hardening of the terms of 'soft' loans, as Malawi was obliged to borrow some of its World Bank money on 'Third Window' terms, as well as continuing to borrow from IDA. On the other hand, some very soft loans were written off by a number of donors; this reduced total debt considerably, but had a relatively small effect on debt service because of the generous original terms of the loans.

Table 5.4 shows that while external debt slightly more than doubled, debt service (interest and capital repayments combined) increased by a multiple of ten. The figures in Table 5.4 do not show the interest payments on short-term borrowing, which also increased very rapidly

**Table 5.4 External debt and debt service, 1978 and 1981**

(million Kwacha)

| | 1978 | | | 1981 | | |
|---|---|---|---|---|---|---|
| | Outstanding | Debt service | % | Outstanding | Debt service | % |
| Soft loans | 227 | 4 | 2 | 369 | 18 | 5 |
| Hard loans | 13 | 1 | 10 | 135 | 34 | 25 |
| Total loans | 240 | 5 | 2 | 504 | 52 | 10 |

*Source:* Estimates of Revenue and Expenditure 1981/82 (1981); Appropriation Accounts for year ended 31 March 1978 (1978).

*Note:* The sources are not strictly comparable, but probably give a fair picture of overall trends. Percentages are debt service as per cent of outstanding.

during this period (see Table 5.5); nor do they show the much greater uncertainty which attaches to eurodollar and short term borrowing, which carry variable interest rates.

One potential risk, normally associated with rapidly increasing debt service from commercial borrowing, has largely been avoided. During a balance of payments crisis, governments are normally grateful to borrow wherever credit can be obtained. The currency composition of rapidly increasing external debt service is, as a result, largely a matter of chance and so can turn out to be dangerously weighted toward one major currency. This happened to Zambia in the late 1970s, for example, where the large increases in external commercial borrowing were denominated mainly in US dollars, rendering the country vulnerable to an appreciation of the dollar, which did in fact occur. Malawi's external commercial borrowing has a large US dollar content, but also contained significant amounts of Yen and Deutschmarks, which, combined with earlier soft borrowing with a large Sterling and

**Table 5.5 Malawi's net foreign assets, 1977–1981**

(million Kwacha)

| | | | |
|---|---|---|---|
| 1977 | +10.8 | 1980 | −85.5 |
| 1978 | −11.3 | 1981 | −120.0 |
| 1979 | −85.4 | 1982 | −167.8 |

*Source: International Financial Statistics.*

Rand component, gave the government a foreign debt portfolio whose currency composition was reasonably diversified.

Rapidly increasing debt service, as a proportion of exports and GNP, while always of concern, can be quite manageable provided that exports have grown rapidly, and continue to do so. Export growth was in fact part of Malawi's strength. From 1972 to 1981, the current value of exports grew from K64m. to K263m., an annual growth rate of 17 per cent. In volume terms, exports grew at 8 per cent per annum to 1980, although there was a sharp fall in 1981. Only in one year, 1978, did the value of exports fall in money terms. Furthermore, the Malawian economy has managed to grow while using relatively fewer imports. The volume of imports grew only 13 per cent from 1972 to 1980, or about 1.5 per cent a year. Real GNP meanwhile grew by 43 per cent, or about 4.7 per cent a year. As a result the ratio of imports to GDP was maintained at 29 per cent, despite the much larger increase in import prices (239 per cent) than in the GDP deflator (144 per cent). In 1981 this trend was sharply accentuated: import volume fell by 20 per cent while real GDP rose very slightly (by about 1 per cent). As a result, the ratio of imports to GDP actually decreased to 24 per cent. In April 1982, the Malawian Kwacha was devalued by 15 per cent, an action which should reinforce even further the incentive to economise on imports.

Meanwhile, the gross foreign exchange reserves remained about K40m. from 1978 to 1980, looking only at end-year figures, although there were some (mainly seasonal) fluctuations below that level from month to month. Net foreign assets moved sharply negative in 1978 and 1979, though, as short term borrowing was used to finance part of the current account deficits. After holding steady in 1980, net foreign assets deteriorated again in 1981 and 1982, in spite of the recovery on current account, and gross foreign exchange reserves fell to an all time low of K21m. at the end of 1982.

Although Malawi got through the first part of this crisis, created mainly by the quite drastic deterioration in the country's terms of trade, with what appeared to be manageable additions to short and long-term debt, there was a real immediate cost, in that growth fell almost to zero in 1980 and 1981. From 1972 to 1979 real GDP grew at an average of 4.7 per cent, with growth more or less up to the average in 1979 itself. In 1980, however, real GDP hardly grew at all (the recorded figure was 0.2 per cent, well within the normal margin of error for GDP estimates) and 1981 was hardly any better (growth of 0.9 per cent). Because of population growth, this represented a fall in per capita output. So even at the purely macroeconomic level, adjustment to international price changes had a real and immediate cost, apart from the future cost of the **increase in foreign debt and other costs to be discussed below.**

**Table 5.6 Changes in gross fixed investments, 1977–1981**

(per cent)

| | 1977 | 1978 | 1979 | 1980 | 1981 |
|---|---|---|---|---|---|
| *A. Current prices* | | | | | |
| Public investment | +29 | +60 | + 4 | +20 | −26 |
| Private investment | + 1 | +82 | + 2 | −37 | −55 |
| Total | +17 | +68 | + 3 | − 2 | −34 |
| *B. In constant prices (using GDP deflator)* | | | | | |
| | 1977 | 1978 | 1979 | 1980 | 1981 |
| Public investment | +19 | +54 | −11 | + 2 | −39 |
| Private investment | − 6 | +76 | −12 | −46 | −63 |
| Total | + 8 | +62 | −12 | −17 | −45 |

*Source:* Reserve Bank of Malawi *Annual Report*, 1980; *Economic Report*, 1982 (not wholly consistent with other source, but basic picture consistent in both).

The most severe effect of the crisis was in fact on private sector investment (see Table 5.6), reinforced by a rapid slowdown in bank lending to the private sector. Net domestic credit to the private sector rose by 39 per cent in 1978 and by 40 per cent in 1979; the restrictive measures taken by the authorities in August 1979 slowed down this rapid growth in 1980 and 1981 to 7 per cent and 5 per cent respectively, which represented a continuous fall in real terms over the two years.[11] Growth in net domestic credit to the official sector (including statutory bodies) did slow down, but only from 56 per cent in 1979 to 33 per cent in 1980. And in 1981, rapid growth resumed and was 61 per cent, more than accounted for by the increase in lending by the Reserve Bank to the government. This sharp discrimination in the availability of bank credit contributed to a near collapse of private sector fixed investment in 1980, to its lowest point since 1973 (in real terms); in 1981, private sector fixed investment was so low, at K33m., that it was well below the level needed to maintain the capital stock.[12]

At the same time as private fixed investment was falling, it was estimated that private consumption continued to rise quite rapidly in 1979 and 1980, by 8 per cent and 10 per cent *in real terms*, and only falling by 6 per cent in 1981. Government current expenditure, on the other hand, was controlled tightly enough to rise only slightly in 1979 and to fall in 1980 and 1981, in real terms again.[13]

Despite these adverse trends, one can argue that Malawi had so far managed to cope quite well, at least at the purely macroeconomic level, with the loss of real income caused by sharply worsened terms of trade. There may have been too great a reliance on credit restraint, so that private investment fell rapidly.[14] Lack of investment, plus the increased debt service payable in the future because of additional foreign borrowing, may have postponed rather too much of the current burden to the future. Crucially, though, exports continued to grow, even if a little fortuitously in 1981, and so long as that continued it would remain possible (and manageable) to borrow in order to maintain growth and development. The question that remained was whether current policies were likely to sustain that growth, and what form that growth would take.

**Agricultural exports: smallholders versus estates**
Growth of exports in the 1970s came mostly from the estate sector. The mechanism for this seems to have been a combination of low prices from Admarc for smallholder crops (estates sell direct to foreign markets), investment by Admarc and financial institutions in the estate sector, and a flow of labour pushed out of smallholder production, by low returns, into wage employment on agricultural estates despite a falling real wage in that sector. Labour was also made available to the estate sector by restrictions on the flow of Malawians to work on the South African mines.[15] Most strikingly, Admarc purchases per worker in smallholder agriculture in constant prices actually declined on average from 1964 to 1980, even though there was quite a large implicit subsidy on rice and maize. The policy of low food prices (until 1980) helped to keep labour costs exceptionally low, although it must also have been a major reason for Malawi becoming a net maize importer. The prices paid by Admarc for tobacco, groundnuts and cotton were substantially below export parity, enabling Admarc to make large profits, more than half of which were invested in estate agriculture.

This pattern ended, however, in the late 1970s. In 1977/78 Admarc made a crop trading profit of K40m., up from K34m. the year before. But in 1978/79 this figure fell to K5.5m. and in the following two years it disappeared completely (K0.1m. and K0.3m. respectively). Taking into account Admarc's other income, mainly dividends and interest on its investments and loans, and its much larger other expenses, mainly losses on fertiliser and farmers' aids and interest payable on its own borrowing, the corporation ran at a loss in 1979/80 and 1980/81 (K4.7m. and K6.2m. respectively).

There was a more positive way of looking at the collapse of Admarc's profits. It could be argued that the gap between Admarc's buying prices and export parities (adjusted for trading expenses) was justified as a precaution against the risk of falling export prices, and that the events of 1979 to 1981 justify this point of view. Admarc's ability to sustain its buying prices during these years was, in this sense, made possible by the earlier 'conservative' policy. Also in support of Admarc's past policies it could be said that the corporation had at least provided a market for smallholder produce in a comparatively efficient way, comparative that is to the marketing available to smallholders in other African countries. The rise in Admarc's administrative expenses in 1979/80 and 1980/81, as a percentage of the net sales value of crops purchased, was probably no more than could be explained by rising transport costs and a rising share of maize among total crops handled.[16]

However, if Admarc's crop trading surpluses had really been intended to be a buffer against bad years, first, rather more would have been held in liquid cash form and, second, the corporation would not have maintained a profit margin on crop trading amounting to an average of 31 per cent of net sales value of crops purchased over the *seven-year* period 1971/72 to 1977/78, the percentage never falling lower than 22 per cent.

By 1981 Admarc's net liquidity was negative since overdrafts were bigger than cash in hand; there was no way, therefore, of using the corporation's accumulated surpluses to raise prices to smallholders, because they were invested mainly in long-term investment and equity participation, mostly in estate agriculture but also in other sectors of the economy. In these circumstances, it was difficult to see where the resources could be found to generate further growth in agricultural exports: Admarc could neither raise smallholder prices nor continue to invest in estate agriculture – the two most obvious avenues of future growth – and the commercial banks could not increase their agricultural lending at the speed of the 1970s (commercial bank lending to agriculture, nearly all of it to the estate sector, rose from K6m. in 1973 to K93m. in 1980, and from 20 per cent to 54 per cent of total advances).[17] To do so would have made the balance of payments worse in the short term, which would have been difficult to finance in current circumstances, as well as being contrary to the conditions of IMF credit. Nor was the government able to subsidise Admarc: domestic borrowing to finance the budget deficit increased sharply in 1980/81, despite a 27 per cent increase in external borrowing, and this got worse in 1981/82 as the monetary authorities increased their lending to the government.[18] Meanwhile, the other sources of investment in estate agriculture, the profits of the estates themselves, had also been sharply reduced. Indeed, the increase in bank lending to agriculture in 1980 of K11m. was thought to be required to finance losses rather than new investment.

## Domestic adjustment

Malawi's basic policy was to allow international prices to feed through into domestic prices, and then to proceed pragmatically. That is, public-sector activity was mainly evaluated according to market criteria, with rather fewer exceptions than might be considered usual; and there was also unusually little interference in private sector activity, the most notable exceptions being the direction of a growing proportion of bank lending to the agricultural estate sector, and the use of Admarc surpluses accumulated at the expense of smallholders for investment in the same subsector, as detailed above. The World Bank has calculated a 'distortion index', which has a higher value the greater is the amount of distortion (from a 'free market' situation) in the economy. Of 31 developing countries studied, Malawi ranked as least distorted, by a substantial margin, with an index of 1.24. The next country on the list (Thailand) had an index of 1.43; the most distorted was Ghana (2.86), and the average was 2.01[19] The government also acted to reinforce the relative rise in the price of energy, by increasing the percentage of tax in the retail price of petrol from 31 per cent in 1976 to 45 per cent in 1981. A similar policy was followed for diesel fuel, although diesel prices remained 9 per cent below petrol prices despite a similar import cost. As a result, the volume of petrol and lubricant imports rose even more slowly than total imports, being roughly constant throughout the 1970s; their cost rose from 6 per cent to 12 per cent of imports.

Malawi was little affected (until 1980) by the international price changes of basic foods, since cereals were only imported in exceptionally bad years, with surpluses sometimes being available for export in good years. All food imports were 6.7 per cent of total imports in 1971, and this figure had fallen to 4.9 per cent by 1979. Even in 1980, a year of exceptionally bad rainfall, food imports were only 6.4 per cent of the total. However, as already noted, Malawi appears to have become a net importer of maize and the cost of importing and subsidising maize contributed heavily to Admarc's deficits in 1980 and 1981.

There was almost no change in import and exchange controls, with most current account transactions permitted. There were quite strict controls on capital movements. As a result of this policy being sustained, economic activity was able to proceed quite normally, with factories, farms and other producers normally able to get imported inputs. Shortages occurred mainly as a result of physical problems with transit routes in Mozambique, rather than as a result of controls; a wide range of imported consumer goods was available. A case reported in the press in July 1982, after the 15 per cent devaluation, suggested that, on small transactions at least, the black market rate of exchange was only **about 14 per cent above the official rate.**[20]

Meanwhile the availability of unskilled labour, increased by the induced fall in migrant labourers to other countries, and reinforced by the producer pricing policies of Admarc for smallholder crops, was allowed to cause a steady fall in average real earnings – from K331 per annum in 1970 to K191 per annum in 1980 at constant 1970 prices.[21] This fall overstates the fall in the real earnings of the average worker, because employment grew quite rapidly; the biggest increase was among the relatively low paid workers on agricultural estates, a process which would tend to drag down the average.[22] However, as already noted above, *within* the agricultural estate subsector, real wages also fell.

An important exception to the use of international market prices, apart from the crucial policy of paying below export parity for smallholder export crops, was Admarc's policy of uniform pricing throughout the country. The cost of this policy, especially for maize and for rice (which was grown mainly in the remote north of the country), increased sharply as transport costs rose. But the policy was not changed.

Most other policies which might have been affected by the increased cost of energy were not changed. Industrial policy offered relatively mild incentives, and industrial location policy consisted mainly in hoping that not every new industry would locate in Blantyre or Limbe, without any very severe pressure to locate elsewhere. The building of a new capital at Lilongwe has obviously shifted the balance in favour of the central region; it was too major a policy politically to alter in the light of higher transport costs. Electricity supply increases were dominated by a big hydroelectric scheme, which was planned before the oil price rises and which still had spare capacity in 1982; the government was said to have decided to eliminate local diesel-powered generation of electricity in favour of a national grid or local hydro schemes. The use of lake transport did not, as might have been expected, increase as oil prices rose; this was probably because of the huge cost of building, taking apart, transporting and rebuilding ships at Lake Malawi, and the lack of a local ship-building industry. Being a sugar producer, Malawi was able to build an ethanol plant and local petrol included a percentage of ethanol from the second half of 1982. Agricultural policy in the form of technical advice offered to smallholders did not apparently change as the result of higher fertiliser prices (which were passed on to farmers, more or less): smallholders were reputed to ignore that advice anyway.[23]

## Imported inflation and income distribution

Table 5.7 compares the import price index with Malawi's high and low income price indices for urban areas. It is clear that Malawi's domestic inflation was greatly influenced by imported inflation: all the indices had their highest rates of increase in the two periods 1974/75 and 1979/80. But domestic inflation showed less violent fluctuations than imported inflation, particularly for low income groups. Thus domestic inflation was lower than imported inflation for both income groups in 1974/75, and for the low income group in 1979/80.

### Table 5.7 Imported and domestic rates of inflation

| Year | Import unit prices Index | Annual change (%) | Low-income group Index | Annual change (%) | High-income group Index | Annual change (%) |
|------|-------|------------|-------|------------|-------|------------|
| 1970 | 100   |            | 100   |            | 100   |            |
| 1971 | 106.4 | 6.4        | 108.2 | 8.2        | 108.3 | 8.3        |
| 2    | 111.9 | 5.2        | 112.1 | 3.6        | 112.5 | 3.9        |
| 3    | 129.1 | 15.4       | 117.8 | 5.1        | 118.9 | 5.7        |
| 4    | 174.4 | 35.1       | 135.9 | 15.4       | 140.0 | 17.7       |
| 5    | 212.0 | 21.6       | 157.0 | 15.5       | 167.5 | 19.6       |
| 6    | 242.6 | 14.4       | 163.8 | 4.3        | 187.7 | 12.1       |
| 7    | 269.8 | 11.2       | 170.7 | 4.2        | 212.0 | 12.9       |
| 8    | 271.0 | 0.4        | 185.2 | 8.5        | 240.8 | 13.6       |
| 9    | 308.7 | 13.9       | 206.1 | 11.2       | 278.3 | 15.6       |
| 1980 | 376.1 | 21.8       | 243.9 | 18.3       | 352.2 | 26.6       |
| 1    | 439.5 | 16.9       | 267.2 | 9.6        | 388.9 | 10.4       |

*Source:* Reserve Bank of Malawi, *Financial and Economic Review.*

Note:    Domestic indices based on 1970 household budget survey; excludes costs of dwelling expenses, medical care, donations, dowry and marriage settlements and personal taxes.

The main reason why the domestic indices have increased less than the cost of imports, and why the low-income index has increased less than the high-income index, is the relatively low rate of increase in the cost of food – which has a 48 per cent weight in the low income index, and only 23 per cent in the high income rate. Clothing, mostly produced locally using low-paid labour, was also relatively cheap. The main cause of the higher rate of inflation for richer people was an increase to 575 in their index for transport and vehicle equipment (with a 26 per cent weight) and an increase in the index for other, mainly imported, goods to 466 (with a 19 per cent weight). In the low-income index these categories increased much less in price and anyway had weights of only 2 per cent and 4 per cent.

So Malawi's lack of dependence on food imports, and the low income group's lack of dependence on imported transport equipment (and other imported luxuries) meant that the country was at least partly insulated from directly imported inflation, and that its effects had a relatively greater effect on the items bought by the higher income groups. However, it would be wrong to deduce from this that income distribution was improved, because of the fall in real wages that occurred for the majority of workers, and the fall in cash income of smallholders, over the period in question.

**Conclusion**
Malawi has been relatively fortunate in that

(a)  oil imports were a small (6 per cent) proportion of total imports in 1970
(b)  the country was normally self-sufficient in grain
(c)  the country is, by African standards, small and densely populated, relying on small intensively cultivated farms, using relatively little imported energy.

In other words, in 1970 Malawi had not reached a stage of high dependence on imported oil and managed to increase exports through the 1970s by making more intensive use of (cheap) unskilled labour and, to a lesser extent, land. The energy crisis in Malawi relates much more to wood: 82–94 per cent of estimated energy consumption was of wood in 1979. Wood is used for cooking and flue-curing of tobacco; shortage of woodland is becoming acute in many areas. Switching to sun-cured burley tobacco is possible, but would require a reversal of the policies favouring estates over smallholders.

The macroeconomic situation, although less serious than in many other countries in Africa (there has been a much larger decline in terms of trade of base metal exporters, for example) appeared likely to prevent Malawi from continuing to grow as in the 1970s without a recovery in the terms of trade: all three sources of finance for export growth in the 1970s (estate profits, Admarc surpluses, bank credit) were not available in 1982. Although some large and lumpy investments (railway extension, capital city, airport, road programme) were by then complete, some will require indefinite funding from the government, which is already deeply in debt, still heavily in deficit and without many possibilities for expenditure savings since the public sector is already underfunded.

The cost to Malawi of adjusting to external circumstances was quite considerable: an almost complete halting of economic growth from 1980 to 1982 and, more seriously, the elimination of much (if not all) of the possibility of a resumption of growth thereafter. Meanwhile, macro-economic adjustment was only achieved at the cost of a very rapid build-up of expensive external debt. The latter problem was partly relieved by a rescheduling exercise in the second half of 1982. The relative ease with which agreement was reached was no doubt a product of Malawi's relatively successful macroeconomic management and of the fact that an agreement with the IMF had already been reached and adhered to for a period; but rescheduling of itself could make it more difficult for Malawi to borrow than it was beforehand, at least in large enough quantities to finance a resumption of growth.

### Notes and references

1  This paper is based on two earlier papers and the comments received on them: 'Malawi's adjustment policies' paper presented to a conference at the University of Malawi, July 1982; and 'The case of Malawi' in *IDS Bulletin*, January 1983. I owe grateful thanks for extensive comment and discussion of the paper to Robert Laslett and Reg Green in particular; to Rachel Jones for help in obtaining materials on the Malawi economy; and most of all to Jonathan Kydd for detailed written and verbal comments at the November 1982 Workshop on the project.
2  Statistics in this section are taken from World Bank *Accelerated Development in Sub-Saharan Africa: An Agenda for Action*, Oxford University Press, 1982; and from *International Financial Statistics*.
3  Jonathan Kydd and Robert Christiansen 'Structural change and trends in equity in the Malawian economy: 1964–1980', University of Malawi, Centre for Social Research, Income Distribution Project, Working Paper no. 2, 1981. In 1980, for example, Malawi had to import large amounts of food; these imports were partly financed by donors, partly by the government through its marketing board, and partly by borrowing from a South African bank.
4  It has been argued that this growth rate is too high, mainly because it includes growth of 2 per cent a year in subsistence sector output while full-year male participation in subsistence agriculture has been falling, implying a growth in productivity for which there is little or no evidence. Subsistence output was estimated to be more than 35 per cent of GDP in 1970. Jonathan Kydd and Robert Christiansen 'Structural change in Malawi since independence: Consequences of a development strategy based on large-scale agriculture', *World Development*, vol. 10 no. 5, May 1982. The authors suggest, however, that even if they are correct in believing that the growth rate has been overestimated, growth has nevertheless been higher than in most African countries.
5  Malawi was not likely to be much affected by international food prices being at that time largely self-sufficient in food, except in bad harvest years when food had to be imported.
6  There was some connection between the rise in imports and capital inflows, since some large aid-financed projects were undertaken.
7  Including a new boarding school with Latin as a compulsory subject.

8 By 1980 the terms of trade accounted for the greater part (K94m.) of the worsening of the balance of payments since 1977 (K121m.). These rough calculations were done by assuming 1977 trade volume and 1980 import and export prices.

9 Net inflows of short term capital have here been amalgamated with errors and omissions in the balance of payments statistics, as has been done in some years but not others, in the official figures. See Reserve Bank of Malawi's *Annual Report*, 1980, p. 22.

10 World Bank *Annual Report*, 1981; new credits information valid in 1981.

11 The GDP deflator rose by 17.9 per cent in 1980: this is probably the broadest available measure of inflation. The indices of Blantyre retail prices rose by 20.6 per cent (low income index) and by 23.6 per cent (high income index). Reserve Bank of Malawi *Annual Report*, 1980.

12 Three years earlier, depreciation in large firms only was K40m. (private communication.)

13 The official estimates for rises in the volume of private consumption may turn out to be over optimistic, given the fall in real wages that was taking place. These figures are from Reserve Bank of Malawi, *Financial and Economic Review*, adjusted using the Blantyre Low Income Price Index. Other sources give different numbers, but also show real private consumption rising in 1979 and 1980.

14 Not all the earlier increase in credit to the private sector was for investment, since some was used to cover deficits, for example in estate agriculture, see J. Kydd and R. Christiansen 'Structural change in Malawi since Independence: Consequences of a development strategy based on large scale agriculture', University of Malawi, 1981.

15 The extremely convincing evidence for these generalisations is contained in two papers by Kydd and Christiansen, the one cited in the previous footnote, and 'Structural change and trends in equity in the Malawi economy 1964–80', University of Malawi, Centre for Social Research, Working Paper no. 2, 1981. Numbers of Malawians recorded as working in the South African mines fell from over 123,000 a year in 1972 and 1973 to below 20,000 a year in the late 1970s. The official reason given for reducing the recruitment of Malawians to work in South Africa was an aircrash in Botswana in 1974 which killed a number of returning workers; however, the estate sector in Malawi has been short of labour throughout its history. There is also evidence of pressure on the government to restrict the flow of migrant workers abroad, both recently, and throughout the period since estates first began to employ labour in Malawi. For example, in 1901 hut tax was reduced from 6/- to 3/- if a man had worked for a European employer; this was to discourage Africans from going abroad to earn money to pay hut tax: R.B. Boeder 'Malawians abroad: the history of labour emigration from Malawi to its neighbours from 1890 to the present', Ph.D. Michigan State University 1974, p. 56.

16 Admarc *Annual Reports*. There is no one measure of inflation in Malawi, but the statement in the text is true whichever measure is used.

17 Reserve Bank of Malawi, *Financial and Economic Review*, vol. 13 no. 3, 1981, p. 75.

18 In the calendar year 1981, monetary authorities' claims on government rose from K58m. to K143m: *International Financial Statistics*.

19  *World Development Report 1983*, Table 6.1, pp. 60–61.
20  The case concerned a Zambian who sold several hundred Kwachas worth of travellers cheques to a trader and was arrested on leaving Malawi with a large amount of cloth. He was acquitted as the exchange control laws only forbade the sale of foreign currency to anyone not authorised by the Reserve Bank; the sale of travellers cheques to a non-authorised person was legal. This illustrates the relatively relaxed nature of Malawi's exchange control regime. It may be, of course, that the premium would be larger for larger amounts, since the controls are much more severe for capital as opposed to current transactions.
21  National Statistics Office, *Reported Employment and Earnings, Annual Reports*, using Low Income Retail Price Index as a deflator.
22  Wage employment in agriculture, forestry and fishing rose from 44,000 in 1968 to 183,000 in 1980, and from 33 per cent to 51 per cent of the total. The 1980 figure is based on a more complete statistical coverage, but the growth in share is not thought to be much affected by this. Kydd and Christiansen, *World Development*, May 1982, p. 364, and Malawi Government sources quoted there.
23  Information in this paragraph based on interviews in Malawi in 1982. In the nature of things it is harder to be sure of such negative findings, that is of no or negligible changes in policy, but the sources were very consistent in giving that impression.

# 6 The Impact of the International Environment on Brazil: From 'Miracle' to Recession*

*Marta Bekerman*

The objective of this paper is to observe the effects that the changes in the international environment during the 1970s have produced in an economy that followed the Brazilian pattern of development. We will look not only at the macroeconomic effects but also at possible structural adjustments that could take place because of changes in international relative prices. The policies pursued by the government in response to the new international conditions will also be examined.

Section 1 provides a brief introduction outlining some structural characteristics of the country. Section 2 explores the influence of external factors during the 1970s. Section 3 analyses the contribution of internal factors to the present imbalance by looking at the growth experience before 1973. Section 4 focuses on the macroeconomic policies pursued in response to the new world conditions. Section 5 looks at the impact of changes in the international environment and in national policies on the macroeconomic variables. Section 6 examines microeconomic policies followed in the food and energy sectors and their impact on development. Section 7 will attempt some conclusions.

*I would like to thank the participants of the Imported Inflation Workshop (Sussex, November 1982) for valuable suggestions, the members of the Instituto Brasileiro de Economia of the Fundacao Getulio Vargas for their collaboration, and Stephany Griffith-Jones for her comments on a previous draft.

## Introduction

One of the striking characteristics of Brazilian society is its degree of income concentration. At the beginning of the 1970s, Brazil was the developing country with the fourth highest income concentration, after Ecuador, Kenya and Mexico (Ahluwalia 1974).

GDP per capita reached US$1,850 in 1979. The lowest 20 per cent of the population received 3.4 per cent of income in 1970 against 46.7 per cent for the highest 10 per cent. There is also a large income disparity among regions, for example income per capita in the South-East is about four times that of the North-East (Reboucas 1980). Unequal income distribution is linked to a high level of ownership concentration in land: about 78 per cent of the cultivated area is under the control of 23 per cent of the owners. On the other hand 12 per cent is owned by 72 per cent of minifundistas (Dos Santos Neto 1981).

The country went through a process of import substitution during the 1950s and early 1960s that contributed to a closing of its economy. Exports plus imports of goods and services amounted to 14.3 per cent of GDP in 1970. This coefficient peaked in 1974 (17.2 per cent) to decrease slightly thereafter.

Brazil is a large oil importer: about 85 per cent of its oil consumption was imported in 1973. The incidence of oil in the total value of imports increased from 11 per cent in 1970 to 45 per cent in 1980. The bulk of imports apart from oil are raw materials and capital goods. Primary goods accounted for 70 per cent of total exports during 1971, but their share decreased during the 1970s because of the substantial increase in manufacturing exports which almost doubled their share to 42 per cent in 1980 (see Table 6.1).

Another important aspect of the Brazilian economy is the increasing participation of the state. During the 1930s the state's role was mainly in

**Table 6.1 Value and composition of exports, 1971 and 1980**

|  | 1971 | | 1980 | |
|---|---|---|---|---|
|  | *Value* (billion US$) | *%* of total | *Value* (billion US$) | *%* of total |
| Coffee | 0.8 | 28.4 | 2.8 | 13.9 |
| Other primary products | 1.2 | 42.2 | 6.8 | 33.8 |
| Semi-manufactures | 0.3 | 8.2 | 2.1 | 10.4 |
| Manufactures | 0.6 | 21.2 | 8.4 | 41.9 |
| Total | 2.9 | 100.0 | 20.1 | 100.0 |

*Source:* Banco Central do Brasil, *Boletim Mensal.*

regulating the export of primary products like sugar and coffee. In the 1950s and 1960s it was dedicated to the production of basic inputs such as oil, iron, steel and electricity. During the 1960s and, particularly, the 1970s state participation in production mushroomed; about 46 per cent of existing state companies were created during the 1970s. State companies were created mainly in key sectors; they had easy access to finance. Therefore, apart from the more traditional functions of administration and provision of public services, the Brazilian state is engaged at present in the productive process to an extent not very common in a capitalist society. The participation of state companies in total gross fixed capital formation reached 39 per cent in 1979 (Bresser Pereira 1982).

The major role of the state is an important factor in understanding the peculiarities of Brazilian development in relation to other countries undergoing a late industrialisation process. The differences are very clear in comparison with Argentina, for example, where the state plays a lesser role in transferring resources among sectors and in production.

## International determinants

### Terms of trade

The rapid increase in trade and liquidity that took place in the international economy from the mid-1960s until 1973 worked very favourably for the expansion of the Brazilian economy.

The terms of trade improved during the early 1970s until 1973, but a substantial decline took place following the first rise in the oil price. The decline between 1973 and 1975 was reversed during 1976 and 1977 (see Table 6.2) because of good international prices for some primary exports. After 1977 the terms of trade deteriorated again.

Import prices increased at a rapid rate, averaging 15 per cent per year, during 1971–81; they were strongly influenced by the two major oil price increases. Between 1973 and 1974 import prices rose by 60 per cent. Large rises in those prices were observed again during 1979–80, but were less pronounced than during the 1973–74 period. There was a significant rise in the price of primary products (excluding oil) between 1971 and 1974, and an acceleration in the price of capital goods thereafter (see Table 6.3).

It is important to mention that the international prices of some commodities may be affected by domestic events: the case of coffee is perhaps the clearest example. The large expansion in coffee prices that took place in the international markets during 1976–77 was related to the frosts that affected Brazil in 1975.

The increase in export prices averaged 10.7 per cent a year between

## Table 6.2 Terms of trade indices, 1970–1981

(1970 = 100)

|      | Export prices | Import prices | Terms of trade | Purchasing power of exports[a] |
|------|-----------|-----------|-----------|-----------|
| 1970 | 100.0 | 100.0 | 100.0 | 2,739 |
| 1971 | 96.5  | 104.0 | 92.8  | 2,792 |
| 1972 | 109.0 | 111.0 | 98.2  | 3,595 |
| 1973 | 150.0 | 139.0 | 107.9 | 4,460 |
| 1974 | 189.0 | 214.0 | 88.3  | 3,715 |
| 1975 | 189.0 | 221.0 | 85.5  | 3,922 |
| 1976 | 218.0 | 227.0 | 96.0  | 4,460 |
| 1977 | 266.0 | 236.0 | 112.7 | 5,135 |
| 1978 | 239.0 | 253.0 | 94.5  | 5,006 |
| 1979 | 269.0 | 302.0 | 89.1  | 5,049 |
| 1980 | 285.0 | 387.0 | 73.6  | 5,199 |
| 1981 | 268.0 | 430.0 | 62.3  | 5,414 |

*Source: Conjuntura Economica,* Fundacao Getulio Vargas (FGV); Banco Central, *Boletim Mensual.*

*Note:* [a] Resulting from multiplying the terms of trade index by the value of exports at 1970 prices.

1971 and 1981; it was more rapid during the 1971–74 period. Manufacturing export prices followed the same pattern as did the prices of other exports.

   Prices of primary commodities decreased considerably in 1981 and 1982 because of the recession in industrial countries (Griffith-Jones 1984). This continued a trend towards high variations in commodity prices shown during the second half of the 1970s. Brazil was relatively less affected because of the diversification of its exports of primary products and the increasing importance of manufactured exports.

### International liquidity

The rapid expansion in private bank lending from the mid-1960s (Griffith-Jones 1984) allowed the Brazilian public and private sectors unprecedented access to foreign credits. From 1969, the net capital inflow financed the current account deficit as well as contributing to increases in reserves.

   The large increase in world liquidity and Brazil's high credit rating allowed a substantial increase in capital inflows from 1974. Foreign exchange reserves even increased between 1976 and 1978, in spite of the

**Table 6.3 Import price indices**

(1963 = 100)

|  | Crude oil | Primary products | Capital goods | General |
|---|---|---|---|---|
| 1971 | 114 | 103 | 79 | 110 |
| 1974 | 519 | 227 | 102 | 226 |
| 1979 | 756 | 231 | 177 | 317 |

*Source:* Serra, J. (1982).

large current account deficit. The level of the foreign debt increased enormously during the 1970s (from US$ 5.3 bn in 1970 to $72.2 bn at the end of 1982); nearly three-quarters of that total consisted of loans with floating interest rates. For this reason, the increase in international interest rates that took place after 1979 was considered in some Brazilian circles as 'the third international shock' that the country had to face.

Although foreign direct investment in Brazil is a large share of the total received by Latin America, it amounts to a small part of the huge increase of capital inflows. John Wells (1973) has suggested that some part of currency loans or suppliers' credits could be a disguised form of foreign direct investment. Multinational corporations may prefer to register a capital inflow as foreign credit rather than as capital investment, because borrowing allows more rapid repatriation of invested capital.

Brazil did not draw any upper credit tranche credits from the IMF during the 1970s. This represented a transitory situation of greater

**Table 6.4 Export price indices, 1971–81**

(1970 = 100)

|  | Total | Total excluding coffee | Mining | Unprocessed products | Manufactures |
|---|---|---|---|---|---|
| 1971 | 97 | 107 | 102 | 86 | 111 |
| 1974 | 189 | 211 | 127 | 152 | 246 |
| 1979 | 269 | 264 | 198 | 259 | 292 |
| 1981 | 268 | 281 | 234 | 161 | 313 |

*Source: Conjuntura Economica* (FGV).

## Table 6.5 Current account balance and variation in reserves, 1971–1981

(billion US$)

|        | Current account balance | Net inflow of foreign capital | Variations in reserves | Level of total reserves |
|--------|-------------------------|-------------------------------|------------------------|-------------------------|
| 1971   | −1.3                    | 1.9                           | +0.5                   | 1.7                     |
| 1972   | −1.5                    | 3.5                           | +2.4                   | 4.2                     |
| 1973   | −1.7                    | 3.5                           | +2.2                   | 6.4                     |
| 1974   | −7.1                    | 6.3                           | −0.9                   | 5.3                     |
| 1975   | −6.7                    | 6.2                           | −1.0                   | 4.0                     |
| 1976   | −6.1                    | 6.9                           | +1.2                   | 6.5                     |
| 1977   | −4.0                    | 5.3                           | +0.6                   | 7.3                     |
| 1978   | −7.0                    | 11.9                          | +4.3                   | 11.9                    |
| 1979   | −10.7                   | 7.7                           | −3.2                   | 9.7[b]                  |
| 1980   | −12.8                   | 9.7                           | −3.5                   | 6.9[b]                  |
| 1981[a]| −11.7                   | 12.9                          | +0.6                   | 7.5[b]                  |

*Source:* Banco Central, *Boletim Mensual;* and *Conjuntura Economica* (FGV).

*Notes:*   Figures do not add because of non-inclusion of errors and omissions.
[a]Preliminary.
[b]With gold valued at two-month moving averages according to the quotations on the London Market.

freedom from the economic directives of that institution, but implied higher costs in terms of interest rates paid for commercial loans, and the requirement to maintain large levels of foreign reserves as a guarantee for the foreign debt.

### Growth pattern before 1973
The economic strategy followed since 1967 can be defined as one of accelerated growth with external indebtedness, or 'debt-sustained growth'. The economy grew at over 10 per cent a year from 1967 to 1973, while inflation decreased. The question is to what extent this form of growth was vulnerable to exogenous changes taking place in the international economy. Rapid industrialisation since 1967 was made possible by growth in durable consumer goods. Since 1969 there was also strong growth in the capital goods sector. The high levels of growth reached during the period were made easier by the existence of idle capacity and by good international conditions regarding opportunities to export and borrow.

**Table 6.6 Debt service**

|      | Value (billion US$) | | | Ratio: |
|      | Interest | Amortisation | Total | as % exports |
|------|----------|--------------|-------|--------------|
| 1971 | 0.3 | 0.9 | 1.2  | 40 |
| 1973 | 0.5 | 1.7 | 2.2  | 35 |
| 1975 | 1.5 | 2.1 | 3.6  | 41 |
| 1977 | 2.1 | 4.1 | 6.2  | 51 |
| 1979 | 4.2 | 6.4 | 10.6 | 69 |
| 1980 | 6.3 | 5.0 | 13.3 | 64 |
| 1981 |     |     | 16.8 | 72 |
| 1982 |     |     | 18.1 | 86 |

*Source:  Conjuntura Economica* (FGV) Marco 1982; and Conselho Monetario
Nacional (1982).

Rapid expansion in the economy generated structural disequilibria
among economic sectors. In spite of the expansion in the production of
capital goods since 1969 there was a considerable lag in the growth of
this sector in relation to consumer durables and construction. As a
result, the share of capital goods imports in total supply increased from
22 per cent in 1967 to 29 per cent in 1975 (Malan and Bonelli 1977). The
easy availability of foreign funds encouraged this import-intensive
pattern. The presence of foreign firms in the Brazilian economy may
have helped this process because of a tendency observed in those firms
to spend relatively more on imports.

Another source of structural disequilibrium was the slow growth of
agricultural production for the domestic market compared with the
expansion in industry and employment. During the period 1967–73 the
amount of food per capita decreased by 3 per cent against an increase in
income per capita of 56 per cent (Serra 1982). Thus the 1973–74
increases in petroleum prices and the 1974–75 world recession took
place at a moment of strong expansion of output in Brazil, based on an
import-intensive strategy made possible by a large increase in foreign
borrowing on commercial terms.

There are two different approaches to explaining the change in the
pattern of growth and inflation occurring in Brazil after 1974. The first
one stresses the role of oil price increases and the following international
economic recession as the main reasons for the interruption of high
growth rates (Balassa 1979). This approach also stresses the role of
short-term adjustments to restore external and internal equilibrium.

A second approach observes a strong cyclical component in Brazilian
growth before 1973. The main reasons given to explain the balance of

payments problems and the renewed inflationary pressures are the import-biased nature of that growth and the structural imbalances in the pattern of industrialisation; for example, Bacha (1980) wrote: 'The oil crisis only anticipated in time a trade deficit that would occur a few years hence, even under the unusually high 1970 terms of trade'. According to this line of argument, the increase in oil prices was not the main reason for the changes that took place in Brazil after 1974. This approach involves a critique of the pattern of industrialisation followed during the 1967–73 period, stressing the importance of long-term adjustments. Although an adjustment of the growth pattern prevailing in Brazil up to 1973 would have been required eventually there is no doubt that, because of the changes in international relative prices, the structural adjustments became much more necessary and urgent in an economy based on such an energy-intensive and import-intensive growth pattern.

## Macroeconomic policies after 1974

The new government that assumed office in March 1974 was under pressure from different groups to lead the country towards political liberalisation. The government sought electoral support through a policy of sustained growth and some increases in minimum wages.

The first government reactions to the new problems that affected the economy in 1974 – the huge deficits on current account and a higher rate of inflation – tried to minimize their effects on the Brazilian economy. The political environment, dominated by the victory of the opposition party in the November 1974 legislative elections, made the government try to avoid economic recession. Planning Minister Velloso referred to that option as economically ineffective and politically inconsistent: 'To attempt to resolve the trade balance problem through a recession, which would bring a sharp reduction of imports would have merely postponed the balance of payments problem while raising unemployment and lowering living standards' (Velloso 1978).

In 1975 the government pursued an expansionary policy. It increased public expenditure and allowed small rises in real urban wages. This decision to return to an expansionary policy, at a time of serious external disequilibrium, showed a Brazilian response very different from policies pursued by many other developing countries at the time. It helped to avoid a severe deflation and led to a postponement of adjustment largely via an increase in the foreign debt.

Two major policy alternatives were discussed in government circles to cope with the severe external disequilibrium. The first, originating in the Planning Ministry, was oriented to a new process of import substitution. In the words of Minister Velloso:

The alternative Brazilian option involved only a moderate degree of deceleration in growth, combined with aggressive efforts, including increased oil exploration and massive investment, to find substitutes for imports of raw materials, basic industrial inputs and capital goods. (Velloso 1978)

The other alternative, represented by the Finance Minister, M. Simonsen, was based on a continuation of the strategy followed up to 1973. It aimed at obtaining a rapid export growth through additional incentives to exporters and substantial devaluation. The strategy followed during 1975–76 was closer to the first alternative, as measures of import protection were more important than were incentives granted to exports. Import substitution was further encouraged until 1976 by large increases in public expenditure oriented mainly to the development of basic products such as steel, petrochemicals and minerals.

An important shift in policy occurred at the time of the second rise in the oil price. New priorities for development were established in 1979. The sectors given special incentives were export industries, energy and agriculture. A diminished role was given to sectors previously given priority, such as production of basic industrial inputs and capital goods.

By the end of 1980, the external sector was perceived as the main problem, to which economic growth was to be sacrificed. The high level of foreign debt, the large rise in international interest rates and decreasing gross inflows of private loans showed the impossibility of relying on foreign finance to the same degree as in the mid-1970s.

The policies followed after 1979 (including a maxi-devaluation) led Brazil, for the first time since 1973, to undertake a more orthodox adjustment to the external deficit. An economic recession (GDP decline of 3.5 per cent) took place in 1981.

*Monetary and fiscal policies*
From 1974 the conflicting objectives, of maintaining high rates of growth and keeping inflation and the balance of payments deficit under control, led the Brazilian authorities to follow a 'stop-go' policy with periods of monetary and fiscal expansion and periods of more contractionary policy.

The decision to follow an import substitution policy after 1974 implied an increase in public investment during the 1974–76 period from its already high levels. In 1976 the government concluded that growth was becoming too rapid, bringing high inflation and loss of reserves. A new strategy of progressive deceleration of growth to around 5 per cent a year until 1980 was announced. This was followed by tighter monetary policy and the freeing of interest rates. As a result, a substantial increase in real interest rates occurred. The policy of freeing interest rates was very closely related to the objective of stopping the outflow of foreign reserves. The resulting large inflow of foreign funds counteracted the policy of monetary restraint.

In 1980, a very rigid limit on credit expansion and an outflow of foreign reserves led to a severe monetary restriction. The money supply expanded by 70.2 per cent during 1980, less than wholesale prices. This marked the end of the Brazilian era of delaying adjustment to external shocks.

There was a different monetary response to the two external shocks reflecting the different economic strategies adopted to face them. After the first shock, monetary policy fluctuated between a period of expansion (end-1974 to early 1976) and more restrictive phases (e.g. 1974 and 1977); the restrictions on credit expansion were limited by the fear of an economic recession. In 1979, after a short initial attempt at expansionary policy, the severity of the financial situation led the authorities to restrict monetary aggregates, a policy which had taken effect by 1980.

*Policies related to the external sector*
Until 1968 exchange rate policy was based on intermittent, large depreciations designed to compensate for the loss in competitiveness resulting from domestic inflation. From 1968 until 1974, a crawling peg policy was established to adjust smoothly to inflation differentials between the domestic and the international economy. The objective of this policy was to avoid the disruption caused by large devaluations and to discourage speculation in the exchange rate market.

In spite of the worsened situation in the foreign sector in 1974, Brazil did not carry out a major devaluation in real terms. The authorities decided to continue with mini-devaluations, applying instead new restrictions to limit the expansion in imports (higher tariffs, advance deposit requirements and quotas were established after 1974).

The exchange rate policy has been heavily criticised, for example by Cline (1981), on the grounds that it failed to give the proper signals needed to adjust to the severe deterioration of the external accounts. There were several reasons explaining the government's decision not to adopt a large devaluation, such as its effect on companies with large foreign debts, and fears of increasing inflationary pressures.

There is another element to consider when evaluating an exchange rate policy: the movement in wages. Given a level of protection, the economy's competitiveness is influenced by the relation between the exchange rate and the wage level; the objective of a devaluation is to increase that ratio. If wages are indexed to the cost of living, wage costs will rise, counteracting the effect of that devaluation. After 1974 wage adjustments were put in line with observed inflation. In 1979, after a number of labour disputes, the government established that, in addition to automatic wage adjustments, negotiations could take place to cover productivity increases. Because of the sharp acceleration in inflation during 1980, wage indexation started to take place twice a year. Increased pressure from 1974 onwards to maintain or even increase real wages, after several years of wage restraint, reduced the possible effects of a devaluation. For this reason, it has been argued that an active devaluation policy is not the right instrument to shift relative prices in Brazil (Cardoso 1979).

On export promotion, it is important to mention the Befiex programme, established in 1972, but which had a significant influence in the expansion of manufacturing exports after 1974. In exchange for signing long term export commitment contracts with the government, firms were exempted from paying import taxes on raw materials and capital goods incorporated into the exported products.

## The impact of changes in international conditions and national policies

*On the balance of payments*
The year 1974 showed the impact of deteriorated terms of trade and of large increases in the volume of non-oil imports on the current account.

**Table 6.7 Average annual growth rates of exports and imports**

(per cent)

|  | 1970/73 | 1974/78 | 1979/81 | 1982[a] |
|---|---|---|---|---|
| Total exports | 28.0 | 15.3 | 22.5 | −9.9 |
| Primary | 23.2 | 8.9 | 14.2 | −3.1 |
| Industrialised[b] | 42.6 | 25.7 | 30.2 | −14.6 |
| Total imports | 32.8 | 17.2 | 17.3 | −7.2 |
| Crude oil | 42.4 | 46.3 | 37.7 | −4.7 |
| Other | 31.9 | 11.5 | 6.1 | −9.6 |

*Source:* Conselho Monetario Nacional (1982).

*Notes:* [a] Preliminary estimates.
[b] Includes manufactured and semi-manufactured goods, excluding refined sugar and soluble coffee.

Import demand was very strong in 1974 because of high industrial growth and stockpiling by the private sector in advance of a possible high devaluation or of increased protectionism.

As a consequence of increases in import prices and quantities, the value of imports more than doubled in 1974 leading to an explosive jump in the current account deficit. The trade deficit decreased after 1975 because of (a) the policy of import restraint that helped to keep the import bill almost constant until 1979; (b) good prices for some primary goods during 1976–77; and (c) a successful policy of expanding industrial exports.

The rapid growth of Brazilian exports of industrial products can be explained by export potential as well as by export promotion policies. By the 1970s Brazil had achieved a relatively sophisticated industrial development with a very small part oriented to the foreign markets. Another important strategy was diversification of markets, particularly to other developing countries, whose share in Brazilian total exports increased significantly during the 1970s, while the US and EEC shares decreased.

In 1979, the second oil price rise and the increase in international interest rates led to a new jump in the current account deficit. But unlike what happened in 1974, when the main source of the current account deficit was the trade account, *from 1979 the main cause was the deficit in services.* This was due to the large rise in international interest rates in the context of a much larger foreign debt.

The balance of payments problem became critical during the early 1980s. The debt service ratio reached 86 per cent in 1982 (see Table 6.6). Due to the debt problems of Brazil as well as other countries in the area, foreign bankers became reluctant to grant new credits to Brazil. In fact we can distinguish two distinct periods, as regards supply of foreign funds to Brazil. During the 1970s, the supply of foreign funds to the country was to some extent elastic. It can be said that the additional liquidity increased the degree of economic autonomy of the Brazilian state and allowed a postponement in adjustment.

From 1980 the supply of foreign funds and the external sector in general became *the* exogenous variable to which the whole economic system had to adapt so that the autonomy of economic policy was substantially reduced. The general economic strategy for 1983 was based on obtaining a trade surplus of US$6 billion (by cutting imports by US$3 billion) which with an expected volume of loans of US$10.6 billion would have balanced the external accounts. The postponement of adjustment to the first oil crisis by a rapid increase in foreign debt made the situation more difficult when other external shocks occurred.

*The impact on domestic inflation*

The inflation rate steadily declined after 1968 to 17 per cent by 1973. It then accelerated again, reaching 48 per cent in 1976, 80 per cent in 1979 and 120 per cent in 1980.

The influence of the external environment and of national policies on domestic inflation in Brazil takes place via (a) the monetary channel or (b) direct price effects (Lemgruber 1977). The monetary channel works through large increases in foreign reserves not sterilised by the government, leading to an expansion in the money supply. Cline (1981) found a relatively close correlation between the growth in reserves and the expansion in the domestic money supply in Brazil between 1962 and 1977, suggesting that reserve changes had a dominant role in the behaviour of money supply during 1970–73. The expansionary effect of capital inflows disappeared during 1974–75 when foreign exchange reserves fell. When the government decided to pursue a tighter monetary policy and free interest rates, large foreign capital inflows occurred which offset the restrictions on monetary expansion.

The direct price effects reflect increases in export and import prices, and policies such as devaluation, export subsidies and import tariffs. Mini-devaluations to maintain parity implied a neutral role for the exchange rate in the transmission of world inflation to internal prices. The maxi-devaluation at the end of 1979 increased the price in cruzeiros of traded goods and accelerated domestic inflation. As mentioned above, Brazil avoided a maxi-devaluation after the first oil crisis by increasing import protection; the inflationary impact of a large devaluation was given as an important reason for not devaluing at that time. However Cline (1981) suggests that the increase in protection that took place in 1975 contributed considerably to the acceleration of inflation by 1976.

The inflationary impact of changes in external prices of agricultural crops and oil and of domestic policies to face them, can be derived by observing the contributions of those products to the increase in the wholesale price index (see Table 6.8). For all the years shown the Table demonstrates that in Brazil food made a much higher contribution to inflation than oil because the weight of food in the WPI is substantially higher than that of oil and lubricants.

The policy of wage restraint followed by the government until 1973 helped slow down inflation. After 1974 wage adjustments followed observed inflation, making Brazilian inflation more vulnerable to the effects of imported inflation (Bacha 1980). The accuracy of the official inflation indicators has been questioned and some Brazilian institutions produce their own price indicators. However, because of the political pressures faced by the government, incomes policy after 1974 could not be used to moderate the impact of external inflation.

**Table 6.8 Contribution of food and oil to the increase in the wholesale price index (WPI)**

| | Increase in the WPI (%) | % of total increase in the WPI due to: | | |
| --- | --- | --- | --- | --- |
| | | Food | Oil & Lubricants | Both |
| 1971 | 21.5 | | | |
| 1972 | 15.9 | 37.9 | 5.8 | 43.7 |
| 1973 | 15.6 | 30.0 | 4.0 | 34.0 |
| 1974 | 35.4 | 38.6 | 7.7 | 46.3 |
| 1975 | 29.3 | 41.9 | 9.1 | 51.0 |
| 1976 | 44.9 | 42.5 | 7.7 | 50.2 |
| 1977 | 35.4 | 41.8 | 7.2 | 49.0 |
| 1978 | 43.0 | 48.5 | 4.7 | 53.2 |
| 1979 | 80.1 | 45.1 | 12.2 | 57.3 |
| 1980 | 121.4 | 47.2 | 8.3 | 55.5 |
| 1981 | 94.3 | 41.6 | 9.3 | 50.9 |
| 1982 (Sept.) | 68.4 | 39.9 | 7.6 | 47.5 |

*Source: Indices Economicos;* 'Suplemento Especial', *Conjunctura Economica* vol. 33, no. 11.

*The impact on growth*

It is interesting to observe how official objectives on growth have changed since 1973 due to external and internal events. In 1974 the Second Development Plan established a growth rate target of 10 per cent for the following years, in spite of the decline in the terms of trade. This led to a policy of high public investment until 1976. In that year, a growth target of 5 per cent until 1980 was announced; this moderation in growth was not achieved. The fluctuations in monetary policy led the economy to a high and fluctuating level of growth with rates such as 9.7 per cent in 1976 and 4.8 per cent in 1978. Since 1980 there have been no growth objectives in the economy as the external sector became the main problem.

Average growth reached about 7 per cent during 1974–80. In spite of the balance of payments constraint and increasing inflation, Brazil avoided a severe recession, as happened in many oil importing countries. Table 6.9 shows the close correspondence in 1970–80 between the industrial and the overall growth rate, while agriculture showed lower growth. This correspondence disappeared with the recession (1981) when growth of the agricultural sector helped avoid a larger fall in GDP.

Growth did decline somewhat after 1973, influenced by monetary

**Table 6.9 Average annual growth rates of GDP, 1971–1981**

(per cent)

|  | Total GDP | Agriculture | Industry |
|---|---|---|---|
| 1970–73 | 11.3 | 5.1 | 12.7 |
| 1974–78 | 7.0 | 5.0 | 7.7 |
| 1979–80 | 7.3 | 5.6 | 7.2 |
| 1981 | −3.5 | 6.8 | −8.4 |

Source: 'As Contas Nacionais ate 1980', *Conjunctura Economica* (FDV), Dezembro 1981.

and fiscal policy. In 1971–73 growth rates were high for all demand components (see Table 6.10).

Gross fixed investment continued to grow at high rates up to 1976 because of large public investment. From 1977 there was a substantial decline in investment and government consumption growth, while private consumption grew rapidly. The purchasing power of exports showed an important fall in 1974, recovering afterwards. In spite of its small share in GDP, the fluctuation in the growth of exports affected the overall growth rate. On the other hand, the control of imports helped avoid larger recessionary effects by diverting demand from foreign to domestic goods. In brief, it could be said that the Brazilian policy after 1974 avoided the worst effects of the external shocks on growth by maintaining high levels of consumption and investment.

## Microeconomic policies after 1973

*The energy sector*
Rapid industrialisation followed by Brazil since the 1940s was based on

**Table 6.10 Real growth and final demand**

(In constant 1970 cruzeiros; % annual average rates of change)

|  | 1971–73 | 1974–76 | 1977–80 |
|---|---|---|---|
| GDP | 12.4 | 8.3 | 6.2 |
| private consumption | 10.3 | 8.7 | 8.2 |
| government consumption | 10.4 | 9.0 | 2.9 |
| gross fixed investment | 15.4 | 12.7 | 3.4 |
| exports (purchasing power) | 20.0 | 1.4 | 4.6 |
| imports | 21.9 | 7.7 | 1.5 |

Source: 'As Contas Nacionais ate 1980', *Conjunctura Economica*, Dezembro 1981.

availability of cheap energy and on a sharp alteration in energy consumption patterns. Wood and biomass represented 78 per cent of total energy consumption in 1941 but decreased to 25 per cent in 1979. Migration to the cities and changes in consumption patterns explain that decline, which was accompanied by a sharp increase in the use of oil (from 9 per cent of total energy consumption in 1941 to 45 per cent in 1972) and hydroelectricity – from 7 per cent to 21 per cent (Gianetti da Fonseca 1981). As local oil production remained stagnant from the mid-1960s, domestic consumption depended increasingly on imports. About 85 per cent of oil consumption was imported in 1973. Perhaps few countries in the world are so deficient in fossil fuels as Brazil. Oil reserves in 1979 were estimated at 155m. tonnes (equivalent to three years' consumption).

The importance of road transport increased Brazilian dependence on oil. Table 6.11 shows the relative share of different cargo transport systems in Brazil and some developed countries. This was not seen as a problem until the first jump in oil prices.

**Table 6.11  Share of different cargo transport systems in Brazil and other countries, 1975**

(per cent)

|  | Railway | Motorway | Water | Other | Total |
|---|---|---|---|---|---|
| USSR | 77.2 | 7.2 | 5.1 | 10.5 | 100.0 |
| USA | 38.7 | 23.0 | 15.8 | 22.5 | 100.0 |
| Canada | 33.6 | 9.4 | 27.1 | 29.9 | 100.0 |
| Brazil[a] | 16.3 | 70.5 | 10.1 | 3.1 | 100.0 |

*Source: World Highway* and *Anuario Estatistico das Transportes,* Geipot 1979, quoted by Goncalves de Oliveira (1981)

*Note:*  [a] 1979

The energy crisis imposed a serious threat to the Brazilian development pattern. Its solution in a country like Brazil could have been attempted through two basic strategies which do not exclude each other but would require a different emphasis (Gianetti da Fonseca 1981). The first one would be based on substitution of imported oil by alternative domestic sources, to continue as far as possible the development patterns followed up to 1973. The second alternative would attempt a major reorientation of productive processes, restructuring of the transport system and the redefinition of urban styles. This would imply a modification in the demand profile for energy, to reduce dependence on oil and at the same time correct serious distortions in urban planning and income distribution. We will examine Government policies to attempt to evaluate to what extent policies implied a response to the increase in oil prices and which of the two strategies outlined was being adopted.

*Energy policy after the first rise in the oil price*
The economic response during the years that followed the first oil price rise was rather weak. The reasons seemed to be lack of understanding by the government regarding the seriousness of the energy problem, pressures to continue with a growth pattern which was very intensive in energy consumption, and higher costs of the alternative sources, particularly as the price of oil fell considerably in real terms after 1975.

The main measures included in the energy policy for 1974–78 were:

(a)  A massive programme of oil exploration and production through higher investments by Petrobas and agreement of risk contracts with foreign companies.
(b)  The establishment of the Alcohol National Programme to produce alcohol to replace petrol.
(c)  The nuclear agreement with West Germany to build eight nuclear power stations.
(d)  The announcement of new incentives to increase use of coal.

By 1978 this policy was proving not very successful, except for alcohol production. In those years low international sugar prices encouraged transformation of sugar cane into alcohol. Distillery units were established as annexes to sugar mills, even though the number was far below that contemplated in the programme. There was also an intensification of investment in oil exploration during the period, but the production of oil remained stagnant. The nuclear programme established in 1975 was behind schedule and proving very costly.

*Energy policies after the second oil price rise*
Energy policy during 1974–78 failed to give a proper answer to the energy problems faced by Brazil, problems which were made more crucial after the second increase in oil prices. Apart from the lack of solutions to dependence on imported oil, by 1979 the country had a very heavy foreign debt which limited future increases in foreign finance. In mid-1979 the government declared 'a war economy' in order to solve the energy problem and an energy plan *(Modelo Energetico Brasileiro)* was published.

The *Modelo Energetico Brasileiro* estimated oil consumption at 1.7m.

bpd by 1985, assuming 6 per cent GDP growth. About 200,000 bpd would be saved by a conservation policy leaving 1.5m. to be supplied, one-third each by domestic production, alternative sources and imports.

The programme implied that domestic oil production was to be raised from 200,000 to 500,000 bpd and that dependence on oil imports would be reduced to 30 per cent from the present level of nearly 85 per cent. Electricity and oil would be kept in state companies' hands (apart from risk contracts for oil exploration), but the alternative sources would be developed by the private sector, based mainly on alcohol (170,000 bpd), coal (170,000 bpd), charcoal (120,000 bpd), and oil-bearing shale (25,000 bpd).

The programme did not attempt any articulation between the energy objectives and policies in agriculture and transport. This created conflicts between the energy and agricultural policies in the case of the alcohol programme. The actual costs of producing energy from different sources was not discussed in the programme either.

The large expansion in energy planned was reflected in the total investment allocation for that sector which was estimated at a minimum of US$13bn. per year from 1980 to 1985, representing over 20 per cent of the country's total gross capital formation component compared with around 10 per cent before 1980 (da Silva Pinto and Rodrigues 1980).

It has been estimated that transport absorbs 58 per cent of total oil consumption (Goncalves de Oliveira 1981). Oil substitution in transport is taking place basically through the alcohol programme. The substitution in industry is a newer process. Industry accounts for a high proportion of total consumption of fuel oil and since 1981 there is a clear policy attempting its substitution. The government has recently signed agreements *(Protocolos de Substitucion)* with some industrial sectors (e.g. paper, cement and steel), establishing goals for gradual substitution of oil derivatives. A recent regulation establishes that from January 1983 fuel and diesel oil are not going to be provided to firms for consumption in boilers and furnaces, which will have to be fed mainly with wood or electricity.

*The alcohol programme*
Different periods can be observed in the development of the alcohol programme, reflecting the government's attitudes to the energy crisis. The existence of conflicts among different economic groups, including the estate companies, for the control of the different stages of the programme inhibited its development during the period 1975–78. At that time the programme was mainly supported by the owners of the sugar mills who saw it as a new market.

The second oil price rise and problems of oil supply completely changed official attitudes towards the development of the programme. To get a secure supply of energy became the primary objective, independently of the costs of obtaining it. The government announced in 1979 the goal of 10.7bn. litres by 1985, with an investment of US$5bn. in a four year period. The alcohol produced under the programme would be bought by official institutions. Loans, with very favourable conditions, were granted by the government to cover 80 per cent of the costs. These loans were to be serviced by the sales taxes on petrol and taxes on roads (Colson 1981). Alcohol production increased very rapidly: 115 distillery projects were approved during 1980, increasing production capacity by 2.8m. litres to a total of 8.9m. This represents nearly three quarters of the goal established by 1985, clearly a big quantitative success when compared with other goals of the energy programme.

The rapid development shown by the production of ethanol affected the motor car industry. The government encouraged the substitution of gasohol by hydrous alcohol (which cannot be mixed with petrol) by promoting the production of vehicles with alcohol powered engines. This required a coordinated national supply of the new fuel, and by the end of 1980 there were 3,500 alcohol pumps (Colson 1981). The big jump in domestic petrol prices during 1980 stimulated demand for alcohol powered cars. About 647 cars were produced in January 1980; by December the number reached 51,000. The total for 1980 reached 195,000 new cars and 29,015 converted ones. The alcohol programme also promoted expansion of capital goods producing distillery and milling machinery; new suppliers entered that market during 1980. The programme suffered new problems in extending the area cultivated with sugar cane with the speed necessary to reach the 1985 goal.

The problem of cost is another element to be considered when trying to detect the future of the programme. It is estimated at between US$50 and $70 per equivalent barrel of petrol, considerably higher than the present cost of imported oil. Different ideas about future behaviour of oil prices will influence alcohol investors in the Brazilian market. This uncertainty was reflected in the fluctuations in the sales of alcohol cars, which declined by the end of 1981. The government confirmed its support for the alcohol programme with a new regulation which established that for two years the price of hydrous alcohol would be 59 per cent of the petrol price.

Another element that could improve the future of the programme is development of new technologies. The main problems at the moment are the destination of the alcohol distillery residuals *(vinhoto)* and the need for improvement in car engines to make them more efficient in the use of alcohol. It is interesting to observe the different approaches to the alcohol programme shown in the literature. For Colson (1981), what made the programme fascinating to the observer 'is the extent to which it has now become a major component of a coherent strategy designed to take advantage of structural shifts within the economy'. For other commentators, the alcohol programme shows deep conflicts with agricultural development and could lead in the medium and long-term to serious changes in the agricultural structure (Quadros 1981).

*Effects of the alcohol programme on agriculture*
Sugar cane production expanded rapidly during the 1960s and early 1970s because of favourable conditions on the international markets. That expansion was accompanied by investment to modernise and increase production capacity. The deterioration in international sugar prices after 1975 threatened to create idle capacity in the sector. This seems to have been very decisive in the initial development of the alcohol programme. The interests of sugar producers, capital equipment suppliers and motor car companies converged at the time. It has been argued that it was because of this convergence, rather than technical reasons, that alcohol was produced from sugar cane (ethanol) rather than from wood (methanol) (Wohlers de Almeida 1981).

The explicit objectives of the alcohol programme were to substitute oil imports, to reduce regional income disparities and to increase employment. There is some evidence that the expansion in the area sown with sugar, required for the production of ethanol, is having contrary effects:

(a) It tends to concentrate most resources in the centre-south (the most advanced area) to the detriment of the poorer states. By the end of 1979 the centre-south region had about 66 per cent of distilleries and 70 per cent of the productive capacity. Sao Paulo had 48 per cent of total alcohol pumps at the end of 1980.

(b) Sugar cane is displacing other crops, particularly food. This phenomenon had already taken place in the past. Between 1953 and 1971 there was an expansion of 63 per cent of sugar cane in the northeast region accompanied by reductions in the production of manioc (12 per cent), millet (50 per cent) and beans (32 per cent) (Quadros 1981). Data on sown areas for Sao Paulo between 1976 and 1980 show a large expansion in sugar (337 per cent), beans (209 per cent) and soybeans (166 per cent), and decreases in pastures (−699 per cent), millet (−220 per cent) and rice (−306 per cent). The reduction in the sown areas for food production can push up food prices, with an adverse effect on distribution of income.

(c)  There seems to be a trend to land concentration in the production of sugar cane, which continued after 1973. (Filho *et al.* 1981).

(d)  The number of working days increased by 15 per cent in São Paulo during the period 1976–80. However, there was a higher proportion of seasonal employment because sugar harvesting was concentrated in a few months of the year (Homem de Melo 1981). Given the precarious conditions for seasonal workers regarding salaries, housing, health and education, the alcohol programme does not provide an ideal solution to the problem of unemployment.

*Pricing policy*

The growth in domestic prices of oil derivatives after 1974 was slower than the growth in the cost of imported oil, plus transport and refinery expenses (see Table 6.12). Therefore, the whole impact of the oil price increases was not immediately transmitted to the economy. There was a recovery in the coefficients in 1977–78 to decrease again from 1979 following the second jump in imported prices. Since 1977, there were other measures to limit petrol consumption such as controlling speed and closing the pumps on Saturdays.

A sharp alteration in domestic relative prices of oil derivatives occurred during the period. Petrol prices increased much faster than those of diesel oil. There was a sharp fall in the relation between the domestic price of diesel and the cost of imported oil after 1974 because

**Table 6.12 Relations between domestic prices of petrol and diesel oil, and cost of imported oil, 1973–81**

(US$ per barrel)

|  | Consumer price | | Imported oil | Price relations | |
|  | *Petrol (A)* | *Diesel (B)* | *price (C)*[1] | *A/C* | *B/C* |
| --- | --- | --- | --- | --- | --- |
| 1973 | 20.7 | 16.3 | 4.3 | 4.8 | 3.9 |
| 1974 | 36.3 | 21.0 | 14.9 | 2.4 | 1.4 |
| 1975 | 46.9 | 25.0 | 14.6 | 3.2 | 1.7 |
| 1977 | 65.5 | 34.9 | 14.6 | 4.5 | 2.4 |
| 1979 | 70.5 | 42.1 | 19.7 | 3.6 | 2.1 |
| 1980 | 102.2 | 44.1 | 32.9 | 3.1 | 1.3 |
| 1981 | 122.2 | 64.8 | 39.6 | 3.1 | 1.6 |

*Source:* Homem de Melo (1982).

*Note:* [1]Import price plus a margin of 20 per cent to cover transport and refinery expenses.

the government tried to minimise the inflationary impact by keeping diesel oil prices down.

The ratio between diesel and petrol decreased from 0.82 in 1973 to 0.53 in 1981 due to higher taxation on petrol. In 1981 the tax on petrol reached US$65 per barrel against US$10 per barrel of diesel oil (Homem de Melo 1982).

A freeze in electricity prices in 1975 caused electricity's price in real terms to fall. This policy has led Electrobras, the state electricity company, to borrow heavily abroad since 1975 to finance its operations. It is estimated that the company had borrowed US$7bn. by the end of the 1970s, more than 10 per cent of the total foreign debt. Table 6.13 shows the evolution of electricity fees in relation to the prices of energy derived from oil.

**Table 6.13 Ratio between average price of MWh 'forhecido light' and the average price of a tonne of oil**

| | |
|---|---|
| 1973 | 0.57 |
| 1974 | 0.45 |
| 1975 | 0.44 |
| 1976 | 0.43 |
| 1977 | 0.38 |
| 1978 | 0.40 |
| 1979 | 0.39 |
| 1980 | 0.35 |

*Source:* Joao Sayad, 'Energia e Inflacao' in *Estudos Economicos*, vol. 11, Sept. 1981.

While the price of fuel oil increased by 883 per cent between January 1979 and September 1981, electricity fees grew by 260 per cent (da Silva Pinto and Rodrigues 1980), leading to a process of substitution of oil derivatives by electricity in some sectors. During 1974–80, electricity consumption increased by 12 per cent a year against a GDP growth of 6.5 per cent; this contrasts with the period 1970–74, when GDP and electricity consumption grew respectively by 12 per cent and 13 per cent.

*The present situation*

The acceleration in oil prospecting has led to a substantial increase in output since 1980. Little was done in the development of the coal programme, and it is unlikely that its goal will be reached by 1985. Coal is not a competitive alternative for energy because the reserves are located in the extreme south, far from the big consumer centres and they are high in ash and sulphur. The distance problem is aggravated by the inadequacy of the railway transport system, making the use of trucks run by fuel oil necessary. Therefore, apart from the funds required to develop the programme, a high level of investment to improve transport facilities would be needed. Alcohol is being substituted for petrol in the car sector but this process has not been extended to heavy transport for technical reasons.

The industrial sectors that consume most fuel oil are cement, chemicals, steel and paper. The cement industry is introducing steam coal as a substitute for fuel oil. The industry should be 100 per cent coal powered by 1985. A process of substituting electricity for fuel oil is also taking place in new industrial plants. The number of furnaces using fuel oil has been reduced and all the new plants use electricity which has shown a decline in the consumption of fuel oil because of conservation and substitution by gas self-generated in furnaces. This can be seen in Table 6.14. The paper industry is increasing the use of wood in substitution of fuel oil to heat the boilers.

**Table 6.14 Evolution of steel production and specific consumption of fuel oil, 1975-80**

(per cent)

|  | Increase in steel production | Reduction in specific consumption of fuel oil[a] |
|---|---|---|
| 1975 | 10.7 | −11.6 |
| 1976 | 10.4 | − 9.7 |
| 1977 | 21.8 | − 4.5 |
| 1978 | 8.4 | −10.2 |
| 1979 | 14.7 | −13.0 |
| 1980[b] | 10.1 | −19.2 |

*Source:* Companhia Energetica de Sao Paulo, *Energia na Industria,* 1981.

*Notes:* (a) Consumption of fuel oil per tonne of steel.
(b) Estimated.

*The agricultural sector*
During 1968–73, good international prices for agricultural products and the policy of mini-devaluations helped expand agricultural exports. This process led to the existence of two groups of products with differential access to technology: (a) the export sector with internationally determined prices and larger possibilities for investment and modernisation: soybeans, coffee, sugar, orange juice; (b) the domestic

sector with prices usually more controlled by the government – food crops like manioc, black beans, rice, millet, tomatoes and potatoes (Barros and Graham 1978).

The major tool of agricultural policy since 1972 was large credit expansion. In some years (e.g. 1975), the credit flow to the sector actually exceeded the net value of output. Those credits were heavily subsidised with negative interest rates. Credit was concentrated on the large export crop farmers. During 1975–79, about 80 per cent of loans for production went to six crops: soybeans, rice, wheat, corn, coffee and sugarcane. A study of a sample of 6,000 farms in São Paulo in 1977 showed that the amount of credit used by the farms was positively related to size (Instituto de Economia Agricola 1979); Central Bank figures also show a concentration in the distribution of credit by area.

The government also established a policy of minimum prices at the beginning of the sowing season. Those prices increased in real terms between 1967 and 1973 but were allowed to decline during the rest of the 1970s as a measure against inflation. The minimum price policy lost relevance after 1973 as market prices were in general higher than those officially guaranteed. Problems of food scarcity led the government in 1979 to raise the level of minimum prices for crops like black beans, manioc and corn to give incentives for production.

The result of domestic policies and of good international prices led to a large expansion in export crops during the 1970s and to a relative decline in the production of food, particularly beans, manioc, rice and sweet potatoes. Soybean output grew from 2m. tonnes in the early 1970s to a record of 12m. tonnes in 1977. The expansion of the sown area increased by about six times and was mainly located in the centre-south area which, during the early 1970s, produced about two-thirds of food. Table 6.15 shows the variation in sown areas and in productivity for different crops during the period 1975–79 in relation to 1966–70.

The reduction in food crop production helped accelerate the rate of inflation during the 1970s. The food wholesale price increased 45 times during 1973–81 against a rise of 38 times in the general wholesale price index.

Wheat is shown separately in the table because the government established subsidies to consumers in 1972 and encouraged a process of import substitution by paying the farmers higher prices than those of the international market.

Higher levels of export crop prices led to better profits for farmers and an increase in rents. Higher rents increased costs for producers of domestic crops, and therefore the prices of these goods.

The declining trend in the production of food crops because of the expansion in export crops was aggravated by the new expansion in sugar

**Table 6.15 Variations in sown areas and productivity**

(1975–79 as a proportion of 1966–70)

|  | *Sown area* | *Productivity* |
|---|---|---|
| Industrial and export crops: | | |
| Sugar cane | 1.33 | 1.12 |
| Soybeans | 8.73 | 1.44 |
| Coffee | 0.65 | 1.31 |
| Oranges | 2.49 | 1.12 |
| Domestic crops: | | |
| Black beans | 1.22 | 0.77 |
| Manioc | 1.19 | 0.84 |
| Rice | 1.28 | 1.04 |
| Millet | 1.19 | 1.08 |
| Potatoes | 0.98 | 1.40 |
| Groundnuts | 0.44 | 1.15 |
| Wheat | 2.79 | 0.87 |

*Source:* Lyra and Ryff (1980).

cane required by the alcohol programme. The availability of calories and proteins derived from the five principal food crops declined by 25 per cent between 1967 and 1979 (Homem de Melo 1982a). However, there was a rapid increase in the domestic consumption of wheat from 1972 because of the subsidy established. Homem de Melo (1982a) attributes this to an attempt by the government to compensate for the scarcity of domestic crops with higher imports of wheat. The increase in wheat consumption helped the availability of proteins and calories to recover after 1975 (when the levels were very low); by 1979 the amounts of proteins per capita were slightly higher than in 1967. Therefore the trend was towards a decrease in the consumption of domestic crops and an increase in the consumption of wheat. High increases in food prices affected mainly the low income families that spend more on food.

From 1980 the domestic supply of food started to increase because of changes that took place in the internal and international stituation. On the domestic front, the government followed a more realistic policy of minimum prices to encourage production. On the international side, there was a significant decline in the price of commodities since 1980 that has affected the Brazilian export crops (particularly soybeans).

It is interesting to mention that, during the 1950s, an expansion was feasible in both export and domestic crops because of the possibilities of expanding the agricultural frontier. This is more limited now because the nearest agricultural frontier is already incorporated in production. The remaining area is perhaps less fertile and its distance from the consumption centres would make a large investment in transport necessary.

## Conclusions

The Brazilian experience during the 1970s shows that even a large and relatively closed economy could not escape the impact of external shocks. Brazil suffered from adverse terms of trade, fluctuations in international lending, world inflation and recession as well as increased protectionism in industrial countries.

Was Brazil able to adapt better than other countries to the international shocks that took place during the 1970s? Why? As was observed above, in spite of an initial serious disequilibrium in the balance of payments and increased inflationary pressures, Brazil had relatively high growth rates until 1980, compared to most other developing countries. Foreign finance availability was a crucial element for this strategy but not the only one. Some of Brazil's main primary exports enjoyed good international prices in some years after 1974. The policy of import substitution that followed the first rise in the oil price succeeded in curbing the growth of imports in relation to that of the GDP; and the policy of export promotion helped expand the volume of manufactured exports, which increased substantially as a percentage of total exports. These results were obtained through a strategy which, in open contrast with the Southern Cone Latin American countries, was based more on state intervention than on free market policies.

Economic policy after 1974 was, however, basically oriented to postponing external adjustment and increasing indebtedness in the belief that the expansion in the productive structure would solve future balance of payments problems. Such a strategy was highly risky. From 1980 there was a reversal in some external events that even after 1974 had helped maintain growth. The effect of the large jump in international interest rates on the Brazilian balance of payments was even larger than that of the second large increase in oil prices. Therefore debt service became the main reason for the negative balance in the current account. Furthermore, foreign loans started to be scarce after the crisis of confidence that followed the Mexican and Argentinian debt crises.

The rise in international interests rates also had an indirect impact on the Brazilian external sector through its effect on commodity prices. High interest rates tend to diminish demand for commodities, thus depreciating the price. This was reflected in the low prices of Brazilian primary exports after 1981. Brazilian manufactured exports were affected mainly by recession in the industrial countries but also by low commodity prices which reduced the capacity of developing countries to import.

Brazil was forced to come to terms with its external deficit. The relatively high degree of autonomy in economic policy possible in the mid-1970s due to the availability of private credits was replaced in 1982 by a narrow scope for economic manoeuvering because of the external situation. This limit to economic policy autonomy will influence politics and the process of *apertura*. However the socio-political reality itself establishes limits on the adjustment process, reflected in strong pressures against reducing real wages and transferring the costs of adjustment to the workers. A policy of manoeuvering between the external and the internal constraints is most likely to take place during the next few years. Growth will probably be lower than that after 1973 but the extent of the recession may be limited by the possible political conflicts which it would generate. It is quite common in Brazil now to hear criticism of the rapid growth policy followed after 1974, on the grounds that it transferred too large a burden to the future (a future that has arrived!).

Another way to look at the past strategy is to ask to what extent the large use of foreign funds since 1974 contributed to reducing income inequalities, one of the most serious socio-economic problems faced by the country. Table 6.16 shows the evolution of income distribution. Since 1974 there has been a reversal of the trend to declining minimum real wages, but this process did not stop a deterioration in the relative distribution of income by 1980. The results are no better when looking at the distribution of income by regions. The development strategy followed by Brazil during the 1970s tended to increase the importance of the centre-south in relation to other poorer regions. The alcohol

**Table 6.16 Income distribution by groups, 1960, 1970 and 1980**

|  |  |  | (% of total income) |
| --- | --- | --- | --- |
| *Group* | *1960* | *1970* | *1980* |
| Lowest 20% | 3.9 | 3.4 | 2.8 |
| Lower 50% | 17.4 | 14.9 | 12.6 |
| Highest 10% | 39.6 | 46.7 | 50.9 |
| Highest 5% | 28.3 | 34.1 | 37.9 |
| Highest 1% | 11.9 | 14.7 | 16.9 |

*Source:* Bresser Pereira (1982).

programme is a good example of this. The situation of the northeast showed a relative deterioration during the 1970s, as income per capita, in relation to the national average, declined.

Although the high rate of growth helped incorporate more people into the labour market and therefore to increase the total number of salaries paid, the debt-led growth strategy followed by Brazil during the 1970s did not help correct the problems of the relative distribution of income which in fact deteriorated during that period.

*The effects of energy and agricultural policies on the patterns of development*

The energy policy up to 1978 was mainly based on pricing, which generated some shifts in consumption from petrol to fuel and diesel oil and increased the use of electricity.

Since 1979, the main objective of the energy policy has been to increase oil production and search for alternative sources. There was some increase in oil production from 1980 and the alcohol programme is one of the most developed alternative sources sponsored by the government. A process of substitution of other sources for fuel oil in the main consuming industries has recently started, encouraged by the government.

In the transport sector there was a trend to substitute alcohol for petrol in private cars and for diesel in heavy vehicles. The substitution of diesel for cargo and passenger vehicles has become a major problem. No major attempt to change the production structure and the demand profile has been made in response to changes in relative prices. In the transport system there was no attempt to expand railways and water transport in spite of the fact that they consume less energy than road transport. In the case of urban road transport there was no special encouragement of the public transport's supply, which did not show a major increase.

A very important effect of energy policy is taking place in the agricultural sector as a response to the alcohol programme. The expansion in the area sown with sugar cane, which will have to be doubled to reach the official 1985 alcohol target, has generated a process of substitution of sugar cane for food crops, a concentration in land ownership, and a higher level of employment with a stronger seasonal base.

Since 1974 good international prices for some Brazilian export crops helped consolidate a trend to extend the cultivated area in those products and contract that dedicated to domestic crops. The effect was a large increase in the price of food and lower availability per capita of food crops. The latter effect was partially compensated by an increase in the consumption of imported wheat. The increase in food prices had an adverse effect on the distribution of income. Since 1980 the international fall in commodity prices and a new policy of minimum prices for food seem to be reversing that trend (perhaps temporarily).

## Appendix

**Table 6.17 Export quantum indices 1971–1981, for selected years**

(1970 = 100)

|  | Total | Manufactures[a] |
|---|---|---|
| 1971 | 106 | 104 |
| 1973 | 155 | 177 |
| 1975 | 174 | 206 |
| 1977 | 177 | 265 |
| 1979 | 220 | 355 |
| 1981 | 323 | 544 |

*Source: Conjuntura Economica* (FGV).

*Note:* (a) Includes wood, textiles and foodstuffs.

## Notes and references

Ahluwalia, M. (1974) 'Income inequality: Some dimensions of the problem' in *Redistribution with Growth,* Oxford University Press.

*Agropecuaria* (1979) Centro de Estudos Agricolas, Fundacao Getulio Vargas (FGV).

Assis C.A. and Rodrigues Lopes, L. (1980) 'A ineficiencia da politica de precos para conter o consumo dos derivados de petroleo', *Revista Brasileira de Economia* July/September.

Bacha, E. (1977) 'Issues and evidence of recent Brazilian economic growth' *World Development* vol. 5 Nos. 1 and 2, January–February.

Bacha, E. (1980) 'Selected issues in post-1964 Brazilian economic growth' in Taylor, *Models of Growth and Distribution in Brazil,* IBRD.

Balassa, B. (1979) 'Incentive policies in Brazil', *World Development* vol. 7.

Barros, J.R. de and Graham, D.H. (1978) 'A Agriculture brasileira o problema de producao de alimentos' *Pesquisa e Planejamento Economico,* December.

Barros, J.R. de and Magalhaes Gomes, F. (1981) 'La crisis energetica, una perspectiva Brasileira' *Comercio exterior* (Mexico) November.

Baumgarten, A.L. jr. and Dunha, L.R. (1978) 'A politica industrial e o desempenho do setor na ultima decada (1968–1977)' in Dias Carniero (ed) *Brasil: Dilemas da Politica Economica.*

Bresser, Pereira (1982) *Economia Brasileira: Una Untroducao Critica, Brasiliense,* *São* Paulo.

**Table 6.18 Balance of payments, 1971–81**

(billion US$)

| | 1971 | 1972 | 1973 | 1974 | 1975 | 1976 | 1977 | 1978 | 1979 | 1980 | 1981[a] |
|---|---|---|---|---|---|---|---|---|---|---|---|
| Trade balance | −0.3 | −0.2 | — | −4.7 | −3.5 | −2.2 | 0.1 | −1.0 | −2.8 | −2.8 | +1.2 |
| Exports | +2.9 | +3.9 | +6.2 | +7.9 | +8.7 | +10.1 | +12.1 | +12.7 | +15.2 | +20.1 | +23.3 |
| Imports | −3.4 | −4.2 | −6.2 | −12.6 | −12.2 | −12.3 | −12.0 | −13.7 | −18.1 | −22.9 | −22.1 |
| Services | −1.0 | −1.2 | −1.7 | −2.4 | −3.2 | −3.9 | −4.2 | −5.0 | −7.9 | −10.2 | −13.1 |
| Interest & profits | −0.4 | −0.5 | −0.7 | −1.0 | −1.5 | −1.8 | −1.6 | −1.7 | −2.4 | −3.2 | −3.5 |
| Other | −0.5 | −0.7 | −1.0 | −1.5 | −1.7 | −2.1 | −2.6 | −3.3 | −5.5 | −7.0 | −9.6 |
| Current account deficit | −1.3 | −1.5 | −1.7 | −7.1 | −6.8 | −6.1 | −4.0 | −5.9 | −10.7 | −12.8 | −11.7 |
| Capital account | +1.8 | +3.5 | +3.5 | +6.2 | +6.1 | +6.9 | +5.3 | +9.4 | +7.7 | +9.7 | +12.9 |
| Overall balance | +0.5 | +2.4 | +2.2 | −0.9 | −1.0 | +1.2 | +0.6 | +3.9 | −3.2 | −3.5 | +0.6 |

*Source:* Banco Central do Brasil, *Boletim Mensual.*

*Note:*   (a) Preliminary.

Cardoso, E. (1979) 'Minidesvalorizacoes e indexecao salarial: Alguns aspectos de experiencia Brasileira na decada de 70' *Pesquisa e Planejamento Economico,* December.

Castro, P. (1981) *Organizacao Fundiaria e Desenvolvimento,* Rio de Janiero, Cedes.

Carneiro Netto Dioniso, D. (1978) *Brazilian Economic Policy in the Mid-Seventies,* Brazilian Economic Studies no. 4.

Cline, W. (1981) 'Brazil's aggressive response to external shocks' in Cline, W. *World Inflation and the Developing Countries,* The Brookings Institution, Washington.

Colson, R.F. (1981) 'The proalcohol programme. A response to the energy crisis' *Bolsa Review,* May.

Conselho Monetario Nacional (1982) *Programacao do Sector Externo Em 1983,* Brasilia.

da Silva Pinto, L.F. and Rodrigues, J.A. (1980) 'Economia energetica no Brasil', *Conjuntura* (FGV) November.

Dos Santos Neto, A.P. (1981) 'A estrutura fundiaria Brasileira', *Revista Pernambucana de Desenvolvimento,* July/December.

Filho E. Gatti and Cardozo de Mello, N. (1981) 'O Programa Nacional do Alcool e seus impactos na agricultura paulista', *Estudos Economicos,* September.

Galveas, E. (1980) 'The energy issue and the balance of payments' in *Energia 80,* Apec Editoria.

Gianetti da Fonseca, E. (1981) 'Energia e a economia brasileira' *Estudos Economicos* vol. 11, September.

Goncalves de Oliveira Edem (1981) 'Transporte de carga e posicao das industrias' *Revista Brasileira de Economia,* Oct./Dec.

Griffith-Jones, S. (1984), 'Impact of world prices on development: The international environment' (Chapter 1 of this book).

Homem de Melo, F. (1980) 'A agricultura nos anos 80: Perspectiva e conflitos entre objetivos de politica', *Estudos Economicos,* May–August.

Homem de Melo, F. (1981) 'Proalcool e emprego' *Estudos Economicos* September.

Homem de Melo, F. (1982) 'A questao dos "subsidios" ao oleo diesel' *Conjuntura* (FGV) July.

Homem de Melo, F. (1982a) 'Disponibilidade de alimentos e efeitos distributivos: Brasil 1967–79' *Pesquisa e Planejamento Economico* August.

Instituto do Acucar e do Alcool, *Relatorio 80.*

Instituto de Economia Agricola (1979), *Informacoes Economicas,* May.

Lemgruber, A.C. (1977) 'Inflation in Brazil' in *Worldwide Inflation,* Krause, L. and Salant, W. (eds), The Brookings Institution, Washington, DC.

Lyra, Ines and Ryff, T. (1980) 'Agricultura de abastecimento interno: Problemas e perspectivas' *Revista de Economia Rural,* Brasilia, July/September.

Malan, P. and Bonelli, R. (1977) 'The Brazilian economy in the seventies. Old and new developments', *World Development* vol. 3 no. 1/2.

Quadros, S. (1981) 'O programa do alcool-expansão e conflito', *Conjuntura* (FGV) May.

Reboucas, Osmundo (1980) 'Politica fiscal y disparidades regionais no Brasil', *Revista Pernambucana de Desenvolvimento,* 7/1 January–June.

Rezende Gervasio, Castro de (1982) 'Credito rural subsidiado e preco da terra no Brasil' *Estudos Economicos,* São Paulo, August.

Serra, J. (1982) 'Ciclos y mudancas estructurais na economia brasileira do apos-guerra' *Revista de Economia Politica,* São Paulo, April–June.

Suzigan, W. *et al.* 'Crescimento Industrial no Brasil'. IPEA, *Relatorio de pesquisa* no. 26.

Velloso (1978) *Brasil: A Solucao Positiva* Abril Tec Editora, Sao Paulo; quoted by Cline, W. 'Brazil, aggressive response to external shocks', in Cline, W. *et al. World Inflation and the Developing Countries,* The Brookings Institution, Washington 1981.

Wells, John (1973) 'Euro-Dolares, divida externa e o milagre brasileiro', *Estudios Cebrap* no. 6 Oct.–Dec.

Wells, John (1979) 'Brazil and the post-1973 crisis in the international economy' in *Inflation and Stabilization in Latin America* Thorp, R. and Whitehead, L., Macmillan, London.

Wohlers de Almeida, Marcio (1981) 'Autonomia empresarial do estado e impasses da politica energetica' in *Estudos Economicos,* September.

# 7  The Republic of Ireland: The Impact of Imported Inflation

*Reginald Herbold Green*[1]

## Introduction

At first glance the Republic of Ireland may seem a very odd economy to include in this volume. It is Western European – indeed a member of the EEC. It is classified by the World Bank[2] as an 'industrial market economy' – albeit with the lowest per capita GNP in the category, below that of 'upper middle' income Trinidad and Tobago and Singapore and only marginally ahead of Hong Kong but still over twice that of Brazil and three times that of the Republic of Korea. It is in the 'rich country club' (OECD) and has an aid programme. Further, its industrialisation – in one sense – is hardly recent. In the 17th and 18th centuries the Dublin area was among the leaders in the United Kingdom (as it then was) industrial revolution.[3]

However, closer examination shows a range of similarities with other economically 'peripheral' economies. Ireland is heavily dependent on exports – and in particular raw-material based and labour-intensive manufactured exports – to larger, richer economies. Its structure of production is much more similar to that of the 'upper middle income class' (and in particular Korea and Brazil) than to that of other industrial market economies in respect to the relative weights of agriculture and of industry, while its industrial structure – especially the low share of machinery, transport equipment and basic metals – is by normal criteria less developed than those of Malaysia or Yugoslavia (let along Korea, Argentina and Brazil), albeit more so than those of

Venezuela and Tunisia. In addition, its early industrialisation failed and its re-emergence as a significant manufactured goods exporter in the 1960s makes it arguably the first of the NICs.[4]

Further, like a number of other countries whose economies are analysed in this volume, Ireland was able to adjust to the 1973–74 international economic shocks successfully but fared much worse after 1979. Its external balance and recurrent government balance went into (and remained in) very substantial deficit with unemployment and inflation rising rapidly and GDP growth falling away to a negative rate by 1982. Another parallel to several other countries is that Ireland, despite entry into the EEC and major consequential benefits from the Common Agricultural Policy (both as to price and as to market access) on top of fiscal policies (on tax and expenditure side) viewed as favourable to farmers, has seen an erosion in the real incomes of its farmers. One difference is marked: Ireland, despite a nearly fourfold increase in official external debt over 1979/1981 to 48 per cent of GDP[5] (above Brazil, Mexico or Poland), has not been seen as a potential credit risk by international lenders and has retained easy access to net new borrowing.

## 1960–1981: An overview

Ireland, therefore, can be viewed as a newly industrialising country with a substantial traditional export base. Its active pursuit of export-oriented manufacturing, largely by foreign transnational corporations, dates to the late 1950s.[6] It was – contrary to the policies of Korea and Brazil – paralleled by an opening of the protected domestic market to imports culminating in a free trade agreement with the UK and accession to the European Economic Community in 1965 and 1973 respectively.[7] The protected pre-NIC industrial sector has played little part in export expansion and has suffered increasing import penetration in its home market.[8]

Until the late 1970s the external balance of Ireland was moderately stable, with capital inflows from foreign investors and moderate government borrowing plus substantial net invisible earnings, private transfers (largely from emigrants to families or relatives) and – after EEC accession – official transfers, offsetting substantial merchandise deficits. The government borrowing also served to bridge the gap between revenue and expenditure caused by provision of infrastructure, buildings and capital grants for new, export-oriented ventures while virtually totally exempting them from taxation. The post-1978 crisis manifested itself in a sharp increase in both the merchandise trade deficit and the government's borrowing requirements leading to the very rapid increase in external debt.

The first two decades of Ireland's externally-oriented strategy were reasonably successful – GDP per capita rose 3.1 per cent a year. However, because Ireland has averaged only 1 per cent a year population growth over the period the overall GDP growth was 4 per cent a year versus almost 7 per cent for upper middle income countries as a group and about 5.5 per cent for industrial market economies.[9] It was nonetheless substantially above any previous period since the Republic of Ireland (then the Irish Free State) became independent in the early 1920s.

The engine behind this was export growth which averaged 7.1 per cent a year in the 1960s and 8.4 per cent in the period 1970–81 – rates above the upper middle income country averages and in the latter period above that of industrial market economies as well.[10] These rates are comparable to those recorded by Brazil (5.0 per cent and 8.7 per cent respectively) which had a similar structure of traditional plus new manufactured exports. However, Ireland had a different market orientation than other NICs, with very heavy concentration on the UK and increasingly, other EEC members and the USA. Relatively little was exported to other NICs or developing countries. The market penetration share has remained relatively low and – apart from the entry into continental markets – has not grown rapidly.[11]

It would appear that, especially in the 1970s, the continued rapid growth of Irish exports was heavily dependent on the rate of growth of EEC and US manufactured goods imports. This helps explain why a 17 per cent deterioration of the terms of trade over 1974–75 had a less severe impact that that of 14 per cent over 1979–81;[12] in the former case export growth recovery was rapid while in the latter the terms of trade decline was succeeded by two years of stagnant world trade.

## An historical aside

The Republic of Ireland became independent in 1922 after several centuries of British colonial rule. While the initial years of independence were marked by civil war, Ireland since the late 1920s has been politically stable with two major and one secondary party dominating elections and both major parties forming governments.

Economic strategy and its major policy components have not been a source of major difference between the two major parties (Fiana Fail and Fine Gael)[13] which are both farmer, middle-class and business oriented but also appeal to working class voters. Labour, which is worker oriented, has been a secondary force throughout (indeed, has declined in recent years) and has not differed fundamentally on major economic issues[14] from the two more clearly bourgeois parties.

The traditional Irish economic policy has been described as conservative populism. From the 1930s through the later 1950s its major components were a combination of agricultural subsidies (following the land reforms against expatriate British landlords in the 1920s), manufacturing protection (leading until the 1950s to relatively rapid growth of employment in this sector), fiscal balance and moderate levels of taxation at the expense of relatively low levels of social services and especially of social security. Apart from the protection, the policy was not primarily business oriented. Over the entire period economic growth was relatively low, about 2 per cent a year, and population declining (over 1 per cent a year for the entire period but rising to 1.5 per cent by the late 1950s).

In the 1950s this strategy was increasingly perceived to be played out and by 1960 had been replaced with 'industrialisation by invitation' giving assistance and tax exemption to new export-directed manufacturing enterprises.[15] As noted earlier, over 1960–81 this led to a more rapid increase in GDP, exports, employment and population (reversing the historic downward trend). It was accompanied by a moderately less rigorous fiscal policy (albeit until the late 1970s recurrent budget deficits were avoided) and was paralleled by an increase in levels of social and welfare services. After 1973 farm subsidies grew rapidly under EEC auspices but were increasingly financed by net transfers from other EEC members, which by 1982 reached almost $200 per capita or 4 per cent of GDP and a much higher share of agricultural income.[16]

By the 1970s Ireland was a net exporter of food and manufactures but a heavy net importer of energy, raw materials and components. Its manufacturing sector was increasingly dominated by low value-added enterprises (in the established food processing sector and the new foreign-owned export industrial one) which bought little beyond labour and services in Ireland and highly dependent on growth of European trade in manufactured goods. Over the 1960s it had benefited from its location, its European status, relatively low labour costs and its early start as a NIC (as well as its traditional favoured access to UK markets). The favoured access – for both food and manufactures – was reinforced and broadened after 1973 by EEC membership.

## Macro-economic policies 1970–81

Ireland maintained expansionist policies – primarily to maximise employment – throughout the 1970s. This changed only in mid-1981 under the first Fitzgerald administration and serious progress towards reducing the recurrent budget and merchandise trade deficits was not achieved until the second half of 1982. The basic perceived political constraint on earlier adjustment related partly to sustaining growth of employment (especially as the growth of jobs for Irish workers in the UK declined and turned negative after 1979) and partly to a desire to avoid increased taxation or wage restraint. These constraints were exacerbated by the near balance between Fiana Fail and the Fine Gael-Labour coalition.

Monetary and fiscal policy therefore contributed to growth through 1981 (especially in 1972–73 and from 1979 onwards). It did not result in an external-balance crisis prior to 1979 largely because of increased foreign borrowing, substantial and growing EEC transfer payments from 1974 on, and a high level of reserves only slightly reduced in 1973 and only moderately lower in real terms at the end of 1981 than in 1972.[17]

Trade policy – beyond continued pursuit of export industries – was very limited. On the one hand the incentives for export industries – including complete company tax exemption, infrastructure and contributions toward capital cost – were already very high. On the other, direct import constraints were ruled out by EEC membership.

Exchange rate policy despite being basically passive was a positive influence on the balance of payments over most of the period. Until 1979 the punt (Irish pound) was at a fixed 1 to 1 parity with the British pound and, therefore, fell by more than one-third relative to the SDR.[18] In 1982, following Ireland's accession to the EEC a further decline of about one-fifth occurred. However, in neither period was an active policy pursued. Taking Ireland's 1970–81 inflation rate of 14.2 per cent together with the 9.8 per cent for all industrial market economies,[19] the effective real devaluation was about 20 per cent. European Monetary System (EMS) membership has entailed the institution of exchange controls (especially on outward-bound portfolio investment) and an overt statement that the 'prime objective' was maintaining 'external reserves adequacy' consistent with the stability of the Irish pound within the EMS.[20] This meant that over 1979–82 Ireland was losing competitiveness in its main export market as Irish inflation was markedly higher than the EEC average.

External capital transactions, and particularly official debt, were the main balancing item – again more consequentially on trade and government deficits than as an active policy measure. While debt levels began to rise significantly in 1974, the explosive growth took place over 1979–81. At the end of 1978 government external debt plus net external liabilities of state sponsored bodies stood at P1,585 million; by the end of 1981 it had soared to P5,071.[21] The ratio of reserves to official external debt declined from over 50 per cent to slightly above 20 per cent over that period.[22]

## Imported inflation: Macro-economic impact

At first glance the Irish economy's evolution over 1970–81 appears to correlate closely – both with regard to inflation and trade deficits – with the 1973–74 and 1979–80 oil price increases. However, closer inspection raises doubts because of the nature of domestic policy, because of the limited share of oil in the import bill, and because of the rapid growth of exports, export prices and fixed investment over the period.

The price increase indices rose through 1975 (with the odd exception of 1974), declined through 1978 and rose again through 1981, with the 20 per cent growth in the Consumer Price Index in that year approximating its 1975 peak of 21 per cent. However, budgetary policy was sharply expansionary in 1972–73 and again in 1978–79 through 1980–81 but relatively contractionary over 1973–74 – a pattern corresponding equally well with the price movements and quite independent of oil prices. Two exercises[23] suggest that perhaps one-seventh to one-fifth of inflation was directly caused by increased oil prices and that Irish inflation rates were highly correlated with international – and especially British – prices.

Money supply rose more rapidly than prices, by about 2 per cent a year over the decade but this inflationary (as opposed to accommodationist) policy was in fact concentrated in 3 years – 1973, 1978, 1979. Interest rate changes broadly paralleled those in money supply. They were negative in real terms in 9 of the 12 years from 1970 through 1980. However, the basic influence on interest rates appears to have been external. Through 1978 *de facto* integration of British and Irish banking meant that rates were virtually identical and dominated by British policy. From 1979 onward Ireland's position within the EMS, and its need to raise substantial external funds to cover its trade deficit, required high interest rates.

The balance of payments' evolution corresponds to the sharp movements in oil prices. However, oil as a share of total imports rose only from 9 per cent in 1971 to 14 per cent in 1975 and 15 per cent in 1981 suggesting that any oil shock explanation must be largely indirect, at least for the 1979–81 period.

Exports and imports, in nominal terms, grew about 25 per cent a year over 1971–81, 26 per cent a year until 1979 and 18 per cent thereafter. This suggests that the dominant factor on the export side was buoyancy of world trade in manufactures and that the rapid recovery of OECD growth rates of GDP and imports after 1975, and their contrasting stagnation after 1982, was a dominant factor in the divergent Irish experience after 1973–74 and 1979–80.

Exports of manufactured goods (excluding processed food) rose significantly more rapidly than those of food (31 per cent as against 20 per cent over 1971–81) with the former rising from 34 per cent to 58 per cent of total exports and the latter falling from 47 per cent to 33 per cent. The average growth of exports in physical terms was 7 per cent and of export prices 18 per cent to 19 per cent (higher for manufactured goods).[24] The latter was, surprisingly, significantly higher than either the GDP deflator, the CPI or non-oil imports so that except in 1973–74 and 1979–81 Ireland's terms of trade tended to improve.[25]

Changes in export patterns were also significant in respect to export destinations, with the UK share falling from 65 per cent to 40 per cent and that to other EEC members rising from about 20 per cent to 45 per cent. However, the UK's share in Irish imports remained constant at about 50 per cent while that from other EEC members declined. Thus there was a growing trade deficit with the UK (and the emergence of a deficit with the USA) and a swing from deficit to surplus in respect to the continental EEC members.

Ireland's share of exports to developing countries remained small, growing from 4 per cent in 1960 to 14 per cent (of which 3 per cent to high income oil exporters) in 1981.[26] This growth was apparently concentrated in food exports, as in 1980 92 per cent of Ireland's manufactured exports were destined for industrial market economies.

Until 1974 official external borrowing had been minimal. From 1974 through 1978 it was significant at a net rate of about P200 million a year while from 1979 through 1981 it soared to an average of over P1,200 million a year.[27] By the end of 1981 external public sector debt was 50 per cent of GDP versus 22 per cent in 1978 and under 5 per cent in 1971. Debt service rose to P954 by 1982 or over 7 per cent of GDP and over 17 per cent of merchandise exports. The relatively low official debt service/exports ratio is partly because of Ireland's high credit rating and partly because of a large share of Deutschmark denominated, and therefore relatively low interest, borrowing. However, it is somewhat deceptive because the very recent raising of most of the external debt meant that the 1982 principal repayments were P440 million, versus a figure of P650 million had the debt been more balanced in time of drawing. In that respect Ireland's late 1970s policy of lengthening the average period of external loans has contributed to the moderate debt-service ratio. Further, the high import content of Irish manufactured exports suggests that the ratio to GDP may be more meaningful in this case.[28]

Until 1979 private capital movements were more important than government borrowing. These primarily took the form of reduction of net external (UK) asset positions by Irish banks and increased lending in Ireland by foreign bank branches. Direct foreign investment was under

15 per cent of total capital inflow over 1970–81 and exceeded 25 per cent only in 1975 and 1978.

As noted earlier, real output growth was healthy over the 1970s taken as a whole. Within that growth a leading role was played by manufacturing for export as, except for the initial impact of EEC accession in 1974–78, the volumes of both agricultural production and food exports were stagnant. As a result agriculture declined from 21 per cent of GDP in 1961 to 15 per cent in 1971 and 11 per cent in 1979 while manufacturing rose from 27 per cent to 33 per cent to 36 per cent. The contribution of public administration and defence to GDP remained relatively low and virtually static, rising from 5 per cent in 1961 to 6 per cent in 1971 and 1981.[29]

Ireland's experience in the 1970s does not appear to reflect either a private consumption boom or a rapid increase in government expenditure on real GDP. Personal consumption fell from 70 per cent of GDP in 1970 to 64 per cent in 1976 while government consumption rose from 16 per cent to more than 19 per cent over the same period. Meanwhile physical capital formation remained relatively constant around 26 per cent.[30] Personal savings relative to personal income rose from 11 per cent in 1970–71 to 17 per cent in 1973–74, 21 per cent in 1975–76 and 20 per cent in 1978–79.[31]

Within investment there was a slight rise in the proportion of plant and equipment as opposed to construction – each making up about half Gross Fixed Capital Formation in 1979. Within construction dwellings grew 10 per cent a year in contrast to 6 per cent for other construction.[32] In fact this breakdown suggests that the decline in personal consumption and rise in personal savings represent a shift from consumer goods to housing more than any basic alteration in overall resource allocation. However, it did have the clear result of increasing demands on the construction sector which contributed to raising the overall inflation rate.

Ireland did not benefit in any significant way from the higher incomes of oil producing countries. Its overseas workers were concentrated in the UK and its banking system was not a recipient of large deposits from oil exporters. Unlike Brazil and Korea it did not build up substantial merchandise or construction exports to oil exporters – in part because of a less interventionist and targeted government policy, but probably more because its export industries were designed to serve the EEC market.

Overall, therefore, it appears that Irish inflation and growth rates were dominated not by oil prices but by inflation rates in the EEC (and especially the UK whose 14.4 per cent inflation rate over 1970–81 is almost identical to Ireland's 14.2 per cent) and the rate of growth of EEC manufactured goods imports.

## Sectoral and microeconomic evolution, 1970-81

Household expenditure pattern changes in the 1970s appear to have owed relatively little to relative price changes. Transport and travelling stayed at about 11 per cent.[33] Increases in housing, transport equipment and consumer durables appear to reflect rising incomes – and the low base levels – more than relative price changes. While food prices rose somewhat less than the overall consumer price index (300 per cent to 330 per cent) and fuel light and transport distinctly more rapidly (415 per cent) these relative price shifts were clearly dominated by changes in expenditure determined by rising incomes.

The agricultural sector has responded quite dramatically to relative price and market access changes, but these appear to relate basically to EEC prices and to 1979-81 interest rates and only secondarily to rises in fertiliser prices caused by oil price increases. Over 1970-73 cattle herds were built up in response to the imminent access to EEC membership, high EEC beef prices and relatively low fertiliser/beef price ratios.[34] However, the 1973 fall in EEC beef prices and the 1974 explosion of fertiliser prices led to large scale disposals at depressed prices.

Over 1975-78 cattle prices recovered and input prices fell relative to them. Easy credit induced herd expansion augmented the price rise. At the same time farmers made heavy investments in buildings, equipment and land (whose price per acre rose 14-fold over 1970-79).[35] Outstanding loans by the end of 1980 stood at P512 million.[36] Both the degree of mechanisation and possession of consumer durables and household amenities grew markedly.[37]

EEC prices peaked in 1979 and declined moderately thereafter. This negative development was paralleled by sharp increases in input costs, the CPI and interest rates. As a result there was a sharp decline in net incomes. Over 1972-81 average real net farm income declined 9 per cent. 1972-75 saw a 4 per cent fall, 1975-78 a 12 per cent rise and 1978-81 a 16 per cent fall.[38] Thus Irish farmers – despite the once-and-for-all gain of EEC entry – were in a similar position to developing country primary export producing peasants with falling real incomes at a time when real wages were rising. Their response was also similar (except that over 1975-78 farm output stagnated).

The manufacturing and service sector is divided into four fairly separate sub-categories: agricultural export processing; import competing 'traditional' manufacturing; non-import competing manufacturing and construction; foreign controlled 'new' export manufacturing.

The first has expanded slowly because of the slow growth of its basic inputs. Import-competing manufacturing is in large part a legacy of the 1930-55 policy of import substitution. It has suffered from the move to free trade and from rising real wages much more than from increases in energy prices or interest rates. While a few firms in this sub-sector have broken through into substantial exports, this is uncommon outside food and beverages. The most marked decline has been in textiles and garments (which, unlike other NICs, were never a central source of exports), suffering from increased EEC, USA and NIC competition. However, there was expansion in other portions of this sub-sector, at least through 1979, so that overall output rose (although employment declined).

Non-import competing activities such as cement and construction materials, brewing, construction, transport and business services appear to have benefited from the growth and, perhaps, the inflation of the 1970s. High capacity utilisation, demand growth, shifts in demand and ability to raise prices were apparent, especially in construction materials and construction.

Indigenous Irish manufacturing is largely made up of these sub-sectors. Over 1973–80 total manufacturing employment rose by 5,000 to 158,000 with 53,000 jobs gained and 48,000 lost.[39] In general the losses exceeded gains in import-competing 'traditional' manufacturing while the reverse was true of industries sheltered from import competition such as cement and construction materials.

The 'new', basically foreign-controlled export industrial sector was, as noted, the major engine of Irish economic growth. On the face of it changes in this sector's output makeup in the latter half of the 1970s – toward electronics and pharmaceuticals and away from synthetic textiles – appear to reflect a response to higher energy prices by a shift to less energy-intensive branches. However, it can be argued that they were more influenced by changes in the overall pattern of world trade (including rapid expansion of textile production and exports by newer NICs).

On the output side this sub-sector appears to have benefited from relative intra-industry price changes. Electronics and pharmaceuticals prices rose more rapidly than those of other manufactures and the overall 20 per cent annual price increase for Irish manufactured exports was above the world average (or that for Irish manufactured imports).

Since 1979 this sector has done relatively poorly because of declining rates of growth of world trade. New entrants' production has more than offset closures but the growth rates of most established firms appear to be low. The entry of Greece – and presently of Spain – into the EEC will increase the number of NICs within the Common Market. Ireland's relatively low import penetration, despite an early start, suggests that post-1983 recovery of export growth in manufacturing may not be rapid.

**Energy: policy and performance**

Irish policy in respect to energy prices was relatively passive in the 1970s with the exception of renewed emphasis on increased domestic production of electricity and peat. As noted, household expenditure on fuel and travel remained a relatively constant share of total spending and in agriculture the ratio of fuel inputs to output probably rose although in manufacturing there appear to have been shifts to less power intensive product mixes and micro savings within enterprises.

This broad impression is borne out by overall energy sector data. [40] Over 1960–74 energy consumption growth was 5.0 per cent a year and over 1974–80 only marginally lower at 4.6 per cent – both significantly above GDP growth. In contrast the average consumption growth rates for industrial market economies were 5.4 per cent over 1960–74 and 0.8 per cent over 1974–80, a much more marked decline. Energy production in Ireland declined 0.1 per cent a year over 1960–74 but rose 4.7 per cent a year over 1974–80, a marked response to the sector's relative price changes (more specifically the external balance impact of higher petroleum costs).

Fuel prices rose substantially over 1973–80. There were no subsidies, with the arguable exception of peat. Government pricing policy was basically passive, i.e. it failed to raise taxes on petroleum products by anything like the crude oil price or to raise the price of industrial electricity and gas as rapidly as that of fuel oil. The most rapid increases were for products (notably gas oil and fuel oil) which had lower taxes to begin with and where, therefore, there was little room to dampen consumer price increases by not raising them.

In general the price of household fuels (including that for motor cars) rose less than for industrial fuels.[41] Peat rose 128 per cent, household coal by 260 per cent, derv by 212 per cent, gasoline by 281 per cent, domestic electricity by 312 per cent. Deflated by the CPI this gives annual real price increases of 3 per cent to 6 per cent a year. Industrial fuel cost increases were 371 per cent for industrial electricity, 428 per cent for gas, 619 per cent for fuel oil and 719 per cent for gasoil, giving real rates of annual increase ranging from 6.5 per cent to 10 per cent.

A study of demand elasticities for total energy demand in Ireland over 1958–77 suggests an elasticity of 1.5 in respect to GDP and long and short term price elasticities of –0.70 and –0.28.[42] A similar study in respect to gasoline[43] gave somewhat higher elasticities in respect to personal expenditure and lower ones in respect to price. The 1973–76 experience of relatively static energy consumption when GDP growth was under 3 per cent and average real energy price increases over 7 per cent a year is broadly consistent with these calculations, as is the 1977–

79 renewed growth in energy demand as GDP growth recovered and real energy prices fell (except for industrial electricity).

Within the energy sector there were changes among fuels both absolutely and in relation to past trends.[44] Oil, after rising rapidly in the 1960s, peaked at 74 per cent of total energy use over 1973–1978 and then declined sharply to 62 per cent, largely consequential on the bringing into production in 1979 of natural gas, which by 1981 accounted for 11 per cent of total energy. Coal held or increased its share at about 10 per cent, albeit (since most is imported) this shift had relatively little impact on the balance of payments. The division of energy use by sector was fairly stable over 1971–1980;[45] however, industrial as a percentage of total use declined from 32 per cent to 29 per cent, despite its more rapid rate of output increase than that of overall GDP, suggesting some energy conservation in that sector.

The household sector does not seem to have economised on overall energy use – partly because of a shift to centrally-heated houses in the 1970s building boom.[46] However, after 1973 (and especially 1979) there was a shift in central heating away from gas and oil to solid fuels.[47]

Manufacturing seems to have engaged in three types of energy saving: small scale conservation within a given production process without major re-equipment or change of fuel; major changes in fuel burning and later stages of the production process, involving substantial new equipment and often change of fuel; and shifts in the industrial structure toward less energy-intensive branches.

The first shift was marked over 1974–75.[48] Among the major firms involved were cement and cigarettes.[49] Substantial adjustment was largely delayed until after 1979 because of the actual time it involves and the 1975–79 relative stagnation or decline of deflated fuel prices. Over 1979–83 major industries making shifts from oil to coal included cement, drainage pipes, brick manufacture, sugar and brewing.[50] However, the total energy saving seems to have been under 2 per cent of oil consumption. In brewing and cement substantial alterations in production technology were made at least partly to reduce fuel requirements.[51] As noted earlier, the 'new' export manufacturing sub-sector shifted toward less energy intensive lines in the 1970s but it is problematic whether this owed much to relative fuel prices as opposed to relative market growth rates.

**Summary and review**

The overall economic record of the Republic of Ireland in the 1970s paralleled that of other NICs, albeit with rather lower than average rates of growth of GDP and of prices. It is quite unconvincing to argue that its economic performance was primarily determined by the direct impact of oil prices. This is especially true from 1979 on when the petroleum share in total imports increased by only 1 per cent and fertiliser prices did not skyrocket as they did over 1972–75.

In fact, growth performance and price increases for the period as a whole have been dominated by the EEC's rate of growth of imports (itself largely dependent on GDP growth) and the United Kingdom's inflation rate. However, this relationship was much weaker over 1979–81 than over 1973–76. In the former period Irish policies were broadly similar to those of the OECD countries as a group, and to those of the United Kingdom in particular; but in the latter period Ireland reversed its expansionist policy relatively late, preferring maintenance of employment and external borrowing until EEC import growth revived rather than speedy adjustment of the balance of payments and the government deficit and reduction of the rate of price increases by a contractionist policy.

Only in the sense of being out of step with the OECD consensus from 1979 on can Ireland's domestic macroeconomic policy be said to be a major contributory factor to 1970–81, and in particular 1979–81, performance. It is true that lack of an active energy policy on the use side led to higher rates of growth of energy use than either GDP or, *a fortiori*, the average for industrial economies. But even had the rate of growth of energy used after 1973 been halved – which would have required massive tax and price increases for coal and gas as well as oil – the result would have been to reduce the 1980 and 1981 trade deficits by under 10 per cent.

The post-1979 exchange rate policy which, as noted, led to substantial real appreciation of the punt against most EEC currencies other than the pound sterling, was in large measure an attempt to delink from British inflation – one which went wrong. The punt's parity was basically held constant to maintain assured access to capital markets and to avoid yet more rapid inflation. Whether the effects on exports were serious during 1979–82 is debatable although the increase in real labour costs relative to major continental EEC economies suggests that it probably had some negative impact.[52] The impact on farmers' incomes was clearly negative and that on imports and import-competing manufactures also negative, albeit tempered by the high proportion of imports coming from the UK (one of the currencies against which the punt's real exchange rate fell). The argument that the exchange control restrictions on capital exports introduced to sustain the parity of the punt aggravated inflation[53] is distinctly dubious. The rise in the government deficit offset the relatively weak enterprise demand for bank borrowing. It is arguable that moderately increased bank liquidity may have led to greater expansion of consumer credit and as a result more imports reinforced the fixed exchange ratio damage to the balance of payments.

A more basic question arises in respect to Ireland's overall growth, and especially export growth, strategy. This is not to argue that Ireland should (or could) have returned to an inward-looking strategy of the 1930–1958 variety. The domestic markets for sustained growth did not exist any more than in the 1950s. The aborting of EEC entry and loss of duty free access to the UK market consequential on reversion to protectionism would have had major negative effects on the growth of manufactured exports and the absolute level of (and prices received for) agricultural exports. In addition, it would have caused a direct GDP reduction of 4 per cent by 1981 through the absence of net EEC transfer payments.

However, the massive tax and capital subsidy concessions and the non-selectivity in respect to new export-oriented enterprises and to markets had the effect of accelerating inflation, probably weakened Irish export growth and, in particular, weakened the ability to sustain export growth from 1979 onward.

The exemption of export manufacturing from company tax narrowed the tax base and, since it was the most rapidly growing sector, reduced revenue buoyancy with respect to GDP growth. The provision of infrastructure and capital grants raised expenditure. Ireland's main methods for coping with its increasingly fragile fiscal position were increases in payroll taxes (which were levied on all employers), taking the inflation creep in personal income taxes[54] as a windfall gain and – especially from 1979 on – increasing external and domestic borrowing. All but the external borrowing were clearly inflationary and the payroll tax approach was arguably more damaging to exports by its impact on the cost of labour than a profits tax yielding the same amount of revenue.

The non-selectivity in respect to enterprises and markets is a more problematic point. Ireland certainly promoted the establishment of foreign-owned enterprises producing for export but with relatively little use of the selective incentives and disincentives for specific industries employed by Singapore, Korea and Brazil. Indeed, apart from bargaining on capital grants, there would appear to have been next to no selective intervention.

Similarly Ireland made no attempt to guide its exporters' choice of markets, except by securing improved access to EEC by its 1973 accession. Unlike Brazil and Korea it did not target developing country, and especially oil-exporting country, markets, even though these had the highest import growth rates over the 1970s.

Arguably, a more selective policy could have led to an upgrading of the labour-skills content and increase in the supporting-service content purchased in Ireland, as has been achieved in Singapore. Similarly, selected targeting of industries for special export incentives on the Japanese and Korean model might have been more effective. However, these criticisms do not relate primarily to Ireland's response to 1970s economic shocks so much as to its medium-term industrial and export strategy more generally. It cannot be denied that the strategy pursued did produce relatively satisfactory employment, GDP, export growth and external balance results until 1979, and it is arguable that any benefits of a more selective policy would have been swamped over 1979–82 by the deliberately deflationary policies of major OECD economies who viewed inflation as a much more serious threat than unemployment – a preference Ireland did not share and was only forced to accept in 1982 by the unsustainable level of 1980 and 1981 merchandise trade deficits and government external borrowing.

## Prospects?

Because Ireland's economic performance has been dominated by that of industrial economies in general and those of the EEC in particular it is tempting to assume that it will resume growth in the mid-1980s (possibly with a lag on recovery similar to that on contraction). However, this may not be accurate and even if it is would imply distinctly lower growth rates than in the 1970s.

In the first place Ireland is particularly closely linked to the EEC economies in general and to that of the UK in particular. Their recovery has been slower than that of the USA or Japan and their growth rates seem unlikely to exceed 3 per cent a year over 1984–90. Given Ireland's relatively low rates of sustained market share increase, this would seem to imply export growth (barring a reorientation of export promotion to other markets) of under 5 per cent, which on 1960–81 relationships would imply a growth rate of perhaps 2.5 per cent a year. A possible offsetting factor is that Ireland, as an EEC member, has been, and will presumably remain, immune to the rise of new protectionist barriers confronting other NICs in EEC markets.

Second, the likely course of EEC budgetary and farm policy in the 1980s will have severe negative consequences for Ireland and in particular for its already depressed agricultural sector. Speculation on the impact of Common Agricultural Policy reform – especially if concentrated on dairy products, the one consistently buoyant sub-sector of Irish agriculture – suggests that by the late 1980s it could cause a loss of 3 per cent to 5 per cent of GDP, which would reduce the 2.5 per cent growth rate previously posited to about 2 per cent. While safely above population growth, such a rate would lead to secularly increasing unemployment (especially as small farmers were forced off the land by massive falls in their real incomes) – the most politically unacceptable political-economic result imaginable in the Irish context.

Therefore, it appears to be arguable that Ireland's export-growth-led strategy – both in respect ot manufactured goods and to agricultural products – reached a secular, and not merely a cyclical, impasse in 1979. If that is the case, the only apparent option open would appear to be a more selective policy of targeting specific industries and markets and a radical departure from the anti-planning, overall demand-management oriented, relatively laissez-faire, stance of Irish economic policy over the last 25 years.

This is not to imply that Ireland must engage in central planning on socialist lines or experience a radical political movement to the left – both of which appear quite unlikely whether one considers them desirable or not. It is to argue that the Republic of Ireland would probably find it beneficial to engage in selected, targeted intervention in respect to new investment, production and exports along lines roughly analagous to those pursued by the Republic of Korea, Brazil and Singapore.

It is clear that one medium-term political necessity in Ireland is increasing employment while avoiding further (and reducing recent past) reductions in real wages. It is also clear that neither the employment nor the real wage constraint can be met without export growth significantly above that of GDP. To sustain export growth at such rates – given Ireland's lack of raw materials for industrial branches other than processed foods – requires that real labour costs do not rise more rapidly than those of her main competitors. This either requires reduction of inflation to the EEC average or regular small devaluations against the ECU (both easier said than done) or sharp increases in labour productivity which are not at the expense of employment. The last might be furthered by promotion of industrial branches using more highly qualified labour and larger quantities of specialised services (including relevant specialised education and training), again contributing to the case for more selective investment, production and export promotion policies.

**Table 7.1 GDP at current and constant prices and sectoral origin at constant prices, 1961 and 1971 to 1981**

(million pounds)

| | 1961 | 1971 | 1972 | 1973 | 1974 | 1975 | 1976 | 1977 | 1978 | 1979 | 1980 | 1981 |
|---|---|---|---|---|---|---|---|---|---|---|---|---|
| GDP at current prices (£m.) | 631 | 1,853 | 2,237 | 2,704 | 2,991 | 3,731 | 4,570 | 5,491 | 6,436 | 7,462 | 8,731 | 10,839 |
| per cent change | 3.7 | 14.3 | 20.7 | 20.8 | 10.6 | 24.7 | 22.4 | 20.1 | 17.2 | 15.9 | 17.0 | 18.9 |
| GDP at constant prices (£m. 1975) | 2,090 | 3,146 | 3,335 | 3,474 | 3,602 | 3,731 | 3,804 | 4,064 | 4,303 | 4,409 | 4,530 | 4,580 |
| per cent change | 4.7 | 3.4 | 6.0 | 4.1 | 3.6 | 3.5 | 1.9 | 6.8 | 5.8 | 2.4 | 2.7 | 1.1 |
| Structure of GDP at final cost in constant prices (1975) per cent: | | | | | | | | | | | | |
| Agriculture, forestry and fishing | 24.2[a] | 16.5 | 17.0 | 15.6 | 16.1 | 17.6 | 15.4 | 15.8 | 15.0 | 12.7 | 13.6 | 12.6 |
| Industry | 30.6[a] | 36.0 | 35.8 | 37.0 | 36.4 | 34.7 | 36.5 | 37.0 | 37.8 | 40.0 | 38.1 | 38.4 |
| Services[b] | 23.0[a] | 21.8 | 21.7 | 22.2 | 22.2 | 21.9 | 21.9 | 21.5 | 21.2 | 21.0 | 21.8 | 22.1 |
| Other domestic | 22.2[a] | 25.3 | 25.5 | 25.2 | 25.3 | 25.8 | 26.2 | 25.7 | 26.0 | 26.3 | 26.5 | 26.9 |

*Source:* Ireland Central Statistical Office, *National Income and Expenditure*, 1968, 1977 and 1981, and IMF *International Financial Statistics*, Yearbook 1980 and January 1983, vol. 36 no. 1.

*Notes:* (a) 1961 sectoral structure is at 1961 current prices.
(b) This includes, distribution, transport, communication, public administration, defence and adjustment for financial services.

**Table 7.2 Balance of payments, 1961 and 1971 to 1981**

(Million US$; minus sign indicates debit)

| | 1961 | 1971 | 1972 | 1973 | 1974 | 1975 | 1976 | 1977 | 1978 | 1979 | 1980 | 1981 |
|---|---|---|---|---|---|---|---|---|---|---|---|---|
| Trade balance fob | -195 | -440 | -378 | -527 | -1,082 | -486 | -609 | -820 | -1,067 | -2,283 | -2,121 | -2,225 |
| Merchandise exports fob | 476 | 1,271 | 1,580 | 2,090 | 2,479 | 3,032 | 3,326 | 4,229 | 5,602 | 6,986 | 8,330 | 7,708 |
| Merchandise imports fob | -671 | -1,711 | -1,958 | -2,617 | -3,561 | -3,518 | -3,935 | -5,049 | -6,669 | -9,269 | -10,452 | -9,933 |
| Other goods, services and income (net) | 110 | 129 | 103 | 61 | 83 | 38 | -48 | -142 | -333 | -542 | -746 | -772 |
| Private unrequited transfers (net) | 75 | 115 | 89 | 97 | 101 | 102 | 88 | 92 | 109 | 93 | 123 | 96 |
| Official unrequited transfers (net) | -3 | -4 | 36 | 116 | 203 | 290 | 228 | 495 | 777 | 1,053 | 1,093 | 752 |
| Direct & portfolio investment and other long term capital (net) | 16 | 392 | 249 | 223 | 796 | 409 | 810 | 745 | 562 | 1,017 | 2,307 | 1,936 |
| Net errors & omissions | 16 | 16 | -12 | 32 | 41 | 47 | 32 | 57 | 50 | 73 | 87 | 41 |
| Counterpart items | — | 89 | 44 | -105 | 99 | -134 | -196 | 106 | 218 | 129 | -94 | -223 |
| Total change in reserves | -19 | -297 | -131 | 103 | -240 | -265 | -306 | -534 | -316 | 460 | -649 | 209 |

*Source:* IMF, *International Financial Statistics*, Yearbook 1983 and February, 1984, vol. 37 no. 2.

**Table 7.3 Indices of export and import unit values and of terms of trade, 1961, and 1971–1982**

(Base 1975 = 100)

|  | *(1)* Unit value of exports | *(2)* Unit value of imports | *(3)* Terms of trade (= 1 ÷ 2) | *(4)* % Change in (3) |
|---|---|---|---|---|
| 1961 | 34 | 36 | 93 | −2 |
| 1971 | 49 | 48 | 103 | +11 |
| 1972 | 56 | 50 | 111 | +8 |
| 1973 | 68 | 57 | 120 | +8 |
| 1974 | 85 | 83 | 102 | −15 |
| 1975 | 100 | 100 | 100 | −2 |
| 1976 | 124 | 119 | 104 | +4 |
| 1977 | 142 | 139 | 102 | −2 |
| 1978 | 152 | 146 | 104 | +2 |
| 1979 | 166 | 166 | 100 | −4 |
| 1980 | 181 | 196 | 92 | −8 |
| 1981 | 208 | 232 | 90 | −2 |

*Source:* IMF, *International Financial Statistics: Supplement on Price Statistics* (1981).

**Table 7.4 Price index numbers, 1961 and 1971 to 1981**

(base 1975 = 100)

|  | GDP Deflator Index no. | % annual change | Consumer Price Index Index no. | % annual change | Wholesale Price Index Index no. | % annual change |
|---|---|---|---|---|---|---|
| 1961 | 31 | 3 | 35 | 3 | 36 |  |
| 1971 | 59 | 11 | 58 | 9 | 55 |  |
| 1972 | 67 | 13 | 64 | 9 | 60 | 11 |
| 1973 | 77 | 15 | 71 | 11 | 71 | 17 |
| 1974 | 82 | 6 | 83 | 17 | 80 | 14 |
| 1975 | 100 | 22 | 100 | 21 | 100 | 25 |
| 1976 | 120 | 20 | 118 | 18 | 120 | 20 |
| 1977 | 135 | 12 | 134 | 14 | 140 | 17 |
| 1978 | 149 | 10 | 144 | 8 | 153 | 9 |
| 1979 | 168 | 13 | 163 | 13 | 171 | 12 |
| 1980 | 192 | 14 | 193 | 18 | 189 | 11 |
| 1981 | 227 | 18 | 233 | 20 | 222 | 17 |

*Source:* IMF, *International Financial Statistics, Yearbook* 1983 and *Supplement on Price Statistics,* 1981.

**Table 7.5 Annual percentage changes in money supply (M3), prices and bank interest rates, 1971–1981**

| | (1) Money supply (M3)[a] | (2) Prices (CPI)[b] | (3) MS–P (1–2) | (4) Bank rate[c] | (5) Real bank rate |
|---|---|---|---|---|---|
| 1971[d] | | 9 | | 4.81 | −4.0 |
| 1972 | 10 | 9 | 1 | 8.00 | −0.7 |
| 1973 | 23 | 11 | 12 | 12.75 | 1.5 |
| 1974 | 21 | 17 | 4 | 12.00 | −5.0 |
| 1975 | 19 | 21 | −2 | 10.00 | −10.9 |
| 1976[e] | 18 | 18 | 0 | 14.75 | −3.3 |
| 1977 | 16 | 14 | 2 | 6.75 | −6.9 |
| 1978 | 20 | 8 | 12 | 11.85 | 4.3 |
| 1979 | 29 | 13 | 16 | 16.40 | 3.2 |
| 1980 | 14 | 18 | −4 | 12.75 | −5.5 |
| 1981 | 22 | 20 | 2 | 16.50 | −3.9 |

*Source:* Central Bank of Ireland, *Annual Report*, 1982; IMF, *International Financial Statistics, Yearbook* 1983 and Supplements.

*Notes:* (a) Money supply taken as yearly average of broad money supply (M3) including currency, bank current account balances, deposit accounts and time deposits.
(b) The prices are reflected by the Consumer Price Index change (see Table 7.4 on prices).
(c) End of period rates; Central bank lending rates: 1971–1980, Discount rate; 1981, Short-term facility rate.
(d) 1971 figures on money supply not available due to bank dispute during that year.
(e) Covers average for eight months due to bank strike.

**Table 7.6 Public finance and borrowing, 1961, and 1971 to 1981 (summary)**

(million £)

|  | 1961 | 1971 | 1972 | 1973 | 1974 | 1975 | 1976 | 1977 | 1978 | 1979 | 1980 | 1981 |
|---|---|---|---|---|---|---|---|---|---|---|---|---|
| Total revenue | 147.7 | 581.7 | 634.0 | 758.6 | 911.7 | 1,295.5 | 1,550.9 | 1,779.3 | 2,076.1 | 2,483.6 | 3,256.2 | 4,064.2 |
| Total expenditure | 184.6 | 682.2 | 761.6 | 929.1 | 1,263.9 | 1,794.9 | 2,042.2 | 2,334.9 | 2,932.4 | 3,538.8 | 4,540.9 | 5,853.3 |
| Overall surplus/ deficit (−) | −36.9 | −100.5 | −127.6 | −170.5 | −352.2 | −499.4 | −491.3 | −555.6 | −856.3 | −1,055.2 | −1,284.7 | −1,789.1 |
| Net borrowing | 37.6 | 100.5 | 127.6 | 170.5 | 352.2 | 499.4 | 491.3 | 555.2 | 856.2 | 1,055.2 | 1,284.9 | 1,789.1 |
| External government debt outstanding (as at 31 March for 1971–1973 and then as at 31 December)[a] |  | 89.9 | 107.5 | 126.4 | 311.9 | 471.3 | 1,039.5 | 1,038.5 | 1,063.9 | 1,542.4 | 2,206.8 | 3,793.9 |
| Annual increment in external government debt outstanding |  | 20.3 | 17.6 | 18.9 | 185.5[b] | 159.4 | 568.2 | −1.0 | 25.4 | 478.5 | 664.4 | 1,587.1 |
| Annual increment in external government debt as per cent of net borrowing |  | 20 | 14 | 11 | 53[b] | 32 | 116 | 0 | 3 | 45 | 52 | 89 |

*Source:* IMF, *International Financial Statistics, Yearbook*, 1980, 1983; Central Bank of Ireland, *Annual Report*, 1975, 1977, 1979, 1981 and 1983.

*Notes:* (a) Fiscal year changed after 1973 to coincide with calendar year.
(b) These figures refer to calculations extending from 31 March 1973 to 31 December 1974.

## Notes and references

1  The original drafts of this chapter were written by Richard Stanton. The final text – which differs significantly in some respects – is the sole responsibility of Reginald Green who revised and edited Mr. Stanton's manuscript when other calls on his time prevented him from doing so. Professor Green wishes to acknowledge his debt to his former student, Dr. Sean O'Malley, who taught him most of what he knows about the economy of the Republic of Ireland.

2  World Bank (1983) 'Historical Data'.

3  See O'Malley (1983) pp. 49–57.

4  O'Malley (1983) pp. 110–131.

5  See McAleese (1982).

6  See McAleese (1977) and O'Malley (1983) pp. 110–131.

7  See O'Malley (1983) pp. 110–131 and McAleese (1975).

8  See O'Malley (1983) pp. 146–202 and Stanton (1979).

9  World Bank (1983).

10  World Bank (1983).

11  See O'Malley (1983) pp. 253–281 and McAleese (1975).

12  IMF (1981).

13  Economic issues have figured in elections but more in terms of policy variants or balance than of the basic policies themselves.

14  It is in no sense a socialist party and its primary concerns of increased employment and real wages are well within the Irish political consensus.

15  See McAleese (1977), O'Malley, (1983) pp. 110–131.

16  'Battle Of Brussels', *Sunday Times,* 18 March 1984.

17  IMF (1981 and 1984).

18  IMF (1981 and 1984).

19  World Bank (1983).

20  Department of Finance (1981).

21  Central Bank of Ireland (1982).

22  IMF (1981 and 1984).

23  See Geary (1976) and Henry (1982) but also Browne and Boyle (1982).

24  Central Bank of Ireland, *Annual Report,* various years.

25  IMF (1981).

26  World Bank (1983).

27  See McAleese (1982).

28  See McAleese (1982).

29  Central Statistical Office (1979).

30  CSO (1977, 1978, 1979).

31  CSO (1977, 1978, 1979).

32  CSO (1977, 1978, 1979).

33  CSO (1977, 1978, 1979).

34  See Crotty (1974).

35  See Kelly (1981).

36  See Higgins (1981).

37  See Frawley (1981).

38  An Foras Taluntais (various years), *Farm Management Survey.*

39  *Sunday Tribune,* Dublin, 19 September 1982.

40  World Bank (1983).

41  See Henry (1981).
42  See Scott (1980).
43  See Feeney (1976).
44  Department of Energy (1981).
45  OECD (various years).
46  See Lewis *et al.* (1977).
47  See Carroll (1980), Minogue (1980).
48  Interview by R. Stanton with P. Fleming, Insitute for Industrial Research and Standards, Dublin, September 1982.
49  Interview by R. Stanton with Staff Economist, Cement Roadstone Holdings, Dublin, September 1982.
50  Interview with P. Fleming.
51  Interviews by R. Stanton with Head of Energy Policy Committee, Confederation of Irish Industry and Staff Economist, September 1982.
52  See McAleese (1982). Also interview by R. Stanton with Professor Brendan Walsh, University College Dublin, September 1982.
53  See Browne and Boyle (1982) pp. 14–15.
54  Since taxes were progressive on a tranche system, as nominal personal income rose so did the average incidence of personal income tax.

**Bibliography**

An Foras Forbartha (1980), (National Institute for Physical Planning and Construction Research), *Aspects of Energy Conservation: Proceedings of Seminar,* Dublin.
An Foras Taluntais (Agricultural Institute) (1981), *Economics and Rural Welfare: Research Report 1981,* Dublin.
An Foras Taluntais (various years), *Farm Management Survey,* Dublin.
Boyle, G. (1980), 'Fertiliser demand' (mimeo) An Foras Taluntais, Dublin.
Browne, F.X. and Boyle, G.E. (1982), 'The transmission of world inflation to the small open economy – a missing link' (mimeo), Draft Technical Paper, Research Department, Central Bank of Ireland, Dublin.
Carroll, D. (1980), 'Energy conservation in buildings: Fuel substitution and energy conservation', in An Foras Forbartha (1980).
Central Bank of Ireland (1982), *Quarterly Bulletin,* Winter, Dublin.
Central Statistical Office (various), *National Income and Expenditure,* Dublin.
Confederation of Irish Industry (1980), *The Energy Problem: The Next 7 Years,* Business Policy Department, Confederation of Irish Industry, Dublin.
Crotty, R. (1974), *The Cattle Crisis and the Small Farmer,* National Land League, Freshford, Co. Kilkenny.
Department of Energy (1981), *Energy In Ireland,* Dublin.
Department of Finance (1981), *Economic Review and Outlook 1981,* Dublin.
Feeney, B.P. (1976), 'The demand for petrol', Report RT 162, An Foras Forbartha (National Institute for Physical Planning and Construction Research), Dublin.
Fennelly, D. (n.d. 1981?), 'Coal – the economic decision for the small company' (mimeo), Institute for Industrial Research and Standards, Dublin.
Fleming, P. (1982), 'Irish industrial heat market', mimeo, Institute for Industrial Research and Standards, Dublin.

Frawley, J. (1981), 'Demographic and managerial aspects of family farms' (research summary), in An Foras Taluntais (1981), pp. 28–92.

Geary, P.T. (1976), 'World prices and the inflationary process in a small open economy – the case of Ireland', *Economic and Social Review* (Dublin), pp. 391–399.

Heavey, J.F. *et al.* (1981), 'Farm management survey' (research summary) in An Foras Taluntais (1981), pp. 5–7.

Henry, E.W. (1981), 'Energy imports to Ireland and final energy demand during 1973–1980: Statistics and some economic implications' (mimeo), Economic and Social Research Institute, Dublin.

Higgins, J. (1981), 'Borrowing by Landholders', (research summary), in An Foras Taluntais (1981), pp. 17–18.

IMF (1983), *International Financial Statistics: Supplement on Price Statistics* Washington D.C.

IMF (1983), *International Financial Statistics: Yearbook,* Washington D.C.

IMF (1984), *International Financial Statistics* 37/2, February, Washington D.C.

Kelly, P.W. (1981), 'Price of agricultural land sold at public auction' (research summary) in An Foras Taluntais (1981).

Killen, L. (1981), *Energy: Forecasts for Ireland,* National Board for Science and Technology, Dublin.

Lewis, J.O. *et al.* (1977), 'The use of solar energy for domestic heating', in National Science Council, Energy Group, *National Conference on Energy Production, Conversion and Utilisation: Papers,* Dublin.

McAleese, D. (1975), 'Ireland in the Enlarged EEC: Economic Consequences and Prospects', in J. Vaizey (ed), *Economic Sovereignty and Regional Policy* Dublin, pp. 133–162.

McAleese, D. (1977), *A Profile of Grant-Aided Industry in Ireland,* Industrial Development Authority, Dublin.

McAleese, D. (1982), 'Which way forward? Prospects for the Irish economy' in Central Bank (1982).

Minogue, P. (1980), 'Energy conservation in buildings: Potential saving from insulation', in An Foras Forbartha (1980).

NESC (National Economic and Social Council) (1982), *An Analysis of Job Losses in Manufacturing Industry,* NESC Report no. 67, Dublin.

O'Grady, Walshe T. (1976), 'The growing national debt: Recent trends and implications', in Central Bank of Ireland, *Annual Report 1976,* pp. 104–123.

O'Malley, Eoin (1983), 'Late industrialisation under outward-looking policies: the experience and prospects of the Republic of Ireland', University of Sussex Ph.D. thesis.

Organisation for Economic Cooperation and Development (various years), *Energy Balances of OECD Countries,* Paris.

Scott, S. (1980), *Energy Demand in Ireland, Projections and Policy Issues,* Policy Series No. 2, Economic and Social Research Institute, Dublin.

Stanton, R. (1979), 'Foreign investment and host-country politics: The Irish case', in D. Seers *et al.* (eds), *Underdeveloped Europe,* Harvester Press, Hassocks, pp. 103–124.

World Bank (1983), *World Development Report 1983,* OUP.

# 8 Imported Inflation and the Development of the Korean Economy

*In June Kim*

## Introduction

Korea is a small open economy which has achieved remarkable economic growth over the last two decades. Because of its large degree of openness, external factors have an important impact on Korea's economic development. This paper will analyse the impact of these external factors: emphasis will be placed on how external factors interacted with internal factors in the past, how stabilisation policies have adjusted to cope with external shocks, and whether the outcome of short-run stabilisation policies had any adverse impacts on the Korean economy in the long run.

In the first part of the paper Korean economic development strategies will be briefly reviewed. Emphasis will be placed on structural changes in the Korean economy, the role of the government and the policy instruments it uses, and the consistency of the outcome of short-run stabilisation policies with long-run economic goals. The change in structure of energy demand and energy policies will be briefly reviewed. In the second part, international determinants influencing the development of the Korean economy will be analysed, as well as their impact on output growth, the rate of inflation, the balance of payments, terms of trade and exchange rate. We will also see in what way the Korean economy is linked to international financial markets. In the third part, the impact of the major oil price rises on the Korean economy in 1970s will be examined. We also analyse the adjustment mechanism of the Korean economy, and desirable economic policies to cope with the adverse situation after the major oil price rises. In the final part of this paper, some policy recommendations for the 1980s are made.[1]

## Economic development policies and development of Korean economy

Until the early 1960s, the Korean economy could be characterised as an agricultural one. In 1962, the share of agriculture, forestry and fisheries in GNP was around 37 per cent, while the share of the manufacturing sector was around 14 per cent. During the last two decades, a major shift in Korean economic structure has occurred: the manufacturing sector share in GNP increased to 29.5 per cent in 1981 while the share of the agriculture, forestry and fisheries sectors decreased to 18 per cent in 1981 (see Table 8.1). The share of social overhead capital and other services also expanded from 47 per cent in 1962 to 51 per cent in 1981.

The annual average growth rate of real GNP during the period 1962–1981 was around 8.3 per cent. Underlying the rapid economic growth, the ratio of investment to GNP rose from 12.8 per cent in 1962 to 31.5 per cent in 1980, but was slightly reduced to 27.2 per cent in 1981. In the early 1960s, foreign saving was a major source for investment. Over the last two decades, however, the share of domestic saving to investment has steadily increased to 92 per cent in 1977 but later decline to 73.4 per cent in 1981 (see Table 8.2).

Rapid economic growth and shifts in industrial structure were helped by the surplus of high-quality labour up to the mid-1970s and by a development strategy based on it. The strategy of Korean economic development over the last two decades can be summarised as follows. First, industrialisation has been vigorously promoted, starting from labour-intensive and light industries, and moving toward capital-intensive heavy and chemical industries. Second, Korea has stressed more export-oriented economic growth policies instead of import-substitution growth strategies. Third, foreign capital has been actively attracted, to fill the gap in financing the increased investment requirements necessary for rapid economic growth. Fourth, the Korean government intervened directly in economic activities on many important occasions. The Korean government used monetary policy as an important instrument to attain high growth and influence the resource allocation. The government had a firm grip on financial institutions and controlled access to foreign borrowing.

Since Korea was poor in natural resources and had abundant high

**Table 8.1 Sectoral structure, 1962–81, selected years**

(share GNP, per cent)

| | Agriculture, forestry & fisheries | Mining and manufacturing | | | | Services & others |
| | | Total | Manufacturing | Light industry | Heavy & chemical | |
|---|---|---|---|---|---|---|
| 1962 | 36.6 | 16.3 | 14.3 | 10.2 | 4.1 | 47.1 |
| 1971 | 27.0 | 22.6 | 21.0 | 13.0 | 8.0 | 50.4 |
| 1976 | 23.8 | 28.8 | 27.6 | 14.7 | 12.9 | 47.4 |
| 1981 | 17.9 | 31.0 | 29.6 | 14.0 | 15.6 | 51.1 |

*Source:* Bank of Korea, *National Income in Korea*, 1982.

**Table 8.2 Composition of gross savings, 1962–1981**

(per cent)

| | Investment/GNP | Gross savings | National savings sub-total | Savings of private sectors | Government | Foreign savings |
|---|---|---|---|---|---|---|
| 1962 | 12.8 | 100 | 25.5 | 37.5 | −12.0 | 83.4 |
| 1971 | 25.2 | 100 | 60.9 | 39.4 | 21.4 | 42.5 |
| 1974 | 31.0 | 100 | 66.0 | 58.7 | 7.3 | 40.0 |
| 1977 | 27.3 | 100 | 92.1 | 71.6 | 20.5 | 2.2 |
| 1981 | 27.3 | 100 | 73.4 | 47.1 | 26.3 | 30.4 |

*Source:* Bank of Korea, *Economic Statistics Yearbook*, 1972, 1975, 1981 and 1982.

quality labour in the early 1960s, it was quite natural for it to pursue industrialisation in the early stage of its development. Because of the Confucian tradition and the major emphasis on education under the Lee dynasty and after the 1945 Liberation, Koreans were well qualified and gave great value to hard work.[2]

As a better way of establishing an efficient and low-cost industrial structure, the Korean government stressed mainly an export-oriented growth strategy. There were several reasons for the government to emphasise such a strategy. In the early 1960s, the United States government announced that assistance to Korea would be terminated. Korean policy makers thought that export promotion would be the only way to replace the impending loss of foreign currency. At the same time, suppression of imports by import-substitution policies was perceived to have its own limit, since the share of non-competitive imports to total imports was quite high. Second, as Professor Kwang S. Kim pointed out, Korea had virtually completed import substitution in non-durable consumer goods in the early 1960s.[3] A growth strategy based on import substitution in machinery, consumer durables, and their intermediate products did not seem to be appropriate because of the small size of the domestic market and large capital requirements. Furthermore, relatively low wages and a surplus of well-motivated high quality labour gave Korea a comparative advantage in exporting labour-intensive goods. Finally, the incentive system was believed by the government to be more efficient than direct controls in shaping the economy in the desired direction. By its nature, export-oriented strategy relied more on incentives than on controls; incentives were given contingent upon export performance in highly competitive international markets. The following instruments were included in the incentive system for export promotion: preferential credit; indirect tax exemptions on inputs into export production and sales; reduction in income tax on export earnings; tariff exemption on imported raw materials and equipment for export production; and allowances on imported raw materials for export production.

Foreign capital was actively encouraged. Since capital inflow on the whole was used for productive purposes, especially for quick-yielding export-oriented production, capital inflow itself prior to the first oil price rise generated its own debt service without putting excessive pressure on balance of payments flows. Foreign borrowing was only undertaken with government authorisation and guarantees; thus the government firmly controlled access to foreign capital.

The course of development has been shaped to a large extent by government direction. From 1961 up to 1979, Korea was governed by a highly centralised and authoritarian government, under which political freedom was restricted to some extent. To partly compensate for restrictions on political freedom, the government gave first priority to economic growth, heavily intervening in economic activities and the course of development.

The first five-year plan, covering the 1962–1966 period was established mainly to check the macroeconomic consistency of the overall plan; for lack of necessary data, the plan did not carry out its function very adequately. From the third five-year plan (from 1972–1976) on, emphasis shifted toward policy planning; focus was placed on formulating policies that led to the desired allocation of resources.

The economic policies of the Korean government have preferred high economic growth to more equitable income distribution. The government attempted to solve the poverty of the low-income class with rapid economic growth, pursuing the policy of growth first, income distribution later. In spite of this, the degree of income inequality in Korea is substantially less than that existing in many other less-developed countries. The main reason for this seems to be that Korea underwent a thorough land reform in the late 1940s and in the early 1950s, which increased equality of income; furthermore, the remarkable economic growth of Korea over the last two decades has been achieved without causing an increase in inequality of income.[4]

There has been no substantial shift in income distribution between wage earners and entrepreneurs. When surplus of labour existed in the early stage of development, the rapid growth of the economy provided new jobs to formerly unemployed labourers. When the surplus of labour disappeared in the mid-1970s, wage earners were fully compensated for productivity gains, which helped maintain a stable share of the national income for them. The share of employees' earnings in the national income increased from 39.5 per cent in 1971 to 47.9 per cent in 1981 (see Table 8.3).

Policy formation was in the hands of relatively few decision makers. The highly centralised decision making process had the advantage of facilitating speed and flexibility in policy formation. However, when economic policies are hastily determined by a few decision makers in the face of a rapidly changing economic environment, there may be a greater likelihood that mistakes are made which lead the economy in the wrong direction.

As Korea began to lose comparative advantage in exporting low-skill and labour-intensive goods to other developing countries, such as India and China, the emphasis on electronics and machinery in the early 1970s reflected a shift in Korea's comparative advantage away from labour-intensive towards more skill-intensive and capital-intensive industries. The large amount of investment in heavy and chemical

**Table 8.3 Distribution of national income**

(percentage shares)

| | Compensation of employees | Income from unincorporated enterprises[a] | Agriculture | Income from property | Corporate transfer payments and saving | Direct taxes on corporation | Government: Income from property & enterprises | Government: (Less) Interest on public & consumers' debt |
|---|---|---|---|---|---|---|---|---|
| 1962 | 36.1 | 47.6 | 33.1 | 11.1 | 3.5 | 0.7 | 1.9 | 0.8 |
| 1971 | 39.5 | 42.0 | 24.6 | 12.6 | 2.3 | 2.0 | 2.0 | 0.7 |
| 1975 | 38.4 | 40.8 | 23.3 | 12.7 | 5.3 | 1.9 | 1.5 | 0.4 |
| 1978 | 46.1 | 31.6 | 20.0 | 14.0 | 4.6 | 2.8 | 1.5 | 0.5 |
| 1981 | 47.9 | 27.9 | 16.4 | 18.6 | 1.5 | 2.9 | 2.1 | 0.9 |

*Source:* Economic Planning Board, *Major Statistics of Korean Economy*, 1982; The Bank of Korea, *Monthly Bulletin*, April 1983.

*Note:* (a) Income from unincorporated enterprises includes agricultural income.

industries in the latter part of 1970s, however, seems to have been hastily decided by the government. Investment in heavy and chemical industries exceeded what was permitted by market size, financing capacity and technical and engineering capacity. Excess capacity resulting from overinvestment is most evident in the machinery and plant manufacturing industry. The overinvestment was carried out with subsidised credit, which later contributed to the high rates of inflation. When the economy is simple, mistakes can be easily corrected without paying high costs. When the economy is complicated, the cost of revising past mistakes outweighs the benefits from speedy decision making.

Since the early 1960s, the Korean government has utilised domestic credit and interest rates as important policy instruments in its efforts to attain high economic growth and influence resource allocation. In 1965, interest rates were doubled on domestic deposits and loans, so as to raise domestic savings. In the late 1960s, interest rates on bank deposits exceeded the rate of increase in the GNP deflator by significant amounts. The interest rates charged on preferential loans, however, were significantly lower than those on bank deposits; real interest rates on preferential loans were often negative. To finance preferential loans and programmes such as export promotion, the government allowed the banking system to create additional credit. In turn, commercial banks were allowed to borrow a large portion of preferential loans from the Bank of Korea through a discount window at a lower interest rate. It can thus be said that a large share of investment was financed by forced savings through the expansion of the money supply.

In the 1970s, low interest rates, and often negative ones in real terms, led to an excess of credit demand and the need for credit rationing; this rationing was highly discretionary and frequently politically motivated. Low interest rates also led to a distortion in resource allocation, contributing also to a high debt-equity ratio of the business sector, particularly among big enterprises. Big business found it easier and cheaper to borrow from financial institutions than to finance through retained earnings or equity growth. By raising the debt-equity ratio, they could maximise the rate of return on their equity, as interest rates on bank loans were much lower than the rate of return on their investments.

Low interest rates and rapid expansion of money supply also contributed to a rapid growth of the curb loan market where the availability and cost of funds were free from government control; this undoubtedly undermined the effectiveness of government monetary policies.

It is true that preferential credit allocations and an expansionary monetary policy helped form domestic capital and achieve high economic growth in the early stage of development. With a surplus of high quality labour, a rapid increase in capital formation was necessary to achieve high economic growth and to increase employment.

The process of growth through preferential credit allocations, however, led to an excessive expansion in the money supply, contributing to Korea's high rate of inflation during the last two decades. Even though the high inflation rate was also stimulated by external factors, such as the oil price rises, it was sustained only by a high growth rate of the money supply. After the prolonged high rate of inflation, economic contracts began to reflect the expected rate of inflation. Wage contracts began to reflect more than the high rate of inflation plus productivity gains, particularly when surplus of labour no longer existed in the latter half of the 1970s; this brought about another round of high rates of inflation and the government accommodated it with a high growth rate of the money supply.

The continued high rate of inflation brought about a rapid rise in speculative transactions, uncertainty and inefficiency, retarding the improvement of productivity and technology development, thus making it more difficult to fully exploit the growth potential of the Korean economy. This trend also made the Korean economy more vulnerable to external shocks.

The rapid growth of the economy implied an increase in energy consumption at an annual average rate of 8.2 per cent over the last two decades. During the period, income elasticity of demand for energy was very high (0.94), much higher than in the developed economies. Since Korea has a limited supply of domestic energy resources, it depended heavily upon overseas energy resources. In 1981, 75 per cent of energy needs were met with imported resources. Moreover, the import structure of overseas energy resources is somewhat vulnerable; 88 per cent of the crude oil originated in the Middle East. The demand for oil has grown very fast – dependence on oil increased from 10 per cent of total energy consumption in 1962 to 58 per cent in 1981 – and Korea has no known oil reserves.

According to H.T. Kim's estimate, during the period 1964–1979, income and price elasticity of demand for oil were 2.87 and −0.71, respectively.[5] Even though these figures may not be precise, it is true that the income elasticity of demand for oil is high and the price elasticity is relatively low in Korea, compared with industrialised countries. This implies that the Korean economy has been more vulnerable to large increases in oil prices, in terms of inflation and economic growth, than the industrialised countries.

Before the first major oil price rise, there were no energy policies in

Korea, since no energy policy issues seemed to exist. In the face of the first big oil price rise, the Korean government made major efforts to secure oil supplies. The government also raised the average domestic price of crude oil. The price rise was carried out mainly to reduce oil demand. However, there were no sound criteria employed in determining the relative prices of petroleum products. The government also made efforts to reduce demand for foreign oil through administrative measures and nation-wide energy-saving campaigns, examples of which were extension of winter vacation and shortening of summer vacation of all schools, temperature control in public buildings, enforcement of highway speed limits and banning gasoline sales on Sunday.

However, the effectiveness of such measures was limited and the demand for foreign oil picked up again. During the period 1976–1978, the amount of oil imports grew at an annual rate of 14.3 per cent and the oil import bill increased at an annual rate of 19.9 per cent.

In the face of the second major oil price rise, the government again made major efforts to secure oil supplies and followed the same kind of policies to reduce demand for oil as after the first major oil price rise. In addition, restrictive demand management policies were also taken both to reduce the demand for foreign oil and to suppress the high rate of inflation.

## International determinants and development of the Korean economy

Korea's small open economy has been greatly influenced by international determinants. For example, the favourable world economic environment in the sixties and seventies greatly contributed to the success of export-oriented economic growth. Rapid increase in exports undoubtedly contributed to high economic growth. But, since the ratio of exports to GNP has been so high (reaching 45 per cent in 1981) fluctuations in exports have had a major impact on aggregate demand and on the growth of output.

The average annual growth rate of exports in dollar terms over the last two decades was around 36 per cent and has been accompanied by a significant change in their composition. In 1962, manufactured goods only accounted for 27 per cent of total exports; in 1981, their share had increased to 91 per cent. Among exports of manufactured goods the share of heavy and chemical industrial goods increased very rapidly in the 1970s, increasing from 14.1 per cent of total exports in 1971 to 42.7 per cent in 1981, while the share of light industrial goods declined from 72 per cent in 1971 to 47.5 per cent in 1981.

Export markets have also been diversified. The share of exports to the United States and Japan declined from 64.8 per cent of total exports in

1962 to 43.2 per cent in 1981. The diversification of export markets is closely linked to the shifts in the composition of exports. In the early stage of its development, Korea had exported low-skill and labour-intensive goods; export markets were restricted to industrial countries. In the process of rapid industrialisation, however, Korea came to have a comparative advantage in the production of skill-intensive and capital-intensive outputs over other developing countries, still maintaining a comparative advantage in the production of labour-intensive goods over major industrial countries. As a result, Korean export markets have been diversified.

Korean imports also grew very rapidly, at an annual rate of 26.7 per cent; there have also been shifts in the composition of imports. A rapid increase in imports of raw materials for exports and petroleum between 1962 and 1981 indicates the large share of imports closely linked to exports (see Table 8.4A). Import markets were also diversified in connection with the change in the composition of imports. Imports from the United States and Japan still occupy the major portion of total imports, but imports from the Middle Eastern countries increased significantly due to the increased importance of oil.

The rate of increase in prices of imported goods has a great impact on the rate of inflation in Korea, since the ratio of imports to GNP already reached around 40 per cent in the mid-1970s, climbing to 51.6 per cent in 1981. Since raw materials and petroleum are a large proportion of imports, fluctuations in prices of raw materials and petroleum had a great impact on the price level of Korea (made worse and sustained by monetary policy, as noted above). During the first and second major oil price rises, the rate of increase in prices of imported goods exceeded the rate of inflation. Except for those periods, however, the rate of increase in unit value of import prices was much less than the inflation rate.

Since Korean inflation exceeded that of the United States by a significant amount, Korea should have devalued its own currency periodically to maintain price competitiveness in international markets. But the Korean government avoided devaluation while the world economy remained favourable. In the face of external shocks, however, the adjustment of foreign exchange rates could not be delayed. Therefore, devaluation coincided with external shocks, aggravating the impact of external shocks on the rate of inflation.

Terms of trade improved through the 1960s and had been quite stable before the first oil price rise. Because of the first oil price rise and consequent devaluation of the foreign exchange rate, terms of trade deteriorated sharply from 1972 to 1975; they began to recover from 1976, however, due mainly to the recovery of the world economy. Because of the second oil price rise at the end of 1979 and consequent

**Table 8.4 Exports and imports of type of products, 1971–1981**

*A. Composition of exports (per cent) and total value*

| | Food & kindred | Crude materials & mineral fuels | Light industry products | Heavy industry products | Total value (US$m.) |
|---|---|---|---|---|---|
| 1971 | 8.0 | 5.8 | 72.0 | 14.1 | 1,068 |
| 1973 | 8.3 | 4.5 | 63.4 | 23.8 | 3,225 |
| 1975 | 13.1 | 4.3 | 57.3 | 25.1 | 5,081 |
| 1977 | 10.6 | 3.8 | 52.7 | 32.8 | 10,046 |
| 1979 | 8.0 | 2.9 | 50.3 | 38.6 | 15,055 |
| 1981 | 6.9 | 2.7 | 47.5 | 42.7 | 21,254 |

*Source:* Department of Finance, *Fiscal and Financial Statistics*, February 1981, and February 1983.

*B. Composition of imports (per cent) and total value*

| | Capital goods | Raw materials for export | Raw materials for domestic use & others | Petroleum | Total value (US$m.) |
|---|---|---|---|---|---|
| 1971 | 28.6 | 21.1 | 42.4 | 7.8 | 2,394 |
| 1973 | 27.3 | 36.7 | 29.0 | 7.0 | 4,240 |
| 1975 | 26.2 | 30.0 | 26.3 | 17.5 | 7,274 |
| 1977 | 27.8 | 25.3 | 29.0 | 17.9 | 10,810 |
| 1979 | 31.0 | 19.3 | 34.4 | 15.3 | 20,339 |
| 1981 | 23.6 | 20.5 | 31.5 | 24.4 | 26,131 |

*Source:* Economic Planning Board, *Major Statistics of Korean Economy*, 1982.

devaluation in 1980, terms of trade deteriorated again; the terms of trade in 1981 were almost the same as those of 1975

It is interesting to compare changes in Korea's terms of trade with those of industrial countries. In the case of the United States, terms of trade deteriorated from 115 in 1972 to 100 in 1975. Therefore, the impact of the first oil price rise on the terms of trade was much less significant in the United States than in Korea (see Table 8.5). During the period 1972–1981 as a whole, however, terms of trade in Korea deteriorated by 29 per cent while they deteriorated by 26 per cent in the United States. In the case of Japan, terms of trade deteriorated by 46 per cent during the same period. Therefore, the deterioration in terms of trade of Korea was not much worse than those of the industrial countries.

Because of the accumulated current account deficits caused by two major oil price rises and high growth-oriented economic strategy, foreign debt outstanding amounted to US$37.2 billion at the end of 1982. The ratio of foreign debt outstanding to GNP reached 56.2 per cent and the debt-service ratio of medium and long-term debt reached 15.5 per cent at the end of 1982. If short-term debt is included, the debt-service ratio reached almost 20 per cent. Since a large proportion of foreign debt outstanding came from commercial banks and most commercial loans carry floating interest rates, the amount of interest payments is heavily dependent upon the fluctuation in interest rates in world financial markets. The sharp increase in interest rates after the second oil price rise became a great burden on the Korean economy and contributed to the worsening of the balance of payments. Since Korea borrows large amounts from private financial markets to finance the current account deficits, changes in terms of loans in the world financial markets have a great impact on the Korean economy.

## Major oil price rises and the development of the Korean economy

### 1971–1973

During this period, Korea achieved remarkable economic growth; the annual average growth rate of output was around 10 per cent. Growth in the manufacturing sector exceeded an annual rate of 20 per cent. The high growth rate of the manufacturing sector was linked to a rapid expansion in exports, whose annual growth rate amountd to 54.8 per cent in dollar terms during the period. The share of manufactured goods to total exports already exceeded 85 per cent in 1971.

Korea already suffered from double digit inflation rates during this period. The annual growth rate of the GNP deflator, which is regarded

**Table 8.5 Indices of foreign trade, Korea and USA**

| | Korea | | | USA | | |
|---|---|---|---|---|---|---|
| | Unit value of exports | Unit value of imports | Net barter terms of trade | Unit value of exports | Unit value of imports | Net barter terms of trade |
| 1971–73 | 73.0 | 51.8 | 141.5 | 62.8 | 54.2 | 116.0 |
| 1974–75 | 104.0 | 98.6 | 105.5 | 94.7 | 95.9 | 98.8 |
| 1976–78 | 123.1 | 101.3 | 121.3 | 108.3 | 111.7 | 97.1 |
| 1979–81 | 168.9 | 154.9 | 110.3 | 146.5 | 170.5 | 86.4 |

*Source:* Bank of Korea, *Economic Statistics Yearbook, 1982;* IMF, *International Financial Statistics, 1981,* December 1982.

as the best indicator for a rate of inflation in Korea, was around 15 per cent. Rapid expansion of the money supply (M2), whose annual growth rate amounted to 30 per cent during the period, was mainly responsible for the high rate of inflation. The rate of increase in the unit value of imports was insignificant in 1971 and 1972, but significant in 1973 due to the worldwide commodity boom and the oil price rise. Therefore, we cannot say that imported inflation initiated the high rate of inflation. The growth rate of wages was as high as that of the GNP deflator, but did not reflect the increase in productivity. Therefore, there was no substantial increase in real wages. In such a situation, the increase in wage rate could not be regarded as the cause of high rates of inflation but rather an adjustment to previous inflation.

The balance of payments position in Korea improved during this period. The main factor was the rapid increase in exports due to the booming world economy. The terms of trade had gradually improved through the 1960s and were quite stable during the 1971–73 period, deteriorating by a small amount in 1973 due to the rapid increase in prices of raw materials and oil. Even though the unit value of exports rose by a substantial amount due to the boom in the world economy, the rate of increase in unit value of imports exceeded it.

During 1971–1973 the Korean currency was devalued by only 7.5 per cent, even though the annual inflation rate of Korea was higher than that in the United States of America by almost 10 per cent. Since foreign countries' income elasticity of demand for Korean exports had much greater impact on determining the level of Korean exports than price elasticities, Korea could postpone the adjustment of the exchange rate while the world economy was in boom. The loss in price competitiveness caused by a higher rate of inflation was also partially compensated for by increased subsidies to export sectors. When the world economy turned into recession, however, Korea had to devalue its currency by a significant amount in order to restore price competitiveness and to partially offset the deterioration in balance of payments. Since the downturn in the Korean economy was coupled with devaluation which contributed to domestic inflation, the high inflation rate was sustained in the economic downturn.

### 1974–1975 period
The first oil price rise undoubtedly had a deflationary impact on the Korean economy. The worldwide recession which followed reduced Korean exports by a significant amount at the same time as the country made larger payments for the oil bill. Multiplier effects of reduced consumer demand caused by the oil price rise also contributed to reducing the growth rate of output. The annual growth rate of exports in

dollar terms was reduced from 54.8 per cent in the previous period to 23.7 per cent during 1974–1975. The slowdown in the growth rate of exports contributed largely to reducing the annual growth rate of manufacturing to 14.2 per cent, which in turn, reduced the annual growth rate of output to 7.6 per cent.

The rise in the oil price gave a cost-push impact on the supply side. The rate of increase in unit value of imports was around 55.5 per cent in 1974, accelerating the already high rate of inflation. During the period, the annual rate of increase in the GNP deflator was around 29.2 per cent. Because of the prolonged and persistent high rate of inflation, inflationary expectations were formed and played an important role in wage settlements. The wage rate rose at an annual rate of 31.2 per cent, exceeding the rate of increase in the GNP deflator by a small amount. Since wage earners were only partially compensated for productivity gains, we cannot simply say that the rapid increase in wage rate was the cause of high rate of inflation.

In the face of rapid increases in import prices Korea did not pursue restrictive demand management policies to cushion the adverse impacts of imported inflation on domestic inflation. Money supply grew at an annual rate of 26 per cent, only slightly lower than during the previous period. Therefore, we can say that the high inflation rate was initiated by a rapid increase in prices of imports and sustained by expansionary monetary policies.

Even though the growth rate of output during the period was not so high as previously, wage settlements began to reflect some part of the productivity increase. Entrepreneurs had to pay more to secure additional workers so that real wages began to rise, as the surplus of labour began to disappear in the mid-1970s. High rates of wage increases, however, cannot be regarded in the Korean context as the main cause of high rates of inflation, since wage earners were only partially compensated for productivity gains.

After the first major oil price rise, the current account deficit increased sharply, amounting to 10 per cent of GNP in 1974. This sharp increase was partly attributable to the increased payments for imported oil; the increase in the oil bill accounted for 40 per cent of the increase in current account deficits. The rest of the increase in the current account deficit can be attributed to the increased payments for imports from industrial countries.

Korea did not attempt to make internal adjustments to reduce its current account deficits. Instead, Korea chose to finance them with foreign loans, attempting to minimise the impact of the external shock without revising its export-oriented high economic growth strategy. There were several reasons why Korea avoided taking measures to revise its development strategy in order to reduce the current account deficits and increased external indebtedness. First, Korea felt at the time that there were many transitory elements in the huge increase in current account deficits. The elements perceived as transitory were the abrupt once-and-for-all increase in the oil price, the reduction in the growth rate of output in industrial countries, and the deterioration in terms of trade against industrial countries. The Korean government felt that as soon as those transitory elements vanished, the current account deficits would be reduced by a substantial amount. Second, there were foreign funds available at a relatively cheap price through international private capital markets. Interest rates (particularly in real terms) in industrial countries declined during the very period when demand for private bank credit by non-oil developing countries was very large. Third, foreign debt outstanding in 1974 was not so large, and Korea felt no real need to worry about debt management problems.

Because of the rapid increase in unit value of imports relative to the increase in unit value of exports, the terms of trade deteriorated from 136.4 in 1973 to 100 in 1975. A devaluation of the Korean currency by 21.8 per cent in late 1974 was carried out as a delayed adjustment of the exchange rate to reflect the difference in inflation rates rather than as a means to achieve external balance.

## 1976–1978 period

Korea overcame the first major oil price rise and the recession in industrial countries rather successfully. Thanks to global economic recovery and the expansion of the overseas construction boom, Korea began to show rapid economic growth. The annual growth rate of exports reached 36.5 per cent in dollar terms and receipts from overseas construction jumped from $39 million in 1975 to $2,148 million in 1978. The rapid growth of the Korean economy, however, was attributable not only to the favourable world economic environment but also to expansionary demand management policies, which shifted industrial structure to heavy and chemical industries. These policies enabled the Korean economy to grow at an annual rate of 12.3 per cent although these policies contributed to its subsequent slowdown.

During the period, the Korean government encouraged and initiated the shift of industrial structure to heavy and chemical industries. This shift was promoted too rapidly and abruptly with heavily subsidised loans and with a large amount of foreign capital inflow to these industries. Preferential margins for loans to support this policy were so great that real interest rates were negative; this led to distortions in resource allocation and the establishment of highly capital-intensive industries. Overinvestment financed by expansionary monetary policies

**Table 8.6 Main economic indicators**

(annual average, per cent)

| | Real growth rate of output | Growth rate of GNP deflator | Growth rate of money supply (M2) | Growth rate of wages in manufacturing | Growth rate of unit value of imports |
|---|---|---|---|---|---|
| 1971–1973 | 10.0 | 15.0 | 30.3 | 14.7 | 11.6 |
| 1974–1975 | 7.6 | 29.3 | 26.1 | 31.2 | 29.2 |
| 1976–1978 | 12.3 | 20.4 | 36.1 | 33.5 | 3.3 |
| 1979–1981 | 2.4 | 21.1 | 25.6 | 24.1 | 17.9 |

*Source:* Bank of Korea, *Economic Statistics Yearbook,* 1972, 1975, 1981 and 1982.

contributed to raising the growth rate of output in the short run but became one of the main causes for the recession after 1979.

Inflation stayed at a high level. The annual rate of increase in the GNP deflator was around 20.4 per cent during the period, resulting from the rapid growth in the money supply at an annual rate of 36.1 per cent as well as the rapid increase in wages at an annual rate of 33.5 per cent. Wage increases exceeded significantly the rate of increase of the GNP deflator; wage earners in manufacturing sectors were compensated for more than the inflation rate plus productivity gains. The tremendous expansion of overseas construction and expansionary demand management policies pulled up wages in the manufacturing sector. In addition, there had been a great transformation in the labour market, as labour surplus no longer existed. A sharp and sustained increase in money wages and unit labour costs exerted strong cost-push pressure on the supply side. During the period, the unit value of imports grew at an annual rate of 3.3 per cent; their impact on inflation was quite insignificant. The continued high rate of inflation weakened the price competitiveness of Korean exports making Korea more vulnerable to external shocks.

As mentioned, the construction boom in the Middle East and economic recovery in industrial countries greatly helped improve the Korean balance of payments. In 1976 exports in dollar terms grew by 56 per cent. The current account was in balance in 1977. From 1978, however, the current account of the balance of payments deteriorated rapidly because the overinvestment in the heavy and chemical industries accelerated the growth rate of imports. In addition, Korea began to lose price competitiveness in export markets due to the continued high rate of inflation without adjustment of the foreign exchange rate. When the external environment is favourable, it would seem advisable that the economy should not be overheated. Korea should have attempted to maintain equilibrium in the balance of payments to reduce its reliance on foreign capital while the world economic environment was favourable.

During the period, terms of trade improved. Even though the rate of inflation in Korea was much higher than that of the United States, the exchange rate adjustment was postponed. If the exchange rate had been adjusted to reflect the difference in inflation rates between the two countries, terms of trade would have improved to a lesser extent during the period.

The delay of the exchange rate adjustment also contributed to a large inflow of foreign capital. Without adjustment of the foreign exchange rate, the interest rate charged on foreign loans seemed to be much cheaper on the part of the borrower, since the nominal interest rates on domestic loans reflected the domestic inflation rate, while the nominal interest rates on foreign loans were more related to anticipated inflation in industrial countries. This postponement of the adjustment of foreign exchange rate misled domestic borrowers to underestimate the real cost of foreign borrowing and led to a large inflow of foreign capital.

During the period, Korea did not make much effort to reduce its reliance on foreign oil. The oil import bill increased at an annual rate of 19.9 per cent and the volume of oil imports grew at an annual rate of 14.3 per cent.

## *1979–1981 period*

The second major oil price rise in 1979 had a more severe adverse impact on the Korean economy than the preceding rise because the impact was further aggravated by the expansionary demand management policies previously followed. Worldwide recession following the second oil price rise reduced the growth rate of Korean exports. The annual growth rate of exports in dollar terms fell from 37 per cent in the previous period to 18 per cent in this period. The slowdown in the growth rate of exports contributed to reducing the annual growth of output in the manufacturing sector to 5.2 per cent; this contributed to reduce the growth rate of output (from 12.3 per cent in the previous period to 2.4 per cent).

In 1980, for the first time after 20 years of successful economic growth, Korea recorded a decline in GNP – of 6.2 per cent. Social unrest after President Park's assassination, an unprecedented bad harvest in 1980, the second rise in the oil price, and lagged adverse impacts of the expansionary monetary policies can be listed as factors responsible for the negative growth. In 1981 Korea achieved an economic growth rate of 7.1 per cent. As a result, the level of GNP of 1981 in real terms was restored to its 1979 level. However, Korea still has to cope with the lagged adverse impacts of expansionary demand management policies prior to the second oil price rise.

The rise in oil price had a cost-push impact on the supply side. The foreign exchange rate was devalued by 36.3 per cent and this contributed to the rapid increase in the unit value of imports in 1980. Rapid increase in wage rates also contributed to the high inflation rate. In 1979 and 1980, the growth rate of wages reflected more than the rate of inflation plus productivity gains. On the demand side, the government began to take restrictive demand-management policies from the latter part of 1979. The annual growth rate of the money supply was reduced; it was still (at 25.6 per cent) high enough to sustain a high rate of inflation. The increase in the GNP deflator was above 20 per cent in 1979 and 1980.

From the latter half of 1981, the Korean government decided to combine incomes policies with restrictive demand-management policies.

The government demanded from labour that it sacrifice some portion of the increase in its productivity to lower the inflation rate. It set up wage guidelines and made an effort to prevent inflationary expectations being reflected in wage negotiations. Due to the success of incomes policy and the small increase in import prices, the rate of increase in the GNP deflator fell in 1981, and declined further to single digits in 1982. The weakness of labour unions and the high rate of wage increase in the previous period (above productivity gains) contributed to the success of the incomes policy.

Because of the slowdown in export growth and increased payments for oil, the current account deficits deteriorated rapidly after the second oil price rise. Payment for oil increased by 191.4 per cent, from 1978 to 1981, even though the quantity of oil imports increased only by 6.7 per cent. The large current account deficits resulted in a rapid rise of the foreign debt and management problems.

Due largely to the rise in the oil price, terms of trade deteriorated from 1978 to 1981. The devaluation in 1980 also contributed to raising the rate of increase in unit value of imports. The devaluation was carried out to compensate for the loss in price competitiveness in export markets due to the higher rate of domestic inflation prior to the second major oil price rise (though inevitably it did not make much contribution to restoring the external balance).

## Policy recommendations for the 1980s

We have briefly analysed the development of the Korean economy, the economic policies of the Korean government, and the impact of imported inflation on the Korean economy. Korea suffered from severe external shocks in the 1970s and its labour surplus disappeared in the latter half of the 1970s. In the face of the changing domestic and world economic environments, Korea should have revised its high growth oriented economic strategy coupled with inflationary financing. When the world economic environment turned out to be favourable after the first major oil price rise, Korea should have pursued steady economic growth strategies with emphasis on price stabilisation. Instead, Korea continuously pursued high growth-oriented economic policies and initiated the transformation of its industrial structure with expansionary monetary policies. This undoubtedly aggravated the impact of the second oil price rise and contributed to the stagflation of Korea after 1979. In the future, Korea should not repeat the mistake of overheating the economy with expansionary monetary policies. The prolonged high rate of inflation was very harmful to the Korean economy in the late 1970s, causing speculative transactions, inefficiency and uncertainty. The inflation rate should be reduced to ensure sound economic development in the long run; it is desirable to maintain the rate of inflation at the same level as that of industrial countries.

By maintaining the inflation rate at a low level, it will be much easier to guarantee positive real interest rates, which will contribute to augmenting domestic savings and reducing dependency on foreign savings. If the inflation rate was at the same level as that of industrial countries, a stable foreign exchange rate could be maintained and the problems caused by lagged adjustment of the foreign exchange rate could be solved. The maintenance of a low inflation rate is also a prerequisite of the financial liberalisation necessary for the development of the financial sector in Korea.

In the past, Korea pursued export-oriented economic growth; the rapid growth in exports has undoubtedly been the engine for very rapid economic growth. Some major constraints to the promotion of exports are expected, though. The world economic outlook in the 1980s is not so bright as that in the 1960s and 1970s. After the collapse of the Bretton Woods system, the international monetary order has been in disarray. The advanced countries have undergone a prolonged recession since 1980, and it is not clear when and to what extent their economies will return to their past growth rates. This has increased pressures for higher levels of protectionism. Furthermore, since Korea is already a so-called newly industrialised country and Korean exports already reach almost 1 per cent of world trade, they are bound to face increased protectionism. Also, changes in the composition of Korean exports make it difficult to achieve such a high growth rate of exports in the 1980s as before. The share of heavy and chemical industrial goods increased so rapidly that Korea has to compete in export markets where industrial countries have dominated. We already see a downward trend in the growth rate of Korean exports. Since there is a limit to pursuing rapid economic growth based mainly on the rapid expansion of exports, Korea should make an attempt to achieve steady economic growth based on more balanced growth between its domestic and foreign sectors. Also, to improve the competitiveness and efficiency of domestic industries and to lead the Korean economy into an advanced stage, it would seem preferable to substitute non-tariff barriers for tariff barriers and possibly to gradually reduce tariff rates.

Since, at the end of 1982, the foreign debt outstanding already amounted to $37 billion, Korea should attempt to reduce the debt-GNP ratio. Korea should reduce its reliance on foreign savings in capital formation by raising domestic savings. Steady growth policies with emphasis on price stabilisation will help reduce current account deficits.

In the past, government's heavy intervention in investment activities discouraged creativity and initiative in the private sector. From now on, the Korean government should promote freer competition and allow the market mechanism to play its proper function, gradually reducing its direct intervention, for example in policy loans. The Korean government should not be too heavy-handed in shaping the course of economic development. In the field of energy, however, the Korean government should provide a long-range overall plan to diversify energy sources, and to reduce its dependence on foreign energy.

Appendix

Table 8.7 Main statistical indicators, 1962–81

| | Growth rate (per cent) | | Exchange rate of won to dollar[a] | Nominal interest rate[b] |
|---|---|---|---|---|
| | Real GNP | Manufacturing | | |
| 1962 | 2.2 | 11.7 | 130.0 | 15.0 |
| 1971 | 9.4 | 18.8 | 373.2 | 21.6 |
| 1972 | 5.8 | 14.0 | 398.9 | 15.0 |
| 1973 | 14.9 | 29.2 | 397.5 | 12.0 |
| 1974 | 8.0 | 15.8 | 484.0 | 14.8 |
| 1975 | 7.1 | 12.6 | 484.0 | 15.0 |
| 1976 | 15.1 | 22.6 | 484.0 | 15.5 |
| 1977 | 10.3 | 14.4 | 484.0 | 15.8 |
| 1978 | 11.6 | 20.7 | 484.0 | 16.7 |
| 1979 | 6.4 | 9.8 | 484.0 | 18.6 |
| 1980 | −6.2 | −1.1 | 659.9 | 23.0 |
| 1981 | 6.4 | 6.8 | 700.5 | 19.3 |

*Source:* Bank of Korea, *Economic Statistics Yearbook*, 1972, 1975, 1981, 1982.

*Notes:*  (a) Bank of Korea standard concentration rate at end of period.
(b) Annual average of actual rates on time deposits over 1 year.

**Table 8.8 Composition of expenditure on gross national product, 1971–81, selected years**

(per cent)

| | GNP | Consumption | Gross investment | Exports | Imports | Domestic savings | Foreign savings | Statistical discrepancy |
|---|---|---|---|---|---|---|---|---|
| 1971 | 100.0 | 84.6 | 25.2 | 17.2 | 28.0 | 15.4 | 10.7 | 0.9 |
| 1973 | 100.0 | 76.5 | 25.6 | 31.3 | 35.1 | 23.5 | 3.8 | 1.7 |
| 1975 | 100.0 | 81.4 | 29.4 | 29.1 | 39.5 | 18.6 | 10.4 | −0.4 |
| 1980 | 100.0 | 80.1 | 31.5 | 40.2 | 50.4 | 19.9 | 10.2 | −1.4 |
| 1981 | 100.0 | 80.0 | 27.2 | 43.4 | 51.6 | 20.0 | 8.3 | 1.0 |

*Source:* Economic Planning Board, 'Economic management plan for 1982,' Jan. 1982.

**Table 8.9 Statistics on major interest rates, 1962–81**

| | Nominal interest rate[a] | Loans for export of DMB[b] | Loans for export of BOK | GNP deflator | Real interest rate[c] |
|---|---|---|---|---|---|
| 1971–73 | 16.2 | 6.2 | 3.5 | 15.0 | 1.2 |
| 1974–75 | 14.9 | 8.2 | 3.5 | 29.3 | −14.4 |
| 1976–78 | 16.0 | 8.5 | 3.6 | 20.4 | −4.4 |
| 1979–81 | 20.3 | 12.9 | 8.0 | 20.6 | −0.3 |

*Source:* Bank of Korea, *Economic Statistics Yearbook 1982*; Bank of Korea, *Monthly Bulletin*, Dec. 1982.

*Notes:* (a) Interest rate on time deposits for over 1 year.
(b) Loans for export of deposit money bank.
(c) Calculated by subtracting GNP deflator from nominal interest rate (column 1).

## Table 8.10 Balance of payments, 1971–81

(million US$)

| | Current sub-total | Trade balance | Invisible trade balance | Long-term capital | Basic balance | Overall balance |
|---|---|---|---|---|---|---|
| 1971 | −848 | −1,046 | 28 | 528 | −320 | −172 |
| 1972 | −317 | −575 | 33 | 496 | 125 | 182 |
| 1973 | −309 | −567 | 67 | 597 | 288 | 390 |
| 1974 | −2,023 | −1,937 | −308 | 946 | −1,076 | −1,094 |
| 1975 | −1,887 | −1,671 | −442 | 1,178 | −709 | −151 |
| 1976 | −314 | −591 | −72 | 1,371 | 1,058 | 1,174 |
| 1977 | 12 | −477 | 266 | 1,313 | 1,325 | 1,315 |
| 1978 | −1,085 | −1,781 | 224 | 2,166 | 1,081 | −402 |
| 1979 | −4,151 | −4,396 | −195 | 2,663 | −1,488 | −973 |
| 1980 | −5,321 | −4,384 | −1,386 | 1,857 | −3,464 | −1,890 |
| 1981 | −4,436 | −3,419 | −1,518 | 2,842 | −1,594 | −2,297 |

*Source:* Department of Finance, *Fiscal and Financial Statistics*, Feb. 1981, and Feb. 1983, Bank of Korea, *Economic Statistics Yearbook, 1982.*

## Notes and references

1   For reasons of space we have excluded in this version the Keynesian-cum-monetarist type mathematical model for the Korean economy, presented by the author in the larger version of this paper: Department of International Economics, Seoul National University (mimeo).
2   On the impact of education on the development of the Korean economy, see McGinn, N.F., *et al. Education and Development in Korea*, Cambridge, Harvard University Press, 1980.
3   See Kim, K.S., 'Outward-looking industrialisation strategy: The case of Korea', in Hong, W. and Kreuger, A.O. (eds.) *Trade and Development in Korea*, Seoul, KDI Press, 1975.
4   For further reference, see Mason, E.S., *et al. The Economic and Social Modernization of the Republic of Korea*, Cambridge: Harvard University Press, 1980, Chapter 12.
5   For further reference, see, Kim, H.T., *Korea's Energy Experiences in the 70s and Short to Medium-Term Options to Korea*, Seoul, Korea Institute of Energy and Resources, 1981 (mimeo).

## Bibliography

Branson, W.H., 'A Keynesian approach to worldwide inflation', in L.B. Krause and W.S. Salant (eds.) *Worldwide Inflation*, Washington D.C., The Brookings Institution, 1977.

Cline, W.R. and Associates, *World Inflation and the Developing Countries*, Washington D.C., The Brookings Institution, 1981.

Corden, W.M., *Inflation, Exchange Rates and the World Economy*, Chicago, The University of Chicago Press, 1977.

Dornbusch, R., *Open Economy Macroeconomics*, New York, Basic Books, 1980.

Findlay, R., and Rodriguez, C.A., 'Intermediate imports and macroeconomic policy under flexible exchange rates', *Canadian Journal of Economics*, 1977.

Flanders, M.J. and Razin, A. (eds.) *Development in an Inflationary World*, Academic Press, 1981.

Gordon, R.J., 'Alternative responses of policy to external shock', *Brookings Papers on Economic Activity*, 1, 1975.

Gordon, R.J., 'Recent development in the theory of inflation and unemployment', *Journal of Monetary Economics*, April 1976.

Hong, W., *Trade, Distortions and Employment Growth in Korea*, Seoul, KDI Press, 1979.

Hong, W., and Kreuger, A.O., *Trade and Development in Korea*, Seoul, KDI Press, 1975.

Kim, H.T., *Korea's Energy Experiences in the 70s and Short to Medium-Term Options Open to Korea*, Seoul, Korea Institute of Energy and Resources, December 1981.

Lindbeck, A. (ed.) *Inflation and Employment in Open Economies*, North-Holland Publishing Company, 1979.

Mason, E.S., and Associates, *The Economic and Social Modernization of the Republic of Korea*, 1980.

McGinn, N.F., and Associates, *Education and Development in Korea*, Cambridge, Mass., Harvard University Press, 1980.

Nordhaus, W.D., 'The flexibility of wages and prices: Inflation theory and policy', *The American Economic Review*, May 1976.

Parkin, M., and Zis, G. (eds.) *Inflation in Open Economies*, Manchester University Press, 1976.

Schmid, M., 'A Model of Trade in Money, Goods and Factors', *Journal of International Economics*, June 1976.

Schultz, L., and Associates, (eds.) *Higher Oil Prices and the World Economy: The Adjustment Problem*, Washington D.C., The Brookings Institution, 1975.

Shur, K.J., *Structure of Energy Demand and Energy Policy in Korea*, Seoul, KIEI Press, Seminar Series no. 36, Nov. 1981.

Suzuki, Y., *Monetary Control and Anti-Inflation Policy – The Japanese Experience Since 1975*, Discussion Paper Series no. 8, The Bank of Japan, 1981.

# 9 The Impact of the International Environment on Argentina

*Marta Bekerman*

## Introduction

Argentina has gone through several changes during the 1970s. Many of them were a response more to domestic circumstances than to international events. The effect of external factors is at times difficult to detect and is sometimes neglected in an economy subject to such strong internal forces. However, the country was obviously affected by the changes that took place in the international scene and the objective of this paper is to observe the impact of those changes on the Argentine economy.

After a brief introduction, section 1 looks at the specific international factors that have influenced Argentina. Section 2 refers to the economic policy pursued before 1973. Section 3 looks at macroeconomic policies since 1973. Section 4 explores the impact of changes in the international environment and in national policies on the Argentine economy. Section 5 observes the microeconomic policies carried out in the energy and agricultural sectors and Section 6 attempts some conclusions.

Income per capita was US$2,600 in 1981; manufacturing had fallen to 25 per cent of GDP in 1981, from 32 per cent in 1960. The country is a major food exporter, with 10 per cent and 4 per cent of world exports of maize and meat in 1981. Agricultural goods dominate the country's exports. Exports plus imports, which amounted to 23 per cent of GDP, decreased (because of lower imports) until the mid-1970s. Since then

**Table 9.1 Share of agricultural exports in the total, 1971 and 1980**

|  | | (per cent) |
|---|---|---|
|  | *1971* | *1980* |
| Cereals | 33.2 | 21.7 |
| Meat | 23.9 | 12.1 |
| Oilseeds | 8.1 | 16.6 |
| Other | 19.0 | 23.0 |
| Total agricultural products[a] | 84.2 | 73.4 |
| Non-agricultural products[a] | 15.8 | 26.6 |
| Value (current US$ billions) | 1.7 | 8.0 |

*Source:*  Cepal (1982).

*Note:*  (a) 'Non-agricultural products' are mainly manufactured goods; some processed agricultural products are included under 'Agricultural products'.

the weight of the external sector has increased again to reach 28 per cent in 1980.

Only about 10 per cent of oil consumption has to be imported; the country also has a large hydroelectric and gas potential. Intermediate goods dominate imports, but oil and consumer goods increased their share in the 1970s.

**Table 9.2 Structure of imports**

|  | | (per cent) |
|---|---|---|
|  | *1971* | *1981* |
| Capital goods | 22.4 | 19.6 |
| Intermediate goods | 67.3 | 59.3 |
| Oil and lubricants | 6.5 | 10.3 |
| Consumer goods | 3.8 | 10.8 |
| Total | 100.0 | 100.0 |
| Value (US$ billions) | 1.9 | 9.4 |

*Source:*  Central Bank.

The economy could be divided, until recently, into an export sector, basically agriculture, which is not important as a market for the industrial sector; and the rest of the economy, based on non-tradeable goods because of high levels of protection, and very dependent on imports.[1] Expansion of the economy therefore tends to increase imports without expanding exports[2] so that the external sector can act as a constraint on economic expansion.

During recent decades, military coups or socio-economic crises have led to abrupt changes in economic policy. The non-existence of a dominant social group, at both the economic and political level, made it difficult to carry out a development strategy on a long-term basis.[3]

## 1 The impact of international factors

*Terms of trade*
During 1972–74 Argentina enjoyed high prices for meat, cereals and oil seeds. Export prices increased by nearly 80 per cent during those two years but the trend was reversed during 1975–78.[4] There was a recovery in export prices during 1979–80 because of price increases for meat, cereals and oilseeds.

Argentina, importing relatively little oil, escaped the worst effects of the oil price rises of the 1970s. This does not mean that there were no negative effects on the external accounts. Oil imports rose from US$172m. (8 per cent of total imports) to US$536m. (15 per cent) at the time of the first oil price increase. During the 1979 oil price increase, oil imports jumped from US$470m. (11 per cent of imports) in 1978 to US$1,126m. (16 per cent) in 1979.

The terms of trade peaked in 1973 but their deterioration was not very large thereafter. In fact during 1974 and 1975 the level was still higher than in 1970 (see Table 9.3) but the fall in the prices of primary exports led to further declines in the following years. The impact of the second oil price rise was again counteracted by the increase in export prices during 1979–80.

*External finance*
Although Argentina became a heavy borrower in the Eurocurrency markets by the late 1970s, its participation in those markets began later than did that of other Latin American countries. The amount of international lending by private banks during the Peronist period of 1973–76 was very small, in spite of the large increase in international liquidity that had already taken place.

It was only some time after the military government assumed office that the international bankers began to consider Argentina as a good

**Table 9.3 Terms of trade indices, 1971–1981**

$(1970 = 100)$

|      | Export prices | Import prices | Terms of trade |
|------|---------------|---------------|----------------|
| 1971 | 113.9 | 103.8 | 109.7 |
| 1972 | 131.1 | 110.8 | 118.3 |
| 1973 | 185.3 | 147.1 | 126.0 |
| 1974 | 233.4 | 212.1 | 110.0 |
| 1975 | 219.5 | 206.0 | 106.0 |
| 1976 | 199.3 | 218.9 | 91.0 |
| 1977 | 205.2 | 231.4 | 88.7 |
| 1978 | 212.4 | 255.2 | 83.2 |
| 1979 | 267.4 | 316.2 | 84.6 |
| 1980 | 314.4 | 329.7 | 95.4 |
| 1981 | na | na | 89.1 |

*Source:* Cepal (1982).

risk. The increase in international borrowing started in 1977 and reached record levels in 1979–80. Helped by the inflow of foreign capital the level of reserves rose rapidly between 1976 and 1979. This process was reversed after 1980, when a sharp fall in reserves began.

The increase in international interest rates during 1979 had a strong impact on the external sector. This was because of the large amount of variable interest rate debt contracted with private banks. The cost of financial services (mainly interest on foreign debt) as a proportion of total exports jumped to 35 per cent in 1981, compared with 12 per cent in 1976.

## 2 Economic policy before 1973

A stabilisation policy was implemented in 1967, following a military coup. The new strategy was to promote industrial exports as a way of reducing the high dependence of domestic growth on agricultural exports. It was based on a substantial devaluation of the peso, counteracted by high export taxes (on agricultural exports) and reductions in import duties. In practice the new exchange rate was only a force for financial transactions and non-traditional exports (Braun 1970).

The objective of expanding industrial exports required an improvement in the efficiency of the industrial sector to make it competitive in international markets. The government attempted to improve the economic infrastructure by raising the level of public investment. Because the industrial sector was relatively inefficient, the strategy was based on cheap labour as an international comparative advantage and on the redistribution of the economic surplus generated in the agricultural sector. This was supplemented by a restrictive incomes policy.

The programme was successful in reducing inflation and improving the balance of payments situation during 1968. In the following year the strong opposition of the working class led to a political crisis and the reinstatement of collective bargaining. The political situation produced a crisis of confidence in the stability of the economic programme. Outflows of capital and large current account deficits during 1971 and 1972 led to heavy losses in foreign reserves. The 'political legitimacy' of the armed forces came under attack. Elections were called in 1973 and won by the Peronist coalition.

## 3  Macroeconomic policies after 1973

*The Peronist government (1973–76)*
The Peronist government assumed office in 1973 with the wide support of the working class and of some industrial organisations. It chose to expand the domestic market and non-traditional exports. The interest rate, which remained under government control, was reduced in nominal terms. The reduction in inflation during 1973 led to positive real rates of interest during the second half of that year, but they were negative during the rest of the Peronist period. The Central Bank also controlled the allocation of credit by the commercial banks.

A higher public sector deficit was the result of an expansion in both current and capital expenditures. Real wages and the number of public employees increased; and new investment projects in infrastructure took place. Consequently the public deficit increased from 3 per cent of GDP in 1972 to 15 per cent in 1976 (Ferrer 1977). Workers' and employers' organisations agreed to a 'social pact' on income distribution. Prices were frozen, with reductions for a selected list of goods, while wages were to be frozen after an initial increase of 20 per cent. The government also controlled agricultural sales. At a time of a boom in commodity prices this policy resulted in a real transfer of resources from the agricultural to the urban sector.

Non-traditional exports were promoted by rebates of import duties on inputs, and there were also international negotiations with East European countries to expand sales. Exchange rate policy was based on a fixed nominal rate, with import and export taxes and refunds that resulted in multiple effective rates. The exchange rate was maintained

at the same level even after the reversal in the terms of trade that started in 1974. As domestic inflation accelerated, the overvaluation of the peso became larger. From mid-1974 the government attempted to compensate for the rigidity of the exchange rate by increasing export refunds for promoted goods and reducing export taxes on traditional exports. This produced a very similar effect to a devaluation on the side of exports without increasing import prices. Consequently the volume of imports continued to grow rapidly.

An intensification of social and political conflicts followed the death of General Peron in 1974. A breakdown of the social pact took place in that year, leading to an open fight for the distribution of income. Inflation was out of control by 1975. In that year there was also a balance of payments crisis because of the deterioration in the terms of trade and the large expansion in the volume of imports. In mid-1975 a large devaluation took place, together with an attempt to reverse the increase in the fiscal deficit and in real wages. However, the government was unable to stop a process of hyperinflation derived from a heavy fight for the distribution of income.

By the end of the year the balance of payments crisis led to negotiations with the IMF to borrow under the oil facility and to borrow the country's first credit tranche. A credit of $250m. was obtained. There was also an expansion of short-term foreign loans (swaps) obtained under forward coverage by the Central Bank. A system of crawling peg devaluations was then established to maintain the real value of the exchange rate.

*Macroeconomic policies since 1976*
The stabilisation programme implemented after the military coup of 1976 aimed not only at correcting macroeconomic disequilibrium but also at producing structural changes in the economy by a process of economic liberalisation. The new government blamed the current crisis on large scale intervention by the state and a long period of protectionist policies (Canitrot 1980). It believed that protectionism resulted in an inefficient industrial sector, and in the development of very strong trade unions able to obtain increases in wages greater than increases in productivity; it also believed that the agricultural sector was adversely discriminated against and that this affected its level of production.

Measures to liberalise foreign trade included the reduction of import tariffs, elimination of agricultural export taxes[5] and a substantial decline in export subsidies to non-traditional exports. After 1978, overvaluation of the exchange rate had a major influence in opening the economy to imports.

The financial reform of 1977 reintroduced the full intermediation role of commercial banks, eliminated exchange controls and freed interest rates. The financial sector was to replace the government role in the transfer of income among sectors (Canitrot 1980). The financial reform and the elimination of exchange controls led to a relatively unrestricted movement of capital in and out of the country.

The adjustment mechanism implemented in 1976 to improve the balance of payments and reduce inflation was based on a large change in relative prices: a large reduction (of about 40 per cent) in real wages; the elimination of export taxes on agricultural exports; and the establishment of a very low external value for the peso (see Table 9.4). As the inflation level remained very high a price truce was announced in 1977 and a contractionary monetary policy was established between the end of that year and the first months of 1978. From May 1978 the exchange rate and the public tariffs were adjusted more slowly than inflation. From end-1978 the government decided to act on expectations by announcing in advance a decreasing monthly rate of devaluation. As inflation remained high, that decreasing rate of devaluation led to a large overvaluation of the peso during 1979 and 1980.

**Table 9.4 Exchange rate: Deviation from parity[a]**

(July 1968/June 1969 = 100)

| Year | Value | Year | Value |
|------|-------|------|-------|
| 1971 | 98.3  |      |       |
| 1972 | 110.4 | 1977 | 98.1  |
| 1973 | 84.8  | 1978 | 86.5  |
| 1974 | 84.9  | 1979 | 60.8  |
| 1975 | 94.4  | 1980 | 54.8  |
| 1976 | 139.3 | 1981 | 90.0  |

Source:  *Fide, Coyuntura y Desarrollo. Anexo Estadistico XI*, Buenos Aires, April 1982.

Note:  (a)  The deviation from parity is the ratio between the current exchange rate and a parity rate, defined as the exchange rate of the base year multiplied by the wholesale price index in Argentina and divided by the wholesale price index in the U.S. Values above 100 indicate that the Peso was undervalued, values below 100 indicate that it was overvalued, compared with the 1968/69 base period.

The exchange rate policy was abandoned when a new military administration assumed office in March 1981. Two major devaluations took place in the following months and the exchange rate was allowed to float from June 1981.

## 4 Impact of changes in the international environment and in national policies

*On the balance of payments*

The Peronist administration faced a very favourable international situation during 1973 and part of 1974. The balance of trade was highly positive in 1973 leading to a good foreign reserve situation. The higher income received from abroad was transferred to the government through export taxes on agricultural exports. The government used those funds to increase public investment and also the number and level of real wages of public employees. This led to an expansion in consumption and growth.

The good foreign reserve situation made it possible to maintain the same nominal exchange rate for over two years. The revaluation of the real exchange rate in the context of high protectionism was an advantage for the industrial sector which could buy foreign inputs cheaply.[6]

The reversal in the terms of trade that took place from end-1974, the quantitative restrictions on meat exports to the EEC, and the increase in imports encouraged by an overvalued peso and by expansionary monetary policy, led to a large deficit in the current account in 1975.

The policy implemented by the military government in 1976 led to positive balances in the current account during the period 1976–78. A low external value of the peso and a domestic recession created a large surplus in the balance of trade. The expansion in international liquidity and large international interest rate differentials caused an inflow of foreign currency. By 1978 there was a large accumulation of foreign reserves. This led some official commentators to say that the foreign sector was not a constraint in Argentina any more, or alternatively that the new economic policy had produced a structural change in the economy which made it less dependent on changes in the foreign sector.

The process of revaluation of the exchange rate, accelerated by the inflow of foreign capital, produced important shifts in relative prices and had a strong impact on the balance of payments. Imports became very cheap and expanded sharply in 1979 (64 per cent in current dollars) and 1980 (56 per cent). Tourism abroad also expanded very rapidly. Exports meanwhile increased by 23 per cent in 1979 because of favourable prices and stagnated in 1980. As a result there were deficits in the current account during 1979–80 and increases in the foreign debt to compensate for them.

There was also a change in the composition of imports and exports. Consumer goods increased their share of imports from 6 per cent in 1978 to 18 per cent in 1980, while the share of capital goods decreased from 29 per cent to 23 per cent. On the export side there was a relative expansion in primary exports. However, it is on the financial side where the impact was greatest.

*On foreign debt*

Particularly after 1979, there was a sharp increase in foreign debt contracted by the private sector which helped to increase the reserves to a record US$10.5bn. at the end of the year. The situation of foreign exchange reserves was rapidly reversed during 1980. A financial crisis in March[7] led to expectations of a large devaluation and to a severe run on the peso.

Those expectations were also encouraged by the large revaluation that had already taken place and by the uncertainties generated by the change in government in March 1981. A heavy loss of reserves took place at that time, originating in both the current and capital accounts of the balance of payments. In order to maintain the exchange rate and avoid further losses of reserves the government decided to attract foreign capital by increasing domestic interest rates, and to encourage foreign borrowing by the public sector to counteract the speculative outflow of funds from the private sector. As a result, the gross public debt doubled between end-1979 and end-1981, and the level of reserves fell sharply (see Table 9.5).[8] As Table 9.6 shows, the main cause of the big increase in foreign debt during 1978, 1979 and 1980 was the private demand for foreign currency and for foreign tourism.

**Table 9.5 Evolution of the foreign debt**

(in current billion US$)

| Year end | Gross foreign debt | | | Reserves | Net foreign debt |
|----------|-------|--------|---------|----------|------|
|          | Total | Public | Private |          |      |
| 1973 | 5.0 | 3.3 | 1.7 | 1.5 | 3.5 |
| 1974 | 5.5 | 3.9 | 1.6 | 1.4 | 4.1 |
| 1975 | 7.9 | 4.0 | 3.9 | 0.6 | 7.3 |
| 1976 | 8.3 | 5.2 | 3.1 | 1.8 | 6.5 |
| 1977 | 9.7 | 6.0 | 3.7 | 4.0 | 5.7 |
| 1978 | 12.5 | 8.4 | 4.1 | 6.0 | 6.5 |
| 1979 | 19.1 | 10.0 | 9.1 | 10.5 | 8.6 |
| 1980 | 27.2 | 14.5 | 12.7 | 7.7 | 19.5 |
| 1981 | 35.7 | 20.0 | 15.7 | 3.9 | 31.8 |

*Source:* Banco Central, *Memorias Anuales.*

**Table 9.6 Causes of increase in the net foreign debt**

(in billion US$)

| | Changes in net foreign debt | Trade balance | Non-specified transfers[a] | Other |
|---|---|---|---|---|
| 1977 | −0.8 | 1.5 | — | −0.7 |
| 1978 | +0.8 | 2.6 | — | −3.4 |
| 1979 | +2.1 | 1.1 | −2.3 | −0.9 |
| 1980 | +10.9 | −2.5 | −6.6 | −1.8 |
| March 1981 | +5.8 | −0.5 | −3.9 | −1.4 |

*Source:* Schwarzer (1983) *Argentina 1976–81.*

*Note:* (a) This item includes the outflow of currency caused by tourism and by purchases in the exchange market for an amount lower than $20,000.

A high level of international liquidity was necessary for this peculiar experiment of allowing a free outflow of private capital and an increase in foreign indebtedness in order to maintain an overvalued exchange rate. Meanwhile the country became very much more, rather than less, vulnerable to conditions in the external sector, contradicting the opinion expressed two years earlier about the independence of the Argentine economy from conditions in the external sector. A devaluation took place immediately the new administration assumed office in March 1981 since the situation had become unsustainable; the cost of foreign currency increased by 400 per cent during that year.

In brief, the effects on the economy produced by domestic policies after 1976, and made possible by conditions in the rest of the world, were a large expansion in imports, some increase in exports, a big rise in foreign debt and, as we shall see next, economic stagnation.

*On growth*
The favourable external situation in 1973–74 and the social pact on prices and salaries helped to produce an economic expansion based on a process of income redistribution and higher consumption. This process had reached its own limits by 1974 when the terms of trade began to deteriorate and new struggles over the distribution of income took place following the breaking of the social pact. By 1975 a falling trend in real wages and stagnation in exports and investment led to an economic recession that continued during 1976.

For more than twenty years interest rates were fixed by the government at usually negative levels as a way of subsidising invest-

**Table 9.7 Variation in real GDP, 1971–81**

(% change, constant 1970 prices)

| | | | |
|---|---|---|---|
| 1971 | +3.7 | 1977 | +6.4 |
| 1972 | +1.8 | 1978 | −3.4 |
| 1973 | +3.6 | 1979 | +7.1 |
| 1974 | +6.2 | 1980 | +0.7 |
| 1975 | −0.8 | 1981 | −6.0 |
| 1976 | −0.5 | | |

*Source:* Banco Central.

ment. The financial reform of 1977 led to periods of highly positive domestic rates. When the exchange rate was used as an anti-inflationary instrument, leading to a strong overvaluation of the peso, expectations about a devaluation increased and a higher interest rate was required to avoid a heavy outflow. Highly volatile interest rates encouraged the placing of money in short-term financial assets rather than in productive investment (see Frenkel 1979).

The level of domestic activity was also affected by the penetration of the domestic market by imports. During 1979 and 1980 imports, especially of consumer goods, grew rapidly at the expense of domestic output; industry actually declined at 3 per cent a year from 1975 to 1981.

On the other hand the non-tradeable sectors, especially the financial sector, increased their share of GDP. It is important to recall that this process of almost nil growth in GDP, in the second half of the 1970s, was accompanied by a large increase in the level of the foreign debt.

*On inflation*

The social pact established in 1973 made an important contribution to reducing inflation during part of 1973 and 1974, showing the big

**Table 9.8 Rates of growth of the GDP by sector**

(per cent)

| | Agriculture | Industry | Electricity | Finance, insurance and state business | Mining | Total GDP |
|---|---|---|---|---|---|---|
| 1970–75 | 2.6 | 3.4 | 7.7 | 1.4 | 1.7 | 2.9 |
| 1976–81 | 1.6 | −3.0 | 4.8 | 5.0 | 3.8 | 0.6 |

*Source:* Banco Central.

influence of social conflicts on the level of inflation in Argentina.

The economic policy pursued between March 1973 and June 1975 helped to isolate domestic prices from the effects of external inflation. The revaluation of the peso was an important factor. In addition, export taxes acted as a barrier between international and domestic prices of primary goods: in spite of the international boom in commodity prices in 1973–74, agricultural prices grew less than non-agricultural prices during both years.

Imports at that time were mostly inputs into local production so that price increases were transferred to domestic costs. To avoid this, preferential rates of exchange were granted for imports of essential inputs. The government also required that any increase in import prices should be absorbed by reducing profits. However, during 1974 the impact of external inflation was so strong that some firms began to violate price controls. World inflation also contributed to the expansion of the black market during 1974–75, adding new pressures against a weakened social pact. The breaking apart of that pact in 1974, accompanied by an expansionary monetary policy, produced an upsurge in inflation that went out of control by 1975. The large devaluation that took place in June of that year caused an abrupt transmission into the economy of the increase in international prices.

**Table 9.9 Increases in cost of living and wholesale prices, 1974–1980**

(annual percentage changes)

|  | Cost of living (Buenos Aires) | Wholesale prices |  | Cost of living (Buenos Aires) | Wholesale prices |
|---|---|---|---|---|---|
| 1974 | 24 | 20 | 1978 | 176 | 155 |
| 1975 | 183 | 193 | 1979 | 160 | 150 |
| 1976 | 444 | 499 | 1980 | 101 | 75 |
| 1977 | 176 | 149 | 1981 | 105 | 110 |

*Source:* Ministry of Economy. National Institute of Statistics and Census.

During 1976–77 the relatively low value of the peso (see Table 9.4) and the gradual elimination of export taxes on agricultural goods favoured the transmission of international price rises into the domestic economy. The large decline in real wages and a reduction in import tariffs acted as counteracting factors.

The effective revaluation of the peso from 1978 to 1981 protected the economy from world inflation. However, the prices of non-tradeables, which did not have to face competition from imports, rose rather faster than the prices of tradeables. This shows up in the more rapid increase in the cost of living index (which includes services) than in the wholesale price index in 1979 and 1980.

The policy of currency overvaluation may have caused a limited reduction in inflation. In addition, however, it caused a major recession in some sectors of industry. Moreover, it was only a temporary repression of inflation, since it was based on an increasingly unrealistic rate of exchange that could not be sustained.

## 5  Microeconomic policies after 1973

*The energy sector*
Argentina was in a relatively advantageous situation for facing the oil price rises of the 1970s, given the wide variety and abundance of its energy resources. The structure of confirmed reserves has changed. Coal accounted for 46 per cent of total reserves during the 1940s, but new deposits of oil and gas were discovered during the 1950s and 1960s, and hydroelectric and uranium reserves became significant. The discovery of a new gas field in 1978 increased substantially the confirmed reserves of gas compared with those of oil. Current levels of reserves and production would secure the supply of oil and gas for 14 and 50 years respectively.

**Table 9.10  Energy resources, 1981**

|  | millions of tonnes of oil equivalent | per cent |
|---|---|---|
| Oil | 341.3 | 12.2 |
| Natural gas | 574.3 | 20.6 |
| Coal | 80.4 | 2.9 |
| Uranium | 301.7 | 10.8 |
| Hydroelectricity | 1,430.0 | 51.3 |
| Vegetable fuels | 60.0 | 2.2 |
| Total | 2,787.7 | 100.0 |

*Source:* Guadagni (1982).

The current structure of consumption does not correspond with the structure of reserves. In 1981 oil accounted for 56 per cent of total energy consumption, gas for 26 per cent and hydroelectricity for 11 per cent. About 80 per cent of the consumption of primary energy takes place in the littoral area (the industrial centres of Buenos Aires, Rosario and Cordoba) whereas a similar proportion of energy reserves are located outside that region. As a result, the development of means of transport often became a serious constraint on the expansion of energy supply.

The policies pursued in the energy sector fluctuated widely with changes in government. During the period 1973–76 the role of the state oil company Yacimientos Petroliferos Fiscales (YPF) was expanded by the nationalisation of the sale of oil products. Energy policy at that time included some attempts at energy conservation, such as speed limits and restrictions on the use of private cars for particular areas of the city of Buenos Aires.

*Transport sector*
There was a large increase in real terms in the price of petrol during 1974–75. However, the real price of gas oil was kept almost unchanged in 1974 and reduced in 1975, increasing markedly the differential between the prices of petrol and gas oil.

The policy implemented from 1976 was mainly oriented to the development of oil with increased participation by the private sector. Exploration of oil fields previously explored by YPF, and new areas, were contracted to private firms. The oil obtained had to be sold to YPF at an established price. The oil companies were to be free to sell it in the market once the country reached the point of self-sufficiency. The sale of oil derivatives was also denationalised.

The energy plan for the period 1980–2000 encourages an expansion in gas consumption, because of the high level of reserves. New measures include a gradual reduction in gas prices compared with those of liquid

**Table 9.11 Average annual prices of petrol and gas oil**

(constant 1970 pesos/per litre)

|  | Petrol[a] | Gas oil |  | Petrol[a] | Gas oil |
|---|---|---|---|---|---|
| 1971 | 0.36 | 0.20 | 1976 | 0.44 | 0.23 |
| 1972 | 0.31 | 0.22 | 1977 | 0.46 | 0.21 |
| 1973 | 0.38 | 0.27 | 1978 | 0.43 | 0.30 |
| 1974 | 0.72 | 0.29 | 1979 | 0.36 | 0.25 |
| 1975 | 0.76 | 0.16 | 1980 | 0.39[b] | 0.25 |

*Source:* Ministerio de Obras y Servicios Publicos, (1981). *Programa del Sector Transporte.*

*Notes:* (a) Is a weighted average of high and low octane petrol.
(b) Preliminary.

fuels, and new incentives for the industrial sector to substitute gas for fuel oil. A project to convert nine thermoelectric stations into gas generated plants is under consideration.

The price established by the government for oil in the domestic market was lower than the international price of oil. The differential increased at the time of the second oil price rise (see Figure 9.1).[9] Among oil derivatives petrol prices showed a sharp decline in real terms after the military government took over in 1976 (see Table 9.11). They declined further in 1979–80.

*Impact of international oil prices and of energy policies*
New oil contracts with private firms helped to expand oil production by 14 per cent during the period 1977–80, but there was stagnation thereafter.

**Table 9.12 Production of oil and gas, 1971–1981**

(millions of cubic metres)

|      | Oil  | Gas    |      | Oil  | Gas    |
|------|------|--------|------|------|--------|
| 1971 | 24.6 | 8.117  | 1980 | 28.6 | 13.466 |
| 1974 | 24.0 | 9.427  | 1981 | 28.9 | 13.629 |
| 1977 | 25.0 | 11.663 |      |      |        |

*Source:* Secretaria de Energia (1981b). *Combustibles.*

Sales of natural gas increased rapidly during 1973–80 because of the building of new gas pipelines. More than 20 per cent of gas production (28 per cent in 1979) was wasted after extraction. Wastage is still high because of the lack of investment to reinject it in the wells or to

**Table 9.13 Consumption of energy by sources**

(per cent)

|      | Oil  | Natural Gas | Coal | Solid Fuels | Hydro-electricity | Nuclear | Volume (million oil equivalent tonnes) |
|------|------|-------------|------|-------------|-------------------|---------|----------------------------------------|
| 1971 | 72.3 | 17.4        | 2.7  | 6.3         | 1.3               | —       | 31.9                                   |
| 1975 | 62.2 | 22.3        | 3.4  | 5.8         | 4.2               | 2.1     | 35.4                                   |
| 1980 | 57.0 | 23.9        | 2.3  | 4.7         | 10.5              | 1.6     | 41.5                                   |

*Source:* Fide (1982).

**Figure 9.1**
**Domestic price of oil (sold by YPF to refineries) and price of Arabian light (in US$ per barrel), 1973–1982**

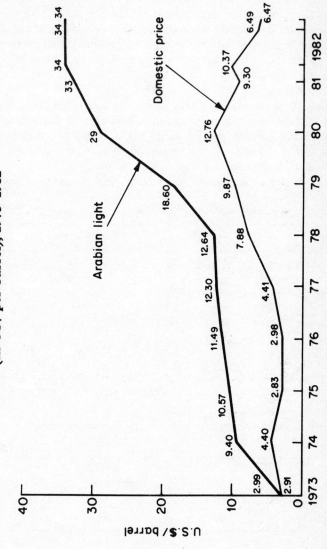

Source: Guadagni (1982).

distribute it by gas pipeline, while a similar amount is imported from Bolivia at high cost.

The expansion in electricity production after 1973 was mainly based on hydroelectric projects. Gas is also being substituted for fuel oil in thermal generation of electricity.

The recession during the second half of the 1970s led to a slower increase in the demand for energy by the industrial sector, which accounted for 34 per cent of total energy consumption in 1980. A continued expansion in the use of gas took place in this sector against a declining trend for gas oil and fuel oil.

The transport sector, which accounted for 31 per cent of energy consumption in 1980, also showed a slow annual increase in energy consumption (2.4 per cent) during 1973–81 together with a process of substitution of gas oil for fuel oil and diesel oil. Cheap prices for gas oil and petrol encouraged the expansion of road transport in areas of competition with rail and water traffic. There were not only more

**Table 9.14  Composition of traffic**

(per cent)

|  | Passenger transport | | | Cargo transport | | |
|---|---|---|---|---|---|---|
|  | 1970 | 1975 | 1979 | 1970 | 1975 | 1979 |
| Road | 84 | 83 | 88 | 49 | 56 | 52 |
| Rail | 13 | 13 | 7 | 14 | 12 | 9 |
| Air | 3 | 4 | 5 | — | — | — |
| Water | — | — | — | 31 | 21 | 20 |
| Pipelines | — | — | — | 6 | 11 | 19 |

*Source:*  Ministry of Public Works, *National Direction of Transport Planning.*

**Table 9.15  Car production by size**

(per cent)

|  | 1959/76 | 1977 | 1979 | 1981 |
|---|---|---|---|---|
| Up to 850 cc. | 24 | 13 | 7 | 2 |
| From 851 to 1400 cc. | 18 | 27 | 29 | 31 |
| From 1400 to 2500 cc. | 28 | 43 | 46 | 55 |
| More than 2,500 cc. | 30 | 17 | 18 | 12 |
| Total number of units ('000s) | 2,372 | 168 | 192 | 139 |

*Source:*  Adefa (1981).

**Table 9.16 Investment in public transport, 1977–1980**

|  | *Total investment (billions of 1970 pesos)* | *Percentage distribution: Highways* | *Railways* | *Water* | *Air* | *Others* |
|---|---|---|---|---|---|---|
| 1977 | 1.8 | 59 | 12 | 19 | 7 | 3 |
| 1978 | 1.6 | 49 | 17 | 14 | 16 | 1 |
| 1979 | 1.4 | 42 | 25 | 16 | 14 | 3 |
| 1980 | 1.5 | 43 | 23 | 27 | 7 | — |

*Source:* Ministry of Economy, *Public Investment Budget 1980–1989.*

private cars on the roads compared to public transport but in addition they were larger cars as the share of the smallest cars fell sharply. The expansion in road transport from 1976 was also encouraged by the distribution of public investment in the transport sector, with 40 per cent or more being spent on highways.

The energy problem in Argentina is perhaps not so much to increase oil production – unless there were a substantial increase in the level of reserves – but to promote its conservation and to make appropriate use of other energy resources. Conservation was not encouraged by the price policy adopted.

Energy price policy since 1976 has implied a virtual isolation from international oil prices. This was particularly so from 1979, when energy prices as well as other public tariffs were reduced in real terms as part of a policy against inflation.

The low level of prices for oil derivatives reduced profits at YPF, so that the company contracted foreign credits, not very long before the large devaluations of 1981. Those credits were not used to buy equipment abroad but to finance the domestic activities of the company (Index Economico, 1982). The current foreign debt of YPF was estimated in 1983 at US$5bn. – nearly 13 per cent of the country's total debt. Since 1978 the policy of cheap oil prices has been financed in the same way as tourism and other capital outflows – by an expansion in the country's foreign debt. The cost will be borne by the population during the next few years in terms of a lower level of domestic activity and lower real wages.

*The agricultural sector*
The Pampas is the most productive region in the country[10] with large comparative advantages at the international level. Its exceptional ecological conditions allow a high degree of substitution and combination between different uses.

Demand conditions in the international markets have a major influence on prices and levels of production of the Pampean region, as a large part of the area's production is exported. Production in the other regions is mainly for the domestic market and usually linked to processing industries. Their products do not enjoy international comparative advantages, but developed rapidly during the period of import protection from the 1930s onwards. Expansion depends on domestic demand. The main crops from the regions outside the Pampas are cotton, tea, 'yerba mate' and tobacco in the north-east, sugar cane in the north-west, grapes in Cuyo and fruits and wool in Patagonia.

Agricultural policies pursued by the Peronist government during 1973–75 (see Section 4 above) caused a transfer of income from agriculture to the industrial sector and the state. In addition, maximum prices were established for meat in an attempt to reduce fluctuations. Exports of oilseeds and edible oil were suspended during 1973–76 to keep down domestic prices. Other policy measures included credits at subsidised interest rates, and a prohibition on the import of nitrogen fertiliser to protect domestic production.

From 1976 to 1978, the new official market-oriented policy markedly increased agriculture income. On the other hand, denationalisation of the exports of cereals and meat made them more sensitive to variations in international prices. From 1978, agriculture lost some of the advantages granted to the sector in 1976. The financial reform of 1977 ended subsidised credit, and the overvaluation of the peso initiated in 1978 reduced domestic prices of tradeable goods, including agricultural

**Table 9.17 GDP of the agricultural sector**

(at factor cost, 1950 = 100)

|  | Cattle | Crops | Total |  | Cattle | Crops | Total |
|---|---|---|---|---|---|---|---|
| 1970 | 117.4 | 157.7 | 138.4 | 1976 | 139.1 | 188.4 | 164.8 |
| 1971 | 120.4 | 154.6 | 140.7 | 1977 | 135.2 | 200.7 | 169.2 |
| 1972 | 128.5 | 151.1 | 143.1 | 1978 | 137.6 | 205.3 | 171.5 |
| 1973 | 132.4 | 177.7 | 158.2 | 1979 | 138.6 | 217.2 | 178.4 |
| 1974 | 134.3 | 187.6 | 163.8 | 1980 | 129.2 | 206.0 | 167.0 |
| 1975 | 136.2 | 176.5 | 157.6 | 1981 | 127.5 | 223.0 | 173.1 |
|  |  |  |  | *Growth rate 1960–1981 (%)* | 0.75 | 3.20 | 2.05 |

*Source:* National Institute of Economic Planning (INPE).

products. A high tax on land established on a non-progressive basis severely affected small land owners. The regional economies were also hard hit by the end of minimum price policies and of credits to co-operatives for the sale of crops.

After a period of stagnation in the 1950s and 1960s, a large increase in agricultural productivity took place during the 1970s because of the incorporation of hybrid seeds and the development of the wheat-soya double cropping system. The sector grew at 2 per cent during the period 1970–81.

Good international prices for beef helped to expand the cattle stock during the period 1970–73. During the second half of the 1970s more land was used for crops, displacing cattle in several areas, in response to international prices and economic policy. In 1980 the USSR replaced the EEC as the main importer of Argentine meat and grains.

The area sown to soyabean increased rapidly from use of the soyabean-wheat rotation and high world soyabean prices. Output of maize and sorghum increased, despite lower areas sown, because of the use of hybrid seeds.

Agriculture outside the Pampean region, selling mainly to domestic markets, expanded rapidly until 1974/75. Thereafter, reduced real wages, the ending of minimum prices and peso overvaluation caused a big fall in real prices: for example the real cotton price fell by 50 per cent in 1980 over 1972–75. In addition higher interest rates endangered both producers and banks in some areas, causing reduced output.[11]

Cotton producers in the north, particularly the middle-sized farmers, were specially afflicted by low prices and high interest rates (small farmers made little use of bank credits). Middle sized fruit producers in Rio Negro were also hard hit; in several cases they were absorbed by the large fruit producers. The crisis had a heavy impact on the level of salaries and employment.

**Table 9.18 Sown areas and production of main grains**

(Area in thousand hectares; production in thousand tonnes)

|          | 1971/1972 | | 1976/1977 | | 1980/1981 | |
|----------|------|------------|------|------------|------|------------|
|          | Area | Production | Area | Production | Area | Production |
| Soyabean | 80 | 78 | 710 | 1,400 | 1,925 | 3,770 |
| Maize | 4,439 | 5,860 | 2,980 | 8,300 | 4,000 | 13,500 |
| Wheat | 4,986 | 5,440 | 7,192 | 11,000 | 6,473 | 7,900 |
| Sorghum | 2,759 | 2,360 | 2,780 | 6,600 | 2,400 | 7,550 |

*Source:* Ministry of Agriculture.

## Conclusions

The increase in international oil prices did not have a strong impact on Argentina as it is only a marginal importer of oil. Moreover, the balance of payments impact of oil and other import price increases in 1973 and 1974 was counteracted by the high price of primary exports. Some deterioration in the terms of trade took place during the period under study (25 per cent between 1971 and 1981) but it was less than for other non-oil exporting developing countries. A large expansion in the volume of agricultural exports compensated for the deterioration in the terms of trade and led to positive trade balances for most of the decade.

Domestic prices of oil were isolated from the evolution of international prices, with the exception of 1974–75, a period too short to produce important changes in the energy sector. Moreover at the time of the second oil price rise the domestic price of oil was reduced substantially in real terms in order to curb inflation. The agricultural sector expanded substantially during the 1970s but this was mainly a consequence of the introduction of hybrid seeds and the wheat-soya double cropping system.

It is on the financial side where the main impact of international conditions on the Argentine economy took place. The access of Argentina to the international capital markets on a large scale started after 1977, much later than in other Latin American countries. How effective was this Argentine response to the increase in international liquidity that took place during the 1970s?

During 1976 the military government pursued a policy of adjustment to the deficit in the balance of payments that took place in 1975. That adjustment was rapidly achieved, contrasting with the difficulties of reducing inflation. From 1978 the accumulation of reserves resulting from high exports, and large capital inflows, enabled the government to pursue an anti-inflationary policy based on import competition with domestic production. The increase in productivity in the agricultural sector and the expansion in exports contributed to maintaining that policy until 1981.

The new policy included a revaluation of the peso and led to a large increase in imports of goods, and of foreign payments for services such as tourism, and since 1980 to a heavy outflow of capital. A large increase in the foreign debt of the public sector took place from 1979. Unlike the experiences of Brazil and Mexico, the rapid increase in indebtedness in Argentina took place in a context of economic stagnation. In Brazil and Mexico, import growth was linked to capital formation. In the case of Argentina, the situation of higher international liquidity worked against the development of the productive sectors. The traditional relations between a high level of domestic activity and a high level of imports was broken. The economic recessions of 1978 and 1980 were not, therefore, generated by an adjustment to a balance of payments deficit but to competition from imports and high domestic interest rates. This was a new experience.

The consequences of the policy could not have been more negative. Apart from the social consequences of the long recession, the country will face the constraints on future growth and income distribution imposed by a foreign debt of over US$40bn. The financial reform and the lifting of restrictions on capital movements led to a process of 'dollarisation' of the economy, by which the reduction in domestic interest rates led to the purchase of foreign currency assets and increased the pressure on the dollar market. This close relationship between the interest rate and the exchange rate put serious restrictions on monetary policy and on the process of economic recovery.

The regions have been particularly badly hit by the policy pursued since 1978. Competition from imports for products like cotton, high interest rates, and the reduction in domestic consumption led to a process of land concentration in some agricultural regions of the country, because many smaller scale producers were driven out of business.

In spite of the heavy weight of the foreign debt it is clear that Argentina has other priority problems to be solved: notably the political future of the country and, in particular, the pursuit of a coherent strategy that can respond to the expectations of the majority of the population. The resolution (or inability to resolve) the political problem seems likely to have a greater impact on the future development of the country than developments in the world economy.

## Notes

1  This protection was reduced after the military coup of 1976 and particularly during 1979–80. As we will see, the opening of the economy that took place in those years extended the spectrum of tradeable goods to the industrial sector.

2  Exports can even decrease in this case because an expansion in income may encourage higher domestic consumption of agricultural products.

3  For an analysis of the political crisis in Argentina from this point of view see Portantiero (1970).

4  Meat prices decreased by 40 per cent during 1975–76 and the export volume was also affected by EEC policy. It took a few years for prices to recover to pre-1975 levels.

5  Export taxes were commonly used to keep domestic prices of agricultural exports at a lower level than the international price of those goods. Their elimination contributed to a fall in real wages because of the heavy weight of traditional exports in wage goods.

6  This effect was partially counteracted by the process of world inflation which was strong during 1973.

7  In that month three large private banks were taken over; they were liquidated later.

8  The large increase in the foreign debt during the period has recently been denounced as illegal and an investigation about its origin is taking place in court. Several statements have been issued condemning that policy. For example, Dr Jose Deheza, former Minister of Justice, has stated that 'a real looting took place in the country during that period by forcing public sector companies to contract foreign debts. The proceed of those debts were used to make possible the most impressive speculative outflow of capital in Argentine history.' He estimated that US$18.8bn. out of an increase in debt of US$22bn. were used to transfer speculative capital abroad (*La Nacion*, 18 February 1983 3rd section). Another case currently in court is about the 'vaciamiento' of Yacimientos Petroliferos Fiscales, the state oil company which was obliged to contract large credits abroad a few months before the large devaluations of 1981 took place.

9  The increase in dollar terms of the domestic price of oil during 1979–80 is only expressing the overvaluation of the peso that reached nearly 40 per cent in 1979. See Table 9.4.

10  The Pampean region generated about 70 per cent of the agricultural GDP in 1970–72. About 72 per cent of the total population live in this region.

11  A good example of this is the critical situation faced by the Banco del Chaco (in the province of the same name) because of the accumulation of bad debts against the cotton producers.

## Bibliography

Adefa (1981), *La Produccion Automotriz Argentina,* Buenos Aires.

Altomonte, H. and Guzman, O. (1980), 'Perspectivas energeticas y crecimiento economico en Argentina', in *Consultor* no. 34, Buenos Aires, Nov.–Dec.

Braun, Oscar (1970), 'El desarrollo del capital monopolista en la Argentina', in Braun, O. *El Capitalismo Argentino en Crisis,* Siglo XXI, Buenos Aires.

Canitrot (1980), 'La disciplina como objectivo de la politica economica', in *Desarrollo Economico* no. 76, January–May.

Cepal (1982), *El Sector Externo. Indicadores y Analisis de sus Fluctuaciones,* Chile.

Ferrer (1977), *Crisis y Alternativas de la Politica Economica Argentina,* Fondo de Cultura Economica.

*Fide, Coyuntura y Desarrollo* (1982), no. 49, September.

Frenkel (1981), 'Mercado financiero, expectativas cambiarias y movimientos de capital', *Estudios Cedes,* vol. 4 no. 3.

Frenkel (1979), 'El desarrollo reciente del mercado de capitales en Argentina', *Estudios Cedes,* vol. 2 no. 10.

Guadagni, A. (1982), 'Balance energetico general', in *Panorama Energetico Argentino,* Camara Argentina de Anunciantes, Buenos Aires, October.

*Index Economico* (1982), Interview with Dr Juan Bustos Fernandez (President of YPF), no. 49, December, p. 14.

Instituto Libre de Estudios Agronomicos (ILEA) (1982). *Situacion de las Economias Regionales.*

Ministerio de Obras y Servicios Publicos (1981), *Programa del Sector Transporte.*

Portantiero, J.C. (1970), 'Clases dominantes y crisis politica', in Braun, O. *El Capitalismo Argentino en Crisis,* Siglo XXI, Buenos Aires.

Santamarina, A. and White, D. (1980). *Evolucion del Sector Agropecuario en la Decade del 70,* Convenio AACREA, BNA, FBPBA, Buenos Aires.

Schwarzer, J. (1983). *Argentina 1976–81. El Endeudamiento Externo como Pivote de la Especulacion Financiera,* Cisea, Buenos Aires.

Secretaria de Energia (1981a), *Programa Energetico 1980/2000.*

Secretaria de Energia (1981b), *Combustibles.*

Teubal, M. (1975), 'Reflexiones sobre la coyuntura economica 1973–74', Annual meeting of the Argentine Association of Political Economy, Mar del Plata.

# 10 Kuwait

*Peter Sadler*

## Introduction

Kuwait traces its history from the end of the 17th century, when the area was settled by a tribe from Central Arabia. They elected their Sheikh from the Sabah family, which has provided its rulers ever since. For sixty years, to 1961, Kuwait maintained a Protectorate agreement with Britain, although it always maintained its independence and no British troops were ever stationed there.

Originally dependent on trade and pearling, the economy's transformation began in 1946 with the first shipment of oil from what is now known to be the world's biggest single oil field. Kuwait's modern history commenced from that date, and is inseparable from the growth in oil output, the increases in oil prices, and the assumption by the country of full ownership of the national oil resources. These were all responsible at different times for increasing GDP, but the really rapid increases in GDP commenced around 1974, with an increase in oil prices, then assumption of local ownership between 1974 and 1979, then further price increases in 1978 (see Table 10.1).

At the beginning of the oil period, the Kuwait Oil Company was jointly owned by Gulf Oil and British Petroleum, paying the country around US12¢ royalties per barrel of oil extracted. The total payments to Kuwait from 1946 to 1950 for almost 300 million barrels of oil were $36.5 million. In 1950 an agreement was reached to share profits equally

## Table 10.1 Oil production, GDP, and government expenditure

| | Crude oil production (million barrels) | Govt. oil revenues (US$m.) (% GDP) | | Government expenditure (US$m.) (% GDP) | | Gross domestic product (US$m.) |
|------|------|------|----|------|----|------|
| 1946 | 5.9 | 0.76 | | | | |
| 1948 | 46.5 | 5.95 | | | | |
| 1950 | 125.7 | 16.09 | | | | |
| 1955 | 402.7 | 281.70 | | | | |
| 1960 | 619.1 | 445.80 | | | | |
| 1965 | 861.5 | 567.50 | | | | |
| 1970 | 1090.6 | 784.00 | 28 | — | | 2769.20 |
| 1971 | 1116.4 | 963.00 | 30 | — | | 3252.00 |
| 1972 | 1201.6 | 1650.00 | 39 | 1040.70 | 24 | 4251.00 |
| 1973 | 1102.5 | 1795.2 | 34 | 1337.60 | 25 | 5328.00 |
| 1974 | 929.3 | 7094.9 | 98 | 3689.70 | 52 | 7223.10 |
| 1975 | 760.7 | 8641.2 | 73 | 3163.70 | 27 | 11902.50 |
| 1976 | 785.2 | 9802.8 | 87 | 3717.50 | 33 | 11214.20 |
| 1977 | 718.0 | 8963.10 | 63 | 4568.40 | 32 | 14145.50 |
| 1978 | 776.9 | 9373.00 | 61 | 6027.80 | 39 | 15266.20 |
| 1979 | 911.0 | 10990.30 | 49 | 6088.80 | 25 | 24409.70 |
| 1980 | 607.2 | 19626.40 | 71 | 8088.50 | 29 | 27494.20 |
| 1981 | 411.2 | 13074.40 | 57 | 9389.10 | 41 | 23087.20 |

*Source:* Ministry of Finance, Kuwait, Budget statements; Central Bank of Kuwait, *Quartley Statistical Bulletins;* Khouja and Sadler, *The Economy of Kuwait, Development and Role in International Finance,* Macmillan, London, 1979.

between the country and the oil companies, and in 1955 the posted price was introduced so that no matter at what price oil was transferred to a subsidiary of the main companies, profit would be assessed at the posted price. The average annual posted prices for Kuwait crude and the government take per barrel, are shown in Table 10.2.

Comparison between Table 10.2 and Table 10.1 shows how the initial increases in output first raised government income, then in 1973–74 how increasing prices achieved this in spite of lower output, then from 1974–78 how the increase in government take also had the same effect, and finally how further price increases from 1979 gave a boost to government income once more.

## The relationship between oil income, government expenditure and GDP

The changes of oil prices from late 1973 may be taken as a milestone from the point of view of the study. The posted price had declined from $1.79 in 1957 to $1.56 in 1961 and remained there for the decade. Only toward the end of the period did the government take improve, so that the proportion of the sale price of oil accruing to the government, 78.11¢ in 1957, only reached 81.34¢ by 1969. By 1973, the price had risen to

**Table 10.2 Average annual posted prices of Kuwait crude and average government take, 1957–1981**

($US per barrel)

|  | *Average posted price* | *Government take* |
|---|---|---|
| 1957 | 1.79 | 0.78 |
| 1958 | 1.85 | 0.80 |
| 1959 | 1.70 | 0.79 |
| 1960 | 1.64 | 0.77 |
| 1961 | 1.59 | 0.75 |
| 1962 | 1.59 | 0.75 |
| 1963 | 1.59 | 0.75 |
| 1964 | 1.59 | 0.79 |
| 1965 | 1.59 | 0.80 |
| 1966 | 1.59 | 0.80 |
| 1967 | 1.59 | 0.80 |
| 1968 | 1.59 | 0.81 |
| 1969 | 1.59 | 0.81 |
| 1970 | 1.60 | 0.86 |
| 1971 | 2.09 | 1.23 |
| 1972 | 2.36 | 1.40 |
| 1973 | 3.11 | 1.85 |
| 1974 | 11.48 | 7.47 |
| 1975 | 11.37 | 10.41 |
| 1976 | 12.09 | 11.10 |
| 1977 | 12.34 | 12.34 |
| 1978 | 12.2 | 12.2 |
| 1979 | 18.3 | 18.3 |
| 1980 | 29.8 | 29.8 |
| 1981 | 35.1 | 35.1 |
| 1982 | 32.3 | 32.3 |

*Source:* Central Bank of Kuwait, *Annual Reports* and *Quarterly Statistical Bulletins;* Central Statistical Office, *Annual Statistical Abstracts;* Ministry of Oil, Kuwait, *Petroleum Intelligence Weekly,* various.

$3.11 per barrel, of which the government received $1.85. After the 1973 meeting, the price was $11.48, with the government taking $7.47. It is important to note, therefore, that the oil price rises, while increasing the government take more than proportionately, did not represent a transfer of purchasing power to Kuwait of anything like the magnitude represented by the total increase in the oil bill.

In 1973 the GDP was $5,328 million, of which the companies received $1,389 million, i.e. 26 per cent. During the following five years, when oil output was gradually reduced, oil price rises were almost insignificant, but the government take increased successively in each year. In the second half of 1974, Kuwait, in line with the rest of OPEC, increased its royalty take from 12½ per cent to 20 per cent, and income tax from 55 per cent to 85 per cent. In December 1975, Kuwait terminated its agreements with Gulf Oil and BP, who jointly handled most of Kuwait's production through the Kuwait Oil Company (KOC) in which they were originally partners, so that effectively the whole of KOC output belonged to the government from then on. The increase in government take per barrel from 1974–1977 ($4.87) was almost as great as the price increase from 1973 to 1974 ($5.62), yet this point is hardly mentioned in discussions on oil prices and their relationship with the world economy.

In 1977, when Aminoil's concessions in Kuwait's share of production offshore the Neutral Zone were ended, Kuwait effectively assumed full control and ownership of all its oil. The effect of these increases in take would have been different if they had not been accompanied by the assumption of ownership of the country's oil by the government. Not until its ownership had been achieved could rationalisation and planning of production be co-ordinated with price policy. From 1973 onwards, crude oil production was successively reduced until 1978 as a matter of policy. Table 10.1 illustrates this. As there are considerable time lags between oil output and receipt of payment for it, the changes in oil production and in government revenues are not directly correlated for each individual year, but the table shows how income rose as a result of increased government take.

The period from 1978 to date is only different because of changed world conditions. The price rises of 1978, coming as they did after the final achievement of complete ownership by Kuwait of its oil resources, gave a further upward impetus to oil prices. However, changed world conditions, under which OPEC changed its output policy, saw Kuwait reduce its output by almost a third in 1981, while a large increase (18 per cent) in the oil price partially compensated for the reduction. This was in line with internal policy, however, as the conservation of reserves, in the face of increasing accumulation of foreign investments, was a declared intention. The fall of world demand due to recession affected oil prices *and* quantity demanded in 1982, however, and anticipated oil output for that year was much below the official ceiling which the country had accepted as its OPEC quota, 1.25 million barrels per day, or 456.25 million barrels per year.

Remembering that oil revenue accrues directly to the government, there is no reverse multiplier effect of taxation normally associated with government revenue through taxation. The increase in GDP occasioned by increased oil revenues has no effect on purchasing power within the economy until it is disbursed by government expenditure, and while rapid increases in oil revenues show almost immediate increases in GDP, the changes in government expenditure tend to smooth out the inflationary tendencies inherent in any such sudden jumps by increasing personal incomes much more gradually, having regard to both the absorptive capacity of the economy and the desired liquidity level. One of the features of the growth of the Kuwaiti economy, especially in more recent years, has been the consistently favourable balance on current account in its balance of payments. To a marked degree, these favourable balances have been invested abroad, whether held by government, institutions or individuals. Thus, investment incomes have formed a growing proportion of GNP, and during 1981 and 1982 have tended to rival government's income from oil in the government's revenue. The way in which these investments have grown is illustrated in Table 10.3.

## Table 10.3 Summary of balance of payments, 1950–1981

(Fiscal years; billion US$)

|  | 1950–60[a] | 1966–77[b] | 1978 | 1979 | 1980[c] | 1981 |
|---|---|---|---|---|---|---|
| Current account surplus (excluding investment income) | 4.76 | 29.7 | 4.77 | 12.20 | 12.62 | 7.07 |
| Investment income | 0.84 | 7.59 | 2.66 | 3.3 | 5.94 | 8.18 |
| Current private transfers | −.56 | −1.32 | −.44 | −.54 | −.70 | −.68 |
| Current government transfers | −.84 | −2.97 | −.80 | −.76 | −.89 | −.86 |
| Net current account surplus | 4.2 | 33.0 | 6.19 | 14.20 | 16.97 | 13.71 |
| (Oil exports) |  |  | (9.39) | (17.01) | (19.45) | (13.57) |
| (Government investment account) |  |  | (4.62) | (9.34) | (11.44) | (9.42) |

*Notes:* (a) Estimates.
(b) Summaries from Central Bank *Annual Reports.*
(c) Central Bank *Quarterly Statistical Bulletins.*

## Imports and export trade

As a traditional trading nation, oil development gave Kuwait opportunities to develop its internal trade and trade with the rest of the Gulf. The absence of any political and legal constraints enabled the economy to respond quickly to increases in demand, but early bottlenecks, especially port congestion, sometimes restricted supply of some goods. Thus, there was an appreciable effect on prices, which was only later alleviated as bottlenecks were cleared in the late 1970s.

The structure of retailing, too, has altered. In earlier years, certain import houses specialised and arranged concessions with large exporters in the industrial economies. This tended to restrict competition, and only in the late 1970s was there a noticeable increase in competition. This affected prices of retail goods quite markedly, but different types of goods were affected in different ways. The franchises for the larger durables were increased (cars, electrical goods, etc.). Retail outlets for other items proliferated, and new suppliers, many from 'non-traditional' market areas, entered the market, while low interest rates made stock-holding cheap. All these changes have blurred the relationship between import prices and retail prices over the last decade.

## Table 10.4 Import and exports 1971–81, selected years

(million US$)

|  | Oil exports | Other exports | Re-exports | Total exports | Imports | Trade balance |
|---|---|---|---|---|---|---|
| 1971 | 2578.2 | 25.8 | 77.4 | 2681.4 | 696.9 | 1984.5 |
| 1976 | 9225.0 | 199.5 | 548.3 | 9972.8 | 3366.9 | 6605.9 |
| 1981 | 14242.6 | 680.4a | 1381.3a | 16304.3 | 6962.8 | 9341.5 |

Source: Kuwait Central Statistical Office, *Annual Statistical Abstract*, 1981. Central Bank of Kuwait, *Quarterly Statistical Bulletins*, 1974–1982.

Note: (a) Division of total non-oil exports between 'other exports' and 're-exports' based on detailed figures for first ten months.

The build-up of oil exports to 1981 is evident from the figures in Table 10.4. The growth in non-oil exports and re-exports, however, which have shown an even greater rate of growth should not be overlooked. Oil exports increased by 452 per cent from 1971 to 1981, while indigenous non-oil exports and re-exports increased by 2,537 per cent and 1,685 per cent respectively.

The exports of manufactured fertiliser, until 1975, occupied some 60 per cent or more of total 'indigenous' non-oil exports, but this commodity was, in fact, a by-product of oil refining and can also be derived from natural gas and LPG. There is also some sulphur and acid contained in the 'other' category shown, so that in reality the 'non-oil' sector does rely heavily on the oil sector for its existence, although it is usually described as part of the diversification of the economy.

## Table 10.5 Non-oil exports, 1970–1980

(million US$)

|      | Fertiliser | Other | Total |
|------|-----------|-------|-------|
| 1970 | 11.8 | 8.7 | 20.5 |
| 1975 | 166.7 | 113.5 | 280.2 |
| 1980 | 91.5 | 297.0 | 388.5 |

*Source:* Central Bank of Kuwait, *Quarterly Statistical Bulletins.*

In the re-export category, the very rapid rise has also some relationship with oil, but in a different way. Here, the market is largely a 'Gulf' market, and the increase is a symptom of the rapidly increasing incomes of many of the Gulf states. But, on a note of caution, it must be remembered that from 1971–1980 the Kuwaiti dinar had appreciated by some 32 per cent against the dollar, so that some of this rise must be attributed to that factor.

### Terms of trade
It is hardly surprising that the terms of trade for Kuwait have shown more than average volatility. The most significant export being oil, the price of oil is effectively the price of exports. Using the IMF index for export prices from industrial countries as Kuwait's import price index, a standard terms of trade index is included in Table 10.6 as column 1; but until the latter 1970s part of the proceeds of each barrel of oil accrued to the concessionaire oil companies as mentioned earlier. This was eroded gradually, eventually terminating in 1977. If we weight the ordinary terms of trade index to account for this, we obtain an 'adjusted net barter' terms of trade index as in column 3 of Table 10.6. This compares receipts per barrel with import prices, reflecting the changing purchasing power of a barrel of Kuwait's oil.

However, the ability to purchase imports is not measured by the barter terms of trade but by the income terms of trade. These measure the changes in prices weighted by the quantities sold relative to import prices. This is shown in column 2, while column 4 shows the same index after a further weighting to take account of the increasing portion of a barrel accruing to the country, as in column 3.

Comparison of the four indices is instructive. While the first gives the purchasing power of a barrel of oil, the second shows how the decrease in oil output offsets some of the increased earning power occasioned by the price rises. Columns 3 and 4 show the picture from the Kuwaiti point of view more accurately, as they take account of Kuwait's

**Table 10.6 Some indices of the terms of trade of Kuwait, 1970–81, selected years**

(1970 = 100)

| | *(1)* Net barter terms of trade (Px/Pm) | *(2)* Income terms of trade (PxQx/Pm) | *(3)* Adjusted net barter terms of trade (Rx/Pm) | *(4)* Retained income terms of trade (RxQx/Pm) |
|---|---|---|---|---|
| 1970 | 100.0 | 100.0 | 100.0 | 100.0 |
| 1974 | 418.8 | 358.1 | 519.4 | 440.1 |
| 1978 | 372.9 | 231.6 | 704.8 | 511.0 |
| 1981 | 854.2 | 262.2 | 1614.3 | 577.9 |

*Source:* Initial data from: IMF, *International Financial Statistics;* Kuwait Ministry of Planning, *Annual Statistical Abstracts;* Kuwait Central Bank, *Quarterly Reports.*

*Note:* For explanation of columns, see text.

changing share in each barrel exported. Column 4 shows that in spite of diminished exports (1,000 million barrels 1970, 300 million barrels 1981) Kuwait's command over imports occasioned by its exports in 1981 was almost six times that for 1970.

It must be borne in mind that much of the income from oil sales did not enter the country but was invested abroad, and this may have had an immediate dampening effect on total demand. But, as the accruing profits and interests are added to income in later years, the 'Retained income terms of trade' progressively understate the changes in the country's total import potential as income from abroad, especially that accruing to individuals, increases the propensity to consume. The concept of the Kuwait economy must encompass foreign investments and foreign income as well as domestic activity.

**Monetary aspects**

The Kuwaiti economy has been characterised by its openness throughout the country's history. This openness reflects the earlier development of the country as a trading centre and has assisted the founding of many banking and financial activities which have stood it in good stead during the oil era.

There are no restrictions on inward or outward monetary flows. There are no income or purchase taxes, and no national debt. Hence the control of the economy, and especially of liquidity, has to be exercised through techniques different from those normally encountered elsewhere, particularly in industrialised countries. The size of the overall GDP depends almost exclusively on oil sales, while the size of the 'internal' GDP, if we could so call that amount of domestic product which is generated and remains active within the country's boundary, is dependent upon the level of government expenditure.

However, the creation of liquidity is quite different from its control. When liquidity is scarce, it can be created by government. When it is in abundance, the problem is more complicated, in that the government, the banking system and many of the general public all have the opportunity to liquidate large quantities of foreign assets at any time, or to borrow against them. Thus, the banking system can always create liquidity by adjusting its foreign portfolio, or by merely giving overdrafts and thereby creating spending power. This latter has hitherto been very prevalent in Kuwait, and although there have been many changes recently, the period over which we are examining the effects of inflation in Kuwait includes times when liquidity was very easy to come by. From 1973 to 1982 bank claims on the private sector grew at rates ranging from 24 per cent to 84 per cent a year, and at an average annual rate of 37 per cent.

From 1974 to 1979 the Central Bank was concerned with the absorption of surplus liquidity due to the narrow absorptive capacity of the economy, which was especially acute until the end of 1977. Activity included the opening of interest bearing accounts for banks with the Central Bank; this was discontinued in 1979 and replaced by Central Bank Bills. In May 1978 swaps were introduced to help mop up surplus funds, and also to create liquidity when necessary.

1979 saw a rapid acceleration of liquidity to finance an increasing level of imports, investment abroad due to increased foreign interest rates, and for the establishment of joint stock companies in the Gulf. To handle this, the bank:

(a) provided low-cost support to the commercial banks;
 (i) by discount and re-discount of commercial paper. The balance of discounts rose from KD 31 million at the end of 1978 to KD 195 million at the end of 1979; and
 (ii) by swaps, which rose from KD 11 million in January 1979 to KD 204 million in December 1979. However, the January activity was to absorb liquidity, the December activity to create it.
(b) prohibited KD denominated foreign loans from November 1979 to October 1980.
(c) made loans where necessary to banks against Central Bank Bills.

These measures had a direct effect and can be said to mark the beginning of the attainment of control by the Central Bank over liquidity.

The rationalisation of credit policy is one of the most crucial aims in Kuwait. In 1976, the Bank fixed maximum lending levels for individual borrowers and later allowed lower rates to be charged for borrowing for productive activities than for other purposes. In 1979, a scheme was introduced to decrease the ratio of overdrafts to other borrowing, especially secured loans, in the commercial banking system. Reduced targets were set for each year (e.g. 1980: 55 per cent; 1981: 45 per cent; 1982: 40 per cent) with the aim of eliminating the overdraft for general longer term transactions altogether.

By active encouragement of the banking sector, especially of branch banking, the Central Bank was able to maintain and spread its influence as an instrument of policy: at the same time this helped the diversification of the economy.

These matters are quoted at length to illustrate the comparative newness of policies and instruments in Kuwait, their different nature, and also the aims of the banking system generally within the context of Kuwait's development. Above all, the control of inflation never appears to have been a prime aim of any policy measure, rather it has been a constraint on the exercise of measures applied in the furtherance of other objectives.

**Subsidies in Kuwait**

The Annual Budget of Kuwait provides explicitly for a programme of subsidising foodstuffs, and some other items of general consumption and use. However, the main bulk of subsidies is provided through the supply of publicly produced goods at prices below economic costs. Notably, these are water and electricity, followed by petroleum products, housing, building materials, and public transport. There are also low interest loans available for approved forms of private capital expenditure.

The word 'subsidy' can be difficult to define. If the government provides cheap public transport and free internal telephone services, should we include the former and neglect the latter? Or again, is a free hospital and education service a social service, and the free telephone service a subsidised one? We will maintain the conventional approach in this study and regard the subsidised commodities as those shown, namely, certain basic foodstuffs, water and electricity, housing, some building materials, petroleum products, and subsidised public transport and other minor items.

The subsidies on foodstuffs were introduced in Kuwait in 1974 when

KD 4 million was allocated for this purpose. They were introduced to protect the prices of basic foodstuffs, especially for poorer families, at a time when the world prices of these were rising rapidly. They operate through co-operative stores and supermarkets. Each family has an allowance and only the quantities included in the allowance are eligible for subsidy. The rest is sold at market prices. The price for each eligible commodity is preset, and the co-operative claims the difference between its own costs and the selling price from the government. The ration allowances are most liberal, and are rarely exceeded by individual families. In fact, the total allowances have generally exceeded total demand. Therefore, only the subsidised prices of the commodities are used in the compilation of the cost of living index.

Table 10.7 shows how the amount spent on subsidised consumer items has changed since 1974. With the exception of meat, the subsidy on each of the other items has fluctuated from year to year rather than increased, so that the subsidy programme has turned out to be as much a price stabilising force as a price reducing one.

The effects of these subsidies on the Kuwait economy in general are extremely modest. They are felt most by the lower income groups. This includes the immigrant workers, who form a substantial part of the labour force (60 per cent of the population in 1981 was non-Kuwaiti). It

**Table 10.7  Amount of subsidy on consumption items**

(000 Dinars)

|                     | 1974   | 1975    | 1976    | 1977   | 1978   |
|---------------------|--------|---------|---------|--------|--------|
| Sugar               | 503.6  | 3548.4  | 2205.5  | 90.9   | 33.9   |
| Rice                | 184.0  | 1508.4  | 1514.1  | 141.9  | 879.6  |
| Vegetable Fat       | 233.8  | 677.7   | 630.5   | 69.9   | 866.6  |
| Milk Powder         | 9.7    | 481.5   | 504.8   | 103.0  | 4.4    |
| Fresh Meat          | 1153.1 | 1619.9  | 2250.0  | 3233.9 | 3895.5 |
| Fresh Milk          | 10.4   | 124.6   | 206.8   | 277.3  | 272.7  |
| Animal Feed         | 99.0   | 323.9   | 236.7   | 288.5  | 469.6  |
| Bakeries & Flour Co.| —      | 1500.0  | 3557.2  | 317.5  | 1522.7 |
| Other               | 55.2   | 415.6   | 601.9   | 521.3  | 482.6  |
| Total               | 2248.8 | 10200.0 | 11707.5 | 5044.2 | 8427.6 |

*Source:*  Ministry of Planning, Kuwait (unpublished).

*Note:*  'Other' consists of lentils, tomato paste, trashbags, tinned cheese, baby milk, baby food, milk, jam, tinned vegetables, vegetable oil, tinned fish and frozen chicken.

is thus probable that there has been a direct benefit to Kuwaiti employers by reducing pressure on wage rates, so that part of the subsidy has in fact been returned to the economy in this way. It is also probable that both by substitution and competition the prices of other commodities have been kept down. Although there is little substitution possible in some major items such as sugar, in some others it could be significant.

While some subsidies are provided through the budget, the major element in the subsidies is the supply of oil and gas to major industries at less than opportunity cost, and the sale of refined petroleum and oil products to the general public at lower than world price equivalents.

Prior to the assumption of control of its resources, the gas associated with Kuwait's oil production was flared. When part of this gas was diverted to use as a domestic power source its opportunity cost was nil. When the facilities were made available for gas liquefication, long-term plans, based on massive long-term energy uses, were already in train. The question arises 'what is the opportunity cost under such conditions?' It is tempting to base this on shadow prices derived from export prices.

But, first, Kuwait sells oil on the world market at a price and in quantities agreed with OPEC. When Kuwait is exporting at its maximum quota level the true value of oil must somehow be related to a future price which will apply at a time when quotas will not be operative. It would be pure accident if the OPEC price reflected that. When oil is not being sold up to quota, to divert locally used oil to export would be bound to affect the price.

Second, the government has only the alternatives of retaining oil underground, investing funds abroad or distributing them domestically. The maintenance of lower prices, thereby increasing real income and encouraging private investment, may be considered preferable to amassing foreign investment or to distributing oil income in other ways. In view of these considerations we would not support the generally accepted view that subsidies in Kuwait can be measured with any degree of accuracy merely by measuring the difference between domestic and world market prices.

Regarding the subsidies available on capital, these too may be regarded as part of a programme of spreading wealth through society. These subsidies have been criticised for their distortion of the economy from an optimum capital/labour ratio, but under Kuwaiti conditions, there is a need to make rapid advances in economic development during the oil era to provide some degree of diversification. Much foreign labour is engaged. When the development period ends, and if those foreign workers leave, the capital/labour ratio will need to be very high indeed for the economy to survive, so that a deliberately distorted current capital/labour ratio could be politically and economically justified if it reduced reliance on immigrant labour.

Electricity and water are considered together, as desalinated water is almost totally produced as a by-product of electricity by the multi-stage flash process. This source provides some two-thirds of total supply of potable water, and it is on desalination that major future expansion will be based. Although the fuel costs are almost always considered as part of the costs of electricity, this is not entirely valid, as water production does imply some reduction in efficiency of conversion of energy into electricity.

A calculation by the World Bank in 1980 (unpublished) shows that with oil at $31.50 per barrel, and basing the price of gas on an oil-price equivalent, the 'real' price of electricity would have been 37 fils (14.5 Cents) per kw. The prices charged were 2 fils (less than 1¢) for domestic users, and 1 fil for industry in the industrial areas.

Oil and gas resources used to provide water and electricity in the year 2000 will be a sizeable proportion of Kuwait's output. We could expect the utilisation of natural gas to climb from 150 billion to 675 billion cu.ft. This is almost equal to the total amount produced at the peak years of oil output (1971–74, when the annual gas output reached 687 billion cu.ft.). With lower output, and new alternative uses, there will undoubtedly need to be some restriction of gas usage or transfer to oil.

The subsidy on water is taken to be virtually nil, as it is produced as a by-product of electricity. As long as the supply of water is surplus to demand or, at least, capacity (without reducing electricity production) exceeds demand, then this may be a reasonable assumption. But if ever there is a shortage at prevailing levels of electricity demand, then other sources of supply will need to be found and a water subsidy will become overt if the current low prices are maintained. Under current conditions this may be not far distant.

The aim to provide housing for the lower and middle income groups has long been part of Kuwait's policy. Only Kuwaiti nationals as heads of households can benefit from the programmes.

The subsidies are in two main forms. One is the adoption into the Housing Authority's accounts of housing units at less than true cost, and the other is the repayment by the beneficiary of the cost of the housing over a long period at nil rate of interest. The true cost inclusive of land of a lower income group (LIG) unit in 1980 was around KD 21,000 ($77,500), but its book value was KD 16,000 ($59,000). 'Repayments' were from KD 6.5 ($24) to KD 15 ($55) per month. For average income group (AIG) housing, true cost included land and was around KD 38,500 ($142,000) while book value was between KD 30,000 to KD 36,000 ($110,000–$133,000), with an annual repayment of KD 780

($2,000). Thus repayments represented between 0.5 per cent and 2.5 per cent per annum of book value depending on the circumstances of the recipient, while the book value could be as low as 76 per cent of building and land costs.

If we look at the building costs above, and neglect the administration and interest element, projected expenditure by the Kuwait Housing Authority (KHA) for the years 1981/82 and 1982/83 were KD 100 million and KD 99.9 million (roughly $370 million). It must be recognised that those who actually receive a housing loan are the only ones to benefit; the large backlog of applicants have to rely on the open market. Although rents must be influenced by KHA housing provision, such a subsidy is not the same as one on food, where all benefit. It has been estimated that at 1980 prices the annual allocation for housing in the budget would need to be increased by 50 per cent to provide equity across the lower income groups and to remove the backlog in the foreseeable future.

Petroleum has always appeared as a small diversion from an enormous output, but with the increase in local demand forecast to be equal to that for electricity (10 per cent for the 1980s and 6 per cent for the 1990s), then the local use would eventually form a substantial proportion of the total. At such rates, the domestic usage in year 2000 will reach around 225 thousand barrels for petroleum and petroleum products or 18–20 per cent of 1980 output.

The use of the telephone for calls anywhere in Kuwait is free. Television programmes are also free, and reception is almost universal, given the small size of the country. Cheap bus transport is becoming increasingly available, but seems to be used mainly by immigrant workers rather than by the local population.

Subsidised foodstuffs comprise, on the author's estimate, about 150 of the 357 relative weights allocated to food. The other items (water, electricity, etc.) cover a further 59 points, so that subsidies cover just over 200 points of the total 1,000 allocated to consumer expenditure. Further, most have remained constant over the decade to 1982. There must be a further dampening effect in that several of the other subsidised items also enter into costs of transport, operational overheads, etc.

The 'subsidy' on such items as petroleum, electricity and water is so heavy that these items account for an artificially low total in the overall weighting system. But these subsidies are part of the government's policy of distributing oil wealth as well as its policy of price stabilisation, and as such do not have the re-distributional effects and consequences normally associated with subsidies met from taxation or government borrowing.

## Price changes[1]

Since 1973 the Central Statistical Office in Kuwait has been publishing a Consumer Price Index. This was based upon a standard basket, weighting factors, and scope decided according to 1972 conditions. Consequently the index was introduced at a time immediately previous to the price adjustments of 1973 which presaged fundamental changes in the economy. These changes affected the size and scope of the economy, the income per capita of the population, and also the range and diversity of the goods available. The structure of marketing was transformed, with the development of shopping areas and supermarket type stores. Consequently, the index of 1973, based upon 1972 conditions, rapidly became outdated.

A new household budget survey was carried out between April 1977 and March 1978 to derive a weighting system for a new index, which was introduced in 1982 with 1978 as base year 100. Although the 1978 index attempted to bring more items within its scope than its predecessor, there are a number of significant items which are not included, and would invalidate any comparison with cost of living indices in many other countries because of the items that are subsidised or provided free. Non-nationals are usually an insignificant portion of total population, but in Kuwait's case they represent a majority. While they enjoy most of the benefits enjoyed by the indigenous Kuwaitis, their expenditure per capita on some items is higher, for example housing. Despite subsidies, in the 1972 index food and beverages showed the greatest increase in the period to 1980, although the reverse was true for 1982 using the 1978 index. Housing also showed a high increase throughout the period.

## Table 10.8  Retail price indices

| *1972 index item* | | | *1978 index item* | | |
|---|---|---|---|---|---|
| | Weight | 1980 level | | Weight | Sept. 1982 level |
| Food and beverages | 371 | 207 | Food | 357 | 122 |
| Clothing etc | 145 | 188 | Beverages and tobacco | 13 | 164 |
| Household appliances | 26 | 180 | Clothing etc | 100 | 127 |
| Housing | 177 | 186 | Housing | 187 | 169 |
| Consumer durables | 140 | 169 | Household goods etc | 110 | 126 |
| Transport etc | 96 | 155 | Transport etc | 153 | 141 |
| Medical, education etc | 46 | 185 | Education; medical | 25 | 166 |
| | | | Other | 55 | 120 |
| Total index | 1000 | 189 | Total index | 1000 | 134 |

*Sources: Annual Statistical Abstract, Kuwait 1981; Central Bank of Kuwait, Quarterly Statistical Bulletins.*

While the retail price index base was changed during the period under consideration the wholesale price index retains the same base, 1972, throughout. Having a common base with the 1972 index for retail prices facilitates some useful comparisons.

If we regard food and beverages in the wholesale index as comparable with the same heading in the 1972 retail index, then up to 1980, retail prices for this category had risen 7.7 points more than the wholesale index by 1980. In clothing and goods for personal care the difference was 25.5 points in the same direction. In household appliances, if we compare these in the wholesale index with the same heading in the retail index, and also with durable consumer goods, the wholesale index rose 5.4 and 15.9 points more than the other two (we have no means of comparing medicine and stationery in the wholesale index with the retail index). If we examine the 1978-based retail prices index, it appears that food rose 21.5 points from 100 in 1978 to September 1982, whereas the wholesale index increased from 172.0 to 223.7 in the same period, or 30.0 per cent. Clothing and footwear increased 27.4 per cent over 100 for the same period in the former, and clothing, etc. increased by 19.1 per cent in the latter. Household goods and services increased by 25.7 points in the former and household appliances by 15.3 per cent in the latter. The changes in marketing structure referred to earlier cannot be discerned by comparing the retail and wholesale price indices.

As so much of the demand for consumer goods is satisfied from imports, and the chain 'imports – wholesale – retail' is very short, it is likely that import prices are generally reflected in wholesale prices, especially as competition has increased over the years in the importing sector. However, many importers are also re-exporters, and the changing economic fortunes in the Gulf, and changing oil prices, usually have some effect on their attitude towards domestic sales.

From Table 10.9, which compares retail prices in Kuwait with the cost of imports, it would appear that Kuwait did manage to keep inflation slightly lower than imported inflation. How inflation is introduced to Kuwait depends upon changes in the prices of goods it imports, which are determined both by the prices of goods which its suppliers export and on the comparative values of the suppliers' currencies and of Kuwait's.

While the weighting of the index of export unit values may not conform with Kuwait's pattern of imports, and the dollar vis-à-vis the dinar may not faithfully reflect changing purchasing power over the average import pattern, the general trend is unmistakable. Only in the years 1972–74 was there a steeper increase in Kuwait's inflation than in import prices. The later improvement reflects the economy's develop-

## Table 10.9  Import prices and Kuwait prices, 1972–81

|      | Import prices[a] | Kuwait prices[b] |      | Import prices | Kuwait prices |
|------|------------------|------------------|------|---------------|---------------|
| 1972 | 100              | 100              | 1977 | 160.3         | 152.7         |
| 1973 | 101.5            | 108.4            | 1978 | 173.4         | 166.4         |
| 1974 | 120.0            | 122.8            | 1979 | 201.2         | 178.2         |
| 1975 | 148.6            | 133.7            | 1980 | 221.9         | 190.5         |
| 1976 | 151.5            | 141.0            | 1981 | 220.0         | 204.5         |

*Source:*  International Financial Statistics; Central Bank of Kuwait, *Quarterly Reports.*

*Notes:*  (a)  Import prices taken as export unit values of industrial countries adjusted for (increasing) US$ purchasing power and Kuwaiti Dinar.

(b)  1978 and 1972 indices, chained.

ment over the decade surveyed, and also the development of instruments of policy and their administration.

## Other policies

For completeness, we should consider briefly the effects of inflation on a part of the Kuwaiti economy not yet covered, namely its foreign investments. After the price adjustments of 1973 the favourable balances on the foreign trading account of Kuwait increased enormously. Due to the lack of absorptive capacity, these were invested abroad, substantially in the world's money markets. The transfer of purchasing power which the increased oil prices represented was loaned back to the rest of the world. Interest rates remained low in real terms during the mid and late 1970s.

By the second round of price adjustments in 1978, the industrial world was roughly back in balance, as the inflated prices of its exports, both to the developing world and the oil producers, had caught up with the higher oil bill. Meanwhile, the oil producers saw a drastic erosion in the real unit value of their output and of the returns on the investments. It was the 1978 adjustments which saw a change in policy and an attack on inflation by the industrialised countries, just reaching a balance after the previous adjustments.

There is no doubt that these shifts in world conditions and policies colour Kuwait's attitude to its own development, both regarding its scope and direction, and its reactions to these shifts are evident in its policies. Whether to invest domestically or abroad, or whether to invest in real capital or the financial market, all have repercussions on the economy, and all are influenced by world events. The influences defy quantification but they are undoubtedly important. Investment in productive capital at home is far more attractive to Kuwait if inflation is eroding values of returns on investments abroad than it would be under stable conditions, just as it would be preferable if foreign investments in real production capacity were likely to be affected by anti-inflationary policies in host countries. But, whereas there have been sudden jumps or changes in policy abroad, Kuwait's reactions to the results of those changes have been more gradual.

We have noted the policy of Kuwait[2] to foster the development of the economy in the non-oil and financial sectors, especially by joint venture and private endeavours. The resources for this come largely from oil revenue which accrues to the government. Consequently, the release of those resources is governed by the consideration of the economy's absorptive capacity, the anticipated level of world inflation, and relative world conditions. These determine the government's view of the quantity of purchasing power it can allow to be available without generating internal inflation. Its aim is, in its policy formulation, to maximise the rate of development within this constraint (and some others such as population and immigration considerations). In this way, inflationary pressure would be generated only by that contained in imports, and whenever possible this would be alleviated by other means.

Up until March 1975 the Kuwaiti dinar was tied directly to the US dollar. Since that date, its value has been fixed by reference to a basket of currencies, details of which are not published. The value is agreed daily, and the strengthening of the KD since the early 1970s, especially against the dollar, has had an appreciable dampening effect on the level of inflation inherent in imported goods. By 1982, the Kuwaiti dinar was worth US$3.47 and SDR 3.14, compared with $2.80 and SDR 2.80 in 1970.

Inevitably, there is a cost associated with every benefit, and although the depreciation of the dollar against the Kuwaiti dinar may have assisted in keeping down inflation, other costs or disbenefits arise. For example, overseas investments, either in dollar-dominated stocks or in dollar-earning capital investments, depreciate in value and their relative earning power falls. Continual appreciation of the dinar can have an effect on both overseas investment and oil depletion policy, in that the first would be discouraged, at least in dollar areas, and the latter biased toward conservation when the investment return on invested oil revenues is seen to be diminishing.

It could be argued that diminution in returns on foreign investment would encourage investment in domestic projects, and thus stimulate diversification of the Kuwait economy, and to an extent this would certainly be true, especially as it would make purchases of capital equipment, on which diversification would depend, proportionately cheaper. On the other hand, given the open nature of the economy, the consumer goods produced would be less competitive and imports would be encouraged, thus adding a counterforce to any movement towards diversification, even that which is pursued as an active part of government policy.

## Conclusions

The previous sections have indicated that world inflation has impinged on inflation in Kuwait almost as severely as in any other country. Indeed, it would be surprising if this were not so, in view of the openness of the economy and the large proportion of internal requirements which are satisfied from imports. But, the way in which this impingement has been countered by public policies has resulted in a dampening of its effect on the economy, and the maintenance of an inflation level well below the average for industrial countries, and even more markedly below the level for developing countries at large.

With the lack of some of the more usual instruments of control, such as income tax, expenditure tax, and a national debt with extensive government paper in the securities spectrum of the financial system, the policies open to the government might appear, at first sight, restricted. However, this is not so, and their effectiveness has stemmed from the willingness, indeed the aim, of the government to fashion instruments and policies with the special requirements of the Kuwait economy in view. The problems of inflation, be they from imported inflation or inflation internally created, are borne in mind in the formulation of budgetary policy, monetary policy, exchange rate policy, commercial policy and even social policy. Furthermore the structure and circumstances of the Kuwait economy have facilitated the handling of inflation in this way without recourse to specific policies directed at inflation as has occurred recently in most of the industrialised countries. It could be argued such policies were introduced by the latter far later than they should have been, and that Kuwait's early and constant response to price inflation in its imports has stood it in good stead over more recent years. Also, the response could be integrated with other policies and combating inflation did not need to be a specific aim to which other policies would be made subservient.

Due to the type of policies adopted, there would appear to be very little 'subdued inflation' in the system, if the term may be used to cover inflation which is still present but which is only temporarily being offset. If world inflation subsides, so will the pressure on Kuwait, and there seems little of this inflation which might then be released. Kuwait is likely to receive and to pass on any benefits of reduced inflation in full to the country. The only reservation one can have is that the rate of development at present contemplated may imply such high future demands on resources, especially of oil and gas, to support continuing extension of these wealth distributing benefits, that the authorities may decide to reduce the level of their support and to raise prices of utilities such as electricity, water, and transport, and also of oil and gas themselves, as a means of rationalising total demand. However, this will not be influenced so much by world inflation as by considerations of domestic development and social policy.

## Notes and references
1  Based on interviews and information from the Ministry of Planning; see also, State of Kuwait Ministry of Planning, 'Consumer price index numbers', June 1982.
2  I am indebted to Mr. Salem Abdul-Aziz Al-Saud Al Sabah of the Kuwait Central Bank for informative discussion of the points in the next four paragraphs.

# 11 World Prices and National Development: The Case of Venezuela

*R. Hausmann and G. Marquez*[1]

During the 1971–81 period the Venezuelan economy was strongly influenced by events which took place at the world level. The reversal in oil price trends in 1971, the oil price rises of 1974 and 1979, the economic slowdown in the major developed countries, the rise in world inflation and the increase in interest rates in the early 1980s, constituted a set of conditions that influenced the path the economy took during the decade. In this paper, we will attempt to show the precise manner in which the international determinants mentioned above influenced economic policy choices, given the particular structure of the national economy. To achieve this goal we will start by characterising the type of development which took place prior to the period under study and which determined the configuration of the economy during the 1970s (Section 1). Next, international determinants (Section 2) and economic policies (Section 3) will be analysed. Finally, in Section 4 the impact on development will be discussed.

## 1 A brief historical review

Venezuela is one of the oldest oil-exporting countries. Oil has been its main export since 1925. During the 1930s, the oil industry stagnated but by 1943 the sector returned to a high growth path which lasted until 1957. Demand increased rapidly at the world level; and a new Hydrocarbons Law (1942) gave the oil companies greatly increased access to the natural resource in exchange for a significant state participation in the revenues generated. The pattern of growth during the 1943–1957 period was characterised by a rapid expansion of internal demand through public spending of the oil income. The pressures on the productive structure oriented investment to the non-tradeables sector (construction and public works, services, commerce) while the petro-dollars permitted a rapid increase in final good imports (see Hausmann 1981).

In 1958, the reopening of the Suez Canal, the world recession, the development of new oil fields in Middle Eastern countries, the 20 per cent decline in oil prices (which grew at an average rate of 6.8 per cent per year during the 1946–1957 period) and the Venezuelan government's decision to increase the oil income tax from 28 per cent to 45 per cent, precipitated an investment crisis in the oil sector which lasted until nationalisation in 1976. During the 1960s the value of oil exports stagnated, while the government's income could only be increased through devaluation (1964) and tax reform (1966). The government reacted to this new situation by imposing a rigid import-substitution policy (1960) which permitted high growth rates with falling imports (see Table 11.1). However, by the end of the decade the substitution

**Table 11.1 The rise and fall of import substitution growth**

| | 1957 | 1964 | 1969 | *Annual rates of growth* 1957–64 | 1964–69 |
|---|---|---|---|---|---|
| Non-oil GNP (billion barrels at 1957 prices) | 16.7 | 27.7 | 35.6 | 7.5 | 5.1 |
| Imports of the non-oil economy (billion US$) | 1.4 | 1.1 | 1.4 | −3.4 | 4.9 |
| Consumer goods imports as a share of private consumption (%) | 22.1 | 8.5 | 6.7 | | |

*Source:* Banco Central de Venezuela (1977).

process weakened and growth fell from 7.8 per cent in the 1960–65 period to 4.6 per cent in 1966–69 period. The government's dependence on oil income and the relative abundance of foreign exchange thwarted the development of the institutions needed to have an effective fiscal and monetary policy. On the one hand, the legal and organisational weakness of the non-oil income tax system and the financial obstacles to internal public borrowing have considerably limited the flexibility of fiscal decisions. On the other, the weight of foreign exchange reserves in Central Bank assets (89 per cent in 1981), the legal and administrative restrictions to rediscounting operations, the limits to open market operations – given the size of the internal capital market and the absolute freedom of international capital flows in the context of fixed exchange rates – made it impossible to have an effective monetary policy.

## 2 International determinants, 1971–1981

*Export prices*

Given Venezuela's dependence on oil, both as a source of foreign exchange and of fiscal revenues, the most conspicuous change in the relevant international parameters during the seventies was the reversal in oil price trends (see Table 11.2). This reversal coincided with the exhaustion of the oil production potential as a result of more than a decade of low investment in the industry. Therefore, the price increases in 1971, 1972 and part of 1973 were offset by a reduction in the volume of exports. It was only in late 1973 that a significant change in export earnings occurred. This rise allowed the government to implement an oil conservation policy which significantly reduced the volume of output. Together with the stabilisation of the export price this situation caused a progressive decline in real export earnings between 1975 and 1978. The second oil price rise permitted a 120 per cent increase in export earnings for 1981 with respect to 1978. However, the unforeseen oil glut in 1982 and the price and quantity reductions in 1983 caused the country to face its harshest reduction in earnings in more than 25 years.

The evolution of the Venezuelan oil export price was not only determined by OPEC and the world market, but also by a qualitative change in the structure of exports. The increase in the relative share of heavier crudes, a consequence of the exhaustion of traditional production zones and the rise in the high-sulphur penalty differentials, caused a fall in quality. In addition, the rise in local gasoline consumption increased the share of residual fuels in the export basket. These fuels are not covered by OPEC agreements making them more sensitive to market fluctuations.

Oil constitutes around 95 per cent of all exports. Until recently iron ore was the second export commodity. However, the government's conservation policy and the development of a national steel industry caused the volume of exports to suffer a 50 per cent decline during the decade. In contrast, the iron ore price tripled in the same period. Nevertheless, due to its small relative size, the balance of payments effects of the iron ore sector are negligible. The newest export product is aluminium, which has taken over second place from the iron ore sector and represents 2.1 per cent of exports.

**Table 11.2 Oil prices, production and export receipts, Venezuela, 1950–1983**

| | Price (US$ per barrel) | Production (million barrels a day) | Export receipts (billion US$) |
|---|---|---|---|
| 1950 | 2.12 | 1.5 | 1.1 |
| 1951 | 2.00 | 1.7 | 1.3 |
| 1952 | 2.11 | 1.8 | 1.4 |
| 1953 | 2.30 | 1.8 | 1.4 |
| 1954 | 2.31 | 1.9 | 1.6 |
| 1955 | 2.29 | 2.1 | 1.8 |
| 1956 | 2.30 | 2.5 | 2.0 |
| 1957 | 2.59 | 2.8 | 2.6 |
| 1958 | 2.48 | 2.6 | 2.3 |
| 1959 | 2.19 | 2.8 | 2.1 |
| 1960 | 2.08 | 2.8 | 2.1 |
| 1961 | 2.10 | 2.9 | 2.2 |
| 1962 | 2.06 | 3.2 | 2.3 |
| 1963 | 2.03 | 3.2 | 2.3 |
| 1964 | 1.94 | 3.4 | 2.3 |
| 1965 | 1.88 | 3.5 | 2.3 |
| 1966 | 1.88 | 3.4 | 2.2 |
| 1967 | 1.85 | 3.5 | 2.3 |
| 1968 | 1.85 | 3.6 | 2.3 |
| 1969 | 1.81 | 3.6 | 2.3 |
| 1970 | 1.84 | 3.7 | 2.4 |
| 1971 | 2.35 | 3.5 | 2.9 |
| 1972 | 2.52 | 3.2 | 2.9 |
| 1973 | 3.71 | 3.4 | 4.4 |
| 1974 | 10.53 | 2.9 | 10.8 |
| 1975 | 10.99 | 2.3 | 8.5 |
| 1976 | 11.25 | 2.3 | 8.8 |
| 1977 | 12.61 | 2.2 | 9.2 |
| 1978 | 12.04 | 2.2 | 8.7 |
| 1979 | 17.69 | 2.4 | 13.7 |
| 1980 | 26.44 | 2.2 | 18.3 |
| 1981 | 29.71 | 2.1 | 19.1 |
| 1982 | 27.47 | 1.9 | 15.6 |
| 1983[a] | 25.17 | 1.7 | 13.5 |

*Source:* Banco Central de Venezuela.

*Note:* (a) Estimate.

*Import prices*

Import prices increased at a rapid and sustained rate that averaged 10.4 per cent per year for the 1971–1979 period (see Table 11.3a). However, only in 1973 and 1974 and again in 1979 and 1980 did the increase exceed 10 per cent a year. These years coincide with two oil price rises.

Import price changes are influenced mainly by the behaviour of US and, to a lesser extent, European export prices (about 50 per cent of imports were from the USA in the 1970s). Since the bolivar maintained a fixed exchange rate with the dollar, the depreciation of the American currency added to imported inflation until 1980. Since then, the increasing value of the dollar has dampened Venezuelan import price increases.

Although the tendency of the general import price index is that of a sustained rise, the prices of the different commodity categories evolved in a differentiated manner (see Table 11.3a). Thus, although the general import price index increased more rapidly in the 1971–1974 period than in the 1975–1979 period, the price of machinery and transport equipment, which accounts for 45 per cent of total imports accelerated in the second half of the decade. On the other hand, the reverse was true of food, raw materials and intermediate products (10 per cent, 5 per cent and 12 per cent of imports respectively).

Consequently, relative prices suffered important changes during the decade. Only foodstuffs maintained the gain in relative prices obtained in the 1971– 1974 period (see Table 11.3b). In contrast, raw materials and intermediate products suffered such a drastic fall after 1974 that their relative prices in 1979 were lower than in 1970. Finally, machinery

**Table 11.3a  Average change in import prices**

(per cent)

|  | Foodstuffs | Raw materials | Intermediate products | Machinery | Total |
|---|---|---|---|---|---|
| **1971–79** | | | | | |
| mean | 14.1 | 21.9 | 10.6 | 10.0 | 10.4 |
| (std. dev.) | (21.5) | (63.1) | (38.0) | (12.3) | (8.6) |
| **1971–74** | | | | | |
| mean | 21.5 | 40.5 | 27.3 | 4.6 | 13.6 |
| (std. dev.) | (27.8) | (69.4) | (48.5) | (8.0) | (11.4) |
| **1975–79** | | | | | |
| mean | 8.1 | 7.0 | −2.7 | 14.2 | 8.0 |
| (std. dev.) | (11.7) | (53.1) | (17.9) | (13.4) | (3.7) |

## Table 11.3b The evolution of relative import prices

(Index, 1970 = 100)

|      | Foodstuffs | Raw materials | Intermediate products | Machinery |
|------|------------|---------------|-----------------------|-----------|
| 1974 | 121.8      | 156.1         | 127.0                 | 73.2      |
| 1979 | 119.9      | 90.8          | 69.2                  | 93.8      |

*Source: International Financial Statistics* and Banco Central de Venezuela.

*Note:* Based on an import price index constructed by the authors. Venezuela does not publish an import price index, so one was constructed from export unit values published in *International Financial Statistics*, weighted by the yearly country composition of imports published by the Banco Central de Venezuela.

and transport equipment recovered their relative price during the 1975–1979 period after a significant fall in the first half of the decade.

*The evolution of the terms of trade*
Because of the oil-exporting nature of the Venezuelan economy, the terms of trade increased fivefold during the period under study. This change occurred in a stepwise fashion during the 1973–1974 and 1979–1980 periods (see Figure 11.1). The present oil glut, produced partly by an energy-substitution process and partly by the world recession, caused Venezuela's terms of trade to deteriorate in the early 1980s.

*The evolution of international liquidity*
The favourable evolution of the oil sector allowed an eightfold increase in foreign exchange reserves by 1975. Then, the increase in imports caused by the internal economic boom produced negative current account results in the balance of payments during 1977 and 1978. Nevertheless, the country's AAA credit rating allowed a significant increase in the foreign debt without affecting the financial conditions of the loans.

By 1979, the increase in the debt, in international interest rates and a pessimistic oil price forecast (which did not anticipate the second oil price rise) induced the government to stop borrowing abroad. This decision was well received by the international financial community, thus preserving the creditworthiness of the country. However, in spite of the second oil price rise and of internal recession, which produced important surpluses in the current account of the balance of payments, the outflow of private capital, induced by the increase in international

Figure 11.1 Terms of trade, 1968–81

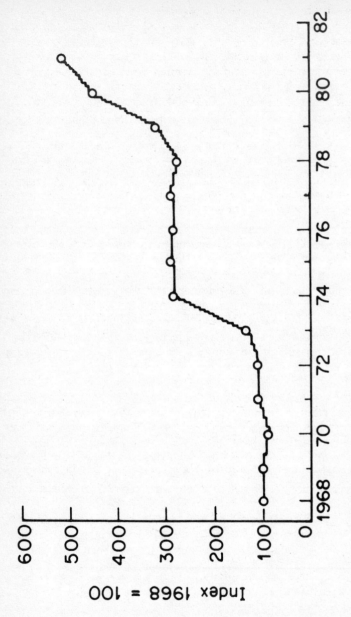

Index 1968 = 100

*Source: IFS* and Banco Central de Venezuela.

interest rates and by the recession itself, prevented a recovery of the foreign exchange situation. This forced both the private and public sectors to seek loans abroad. As a result, by 1983 the external public debt amounted to US$35 billion. In 1982, the fall in foreign exchange reserves (from US$7 billion in December 1981 to US$3.5 billion in December 1982, excluding the oil company's reserves), the decline in export earnings, pessimistic economic forecasts and the general financial instability in the Latin America area (Mexico, Argentina, Brazil, Chile, etc.) caused the nation's financial rating to decline to AA. In addition it prompted the Central Bank to revalue its gold bullion holdings (from $42 to $300 per ounce) and to centralise the oil companies' foreign exchange reserves which had been autonomously managed previously.

By February 1983, the fall in the oil price, the export quantity reductions agreed by OPEC, the intensity of private capital flight, the accumulated over-valuation of the bolivar and a poorly structured foreign debt (US$14 billion of short-term debt maturing in 1983) caused a collapse of the free foreign exchange system. In its place, the government instituted a complex exchange control regime with five distinct exchange rates, a system of import and price controls and a restrictive fiscal policy. It also entered negotiations to reschedule the external debt and stopped repayments of principal.

The poor structure of the foreign debt has been a consequence of decentralised borrowing by public enterprises facing financial problems, and has been accentuated by the requirement of congressional approval for long-term borrowing.

## 3 National policies

The problem of imported inflation, although used often as an explanation for internal inflation, did not constitute an important policy concern during the 1971–1981 period. Instead the maintenance of growth and macroeconomic equilibrium through import-substitution and fiscal policies were the principal concerns. The implementation of these policies had only an indirect impact on the manner in which the rise in international prices affected the internal price level. In order to provide a detailed analysis of the macroeconomic policies pursued, we will divide this section into four parts: the 1971–1973 period, the 1974–1976 period, the 1977–1978 period and the 1979–1981 period.

### The 1971–1973 period

Two major factors dominated the policies which had an impact on imported inflation: import-substitution industrialisation and the dollar devaluations.

During the 1960s, the social democratic *Accion Democratica* party had implemented a very strict import-substitution policy with outright import prohibition on goods which could be locally supplied. This policy was in fact institutionally necessary since the US-Venezuela Trade Act did not allow protective tariffs. In 1969, the social-christian party COPEI, which had always critised the import-substitution policy, took over power. The new industrialisation policy consisted of a relative weakening of protective barriers. This was achieved by transforming import prohibition into high tariffs. This change required the abolition of the Trade Act, a decision which was taken in 1971.

The switch from prohibition to tariffs together with the rise in international inflation during the period made the economy more sensitive to the imported inflation problem. Nevertheless, internal prices increased more slowly than international prices (see Figure 11.2) although at a faster rate than in previous years (2.9 per cent in the 1969–72 period versus 1.4 per cent in the 1965–69 period).

The second policy concern which had an impact on imported inflation was the revaluation of the bolivar. Since oil companies only exchanged the minimum amount of dollars required to pay for their local costs, maintenance of the exchange rate after the 1971 devaluation of the dollar would have allowed the oil companies to make local payments in local currency with the same amount of dollars as before. For this reason, the government revalued the bolivar twice, forcing oil companies to bring in more dollars. The revaluations were decided after each of the two dollar devaluations and amounted to a total of 4.7 per cent (from Bs.4.50 to Bs.4.30 per US$). This had the effect of compensating for the revaluation of european currencies and of limiting somewhat the impact of imported inflation. Nevertheless, by 1973, internal inflationary pressures caused the rate of increase of nationally produced wholesale prices to triple (from 2.7 per cent in 1972 to 7.2 per cent in 1973).

*The 1974–1976 period*
The 1974–1976 period was dominated by two basic concerns: what to do with the revenues produced by the first oil price increase; and how to manage inflation. The rate of imported inflation was seen more as the target for internal inflation than as a specific object for economic policy, given that maintaining internal economic equilibria appeared difficult.

The first question gave rise to what was known as the 'Great Venezuela' policy: big public industrial projects undertaken during the Fifth Development Plan. This policy broke with the government's tradition of promoting private industrial investment through distribution of the oil revenues. Instead, the state was supposed to transform the oil rent directly into accumulated capital. Therefore, it reserved for

Figure 11.2 Ratio of national to import prices
(wholesale prices)

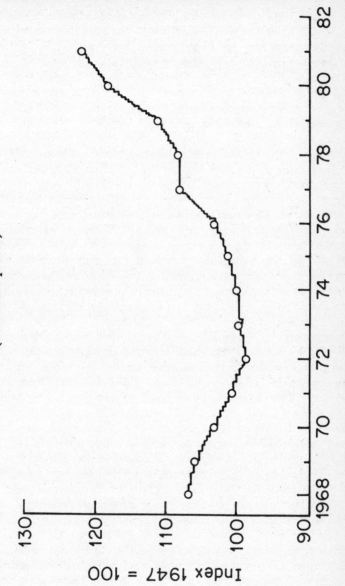

Index 1947 = 100

*Source:* Banco Central de Venezuela.

itself absolute control of industries considered strategic: oil, iron ore, steel, petrochemicals, aluminium and electricity.

The inflation problem was tackled through a set of policies: first, the policy known as *Represamiento* which consisted of an accumulation of external financial assets by the state in order to reduce the growth of internal demand, and second, a subsidy programme designed to reduce the rise in the price of the basic commodity basket, while guaranteeing producers' profitability in order to promote a rapid growth of supply. To this end, debt owned by all agricultural firms to public financial organisations was cancelled in 1974.

Another element was price policy. A strict price regulation system was enacted with the philosophy that costs had not gone up significantly, and that the demand gap should be filled by imports, which increased at a 40.2 per cent annual rate during the 1974–1977 period. Finally, within the first 100 days of taking office, social-democratic president Carlos Andres Perez made good on campaign promises to drive the economy towards full employment and to redistribute income. Two major decrees were issued in this respect. First, with respect to employment, an obligation was imposed on all enterprises to have elevator and bathroom attendants. Second, a general wage increase which varied from 15 per cent to 35 per cent was decreed. In a certain sense, it could be said that these policies accentuated the growing macoeconomic disequilibria of excess demand and manpower shortage (Marquez 1982).

In the context of the inflation problem, the big project strategy of the Fifth Plan was seen as appropriate since its high import content reduced the impact of investment expenditures on internal demand. Nevertheless, its impact on the labour market forced a liberalisation of immigration policy.

### The 1977–1979 period

During the period, a new set of macroeconomic problems appeared. While the government's oil revenues stagnated, the projected investments began to take place. The resulting deficits were financed by massive external borrowing. The explanation behind this policy was that the oil price was expected to rise, so that the debt would be repaid with fewer barrels of oil. The monetary expansion of the 1974–77 period (31.4 per cent per annum) had been based on the rapid increase in foreign exchange reserves, so that the fall in these reserves caused a credit squeeze. To deal with this problem, the government decided to continue with its policy of external borrowing. Furthermore, it enacted a set of regulations in order to reassign the banks' limited loan portfolios to certain priority fields, such as agriculture and low income housing, and away from consumer credit.

*The 1979–1981 period*
In March 1979, the social-christian party took over power and made a major economic policy change. Faced with growing public sector and balance of payments deficits and not foreseeing a change in the oil price (which took place a few months later), the new policy consisted of fiscal austerity and economic liberalisation.

Instead of financing public investment through external debt, the new fiscal policy was based on a drastic reduction in the level of government capital expenditures. Thus, while in 1978 the central government invested Bs.19,795 million and borrowed Bs.10,540 million, in 1979 investment fell by 45 per cent to Bs.10,945 million while borrowing fell by 95 per cent to Bs.493 million. Nevertheless, this drastic policy was unable to reduce fixed capital formation in state enterprises. Fixed investment instead grew nominally by only 4.9 per cent contrasting with a 30.8 per cent rate of growth during 1976–1978. To finance their investment projects, state non-financial enterprises borrowed externally, in a decentralised manner and under more disadvantageous conditions, a record Bs.11,572 million, showing the incapacity of the central government to impose such a major break in economic trends. In 1980 and 1981, the increase in public expenditures permitted by the second oil price rise was used to expand both current and investment expenditures (Table 11.4).

The liberalisation policy consisted of three major measures. First, food subsidies were reduced in order to reduce the fiscal deficit. Second, a generalised price deregulation policy was implemented under the triple assumption that the previous price policy had reduced internal

**Table 11.4 Central government expenditure, 1979–1981**

(million Bs. at current prices)

|      | Total expenditure | Current[a] | Investment[b] | Debt service[c] |
|------|------|------|------|------|
| 1979 | 47.6 | 28.9 | 10.9 | 7.8 |
| 1980 | 68.6 | 36.8 | 22.0 | 9.7 |
| 1981 | 92.2 | 48.8 | 32.8 | 10.6 |
| 1982 | 89.5 | 48.3 | 27.9 | 13.2 |

*Source:* Banco Central de Venezuela.

*Notes:* (a) Includes purchase of goods, services, the wage bill and current transfers.
(b) Includes fixed capital formation and financial investment.
(c) Includes interests and capital payments.

competition, distorted real costs and limited profits in sectors that needed investment. Third, an import tariff reduction policy was implemented with the goals of increasing internal competition, forcing companies to rationalise costs and limiting inflation.

In fact, these policies were abandoned by the end of 1980 since their effects were unexpected and unsatisfactory. Inflation rose from a 7.8 per cent rate in 1978 to 21.6 per cent in 1980. Faced with a rapid decline in real incomes, a generalised worker mobilisation secured a 5 per cent to 20 per cent scaled wage increase effective January 1980. Profits did grow in 1979 and 1980 in real terms but since aggregate real internal demand fell, private investment demand collapsed from Bs.18.9 billion in 1978 to Bs.10.4 billion in 1980.

Furthermore, the production cuts that took place in those industries most affected by the import liberalisation policy (e.g. textiles and clothing) generated significant cost and price increases, further weakening competitiveness and precipitating sectoral crises. By 1981, this caused a return to protectionist policies with outright import prohibitions for certain products and a 'Buy Venezuelan' decree for the public sector, including the oil companies.

In 1982 because of the reduction in fiscal oil revenues, the government announced a new austerity programme based on drastic reductions in investment and to a lesser degree, in current expenditures. However, actual spending was not reduced and the gap was financed through a reduction in government deposits.

## 4 The impact of world prices on development and macroeconomic behaviour

In this section we will discuss how international events affected national economic behaviour, taking into account the mediating role played by economic policy. We will analyse successively the impact of oil price increases, the rise in international inflation and the increase in interest rates.

*The differential reaction to the successive oil shocks*
The behaviour of the Venezuelan economy during the 1971–1981 period clearly shows that the impact of an oil price increase can be very varied. While the 1973–1974 oil price increase permitted a 10 per cent growth in GNP during 1974–1976 (see Table 11.5), the 1979 increase coincided with the longest recession modern Venezuela has ever known. Similarly, the growth rate during the 1971–1973 period (5.9 per cent) was practically equal to that of the 1965–1969 period (4.7 per cent) even though export earnings behaved differently (−1.1 per cent a year during the 1965–1969 period compared with +11.9 per cent a year for the

## Table 11.5 Growth and final demand, 1971–1981

| | (average yearly per cent rates of change) | | | | |
|---|---|---|---|---|---|
| | *1970–81* | *1970–73* | *1973–76* | *1976–78* | *1978–81* |
| GNP (oil excluded)[a] | 5.4 | 5.9 | 10.0 | 5.8 | 0.2 |
| Exports[b] | 11.6 | 11.9 | 16.9 | −4.9 | 16.9 |
| Imports[b] | 11.9 | 4.8 | 23.3 | 20.7 | −3.4 |
| Investment rate (%)[c] | 26.4 | 23.2 | 26.2 | 36.5 | 22.9 |
| Private non-residential investment[a] | 4.3 | 7.5 | 14.4 | 21.1 | −20.0 |
| Public non-oil investment[a] | 17.1 | 33.9 | 25.6 | 11.5 | −4.5 |
| Private consumption[a] | 7.3 | 4.8 | 12.7 | 10.0 | 2.5 |
| Government consumption[a] | 6.8 | 7.5 | 15.6 | 2.1 | 0.3 |
| Inflation[d] | 9.1 | 3.4 | 7.6 | 7.5 | 16.6 |

*Source:* Banco Central de Venezuela and Appendix.

*Notes:* (a) In real terms.
(b) Deflated by the price of imports.
(c) Non-oil non-residential investment as a fraction of GNP.
(d) Rate of change of the cost of living index.

1970–1973 period). Consequently, the impact of the oil price on growth can hardly be understood through a simple multiplier-type model.

The 1971–1973 period clearly shows the exhaustion of the import-substitution growth pattern. In spite of the oil price increases, a significant rise in the investment rate (from 12.5 per cent in 1965–1969 to 23.2 per cent of GNP in 1970–1973) and an above average increase in government consumption, the rate of GNP growth remained below the average for 1960–1969, which was a period of unfavourable external trends. In addition, a conservative incomes policy did not allow a sufficient growth of consumer goods demand, slowing the expansion of the leading growth sectors.

With the presidency of Carlos Andres Perez, incomes policy suffered major changes, as explained in section 3 above. The increase in employment and real wages fuelled a private consumption boom which exceeded 10 per cent per annum during the 1973–1978 period.

Nevertheless, economic behaviour during the 1974–1976 period and 1977–1978 was clearly different. During the initial years of the boom, underutilised capacity allowed an average 10 per cent increase in GNP while the rise in imports helped to control inflation without producing balance of payments deficits. In contrast, during 1977 and 1978 several different problems appeared which limited growth and disturbed the macroeconomic equilibrium.

First, the full capacity constraint and the appearance of severe bottlenecks and labour shortages reduced growth. Second, the rise in demand during the previous period produced a private investment boom, through a delayed acceleration effect. Added to the growth of public investment, this caused an expansion of imports because of the high import propensity of investment. Together with a decline in export earnings, this situation produced significant balance of payments deficits.

The monetary impact of these deficits had an important cooling-down impact, as well as the traditional income and demand effects. Since 1971, the rise in international reserves had become the major expansionary factor in the growth of legal-tender money. In fact, international reserves accounted for about 90 per cent of Central Bank assets. Given the rigidities in monetary management described in section 1 above, internal liquidity became highly dependent on the evolution of the balance of payments.

Thus, while during the 1977–1978 period the rate of growth of the money supply (M2) and of loans to the private sector declined significantly, the credit required by the private investment boom was growing exponentially. The credit shortage that ensued gave rise to the loan portfolio restriction policy described in section 3. Confronted with this situation, private non-financial enterprises undertook massive borrowing from international banks: \$4.3 billion for 1977 and 1978, as compared to \$0.9 billion for 1975 and 1976.

However, the demand-pull private investment boom reduced the financial solidity of this sector. Because of the price regulation policy, the progressive incomes policy and the labour shortage, private profits were held in check. Consequently, they were insufficient to maintain the rate of self-financing of investment, causing an increase in debt-capital ratios and in financial costs. Then in 1979, the stagnation in demand initiated by the public sector reduced the ability of the private sector to pay rising financial costs.

In addition, the tariff liberalisation policy reduced the share of domestic producers in the internal markets, further complicating the financial problems faced by the private sector. Furthermore, the price deregulation policy allowed firms to try and increase their earnings, which, given the stagnation in production, could only come from price increases. The rise in inflation further reduced private demand and precipitated an important economic contraction.

When in 1980 and 1981 the government spent its increased oil revenues, their overall impact was dampened by three major causes. First, inflation reduced the real internal impact of export earnings. Thus, while in 1981 government revenue was 87.2 per cent higher than in 1978, prices were 59.6 per cent higher. Second, debt service expenditures increased from $1.0 billion in 1978 to $10.6 billion in 1981 (see Table 11.4). Third, although government financial investments in state enterprises tripled in the 1979–1981 period to $5.4 billion, their current deficits and previous borrowing ($7.1 billion in 1979 and 1980) forced the new funds to be used to re-establish financial solvency, not for fixed capital formation.

In spite of the favourable trend in external earnings, private investment fell during the 1980–1981 period at a 20.0 per cent rate, due to the negative effect of the accelerator, to the weak financial situation of private firms, to the scarcity of credit and to the rise in international and national interest rates. Furthermore, the depth of the recession increased unemployment while the jump in the inflation rate reduced real wage earnings, thus causing private consumption per capita to fall. In conclusion, the incapacity of the public sector to transform the increased oil revenue into a demand for goods and services and the collapse in private demand explain the paradox of a stagflationist crisis at the same time as an export price increase.

The analysis presented so far relates the oil price change to the aggregate behaviour of production and demand. However, changes in the composition of the GNP were also fuelled both by income and price effects. Two major effects will be discussed below: the tradeables/non tradeables composition of GNP and the energy price differential.

When the first oil price rise made demand increase at an accelerated rate, supply constraints were felt throughout the economy. However, in the tradeables sector, supply could be increased through imports, while for the non-tradeable sector demand could only be supplied locally. Consequently, relative prices and profitability increased in the non-tradeable sector. This differential redirected investment to the non-tradeable sector causing it to grow faster than the rest of the economy.

In the crisis, the decline in demand was partly suffered by imports, making production in the tradeables sector less affected by the downturn than production in the non-tradeables sector. Thus the share of the tradeables sector declined steadily until the 1979–1981 recession (see Table 11.6).

Energy prices in Venezuela are about the lowest in the world. Gasoline prices were kept at $0.13 to $0.30 per US gallon until 1982 when they were increased to $0.30 to $0.86 per US gallon. The abundance of hydroelectric energy and the nearly-zero opportunity cost

## Table 11.6  Changes in the structure of production: tradeables/ non-tradeables

(per cent)

|  | 1970 | 1973 | 1976 | 1978 | 1981 |
|---|---|---|---|---|---|
| $\dfrac{\text{Tradeables}^a}{\text{Tradeables } + \text{ Non-Tradeables}^b}$ | 30.0 | 28.8 | 28.1 | 27.4 | 30.2 |

*Source:* Banco Central de Venezuela.

*Notes:*  (a) Tradeables: Agriculture and manufacture.
(b) Non-Tradeables: Construction, electricity, commerce, transportation, finance, services (government excluded).

of natural gas has kept overall energy prices at well below world levels. Consequently, Venezuela offers comparative advantages for energy-intensive sectors. This fact influenced investment in the private sector and was an explicit government development policy. Thus, steel, aluminium and petrochemicals became major public investment projects.

However, as shown by Porta and Rama (1982), these energy-intensive sectors are among the most capital-intensive and import-intensive, and they also require highly skilled labour.

This type of development merits all the criticisms that have been made concerning the type of technology and its social impact. But in addition, its non-viability in the medium run must be stressed. First, it requires financial investments which can only be made in times of dollar plethora such as 1974–1976. Second, the financial costs associated with massive capital investments are unaffordable and help explain a good part of the 1979–1981 large deficits in state enterprises. Finally, their long gestation periods cause serious macroeconomic disequilibria since for years large investments are made without adding to output.

### The impact of imported inflation
Contrary to most Latin American countries, inflation in Venezuela has been traditionally low, staying within the range of world levels. During the 1970s, internal inflation accelerated, raising the question of the origin of its determinants, whether internal or external.

An econometric study was carried out in order to test the relative importance of each source. The results suggest that internal causes explain the bulk of the inflation. Thus, the equation for the non-oil GNP deflator weights the internal and external components of inflation in proportions similar to their relative weight in the cost structure.

Nevertheless, imported inflation seems a more significant phenomenon as an explanation of nationally-produced tradeable goods prices.

Because internal inflation has been higher than imported inflation since 1975 (see Figure 11.2) and because tariffs are not levied on goods not produced locally, such as capital goods, the relative price of these goods has declined consistently, thus favouring the use of capital-intensive technologies. It has also promoted the continuous adoption of new luxury consumer goods not produced locally.

### The rise in international interest rates

The impact of the rise in international interest rates is varied. First, the increase in debt service has reduced internal demand and reduced the beneficial impact of borrowing. Second, it has influenced the policy on internal interest rates. Until August 1981, internal interest rates were fixed by the Central Bank at a rate which could never exceed 12 per cent. In that context, the effect of a rise in international interest rates was mainly to produce an outflow of private short-term capital. In 1976, when internal liquidity was growing very quickly, this outflow had a stabilising effect.

However, during 1980 and 1981 the decision not to increase internal interest rates, as an incentive for investment, caused such an outflow of capital that credit availability was curtailed, reducing investment. The decision to free interest rates in August 1981 caused the internal rate to rise about three points above international levels. Nevertheless, the outflow of private capital has continued, and even grown, because the fall in foreign exchange reserves led to expectations of a bolivar devaluation.

Econometric studies suggest that the influence of interest rates on corporate investment in the 1971–1981 period is not significant, while the effect of the increase in the volume of credit seems greater. In contrast, the rise in interest rates does seem to affect residential investment.

### Concluding remarks

The economic changes suffered by the Venezuelan economy during the 1971–1981 period have culminated in a long inflationary stagnation. While during the 1960s the growth rate was high in spite of falling real external earnings, the present oil glut has caused a major contraction of non-oil GNP, privately estimated at 2 per cent for 1983 and −3 per cent for 1984. Moreover, there seems to be a need for major reforms in economic policy before any durable return to a growth path can be expected.

The protectionist industrialisation policy permits neither a reduction in imports nor an expansion of production in the context of a stagnant external income. Moreover, the chronic diseconomies of scale aggravated by a tendency of firms to overdiversify their production basket, in a market determined by a highly skewed income distribution (Escobar and Hausmann 1981) have caused a long-run stagnation of industrial productivity.

Furthermore, the increase in internal inflation and the widening gap in productivity, have produced industrial price differentials compared with the world market which vary from 100 per cent to 300 per cent. In this context, the implementation of an effective protection becomes ever more difficult as smuggling profits increase. The market is increasingly penetrated by imported final goods limiting the output of industrial firms which no longer seek to become internationally competitive, but simply attempt to maintain their share in the local market.

The liberal solution to this problem, attempted in 1979, failed because firms reacted to the cuts in production caused by their reduced share of the market with an increase in prices, thus further weakening competitiveness and threatening to cause massive industrial bankruptcies. The return to protectionism decided in 1981 clearly shows that such a policy has lost its progressive role, being defended only as a lesser evil.

Public sector industrialisation policy has encountered major failures (see Hausmann and Marquez 1981). The choice of capital-intensive, technology intensive sectors such as steel, aluminium and petrochemicals seems questionable. Not only are these industries in crisis at the world scale, but in addition, they require capital investments which have been unaffordable since 1977. Furthermore, the complex organisation they require and the politics surrounding their prices have prevented state enterprises from operating profitably. The increase in their debt/capital ratio finally choked investment.

The state's fiscal policy, which concentrated on oil taxes to finance public investment is no longer viable. With the perspective of a stagnant oil income, the problem today is how to finance the growing need for public services. The current tax laws are unable to do so. Yet there has been no political consensus to face this situation. Instead, attention has been centred on government waste, clearly not a source of revenue in the long-run.

Monetary policy also needs major reforms. Venezuela is unable to create the internal means of payment necessary to finance growth unless foreign exchange reserves rise (Hausmann 1981). Present prospects suggest that this condition will not be fulfilled. Therefore, any attempt to return to a growth path without a monetary reform will face a liquidity shortage. Mechanisms to ease internal public debt and rediscounting would be needed, but have not been proposed.

The overvaluation of the bolivar had a serious impact on growth. On the one hand, it reduced the real internal effect of the oil income, while on the other it reduced the share of local production in the internal market. The intensity of private capital outflows in spite of internal interest rates above world levels, the reduction in export earnings and the tightening of international liquidity finally caused a major devaluation and the collapse of the free exchange system.

The severity of the crisis and the weakness of government decisions ahead of elections in December 1983 suggest that the major policy changes have yet to occur. The future of the Venezuelan economy will depend decisively on the choices to be taken at that time.

**Note**
1   We would like to thank Silvia Fernandez and Roberto Smith for computer calculations.

**References**
Banco Central de Venezuela, *Informe Economico,* various years, Caracas.
Banco Central de Venezuela, 1977, *Economia Venezolana en los Ultimos Treinta y Cinco Anos,* Caracas.
Boyer, R. and Mistral, J., 1978, *Accumulation, Inflation, Crisis,* PUF, Paris.
Escobar, G. and Hausmann, R., 1981, 'La productividad en la industria manufacturera Venezolana, 1971–1980', Consejo National de Recursos Humanos, Caracas (mimeo).
Hausmann, R., 1981, 'State landed property, oil rent and accumulation in the Venezuelan economy', Ph.D. thesis, Cornell University.
Hausmann, R., 1982, 'Acumulacion y crisis en una economia petrolera: El caso de Venezuela, CENDES, Caracas (mimeo).
Hausmann, R. and Marquez, G., 1981, 'Analisis critico del VI Plan a la luz del metodo Formeplan', CENDES, Caracas (mimeo).
Porta, F. and Rama, C., 1982, El diferencial energetico, CENDES, Caracas (mimeo).

# 12 Imported Inflation and Imported Growth: The Case of Tunisia's Studied Postponement

*Philip Mishalani*

## Introduction: Unbalanced growth in a mixed economy

Tunisia is the smallest North African Arab country in area (164,000 sq.km.). By the end of the 1970s, its population had reached over 6 million, providing it with a small domestic market. Population growth was somewhat high at an annual average of 2.1 per cent during the decade. Because 47 per cent of its land is agricultural, Tunisia has a favourable population density on agricultural land (78.7 sq.km.) relative to other middle income Arab countries (442.7), or even Latin American ones (94.5). It also benefits from its Mediterranean coast which provides easy and relatively inexpensive transport connections with its main trading partners in Europe. The World Bank classifies Tunisia as a middle-income country; in 1980 and 1981 it rated it as one of the top performers in that group of countries.[1]

Tunisia's development, however, has been marked by continuous structural imbalance. Despite the existence of large phosphate deposits in the desert-like south, economic activity is concentrated in the north, which contains most of the arable land, where cash crops (olives and grapes) are cultivated and rainfall is abundant. Moreover, out of 18 governorates, Tunis (named after the capital) accounts for 48 per cent of the number of industrial establishments and 58 per cent of industrial wage costs.[2]

Population density within the country follows the same pattern. At the extremes, the governorate of Gabes in the south has 9 people per sq.km., while that of Tunis has 708 per sq.km., with the capital itself having 32,185.[3] Internal migration is not only from rural to urban areas, but also between urban centres in favour of large towns in the north, especially the capital. Very rapid urbanisation has led to relative depopulation of the countryside, reflected by a 0.5 per cent average annual population growth in the rural sector between 1966 and 1975, in contrast to 3.8 per cent for the urban areas.

Structural change in Tunisia took place in the context of two distinct periods of the country's political economy. After independence in 1956, the public sector had to compensate for a Tunisian private sector kept weak by French rule. Agriculture, then the major sector, was dominated by the French who represented 7.4 per cent of the total population, but accounted for 40 per cent of agricultural output.[4] But an even heavier role was played by the public sector in the 1960s, the decade associated with the collectivist strategy of the prime minister, Ahmad Ben Salah.

Ben Salah Tunisified the economy, attempting self reliance and agricultural collectivisation along with rapid industrialisation, i.e. import substitution and protection on the one hand, but a heavy import requirement of capital and intermediary goods on the other.[5] This strategy ran into substantial domestic difficulties with the merchants (the majority of the bourgeoisie), who disliked the acute shortage of imported consumer goods, and with the peasants, who did not respond to collectivisation. But it ultimately collapsed due to financial problems. National savings financed little more than half of investment throughout the decade and the growing trade deficit could not be balanced by the two areas developed for that purpose, petroleum exports and tourism.[6] Both were relatively new industries and the international price of oil during that period was still very low. This forced dependence on foreign finance, which grew at an average of 17 per cent per year between 1961 and 1969, largely from official Western sources. In 1969 53 per cent of the drawings were from the USA, 16 per cent from the World Bank, 11 per cent from France, 9 per cent from West Germany and 6 per cent from Italy.[7]

The 'international environment' of the 1960s, relevant in particular to the price of petroleum exports and the external sources of finance, did not permit Tunisia to sustain its development strategy. It is noteworthy that shortly before the fall of Ben Salah in 1969, there was a serious disagreement with the World Bank over its refusal to finance the co-operatives programme in agriculture. The Bank along with other western financial sources disapproved of the 'collectivist' aspects of Tunisia's development strategy.

With the 1970s began the second period of Tunisia's political economy. Elements of continuity with the previous period existed. The foundations laid in the 1960s allowed a vigorous continuation of industrialisation. But changes took place towards liberalisation of import controls, greater private sector involvement and, at least in intention, more investment and concern for agriculture. Within industry the shift was towards an export promotion strategy, which changed Tunisia's position in the international division of labour. International subcontracting was initiated in 1972. Law 72–38 was passed, allowing foreign capital exceptional fiscal and commercial advantages including an industrial free zone, exclusively for export production. In 1974, Law 74–74 was passed giving special advantages for Tunisian manufacturers producing for export.[8]

The economy that emerged in the 1970s was one whose production and employment structure was dominated by services, construction and, increasingly, manufacturing (see Table 12.1). This coincided with strong regional concentration and urban bias. The economy became increasingly open with exports and imports accounting for over 70 per cent of GDP (1971–81) compared with less than 50 per cent in the previous decade (1961–70). Despite its net export position in fruits, vegetables, vegetable (olive) oils and seafood, Tunisia remained an overall net food importer, especially in cereals, meat and dairy products. The 1970s were especially characterised by Tunisia's considerable

**Table 12.1 Main economic structure of Tunisia, 1979**

(per cent composition)

|  | GDP at factor cost | Employment | Export of goods and non factor services |
|---|---|---|---|
| Agriculture | 16.2 | 35.0 | 3.0 |
| Energy and mining | 12.1 | 1.8 | 34.1 |
| Manufacturing | 12.1 | 21.8 | 29.3 |
| Tourism | 4.8 | 1.5 | 20.1 |
| Construction and services | 31.2 | 25.4 | 13.5 |
| Government services | 13.6 | 14.5 | — |
| Total | 100.0 | 100.0 | 100.0 |

*Source:* Ministry of Planning and Finance and IBRD, 1981.

exports of phosphates and fertilisers, as well as a modest net export position in energy, on account of high grade, but limited, oil deposits. Otherwise the country retained its large deficit in capital goods and durables.

Unemployment and underemployment in Tunisia have been estimated at 25 per cent of the labour force. This has been the long-standing problem facing the country's development. International migration has also been a quasi-permanent feature of the country, but it does not seem to have averted the pressure of unemployment. This facet is partly explained by the structure of growth. The most dynamic sectors of the 1970s, energy, mining and tourism, have generated little employment (see Table 12.1). These sectors have held a strategic position for exports, savings and public revenue. They accounted for over half the country's foreign exchange during the decade. Despite its declining share of GDP, agriculture remains crucial for Tunisia partly because it still accounts for over a third of employment (Table 12.1). Planners also regard its performance as a barometer of the economy's health, not only due to the importance of restraining rural-urban migration and expanding domestic food supplies, but also because of the centrality of key agricultural exports, largely olive oil.

Compared to most LDCs, Tunisia has developed socio-economic institutions of reasonable standing. It has elaborated a planning process on which it relies quite seriously, with six development plans to date. Trade unions are established institutions wielding recognised power. In spite of that, however, available data on income distribution does not reveal notable improvements. A comparison between the 1966 and 1975 consumption surveys shows a worsening expenditure distribution for the lowest 20 and 40 per cent of the population, while the top 20 per cent achieved significant improvements.

## The internal and international determinants of inflation and growth

### The importance of 'internal shocks'
Imported inflation in Tunisia during the 1970s occurred in the context of a generally favourable 'international environment'. This is somewhat exceptional. As Griffith-Jones has shown[9] the terms of trade and cost of borrowing elements of this environment were not good for most LDCs.

Tunisia's positive performance is partly reflected in the moderate increase during the 1970s of the rate of coverage of imports by exports (Table 12.2). This however conceals important differences in the price and volume trends of exports and imports. Tunisia benefited during the decade from an average annual gain of 2.5 per cent in its terms of trade, which contrasts with the 2.2 per cent yearly loss during the 1960s; export prices increased at an average of 11.7 per cent per year, while the increase for import prices was 9 per cent.[10] By contrast a massive rise of imports was allowed, reflected in the significantly greater rate of increase of imports over exports in real terms (i.e. at fixed prices or in volume: see Tables 12.2 and 12.3).

The conventional literature covering the experience of LDCs during the 1970s in relation to the 'international environment' usually emphasises what are called 'external shocks'.[11] This largely refers to the steep rise in the price of vital imports, e.g. energy and capital goods, and in the cost of borrowing, and to the negative effects of inflation and recession on the LDCs' export markets. The impact is then seen in

**Table 12.2  Rate of coverage of imports of goods by exports of goods, 1960s and 1970s**

(per cent, current prices)

| Average 1960–70 | 1971 | 1972 | 1973 | 1974[a] | 1975 | 1976 | 1977 | 1978 | 1979[a] | 1980[a] | 1981 | Average 1971–81 | 1982 |
|---|---|---|---|---|---|---|---|---|---|---|---|---|---|
| 57.0 | 63.0 | 67.6 | 62.5 | 81.4 | 60.3 | 51.5 | 50.9 | 52.1 | 62.8 | 64.0 | 61.1 | 61.0 | 58.9 |

*Source:* Banque Centrale de Tunisie, *Statistiques Financières,* nos. 63 and 64, February 1982 and March 1983.

*Note:*   (a) Years of high oil price rises.

**Table 12.3  Annual rates of growth of imports, exports, the trade deficit and GDP by sub-periods**

(volume and current prices)

| | *1971–1974* | *1975–1978* | *1979–1981* |
|---|---|---|---|
| **Volume** | | | |
| Imports | 19.00 | 9.00 | 4.66 |
| Exports | 2.75 | −0.75 | 2.33 |
| **Current prices** | | | |
| Imports | 33.75 | 16.50 | 30.00 |
| Exports | 48.00 | 6.30 | 37.60 |
| Trade deficit (goods) | 11.25 | 55.50 | 22.00 |
| GDP (market prices) | 19.77 | 13.15 | 16.22 |

*Source:* Based on *Statistiques Financières,* Nos. 41, 47 and 63.

terms of effects on the LDCs' growth and balance of payments position. In Tunisia's case concentrating on 'external shocks' would miss the leading role played by powerful domestic factors, or 'internal shocks'. Deliberate policy decisions leading to intensive industrialisation while at the same time liberalising the economy, thus allowing rapidly rising consumption and investment by the private sector, constituted such 'internal shocks'. These were accelerated by rapid urbanisation, expanded consumerism and much higher income and welfare expectations. The type of demand pressures released by such policies is partly reflected by the rapidly growing size of excess expenditure as a percentage of GDP at constant prices, which moved from 4.2 per cent in 1974 to 26.1 per cent in 1978.[12]

Demand pressure on imports came from both the public and private sectors. However, the role played by heavy public sector investments is quite pronounced. Despite the increasing privatisation of the economy, the public sector still claimed around 60 per cent of total investments during the 1970s. It accounted for the bulk of large import-intensive projects.

The period under study roughly coincides with three development plans: the Third Plan (1969–72), the Fourth Plan (1973–76) and the Fifth Plan (1977–81). Along with the liberalisation of the economy the Third Plan declared special interest in agriculture and services. This was intended to signal the change from the austere industrial strategy of the 1960s. But in fact the 1969–81 period witnessed strong emphasis on heavy import-intensive investment. Hence when in 1973 and 1974 the price index for investment increased by 13 per cent and 12 per cent respectively, it was mainly due to the steeply rising cost of imported equipment.[13]

Ambitious investment targets were advanced: 25.2 per cent of GDP at current prices for the Fourth Plan (1973–76) and 31.6 for the Fifth Plan (1977–81). Targets were often revised upwards or exceeded in practice. The Fifth Plan was particularly ambitious, having an average annual increase of the volume of investment 55 per cent above that of the Fouth.[14] Investments exceeded the target by 5 per cent.

The strong positive effect on the demand for imports is also due to the choice of projects and technology, and the sectoral distribution of investment. During the decade there was emphasis on infrastructure (e.g. transport, electrification), petroleum and gas (including refining), phosphate mining and processing and construction materials factories (e.g. cement, steel). The pace and intensity of these investments was often high. Thus one of the most significant developments in the industrial sector affecting imports was the doubling of investments in mining between 1976 and 1978 and their quadrupling in chemical industries in 1978. The latter raised the chemical industry's share of total investments from 8 to 24 per cent in one year.

Within industry there was also a strong bias for capital-intensive projects. This was particularly the case of the Fifth Plan (1977–81) with 47 per cent of investments in capital-intensive projects; building materials and chemicals which accounted for 52 per cent of manufacturing investment, respectively had a 65.7 per cent and 92.9 per cent proportion for such projects.[15] Even in the usually labour-intensive food and agricultural industries as much as 34 per cent of investments were capital-intensive. These proportions are quite high for a middle-income country like Tunisia with a traditional dependence on primary production, modest financial resources and an excess labour supply.

The choice of import-intensive technology in Tunisia was conditioned by the nature of its resources and the positive 'international environment' during the 1970s vis à vis the price of its phosphate and petroleum exports. Having done well out of these two exports (see below), policymakers were encouraged to find more of these goods and to develop them. The heavy import cost of such a strategy is typically exemplified by phosphates.

Tunisia has abundant, but low grade, phosphate deposits. Among LDC producers it has the highest cost of production of phosphate rock; poor grade deposits necessitate additional equipment for mining and purification, forcing either big decreases in sales or price reductions in order to stay competitive.[16] In fact Tunisia's phosphate rock prices were so low in 1978, they were insufficient to cover capital charges, which were in any case not high (10 per cent of plant investment) given the rates of return in other sectors.

Tunisia's answer was to become the leading Third World phosphate processing country in the 1970s. While this option benefits from higher export prices it drastically increases import intensity. The available technology requires large-scale vertically integrated plants producing more than one product if cost-effective production is to be achieved. This needs very expensive inputs not available in Tunisia, notably sulphur. The price of sulphur increased more than threefold between 1976 and 1981. It also has very high transport costs relative to the small quantities purchased. A recent example of the cost of this technology is the Gabes complex whose investment bill ($150–200 million)[17] would alone amount to over half of investment in the chemical industry during the Fifth Plan (1977–81).

The choice of import-intensive technology was however also made in more debatable cases.[18] Planners decided to confront excessive dependence on rainfed agriculture, while shifting the burden of employment creation from agriculture to industry. This entailed heavy investment in irrigation, including several large dams, and agricultural equipment, which together accounted for approximately 60 per cent of total agricultural investment during the decade. These heavy investments in industry and agriculture increased the share of intermediate and capital goods in total imports (Table 12.4) injecting considerable imported inflation into the cost of production, and putting pressure on the balance of trade.

**Table 12.4  Structure of imports and exports by major sectoral origin and by sub-periods**

(per cent)

|  | Imports (cif) | | | Exports (fob) | | |
|---|---|---|---|---|---|---|
|  | 1971–74 | 1975–78 | 1979–81 | 1971–74 | 1975–78 | 1979–81 |
| Food products | 19.0 | 13.0 | 11.0 | 30.0 | 17.0 | 8.0 |
| Primary and semi-products | 41.0 | 39.0 | 49.0 | 64.0 | 65.0 | 71.0 |
| of which: | | | | | | |
| *Energy* | *9.0* | *10.0* | *21.0* | *32.0* | *41.5* | *52.0* |
| *Products of animal or vegetable origin* | *7.0* | *5.0* | *5.0* | *4.0* | *2.5* | *2.0* |
| *Products of mineral origin* | *2.0* | *2.0* | *3.0* | *12.0* | *8.0* | *3.0* |
| *Other semi-products* | *23.0* | *22.0* | *20.0* | *16.0* | *13.0* | *14.0* |
| Finished goods | 40.0 | 48.0 | 40.0 | 6.0 | 18.0 | 21.0 |
| of which: | | | | | | |
| *Capital goods* | *26.5* | *31.0* | *24.0* | *1.0* | *1.0* | *2.0* |
| *Consumer goods* | *13.5* | *17.0* | *16.0* | *5.0* | *17.0* | *19.0* |
|  | 100 | 100 | 100 | 100 | 100 | 100 |

*Source:* Based on Banque Centrale de Tunisie, *Statistiques Financières,* no. 63, February 1982.

The private sector's contribution to imported inflation was mainly via consumer goods. The liberalisation of the economy during the 1970s allowed a notable increase in imported finished goods destined for final consumption (Table 12.4). Hence for example car imports increased from 1.8 million dinars in 1978 to 21.5 million dinars in 1981. However even in some industries where private capital concentrates, import-intensive technology prevailed. This was the case of construction materials industries which grew in response to very high demand for construction and housing in the 1970s. This demand heavily taxed local supplies particularly during the first half of the decade. It partly derives from a strong preference by Tunisians for private housing, which is also a leading item on which remittances from abroad are spent.

But the case of the private sector is altogether different when it comes to the 'free zone' export industries established by the 1972 law mentioned earlier. These industries have little direct consequence for imported inflation. They are intended to attract foreign investment (largely from the EEC) on the basis of cheap labour and available raw materials. They overwhelmingly use labour-intensive technology (e.g. old machinery) and require inexpensive imported inputs.

However, indirectly these industries do have a negative consequence. Law 72–38 which governs the 'free zone' industries restricts their output for export purposes. Hence this sector directs factors of production and pays wages, but it does not help absorb domestic excess demand for the same goods that it produces, which then need to be imported. Thus for example in the case of textiles, which dominate 'free zone' manufacturing, 90 per cent of Tunisia's total exports originate from the 'free zone' factories. If one excludes these exports, Tunisia becomes a seriously deficitory country in textiles. This reasoning is particularly justified since the exceptional provisions and tax exemptions allowed to this sector makes it practically extra-territorial, with minimal linkage effect to the domestic economy. The foreign exchange earned by these industries remains largely under their control and is not tapped by the national economy in paying for alternative imports. No wonder that trade statistics in Tunisia sometimes exclude the output of this sector from the 'national' tables.

### External factors: Terms of trade, access to markets and to foreign finance

The positive effect of Tunisia's terms of trade is precarious and transitory. This arises out of the high commodity and geographic concentration of its trade. Since 1974, six items accounted for between 75 per cent and nearly 90 per cent of the total value of exported goods. These items are: crude petroleum, crude phosphates, phosphate fertilisers, phosphoric acid, olive oil and textiles. Hence improving export performance was largely due to the rise in the world price of key exports, mainly crude oil. As Tables 12.2 and 12.3 show the major positive impact took place in 1973–74 and in 1979–80, coinciding with the sharpest rises in oil prices and portraying the highest rate of coverage of imports by exports. The share of energy in total exports increased throughout the decade, constituting over a half of the total by 1979–81 (Table 12.4).

Apart from oil price rises Tunisia benefited in 1973–74 from the increases of between 200 and 400 per cent in the prices of olive oil, crude phosphates and phosphate products. Although crude phosphate prices declined sharply after 1975, there were further, but less pronounced, increases in the prices of Tunisia's key exports, including textiles whose price doubled between 1978 and 1981.

However several problems of Tunisia's trade performance were evident. At the general level, export volumes were increasing far slower than import volumes. This was partly caused by the vicissitudes of rainfed agriculture for olive oil and the limited proven petroleum deposits. Hence when in 1975–78 import prices accelerated faster than export prices it combined to produce a dramatic increase in the trade deficit (Table 12.3). Moreover, at the sectoral level terms of trade movements were negative for several product groups. Only energy and intermediary products (largely processed phosphates) retained a favourable terms of trade performance (Table 12.5). Particularly worrying was the deteriorating terms of trade for food products, in spite of the sharply rising price of olive oil exports in 1973–74. Food import prices rose faster, particularly cereals, sugar, coffee, tea and soya oil.

Geographic concentration also played a negative role. Despite attempts at diversification, Tunisia continued to concentrate its trade with the EEC countries (notably France, Italy and Germany), which still accounted in 1981 for 66.6 per cent of its imports and 61.2 per cent of its exports.[19] This made it particularly prone to importing European inflation during the 1970s; the depression in Europe also affected demand for Tunisia's exports. Declining growth in foreign demand had a negative effect on export volumes equivalent to 4 per cent of Tunisia's GNP in 1978; it was less than 1 per cent in 1974.[20]

The concentration of trade with Europe also had its effect in terms of access to markets and international competition. The decline of olive oil export prices after 1974 is an example of this situation. The main international market for vegetable oils is the EEC and the Mediterranean countries. Most of these countries were, in the 1970s, replacing olive oil with other vegetable and grain oils. This was due to the gap in price which had a definite effect on substitution.[21] Moreover the EEC has a surplus of olive oil which grew larger with the accession of Greece and will be even more acute when Spain and Portugal join. This affects Tunisia as the leading exporter of this product to the EEC.

The difficulties of competition in the EEC affected Tunisia even when its harvest was good; in 1975 Italy 'closed its frontiers' against foreign olive oil causing Tunisia's exports to decline by 55.9 per cent relative to their value in 1974.[22] Problems of market access also exist for Tunisia's textiles exports. The multifibre agreement with the EEC imposes quota restrictions on Tunisia, which will again become more acute with the accession of Spain and Portugal.

By contrast to the above Tunisia had a favourable position in terms of access to foreign finance. During the 1971–81 period its credit rating

**Table 12.5 Terms of trade by major sectoral origin of imports and exports and by sub-periods**

(1970 = 100)

| | 1971 | 1972 | 1973 | 1974 | Average 1971–74 | 1975 | 1976 | 1977 | 1978 | Average 1975–78 | 1979 | 1980 | Average 1979–80 |
|---|---|---|---|---|---|---|---|---|---|---|---|---|---|
| Food products | 100.3 | 101.8 | 96.6 | 91.8 | 97.6 | 105.2 | 80.8 | 92.6 | 103.1 | 95.4 | 99.3 | 82.5 | 90.9 |
| Energy | 102.3 | 120.7 | 136.0 | 147.9 | 126.7 | 160.4 | 148.8 | 137.9 | 147.5 | 148.5 | 190.8 | 134.6 | 162.7 |
| Primary products of animal or vegetable origin | 118.0 | 113.2 | 95.4 | 90.2 | 104.2 | 102.4 | 90.1 | 117.0 | 115.9 | 106.3 | 89.1 | 87.7 | 88.4 |
| Primary products of mineral origin | 133.2 | 135.9 | 108.5 | 191.1 | 142.1 | 168.8 | 142.5 | 118.7 | 125.0 | 138.7 | 114.8 | 90.4 | 102.6 |
| Semi-products (intermediary) | 97.2 | 101.3 | 125.0 | 165.5 | 122.2 | 129.2 | 98.1 | 129.1 | 119.6 | 119.0 | 165.4 | 251.5 | 208.4 |
| Finished products (incl. capital goods) | 85.5 | 77.4 | 85.0 | 97.9 | 86.4 | 90.5 | 69.6 | 68.7 | 95.0 | 80.9 | 75.4 | 106.0 | 90.7 |
| Total terms of trade | 105.1 | 105.3 | 113.2 | 170.7 | 123.5 | 152.8 | 114.3 | 144.0 | 147.6 | 147.1 | 181.5 | 203.5 | 192.5 |

*Source:* Based on Banque Centrale, *Statistiques Financières*, no. 63, February 1982.

was very high, partly due to a long-standing record clean of defaults. In marked contrast to the 1960s this aspect of the 'international environment' helped sustain the industrialisation strategy of the 1970s. A variety of sources of finance were available, including oil-exporting Arab sources (OPEC countries), particularly after 1973.

Moreover, while most countries faced lending sources which were increasingly private and costly, accumulating large deficits and enormous debts, Tunisia retained strong access to the official sources more typical of the 1960s (see chapter 2 above). The political motives behind the 1960s financial flows, dominated by official sources, were important, as was Tunisia's efficient use of aid. Both factors retained their importance for Tunisia in the 1970s.

*Tunisia's current account and the importance of tourism and workers' remittances*

Tourism and workers' remittances are vital items of Tunisia's foreign current account. They are the main items constituting the country's nearly consistent surplus in its factor and non factor services balance, which has greatly contributed to balancing the continuous merchandise deficit (Table 12.6).

**Table 12.6 Major items in current account receipts and the importance of services and remittances**

(per cent)

|  | 1972 | 1976 | 1980 | 1981 |
|---|---|---|---|---|
| Petroleum | 13.3 | 23.0 | 34.5 | 36.3 |
| Tourism and travel | 23.4 | 20.0 | 20.0 | 17.0 |
| Migrant workers' remittances | 9.7 | 10.0 | 8.9 | 9.7 |
| Phosphates and other minerals | 4.0 | 4.2 | 1.7 | 1.3 |
| Fertilisers | 3.1 | 5.3 | 4.8 | 5.2 |
| Olive oil | 15.0 | 5.8 | 1.8 | 2.7 |
| Textiles | 1.6 | 5.8 | 11.4 | 10.0 |
| Total current account receipts | 100.0 | 100.0 | 100.0 | 100.0 |
| Services surplus as per cent of merchandise trade deficit (net) | 61.0 | 21.0 | 45.0 | 39.0 |
| Services and remittances surplus as per cent of merchandise trade deficit (net) | 100.0 | 42.0 | 73.0 | 71.0 |

*Source:* Calculated on the basis of Banque Centrale de Tunisie, *Statistiques Financières,* nos. 63 and 64, February 1982 and March 1983.

Emphasis on tourism, dominated by the private sector, has been a feature of the more liberal development strategy of the 1970s. Tunisia specialises in inexpensive 'package deal' tourism. To the extent that international prices are higher than domestic ones, it benefits. Spain is a main competitor in this area and has the advantage of a cheaper currency due to devaluation policies. Tunisian foreign exchange policy supports a fixed exchange rate making the Tunisian dinar more expensive for tourists.

Although most visitors to Tunisia are Western European (French and German sources accounting for 59 per cent of tourist revenue in 1981), there has been a change in the direction of Arab visitors. This encouraged government attempts to attract Arab capital into this sector. In 1981 the Central Bank reported that Arab capital from the oil-rich states was backing tourist projects to the total value of US$383 million.[23] On the negative side, French policies in 1983, limiting the amount of money allowed for French tourists abroad, troubled Tunisian planners, causing speculation as to its effects on their country.

The issue of workers' remittances is even more dependent on Europe than tourism. It largely hinges on French policy towards migrant workers.[24] By 1980 there were 90,000 Tunisian workers in Europe (i.e. equivalent to 5.7 per cent of those employed in Tunisia during the same year), 80,000 of them in France. The Tunisian government's pro-emigration policy, aimed at reducing domestic unemployment, had to change in the mid-1970s towards emigrant reinsertion policies. Rising unemployment in France prompted restrictions on emigration and repatriation policies including aid-to-return schemes.

The main alternative for Tunisian workers has been Libya, which after France (60 per cent in 1981), accounts for the second largest share of remittances (17 per cent in 1981). But even here there have been problems arising out of a volatile political environment. In 1976, 13,700 Tunisian workers were abruptly expelled from Libya, consequently destabilising southern Tunisia's labour market as migrants sought to settle and work in their region of origin.[25]

Despite the beginning of net return migration into Tunisia in 1980, remittances kept on increasing until 1981. Remittances do feed inflation in Tunisia, which shares similar, but less acute, problems with other Arab labour-exporting countries in this respect (see chapter 13 below on Jordan).[26] Remittances are mainly intended for consumption or expenditure on construction. A study in the mid-1970s revealed that 87.8 per cent of Tunisians interviewed considered that, directly or indirectly, housing and construction is the main item for their repatriated money; this is consistent with the finding that more than any other immigrant community in France, Tunisians tend to aim at returning to their country.[27]

## Policies and inflation: adjustment versus postponement

Because of the favourable trends in the prices of key exports, the services and remittances surplus and access to foreign finance, Tunisia did not feel the urgency of adjustment to imported inflation during the 1970s. The main trend in policy was to postpone adjustment, particularly in view of the heavy expenditures planned during the decade.

### Adjustment policies

*Fiscal policy:* As discussed above the Tunisian government did not exercise budgetary restraint during the 1970s. The Tunisian government budget is divided into a current account involving most fiscal revenue and current (recurring) payments, and a capital account dealing with development investments and expenditures. On its current account, government revenue rose to very high levels, reaching over a third of GDP after 1977, one of the highest levels of fiscal pressure among middle-income countries. This allowed current account savings which financed 69 per cent of the capital account expenditure during 1976–81.

At the level of restraining private demand taxation policy has been rather ineffective. Direct taxes remained small (5.8 per cent of GDP in 1981) and only increased due to the increase in the tax base. A World Bank study in 1980 revealed that the taxation system is in fact regressive at the higher levels of income, with considerable tax evasion involved. The government mainly concentrated on better tax collection and identification of tax payers in addition to few new taxes, e.g. on capital gains from land and building speculation in 1977. Currently planners are recommending a lowering of the higher levels of taxation in the hope of facilitating tax reporting and collection and encouraging more honest declarations.

The major sources of tax revenue throughout the 1970s have been indirect taxes on imports and direct and indirect taxes on hydrocarbons and phosphates. Towards the early 1980s indirect taxes accounted for around 55 per cent of government revenue with a further 15 per cent from government monopolies, e.g. on tobacco and matches.[28]

Indirect taxes on imports did not play an important role against imported inflation in the 1970s. Because of the overriding importance of industrialisation, various duties on capital and intermediary goods were lowered in 1973, a measure consistent with the massive increase of these imports after that date. However, Tunisia still operated an elaborate system of import controls which, along with selective tariffs, allowed protection (of up to 40 per cent) for some local products and infant industries.

In 1977 and 1978 the high rise of imports, particularly consumer durables, prompted a raising of customs along with higher fees on motor vehicle registration. Taxes were raised on a variety of non-essentials, reaching 300 per cent in the case of luxury cars. However, as evident from the increasing car imports mentioned above, this had limited success in restraining demand. Policy makers continue their efforts in this area as they feel that the food and industrialisation priorities make consumer durables the most favoured imports to restrict. This recreates the same unrest amongst merchants which confronted the 1960s strategy.

*Monetary and credit policy:* Monetary policy in Tunisia has been more effective as it has exercised some control on monetary flows. The Central Bank (CB) has a legal status autonomous from the cabinet and is capable of exercising genuine pressure on government spending. In 1970 a convention was drawn limiting the government's access to indirect domestic financing (a method abused during the 1960s) to 5 million dinars. In the past, the government freely tapped this source mainly constituted by CB deposits with the Postal Checking System.

The aim of Tunisia's monetary policy of limiting the growth of money supply to that of nominal GDP broadly succeeded, with slightly higher increases in the early 1980s. The share of money supply (M1) in GDP remained around 26–28 per cent throughout the decade. Despite the existence of a variety of instruments at the disposal of the CB, the main control mechanism has been the prior approval of credits. The direct control of credit along with a diversified interest rate policy allows the monetary authorities considerable intervention and selectivity in the management of credit according to development priorities.

The direction of funds to longer term development investments, the other major objective of monetary policy is facilitated by the small number of deposit banks (10), two of which are government owned. In the pursuit of the development objective the CB encouraged the increase of savings and time deposits to enhance the capacity for longer term lending. Hence quasi-money's share of GDP increased from 8.8 per cent in 1973 to 16.4 per cent in 1981. Other methods included the introduction in 1975 of a global development finance ratio for banks, fixed at 43 per cent of total deposits. This device includes the mandatory holding of various long-term bonds.

In spite of the positive aspects of a diversified and structured interest rate policy in Tunisia – sensitive to development needs, varying with the purpose of the loan and encouraging longer term deposits and loans – the general level of real interest rates has been very low. This constitutes the main problem of monetary policy. For interest applied to deposits, real rates have been negative between 1971 and 1981, irrespective of the inflation index one uses (e.g. consumer price index, wholesale price index or international deflators).

Apart from encouraging capital-intensive projects, thus increasing import intensity per project and contradicting the employment objectives of the government, low interest discourages savings, even by households. Holding cash balances and imported inventories, and speculative investment in real estate is, by contrast, encouraged, contributing to imported and domestic inflation. Awareness of these aspects has led to an increase in interest rates, e.g. by 20–30 per cent in April 1981.

The above problems related to interest rate policy seem consistent with the increasing orientation of credit in the 1970s towards import-intensive projects, namely industry (including construction and mining) and transport; their joint shares increased from 17 per cent of total medium and long-term loans in 1971 to 52 per cent in 1981. By contrast agriculture and tourism, less import intensive sectors, had their shares decline from 52.1 per cent to 23.7 per cent.

One problem affecting lending to agriculture is the wide margin between prices paid by middlemen to farmers for their produce and the retail prices at which the produce is actually sold. The ratio can be as high as 1 to 5. Profitability of agricultural credit suffers under these circumstances. Along with other problems, e.g. precariousness of collateral and fragmentation of landholdings, this discourages agricultural production which cannot satisfy higher domestic demand, leading to increased imports.

An institutional factor somewhat peculiar to Tunisia also ties credits to imported inflation. The rate of profit applied by private producers and merchants is negotiated with the Ministry of the Economy; the procedure followed allows the inclusion of the cost of borrowing in the general cost on which a percentage mark-up is negotiated. Since the profit increases with the increase of the absolute size of the cost, this encourages excess borrowing (taxing the vigilance of the CB) as well as the import of more expensive products and inputs.[29]

Thus it would seem that despite the restraint of conventional monetary indicators (M1), Tunisian monetary policy could not fully control financial pressure leading to imported inflation. This points to the limitations of monetary policy, particularly in mixed economies, where institutional factors and social behaviour are somewhat more complex. It could also indicate that the high rise in M2 (including quasi-money) is perhaps more relevant to imported inflation.

*Exchange rate policy:* Exchange rate policy in Tunisia is not used as an instrument against inflation. The dinar's rate of exchange is fixed against a basket of currencies of Tunisia's main trading partners. The CB argues that the multiple pressures in the economy (e.g. importers versus exporters) reflected in the highly diversified interest rates applied to different sectors, should not be allowed to operate on the exchange rate. Otherwise, wide conflicts would be encouraged leading to instability in the rate. Tunisia's domestic inflation has not been higher than its trading partners', thus it has not adversely affected the real rate of exchange.

*Incomes and wages policy:* Successive wage increases in Tunisia during the 1971–81 period, led to average annual rises in minimum industrial wages (SMIG) and minimum agricultural wages (SMAG) of 11.9 and 10.5 per cent respectively.[30] Given that domestic inflation increased at an average annual rate of 5.6 per cent (consumer prices), this led to real increases of 6.0 per cent for the SMIG and 4.6 per cent for the SMAG. These increases occurred in the context of two socio-political trends: the explicit social concern of the broadly 'social democratic' ruling party and labour activity by Tunisia's general trade union, the UGTT.

Tunisia's ruling party since independence, the Socialist Destourian Party, had recognised at the outset of the 1970s the dire need for improving wages and standards of living. Distributional and welfare aspects of wage increases were paramount, particularly since the working class had not reaped much benefit from growth in the 1960s. Between 1966 and 1975 the SMIG and the SMAG had increased at an average 1.9 and 1.2 per cent per annum respectively, relative to real GDP's 5.1 per cent rate.[31] In 1971 over 40 per cent of the Tunisian population were still living below the poverty line. These circumstances created pressure for significant wage increases during the decade. A crucial element sustaining wage increases was union pressure, sustained at times by union militancy and strikes. In the late 1970s a spate of strikes was followed by a social pact between unions and the government which eventually broke down.

It can be argued that Tunisia's wage increases have encouraged inflation by pushing up demand and encouraging capital-intensive projects. However there are important qualifications to this conclusion. Apart from the fact that the absolute level from which wages were increased was very low, there are wide differences in average wages according to sector, region and level of unionisation. Moreover, in agriculture the SMAG is admitted by planners to be irrelevant in comparison to labour market conditions, including factors such as migration and seasonal demand.

Wages in Tunisia increase fastest in urban areas of the north, and in large industries and the public sector where unions are strong. The range is widest between agriculture, and mining and energy. The ratio of average wages in this case is 1 to 9. The government is concerned because the gulf between rich and poor is widening and is regionally biased in favour of the northern coastal areas.[32] This is underlined by the index of expenditure concentration which registered 0.43 in Greater Tunis and zero in the south.[33] Moreover, in the export sector employment is largely dominated by non-unionised women; in textiles for example over three-quarters of the workers are women. They are highly exploited and paid very low wages. In 1976, for example, the export sector employed 15 per cent of manufacturing workers, but paid only 9 per cent of this sector's wages.[34]

The case of the export industry reveals a serious contradiction of government policy. The idea is to attract foreign capital partly on the strength of a comparative wage-cost advantage. Thus employment targets are in conflict with the government's social concern. The level of the wages paid can hardly be seen to lead to imported inflation.

*Postponement policies*
*Borrowing policy and foreign finance:* Because of the availability of a good range of foreign finance, Tunisia could rely on borrowing to finance a general budget deficit and to postpone adjustment to imported inflation. The government portrayed good management of foreign debt, following a cautious policy sensitive to changes in the international environment. It thus succeeded in keeping the level of foreign debt at roughly the same level of GDP along with a stable debt-service ratio (see Table 12.7). Hence during the most difficult part of the decade vis-

**Table 12.7 Foreign debt and debt-service ratio (sub-periods)**

|  | *1971–1974* | *1975–1978* | *1979–1981* |
|---|---|---|---|
| Foreign debt (m. dinars of which[a] | 1640.0 | 2899.1 | 3880.0 |
|   Public sector (%) | 77 | 70 | 60 |
|   Private sector (%) | 23 | 30 | 40 |
| Foreign debt/GDP ratio (current prices)[b] | 36.4 | 33.5 | 38.9 |
| Debt-service ratio[b] | 12.5 | 10.1 | 10.9 |

*Source:* Calculated from Ministry of Planning and Finance data.

*Notes:* (a) Total for each sub-period; end of period data
(b) Annual average for each sub-period.

à-vis the trade deficit (1975–78), Tunisia managed to maintain the lowest percentage of debt in relation to GDP (see Tables 12.2, 12.3 and 12.7). Short term credit for adjusting balance of payments problems is usually strictly avoided. The debt-service ratio was kept at reasonable levels.

Tunisia retained strong access to official bilateral and multilateral aid and cheap loans. In fact the World Bank's aid to Tunisia during the 1971–80 period was more than three times the sums it provided during the previous decade.[35] Moreover the growth of OPEC sources of funding after 1973 amounted to 25 per cent of all foreign financing during the Fifth Plan (1977–81). The availability of this extra source of money provided a useful margin for the negotiation of favourable loans.

The structure of lending to Tunisia started improving in the 1970–74 period, when the share of drawings on official loans within total drawings increased from 60 to 75 per cent; in 1974, 80 per cent of official loans had very favourable terms.[36] In 1975, the effective rate of interest payment on outstanding disbursed debt was only around 4.2 per cent. Bilateral loans from Western countries had maturities ranging between 25 and 50 years. The continuation of this situation allowed Tunisia to enter the Fifth Plan (1977–81) period with an overall loan portfolio having an average 20 years maturity, with six years of grace, at an average interest rate of 6 per cent. Relative to world inflation these were very low rates.

Despite the slight hardening of terms during the 1977–81 period, Tunisia retained a similar advantage. In 1980 virtually all borrowing requirements were covered by overseas aid, thus allowing the avoidance of the Euromarket. By 1981, Tunisia's loan portfolio retained the same maturity structure (average 20 years) with average interest rates of 7 per cent.

Part of the increasing cost of borrowing during the latter part of the decade was due to the changing structure of foreign financing. The positive performance of Tunisia justified a decrease in the grant element of foreign finance, increasingly reserved for the poorest countries. As Table 12.8 shows the latter period (1977–81) has a lower share of grants and long-term loans. Tunisia is expecting harder times in the 1980s and has been attempting to increase the share of foreign investment as an alternative. Joint venture investment banks with Arab OPEC countries have been one option. In 1981 and 1982 five joint investment banks with a combined capital of 420 million dinars were established.[37]

*Price support and subsidies:* The main methods of postponing adjustment to imported inflation were the price support system and subsidies to public enterprise. The price-support system is based on a special fund

**Table 12.8 Structure of foreign financing**

|  |  |  | (per cent) |
| --- | --- | --- | --- |
|  | *1972–1973* | *1977–1981* | *Target of Sixth Plan 1982–1986* |
| Special drawing rights | 13.0 | — | — |
| Grants | 17.5 | 4.9 | 2.0 |
| Foreign investment | 19.3 | 25.0 | 27.0 |
| Loans (long-term) | 45.0 | 32.6 | 37.0 |
| Loans (medium-term) | 16.9 | 37.5 | 34.0 |
| Total | 100.0 | 100.0 | 100.0 |

*Source:* Ministry of Planning and Finance data and *VI$^e$ Plan de Developpement Economique et Social,* p. 121.

called the Price Equalisation Fund (PEF). It works like a Treasury account, receiving earmarked tax revenues, mainly on gasoline and luxury goods, and making payments to legitimate producers and distributors. Consequently it helps keep the price of several goods down.

The PEF has a multi-sided rationale including the protection of the purchasing power of lower income groups, the balancing of supply and demand and compensating producers (especially in agriculture) in order to encourage investment and employment.[38] In practice, however, the PEF has been used in reaction to emergencies, usually originating in the foreign sector; this includes for example unusual increases in the world price of wheat, sugar and vegetable oil. It has also been used in times of peak excess demand for specific products (e.g. cement, meat and eggs) or shortages of production (e.g. milk).

As can be seen from Table 12.9, the subsidy rates can be very high. This has produced a distortion of up to 10.9 per cent in the domestic rate of inflation. Although this form of postponement is intended to shield lower income groups as it touches many essentials, a 1975 government study has shown that the main beneficiaries have been middle and upper income groups.[39]

Financial transfers by the government to public enterprises have also constituted a buffer against the impact of imported inflation. Many of these enterprises are import intensive as mentioned earlier. Their low profitability is partly reflected by the degree of self-financing.

Industrial self-financing in general declined from 54.1 per cent of total requirements in 1975 to 31.2 per cent in 1980. Industries in which the public sector predominates had particularly sharp decreases,

## Table 12.9 Inflation and price support in Tunisia, 1982

| Product | Price unit | Real price | Subsidised price | Subsidy rate (%) | Impact on consumer price index of removal of subsidy rate (%) |
|---|---|---|---|---|---|
| Hard wheat | d/q | 12.229 | 8.000 | 35 | 0.36 |
| Soft wheat | d/q | 10.983 | 7.250 | 34 | — |
| Flour | d/q | 14.645 | 10.500 | 28 | 0.03 |
| Semolina | d/q | 18.876 | 12.540 | 34 | 1.71 |
| Bread (700g.) | mill | 130 | 80 | 38 | 1.82 |
| Baquette (300g) | mill | 66 | 50 | 24 | 0.93 |
| Barley | d/q | 9.267 | 3.000 | 68 | — |
| Corn | d/q | 10.314 | 3.100 | 70 | — |
| Soja | d/q | 17.833 | 6.500 | 63 | — |
| Bovine meat | d/kg | 1.661 | 1.041 | 37 | 1.82 |
| Poultry | d/kg | 0.707 | 0.488 | 31 | 0.92 |
| Eggs (unit) | mill | 41 | 28 | 32 | 0.45 |
| Bottled milk | m/l | 230 | 140 | 39 | 0.97 |
| Pasteurised milk | m/l | 270 | 200 | 26 | 0.18 |
| Fresh milk | m/l | 185 | 160 | 13.5 | 0.10 |
| Butter | d/kg | 1.950 | 1.700 | 13 | 0.06 |
| Powder sugar | m/kg | 325 | 240 | 26 | 0.75 |
| Sugar in pieces | m/kg | 385 | 300 | 22 | — |
| Mixed oil | m/l | 359 | 300 | 16 | 0.50 |
| Ammonium | d/t | 125 | 63 | 50 | ⎫ |
| Fertilisers super simple | d/t | 33.6 | 25.4 | 24 | ⎬ 0.30 |
| Fertilisers super triple | d/t | 79.4 | 38.5 | 52 | ⎭ |
| Average rate of subsidy | | | | 35 | |
| Global impact on consumption prices | | | | | 10.9 |

*Source:* Data supplied by Ministry of Planning and Finance, March 1983.

*Note:* (a) d/q = dinars per quintal; mill = millimes (1000 millimes = 1 dinar); d/kg = dinars per kilogram; m/l = millimes per litre; m/kg = millimes per kilogram; d/t = dinars per ton.

chemical industries for example saw their share of self-financing decline from 76.3 per cent in 1975 to 28.9 per cent in 1980. By contrast the largely private textiles and clothing industries, labour-intensive with a high share of foreign investment, maintained higher levels of self-financing.

### The impact of imported inflation on national inflation
The domestic rate of inflation in Tunisia does not reflect the real effect

of imported inflation. This largely arises because of the existence of an elaborate system of pricing in the country.[41] It is the stated policy of the Tunisian government that a free market mechanism is by itself inadequate for development. Supply-side problems could easily produce equilibrium with demand at socially unacceptable prices. Thus for example excess demand for cereals is matched by fluctuating production, hardly any increase in areas cultivated during 1971–81 and a rise in the cost index of cereals' means of production of 248 per cent over the same period. This motivated the protection of consumers via a ceiling on prices, and of producers' incentive to re-invest via a subsidy.

The pricing system in Tunisia involves five different methods. These range from complete freedom for the market mechanism to price ceilings. One of the effects of this system can be seen in Table 12.9; the removal of the price subsidies would lead to an 11 per cent effect on consumer prices. It is not surprising therefore that while the domestic rate of inflation has ranged from around 5 per cent in the middle 1970s to 10 per cent in 1980, import prices have risen faster. The rise in import prices during the 1970s did not have a strong impact on the demand for imports. This is partly due to the high import elasticity of demand (relative to income). For goods in general it was 1.5 between 1970 and 1978, with energy goods scoring the highest elasticity at 2.7.

### Prospects for the 1980s

The 1980s is proving to be a decade characterised by a less kind international environment as far as Tunisia is concerned. Tunisia's energy balance is under increasing pressure from a shrinking world oil market, declining prices of oil and increasing domestic demand for energy brought about by rising private consumption as well as the capital-intensive, import-intensive and fuel-intensive investments of the 1970s. In 1979–81 energy constituted 21 per cent of Tunisia's total imports, a share that rose from 9 per cent in the early part of the decade (see Table 12.4). Fears that Tunisia would become a net oil importer by the mid-1980s have, however, subsided. New oil discoveries and conservation methods at home have helped. Domestic energy prices were raised and domestic consumption of oil fell by 12 per cent in 1982.

The financial burden of the PEF had reached unacceptable levels. The PEF's increasing deficit position drew mounting criticism. Its expenses reached 10 per cent of the government budget and 2 per cent of GDP by the early 1980s. Similarly transfers to enterprises doubled during the Fifth Plan (1977–81) to reach 37 per cent of budgetary expenses, and 9 per cent of GDP. Thus price subsidies were decreased in 1982 and 1983. The subsidy rates in Table 12.9 no longer reflect the current position.

Social concern and labour demands continue to lead to rising wages. In early 1982 an increase of nearly 34 per cent in minimum wages was agreed to, with further increases in 1983. These forces among others have produced a rising rate of inflation, 13.7 per cent in 1982, compared to 8.9 per cent in 1981 and 10 per cent in 1980.

Economic growth in Tunisia has declined to 1.5 per cent in 1982 (at 1980 prices) compared to the 3.5 per cent forecast by the Sixth Plan (1982–86). The trade deficit has increased and reserves have fallen. Tourist trade has declined with a significant decrease in arrivals in 1982 and 1983. Workers' remittances, always important for Tunisia's balance of payments, are not expected to increase at rates similar to the 1970s because of the tightening immigration conditions in Europe and the decline in the oil revenues of the labour-poor Arab oil countries.

Tunisia's borrowing position continues to be relatively favourable. Levels of aid are not expected to retain the same primacy as during the 1970s. However a wide array of sources still exists, with Arab aid, loans and investment increasingly encouraged. Arab sources are expected to cover 50 per cent of the finance needs during the Sixth Plan (1982–86). Tunisia remains a highly fundable country. In early 1983 the Ministry of Planning and Finance was surprised by the protest from financial sources of one particular OECD country for the rejection of their very generous package in favour of an even more generous one.

The political climate in Tunisia and the Arab world is extremely important for the prospects of the country with respect to growth and effective economic policy. Tunisia now holds the prestigious position of being the location of the League of Arab States. Parallel to this, relations with Maghreb countries have improved. The March 1983 pact with Algeria towards establishing a Maghreb common market will hopefully give Tunisian productive capacity the scale it needs. The capacity of policy makers to deal with inflationary pressures during the 1980s is very dependent on the way the ruling party handles the increasing class conflict in the country. Merchants, and quick-profit businessmen form a pressure group to be reckoned with. Left-wing parties, leftists in the ruling party, and unions form another. Holding the middle ground seems to be increasingly difficult. More progressive taxation and less tax evasion may, if successfully instituted, 'buy off' moderation of union demands and increasing acceptance of unsubsidised prices. This constitutes one of several important challenges to Tunisia in the present decade.

The events of January 1984 were apparently triggered off by a 110 per cent increase in the price of basic food products, bread and pasta. This had been announced by the government in November 1983 in order to reduce the cost of the Price Equalisation Fund. This policy has been backed by the World Bank and the IMF and clearly reveals the difficulties of postponing adjustment from the 1970s to the 1980s. Moreover the reports that the riots were started by groups of unemployed youths and first manifested themselves in southern Tunisia underlines the dangers of high unemployment and regional imbalance.

While it is too soon to assess the real significance of these events and their true causes, it is clear that economic policy towards inflation is a critical factor for a peaceful development process. It is also clear that the 'free-market' type of 'advice' coming from Western capitalist institutions retains a destructive element already experienced in many developing countries.

Again the prestige and authority of President Bourguiba has managed to impose itself on the events and control them. But that presence may not be there during the next conflict.

## Notes

1 World Bank, *World Development Report 1981*, Washington D.C., August 1981.
2 République Tunisienne, INS, *Recensement des Activités Industrielles*, 1980.
3 République Tunisienne, INS, *Annuaire 1980*.
4 Yusif A. Sayigh, *The Economics of the Arab World*, London, Croom Helm, 1978, pp. 472–3.
5 Daniel Kamelgarn, 'Stratégies de "self-reliance" et système économique mondial: l'expérience Tunisienne des années 1960', *Peuples Méditerranéens*, no. 13, October–December 1980, p. 115.
6 Ibid., p. 109.
7 Ibid., p. 112.
8 Daniel Kamelgarn, 'Tunisie (1970–77), le développement d'un capitalisme dépendant', *Peuples Méditerranéens*, no. 4, July–September, 1978, pp. 127–8 (henceforth Kamelgarn 1978).
9 See Chapter 2 of this volume.
10 République Tunisienne, Ministère du Plan et des Finances, *Evaluation Préliminaire des Résultats de la Deuxième Décennie de Développement*, Tunis, June 1980, pp. 64–5 (henceforth *Evaluation Préliminaire*).
11 This tends to be done by Balassa. See IBRD, World Bank Staff Working Paper No. 449, 'The policy experience of twelve less developed countries, 1973–78', prepared by Bela Belassa, Washington, April 1981; and Bela Belassa *et al.*, *The Balance of Payments, Effects of External Shocks and of Policy Responses to those Shocks in Non-OPEC Developing Countries*, OECD Development Centre, Development Centre Studies, Paris, 1981.
12 Mahmoud Abd Al-Fadeel, *The Problem of Inflation in the Arab Economy*, Beirut, Centre for Arab Unity Studies, 1982, p. 34 (Arabic text).
13 IMF, *Survey of African Economies*, vol. 7, Washington D.C., 1977, p. 292.
14 République Tunisienne, *VIᵉ Plan de Développement Economique et Social [1982–1968]*, June 1982, p. 78 (Henceforth *VIᵉ Plan*).
15 Ibid., p. 83.
16 UNCTAD, Trade and Development Board, Committee on Commodities,

*Processing and Marketing of Phosphates: Areas of International Cooperation,* Report by the UNCTAD Secretariat, 9 September 1981, p. 54.

17  Ibid., p. 48.

18  For a critique of centralised capital-intensive agricultural strategy of Tunisia, see S. El Amami, J.P. Gachet and T. Gallali, 'Choix techniques et agriculture Maghrebine: le Cas de la Tunisie', *Peuples Méditerranéens,* no. 8, July–September 1979.

19  IMF, *Direction of Trade Statistics Yearbook,* 1982.

20  Belassa, IBRD, p. 8.

21  Mahmoud Allaya and Vassilis Bontosoglou, *Tunisie – Le Secteur Agricole et ses Perspectives à l'Horizon 1990,* Institut Agronomique Méditerranéen de Montpellier, Montpellier, September 1980, pp. 48–57.

22  Banque Centrale de Tunisie, *Rapport Annuel 1975,* pp. 42 and 86.

23  Banque Centrale de Tunisie, *Rapport Annuel 1981.*

24  For issues concerning Tunisian migrants and their effects on the Tunisian economy see Richard Lawless *et al., Return Migration to the Maghreb: People and Policies,* Arab Papers no. 10, Arab Research Centre, London, 1982; and J.P. Garson and G. Tapinos (eds), *L'Argent des Immigrés,* Travaux et Documents Cahier no. 94, Institut National d'Etudes Démographiques, 1981: especially the article by G. Simon on Tunisian workers.

25  R. Lawless *et al.,* p. 42.

26  Abd Al Fadeel, *The Problem of Inflation,* emphasises the inflationary role of remittances in Arab labour-exporting countries.

27  Garson and Tapinos, p. 241.

28  Lloyds Bank Group, *Economic Report 1982, Tunisia,* p. 14.

29  I am very grateful to discussions at the research department of the Central Bank of Tunisia which brought up this point.

30  *VI Plan,* pp. 207 and 416.

31  Reported from Ministry of Planning and Finance data.

32  Lloyds Bank Group, *Economic Report 1983, Tunisia,* p. 5.

33  *Evaluation Préliminaire,* p. 120.

34  On these issues see Daniel Geza, ILO, World Employment Programme Research, Working Paper no. 15: 'The promotion of the exports of manufactured products in Tunisia: The case of international subcontracting', February 1982. And Gerard de Groot, Tilburg University, Development Research Institute, Occasional Papers no. 5, 'Export industry in Tunisia: Effects of a dependent development', 1979.

35  Lloyds Bank Group, 1983, p. 30.

36  IMF, pp. 349–51.

37  *Middle East Economic Digest,* 'Joint banks revitalise industrial investment', 1 January 1982.

38  For a comprehensive review of pricing policy in Tunisia during the 1971–81 period see the semi-official Tunisian periodical *Conjoncture,* 'La philosophie de la politique des prix en Tunisie', no. 61, October 1981.

39  Ibid.

40  République Tunisienne, Ministère du Plan, Institut National de la Statistique, *Recensement des Activités Industrielles,* nos. 7, 10, 11 and 12 (1975, 1978, 1979 and 1980).

41  See *Conjoncture.*

# 13 Jordan: The Case of Inevitable Imported Inflation in the 1970s[1]

*Philip Mishalani*

## The external determinants of precarious existence

The case of imported inflation in Jordan is in principle easy to comprehend. The political and economic structure of the country dictate considerable dependence on external forces, creating almost total exposure to changes in the international environment. Imported inflation during the 1970s and early 1980s has consequently been a major influence on the domestic economy, playing the role of the leading pace-setter for the rate of inflation in Jordan.

The fundamentals of Jordanian political economy also prevail against definite solutions to the problem of imported inflation in the short to medium-term. Speculation about long-term remedies involves a discussion of the prospects of comprehensive progress in Jordan's socio-political, as well as economic development. The structural causes of inflation implicit in the development process and the necessity of comprehensive solutions have long been recognised in the theoretical literature.[2] But, as will be clear from the discussion below, this is of particular relevance to Jordan.

Jordan's actual creation was internationally determined by Franco-British rivalry and agreement over the division of the Middle Eastern territories under the Ottoman Empire. The demise of this Empire during World War I finally brought Jordan (then TransJordan) under British rule. Its largely straight-line borders were almost arbitrarily determined and primarily conceived for geo-political and strategic considerations with economic viability ignored. International events continued to determine the country's fortunes after independence in 1946. The war in Palestine during 1947–48 added the West Bank. Twenty years later, the 1967 Arab-Israeli War witnessed the occupation of the West Bank of Israel.

The trauma that Jordan's development went through as a consequence of losing the West Bank in 1967 should not be underestimated. Although the West Bank constituted less than 8 per cent of Jordan's territory, it contributed around 45 per cent of GNP in 1966, supplied well over 50 per cent of total domestic food supplies (including most of the livestock and dairy products) and contained around half the country's industrial and trade establishments.[3] The services sector, a leading income earner,[4] took a heavy blow, not least due to the loss of the Holy places (Moslem and Christian), the main attraction for foreign visitors. The 1967 War also led to the closure of the Suez Canal, greatly restricting access to Aqaba, Jordan's only port, on the Red Sea.

Between 1967 and 1971, growth, domestic production and the whole investment atmosphere were further impaired by the war of attrition between the PLO and Israel, and by the conflict between the PLO and the Jordanian state. Value added in agriculture and industry declined and it was only in 1972 that Jordan's GDP reached and surpassed the level it had attained prior to losing the West Bank. Of specific relevance to our subject is the capacity of the domestic economy to satisfy increasing demand for food in order to avoid primary inflationary pressures. This was heavily undermined due to the location of the Jordan Valley, the area of maximum agricultural potential, in the 'frontline' of conflict with the Israeli forces. Projects were stopped, and by 1970 economic activity had ceased and the valley was depopulated. With the reduction of tension after 1971 gradual re-occupation and production started.[5]

At the outset of the 1970s Jordan's economy looked extremely precarious. Its area is equal to South Korea (98,000 sq.km.), but with only about 2 million people it has a very small domestic market. Density on agricultural land is very high (around 200), over twice the figure for Latin American countries for example. Only around 6 per cent of Jordan's land is arable, the bulk of the country being either sandy desert or barren mountains. One tenth of arable land is potentially irrigable, with the rest dependent on highly fluctuating rainfall. Water is a scarce resource, as yet not utilised efficiently in agriculture.[6]

The vulnerability of the Jordanian economy is exacerbated by its very narrow range of natural resources. It has no proven oil resources. Exports relied increasingly on high-grade phosphate deposits; in 1980 these constituted nearly 40 per cent of the value of total domestic merchandise exports. Recently the economy has been benefiting from potash production from the Dead Sea. Limestone deposits are also available.

In contrast to its meagre natural resources Jordan has one of the highest rates of population growth in the world, nearly 4 per cent per year, with urban population growing much faster at around 4.7 per cent.[7] Moreover, a main problem is the low participation rate of the labour force which has been declining since the 1960s, from 24.2 per cent in 1961 to 19.6 per cent in 1974.[8] The World Bank has recently given a figure of 20 per cent for 1979. Three main reasons behind this phenomenon are the very low participation rate of females (3.8 per cent in 1976), the high dependency ratio (53 per cent of the population is under 15 years of age)[9] and substantial net emigration of working age groups during the 1970s.

In spite of those fundamental disadvantages, the 1970s were a decade of rapid growth and change. The two development plan periods covering most of the decade, the 1973–75 and 1976–80 plans, averaged a real annual growth rate of 7 per cent and 11 per cent respectively.[10] This is inexplicable in purely national economic terms; the economist must 'look for determinants of development beyond the conventional factors of land, capital and labour and entrepreneurship narrowly defined'.[11]

The key factors behind Jordan's growth are its long-term dependence (in fact since its creation) on aid and concessionary loans, and the special links it developed during the 1970s with oil-exporting Arab countries, towards which it became chiefly a net labour exporter. The money coming from aid and remittances allowed the rapid growth of the 1970s, particularly after the 1973–74 oil-price rises.

Rapid growth in Jordan took place in the context of serious imbalances. Traditionally run by merchant-capital, the economy retained its heavy bias towards services, a matter not helped by the loss of the major commodity producing area of the West Bank. Jordan's production and employment structure placed it on the extreme in terms of reliance on services – 62 per cent of GDP compared to 45 per cent for the middle-income country group, to which it belongs according to World Bank classification. Moreover, urbanisation and geographic concentration of economic activity became more acute. The capital, Amman, has grown to include nearly a third of the total, and half of the urban, population.[12] The governorate region of Amman concentrated in the mid-1970s 71.8 per cent of all industrial establishments, employing 85.4 per cent of all people working in industry and producing 96.6 per cent of total industrial value added.[13]

**Table 13.1 Selected development indicators for Jordan and the average middle-income country**

|  | Jordan | Average middle-income country |
|---|---|---|
| GNP per capita (dollars 1980) | 1,420 | 1,400 |
| Life expectancy at birth (years, 1980) | 61 | 60 |
| Infant mortality rate (aged 0–1, 1980) | 69 | 80 |
| Population per physician (1977) | 1,960 | 5,840 |
| Enrolment in primary school as per cent of age group (1979) | 102 | 97 |
| Enrolment in secondary school as per cent of age group (1979) | 74 | 39 |
| Adult literacy rate (per cent, 1977) | 77 | 65 |

*Source:* The World Bank, *World Development Report*, 1982.

However, Jordanian growth has been accompanied by some noted achievements in the social field, particularly in education and health (see Table 13.1 for international comparison). Of special interest here is Jordan's relative advantage in education over other Middle Eastern countries. This has been largely due to the high educational standards of Palestinians[14] and the extension of this orientation to the whole population, partly due to the efforts of the public sector. This advantage, reflected for example by differential adult literacy ratios in the Arab world,[15] is a major factor behind the high net emigration during the 1970s of Jordanian professionals and skilled labour to the oil-exporting Arab countries. Kuwaiti data for 1975 gives an example of the high percentage of Jordanians (including Palestinians) belonging to these occupational categories amongst expatriate workers.[16]

## The determinants of rapid growth and inflation in Jordan during the 1970s

Rapid economic growth is generally expected to produce inflationary pressures, generated by excess demand over what the domestic economy can supply during the same period. However, when, as in the case of Jordan, rapid population and income growth is met by long-term domestic supply rigidities due to a narrow commodity base, high dependence on services and very low participation in the workforce, then excess demand becomes an endemic characteristic of the economy. Strictly in relation to labour productive of physical goods, a small minority of the people (7 per cent) were working to supply the whole economy in 1979.[17] Although rapid real growth in industry pushed up the share of the commodity-producing sectors from 31.1 per cent in 1972 to 37.3 per cent in 1980, this was largely due to the expansion of phosphate production and construction activity.[18] Food and consumer goods production, given by theory a crucial role in absorbing inflationary pressures, did not expand at a rate capable of satisfying fast-rising demand.

Jordan seems to be an extreme case in the Arab world, which is generally characterised by imbalances in sectoral and population growth relative to supplies; structural causes are given by one economist the leading role in causing inflation in the Arab economies.[19] Jordan's demand structure in relation to domestic production is compared to other middle income oil-importing countries in Table 13.2. On the basis of domestic production, Jordan would have a major structural disequilibrium.

**Table 13.2  Structure of demand for Jordan and middle-income oil-importing LDCs, 1980**

(per cent of GDP)

|  | Jordan | Average middle-income oil-importing LDC |
|---|---|---|
| Consumption | 117 | 82 |
| Gross domestic investment | 41 | 27 |
| Exports of goods and nfs | 54 | 22 |
| Gross domestic savings | −17 | 21 |
| Resource balance (exports-imports of goods and nfs) | −58 | −6 |

*Source:* World Bank data, 1982, supplied by the National Planning Council.

To understand the possibility of sustaining the above structure, one must recall the two key factors mentioned in the introduction: financial aid and net export of labour to the oil-exporting Arab countries, from which Jordan receives substantial workers' remittances. Neither of these two is included in GDP figures. The number of Jordanians working abroad amounts to around two-thirds of the size of the labour force in Jordan (including the unemployed)[20] so that the flow of remittances from these workers becomes a major national income source. Aid (net transfers) is a vital additional source of income (see Table 13.8 in Appendix to this chapter).

Nevertheless, throughout the 1970s tremendous demand pressure on domestic supplies built up and could only be released by an unrelenting rise in imports allowed by Jordan's traditional laissez-faire and highly liberal trading policies. This is reflected by the huge jump in the degree of openness of the economy after 1973: exports and imports as a proportion of GNP moved from a yearly average of 38 per cent during 1960–67 to 47 per cent during 1970–73 and to 81 per cent during 1974–81. Although serious attempts were made to decrease the country's traditionally large trade gap, the coverage of imports by exports rose only from an average of 17 per cent in 1970–73 to 22 per cent in 1978–81.[21]

Jordan is totally dependent on imported oil and capital goods, and to a large extent also on manufactures. Dependence on imported food became increasingly serious during the 1970s. Agricultural imports supplied an increasing proportion of domestic consumption, while local production's share dropped from supplying 40.3 per cent in 1968 to 17.3 per cent in 1979.[22] This took place in spite of absolute increases in production levels, again pointing to the rapidly rising pressure from demographic and income increases. In the mid-1970s Jordan was a serious deficit country vis-à-vis five commodities central to Arab diets, even when compared to other Middle Eastern countries. As a percentage of its total consumption, Jordan had a deficit ranging between 50 per cent and 100 per cent for wheat, rice, sugar, vegetable oils and red meat.[23]

Remittances and aid have been crucial for Jordan's balance of payments (see Appendix, Table 13.8), financing between 90 per cent and 110 per cent of the deficit on goods and services between 1974 and 1981 and have in turn allowed high levels of demand increases, reflected in consumption, investment and imports. The country had a short-run price-inelastic demand for imports ($-.77$), due to the inability to produce substitutes, and a high income elasticity to import (1.26), which rises (to 2.57) in the long run. These calculations covering 1968–79 also yield a high marginal propensity to import (.78), which contrasts with the much lower figure (.24) for the period 1954–1967. Similarly, the 1970s were characterised by a high marginal propensity to consume (.83), leading especially to much higher consumption of luxury goods which came to account for over 50 per cent of manufactured imports during the decade.[24] Thus, these characteristics of demand are more specific to the 1970s due to the high level of income derived from the boom in the Middle East.

Maldistribution of income in Jordan has been aggravating the situation by pushing personal consumption increasingly towards imported luxury goods. Two separate studies based on 1973 data and on the 1979 survey of family expenditures show substantial and little improving inequality: a high gini coefficient by international standards (.6694) and 55 per cent of income going to the highest income group (decile).[25]

However, the development of consumerism in an economy dominated by merchant-capital where people have the option of earning higher income abroad was not restricted to the upper class. The demonstration effect operated both nationally and internationally. Migrant workers abroad develop consumer patterns possible in the rich oil countries. Returned migrants who have acquired these goods generate among non-migrants of the same class or community a feeling of lack of achievement; this leads to associating personal progress not with improving productivity in Jordan, but with more rapid improvements in standards of living achieved by working in the oil-exporting states.[26]

Remittances from Jordanians abroad go primarily to family maintenance and housing, with considerable evidence that they have also fuelled a wave of land and real-estate speculation during the 1975–80 period. Moreover 'despite Jordan's intensive efforts to attract a sizeable part of remittances to productive and investment uses, the evidence made available . . . does not reveal that the desired investment . . . was made'.[27] The effect on importables is evident, for example, in the greater percentage of returned migrants' housholds having electrical appliances, relative to the households of non-migrants and current migrants.

Economic aid to Jordan is also directly related to rising excess demand and imports. Much of the foreign grants to Jordan go into budget support, mainly financing recurring expenditures, e.g. wages and salaries of the civil service and army, thus feeding into consumption. Foreign grants, and to a secondary extent loans, covered from 78 per cent to 99 per cent of the budget deficit between 1971 and 1981.[28]

The funds made available directly by grants and loans, or via the release of other state funds, allowed the two development plans to have a very heavy investment programme. In fact during the 1976–80 plan Jordan achieved one of the highest investment rates in the world, moving from 25 per cent of GNP in 1975 to 33 per cent in 1980. Table 13.3 shows that the bias towards capital-intensive sectors and against agriculture in planned investment was reinforced by the amounts actually spent.

The heavy investment programme fed into imports in a massive way. Despite the high absolute growth of consumer goods (19 per cent per year during 1968–79) the much faster growth of intermediate goods (26 per cent per year) and capital goods (61 per cent per year), pushed up the share of these two categories in total imports (see Appendix, Table 13.10). This evidently follows from the lack of domestic substitutes and

**Table 13.3  Capital expenditure by economic activity in Jordan, 1976–80**

(per cent)

|  | 1976–80 Plan | Realisation ratio[a] |
|---|---|---|
| Agriculture and irrigation | 6.4 | 49.7 |
| Industry and electricity | 34.1 | 104.5 |
| Tourism | 2.7 | 93.4 |
| Transport | 20.5 | 144.3 |
| Communications | 1.9 | 83.1 |
| Housing[b] | 21.3 | 218.2 |
| Construction and other services | 13.1 | 82.6 |
| Total | 100.0 | 110.3 |

*Source:* National Planning Council, *Five Year Plan 1976–1980*, p. 19; and *Five Year Plan 1980–1985*, p. 6.

*Notes:* (a) The realisation ratio refers to percentage of actual capital expenditures out of planned capital expenditures for each sector.
(b) Housing includes considerable construction.

the high income elasticity of demand, particularly for imported capital goods (2.66).[29]

Regional political factors also contributed to demand pressures. The Lebanese civil war which started in 1975 diverted from Beirut regional reliance on a dynamic services sector. Amman, the capital of a country based on a very liberal economy, was one of the natural alternatives. Hence in the mid-seventies a large number of families and businessmen, estimated at 60,000 Lebanese,[30] i.e. equivalent to 12 per cent of the population of Amman at the time, moved from Beirut. This included well over 100 Lebanese and international companies and agencies. Consequently a substantial amount of human and financial capital was transferred, adding to aggregate demand without directly contributing to concrete physical production.

One of the main sectors affected by this sudden transfer, as well as from migrant remittances, was land, real estate and housing/construction. The figures in Table 13.4 on land purchases show high activity as of 1973 and particularly during 1975 and 1976, the first two years of the Lebanese war. The rapid rise in real estate prices and rents in Jordan during the latter half of the 1970s, can very roughly be gauged from

Table 13.4, which suggests that land prices were increasing at a yearly average of 36 per cent with the largest jumps in 1975 and 1976.

The main effect of the Iran–Iraq war was the boosting of services income in Jordan, particularly transport, transit and re-exports. The restriction of Iraq's main sea route in the Gulf diverted a substantial amount of Iraqi trade to Aqaba, Jordan's port on the Red Sea. Re-exports jumped from a yearly average of 34 per cent of the value of Jordanian exports during 1974–78 to 44 per cent during 1979–81. Moreover, the Aqaba Free Zone handled in 1981 112 per cent more tonnage than it did in 1980. The income earned from the windfall gains of the Lebanese and Iran–Iraq wars was sudden and had little counterpart in domestic production, thus increasing inflationary pressures.

**Table 13.4 Revenue of land registration department and the number of buying and selling transactions (1972–79)**

|  | Revenue[a] (JD millions) | Number of transactions ('000) |
|---|---|---|
| 1972 | 1.1 | 56.9 |
| 1973 | 2.2 | 77.3 |
| 1974 | 2.0 | 64.7 |
| 1975 | 5.4 | 93.2 |
| 1976 | 9.3 | 108.5 |
| 1977 | 6.1 | 74.1 |
| 1978 | 9.8 | 86.8 |
| 1979 | 14.4 | 101.8 |

*Source:* Adapted from Bassam K. Saket, *Economic Uses of Remittances – the Case of Jordan* (see footnote 47) p. 24, table 9.

*Note:* (a) Revenues represent around 10 per cent of the valuation of land. Land valuation corresponded only roughly to the true value of land transactions; it has been assumed here that any level of under-valuation was constant.

It would be less than fair to discuss inflationary pressures in Jordan without noting a significant socio-economic determinant. Class structure in Jordan is such that a small percentage of the population, largely merchants, hold enormous economic power. Any visitor to Jordan would notice the high mark-up on retail goods in spite of a very liberal import policy (see next section). During a brief field trip to Jordan, it became evident from discussions with policy-makers and businessmen

294 World Prices and Development

that the minimum acceptable mark-up on cost was high by any standard. These rates can easily involve three digit figures in percentage terms.[31]

Given the tremendous excess demand pressures and the socio-economic patterns leading to inflation, price rises in Jordan during the 1970s seem lower than one would expect. However, 'considerable confusion surrounds the domestic rate of inflation and its current trend'.[32] A new cost of living index based on the new household expenditure survey will, it is hoped, improve the situation.

Between 1967 and 1972 the cost of living in Jordan increased at an annual average rate of 4.8 per cent. It was only after 1972 that the rate went above 10 per cent, particularly during 1973–75, which had an annual average of 14.1 per cent. Comparative Middle East figures show Jordan as having relatively high rates, even by Saudi Arabian standards, particularly in the latter part of the decade (see Appendix, Table 13.9). The highest rates of increase in the cost of living were in clothing and footwear, and other goods and services, the two commodity groups with the highest imported content.

Given the overwhelming role of imports in Jordan's consumption and production, there is no doubt that inflation is largely imported. Some discussion has arisen, however, as to the extent of the imported element's share in national inflation. One estimate put the imported share in Jordan's inflation at around 90 per cent.[33] However a study prepared by the director of research at the Central Bank of Jordan suggested a 65 per cent share, with external factors becoming slightly more important than domestic ones after 1974. This study also finds that the trade and budget deficits between them explain 92 per cent of the variation in inflation. If the implication here is that the budget deficit is an internal factor, then this raises a problem. The only way the government could maintain such a high budget deficit is via the traditional assurance of foreign grants. This makes government expenditures at least indirectly dependent on foreign factors. In this case the 92 per cent figure would largely represent external factors and would come close to the first estimate.[34]

## Table 13.5 Changes in import prices

(1969 = 100)

|  | 1972 | 1973 | 1974 | 1975 | 1976 | 1977 | 1978 | 1979 |
|---|---|---|---|---|---|---|---|---|
| Yearly change, % | 9.0 | 4.7 | 27.0 | 37.2 | −10.4 | 11.4 | −6.8 | 10.7 |

Source: Central Bank of Jordan.

Over the 1970s Jordan's import prices increased at a yearly average of 10 per cent (Table 13.5). The high rise in domestic inflation during 1973–75 was matched by higher rises of import prices (23 per cent on average) during the same period.

The IMF attributes to imported inflation the leading role in Jordan's 1973–75 inflation, but also notes that food prices rose sharply in 1976 due to very high demand for Jordanian food products from the oil countries. This was in fact part of a general regional excess demand, especially for perishable agricultural goods.[35]

## Economic policy and inflation in Jordan

### The generation of inflation and general policy options

The generation of inflation in Jordan during the 1970s has been shown to be heavily dependent on external factors: rising import prices, rapidly rising domestic demand derived from income earned abroad and aid, and rising regional (Middle Eastern) demand affecting the domestic prices of Jordanian consumer products (chiefly food) and inputs (labour). Thus vital conditions of growth and inflation in Jordan are beyond the direct control of policy-makers.

Policy-makers face three general, but not mutually exclusive, options: either domestic production can be increased fast enough to satisfy demand (failing which prices will rise and real wages will fall bringing down consumption); or demand can be restrained via fiscal, monetary and other policy measures; or else imports (a trade deficit) should be allowed to absorb demand pressure. It would seem that the balance of Jordan's policy record over the 1970s came out in favour of the third option, i.e. a huge trade deficit.

In the case of a small country like Jordan which finds it difficult to expand production for structural reasons, and where demand restraint is a complicated matter (see below), but with available sources of money, there could be options worse than imported inflation, i.e. even higher domestic inflation. This is not to imply however that failure to restrain demand, particularly for non-essentials, is acceptable. But at least the availability of imports seems to have placed an upper limit on inflation in Jordan as reflected by the closeness of the rates of increase in the cost of living and the price of imports (approximately 10 per cent per year on average over the decade).[36]

Adjustment-oriented policies, e.g. demand restraint, vis-à-vis imported inflation, were not pursued. But viewing dependence on remittances, grants and loans as postponement-type policies,[37] is in this case slightly problematic. It would partly depend on whether one is studying Jordan with the 'nation-state' as the unit of analysis or understanding it as part of a regional political-economic system encompassing the Middle East and the West. Thus if it could be shown that there are some quasi-permanent features of Jordan that endow it with assured dependence on foreign financial resources, this could reduce the urgency of adjustment and would stretch the horizon within which postponement is acceptable. The underlying danger is that the precariousness of Jordan's position, even as part of a wider system, requires more self-sufficiency and should not allow dependence on foreign resources to be continuously assumed. This is particularly important in Jordan's planning given that 'the only way to plan has been to assume that aid will continue to be available, at roughly the same volume, throughout the plan'.[38]

*Monetary policy*

Monetary policy in Jordan is a relatively recent phenomenon. Prior to 1969 the Central Bank of Jordan (CBJ) had practically no discretionary control over the monetary base in the country, which was essentially determined by changes in the balance of payments. The direct link between 'money' and the CBJ's foreign reserves was broken when the government introduced the first treasury bills and long-term bonds in 1969. Similarly, legal reserve requirements were first introduced in 1969.

High expansion in domestic liquidity (money plus quasi-money) began in 1973. However, the stage had already been set by the changing behaviour of commercial banks and the public. After the introduction of higher-yielding government securities, the banks switched their excess reserves in their direction, thus helping finance government spending. And the Jordanian public's classical preference for hoarding money and holding cash as opposed to demand deposits, a feature reinforced by the turmoil of the period 1967–71, was beginning to change.[39] The gradual increase of stability and increasing sophistication of commercial banking produced a greater demand for deposits and a higher velocity of money.

The years 1973–76 were characterised by very rapid monetary expansion. In 1977 the expansion had over-reached itself. Boom conditions tapered off and monetary expansion decelerated, reflecting the slower pace of business activity in construction and trade. Banks exercised caution in lending as borrowers were facing difficulties in the real estate market and in running down inventories of imports. After 1977, the cycle of expansion restarted, slowing down again during 1981.

Because of the continuing dependence of Jordan's liquidity on foreign factors, the 1981 slowdown was not followed by a new expansion cycle, as happened after 1977. In 1982, because of the effects of the world recession on the oil-countries, general instability in the region accentuated by the Gulf War and the invasion of Lebanon by Israel 'Arab assistance to Jordan dropped considerably and remittances of Jordanians working abroad did not increase at previous rates. The balance of payments account ended up with a small deficit for the first time since the early seventies.'[40] Because the government and public sector were forced to compensate for these reductions by borrowing commercially, credit expansion was considerable (40 per cent above 1981) and became the main generator of liquidity.

Monetary policy in Jordan has had two main objectives: the control of inflationary monetary expansion and the direction of finance to longer-term productive projects. The measures used during the 1970s included: limitations on credit expansion (with exemptions for industry and agriculture), raising the reserve and liquidity ratios, application of a credit-deposit ratio (to constrain the impact of remittances), minimum interest rates on loans, overdrafts and discounts. These measures usually discriminated between goods-producing activities and services to the benefit of the first, and between demand deposits and longer term deposits to the benefit of the latter. They followed the changes in domestic liquidity and business environment as affected by aid and remittances, thus being at their most stringent during 1973–76, then being relaxed in 1977 and again restrictive after that until the early 1980s.

Monetary policy in Jordan has failed to affect inflation. In spite of the use of the various measures mentioned above, continued price rises led 'the Central Bank governor . . . to state flatly in late 1980 that the CBJ does not have much leeway to affect credit volume or inflation, because of the open economy's enormous susceptibility to imported price rises. He said that fiscal restraint would henceforth be adopted as the government's main anti-inflationary tool'.[41] However, this was not the only reason for the ineffectiveness of monetary policy.

The discount rate and the reserve and legal liquidity requirements have been shown to have a very weak statistical relation to money-supply (both M1 and M2).[42] A main reason behind this phenomenon is that the very high availability of funds (from grants and remittances) combined with traditionally conservative banking practices in an often uncertain environment, usually prompts the banks to hold reserves and liquidity in excess of requirements (e.g. a 40 to 50 per cent liquidity ratio compared to a minimum 30 per cent in the late 1970s). Another factor has been the narrow spread between CBJ's discount rate and the other sources of credit which did not attract banks to use it.[43]

Interest rate policy has been equally dubious in its effects. The low rates on borrowing and lending relative to inflation meant that real interest rates were negative. This has encouraged borrowing particularly if it leads to the building up of inventories of imports that benefit from inflation. It has also diverted depositors to similar assets as well as real estate. Bankers therefore have been reluctant to extend long-term lending.

The authorities in Jordan have attempted to absorb liquidity and provide funds for long-term productive projects by creating during the 1970s several specialised financial intermediaries, including a stock market and four government owned institutions. In addition, local syndicated lending has been encouraged. The net effect of all these arrangements on the finance of agriculture and industry has been modest. Credit expansion by the specialised banks has been small. It seems that despite the availability of relatively cheap finance in Jordan the opportunities for investment are limited. Consequently the major share of credit expansion has continuously gone to trade and construction. These two sectors have accounted for 61.6 per cent on average of credit by commercial banks between 1975 and 1979 and 56.5 per cent in 1982.[44] This large share accounts for one of the results of Haddad's econometric analysis, namely that credit expansion has a slight impact on inflation.[45]

In addition, the value of remittances from workers abroad is heavily understated. Although the authorities have attempted to 'surface' as large a portion as possible of total remittances via liberal foreign exchange regulations, allowing the opening of foreign currency accounts for non-residents, widening the spread between interest rates on demand deposits and time deposits and allowing migrants to bring in tax-free goods, there seems to remain a large undeclared percentage.

The above is confirmed by several sources.[46] Moreover, in a survey conducted by the Department of Economics of Jordan's Royal Scientific Society, evidence was assembled showing that 47.8 per cent of returned migrants and 53.4 per cent of current migrants (across income groups) have not used either cheques or the banking system to send money home. The methods used include friends, personal transfers, money exchanges abroad and others.[47] Moreover, in interviews with the staff of the CBJ conducted in May-June 1983, I was informed that the 382 million JDs figure officially presented as remittances in 1982 could easily be anywhere between 700 and 1,000 million JDs (with emphasis on the latter figure). This seemed an informed approximation.[48] The undetected state of remittances could explain the limited effect that monetary policy has had on money supply and inflation.

*Fiscal policy*
Until 1979 fiscal policy was even less of a restraint on excess demand

and inflation than monetary policy. The growth of budget expenditures was higher than that of GNP and GDP throughout the 1970s. As mentioned earlier a deficit budget relying on foreign aid facilitated massive public spending, a leading source of inflationary pressure. However, as of 1980, the year the CBJ governor stated that fiscal restraint would become the main anti-inflationary tool (see preceding section on monetary policy), expenditure growth slowed down and dropped below the rate of growth of the economy (Table 13.6).

The role of taxation was also weak. Government expenditures adjust faster than government revenues to inflation; the long lags in tax collection in Jordan are the main reason behind this disparity, with inflation speeded up the longer the lags.[49]

In fact, domestic revenues as a whole have been decreasing in relation to GDP after a rising trend in the early to mid-1970s. Due to the vast increase in imports during the decade, indirect taxes, largely import duties, have accounted for an increasingly major share of these revenues (Table 13.7). The shortfall of domestic revenues has been compensated by foreign grants and loans, 50 per cent higher than the anticipated allocation of grants for the 1976–80 period.

As in many other LDCs, direct taxation in Jordan is limited and suffers from political, social and institutional obstacles. Income tax is imposed largely on government employees and urban wage earners whose income can be taxed at source. Widespread evasion and under-reporting exist among self-employed people, large businesses and professionals. Furthermore capital gains and property taxes were minimal. Because of the importance of considerable land speculation, trading profits and imports of luxury goods, Jordan was lacking a vital

**Table 13.6 The growth of government budget expenditure, 1972–82**

(Average annual growth rate, at current prices)

|  | 1972–1975 | 1975–1979 | 1980 | 1981 | 1982[a] |
|---|---|---|---|---|---|
| Total expenditures | 25.0 | 25.9 | 9.2 | 14.9 | 11.6 |
| Current expenditures | 21.3 | 22.7 | 4.5 | 16.4 | 18.1 |
| Capital expenditures | 32.9 | 27.1 | 16.8 | 12.5 | 4.4 |
| GNP | 15.9 | 24.8 | 28.2 | 26.6 | 12.2 |
| GDP | 10.3 | 23.8 | 30.1 | 20.8 | 13.2 |

*Source:* World Bank sources, 1980 and CBJ *Annual Report*, 1982, pp. 62–65; also CBJ *Monthly Statistical Bulletin*, May 1983.

*Note:* (a) Preliminary data.

## Table 13.7  Structure of domestic revenue in Jordan and share of GDP (1972, 1975 and 1980)

(per cent)

|  | 1972 | 1975 | 1980 |
|---|---|---|---|
| Tax revenue | 52.2 | 54.0 | 60.2 |
| Taxes on net income and profits | 7.5 | 11.3 | 12.3 |
| Import duties | 26.6 | 29.8 | 40.6 |
| Other taxes | 18.1 | 12.9 | 7.3 |
| Non-tax revenue[a] | 24.5 | 32.2 | 31.7 |
| Other[b] | 23.3 | 13.8 | 8.1 |
| Total domestic revenue | 100.0 | 100.0 | 100.0 |
| Total domestic revenue's share of GDP | 20.7 | 29.3 | 26.0 |

*Source:* World Bank data, 1982, supplied by the National Planning Council in Jordan.

*Notes:*  (a) Licences, fees and interest and profits from public enterprises.
(b) Proprietory receipts, sales of services, export duties, oil transit dues and other miscellaneous items.

instrument for the control of inflation. Despite the slightly rising share of direct taxes in domestic revenue, they still amounted to only 4 per cent of GDP in 1982. The growth of non-tax revenue, mainly profits from public enterprise, undershot the target proposed for it in the 1976–80 plan by 40 per cent.[50]

*Import duties and import substitution industrialisation in Jordan*
In the 1960s Jordan followed an import substitution industrialisation strategy. Despite some success in the early stages, this approach became ineffective in the 1970s, which led to a change in thinking towards the end of the decade in the direction of export expansion. Hence between 1968 and 1977 the industrial sector in Jordan experienced negative import substitution in terms of contribution to output and value added, resulting in foreign exchange dis-saving.[51]

The problems of import-substitution in Jordan are somewhat similar to the classic cases of Latin America.[52] Production is more costly than is feasible, productivity is low (even by Middle Eastern standards) and capacity utilisation is disturbingly low. Industrial investment favoured large capital and energy intensive sectors, i.e. import-intensive sectors.

Two-thirds of industrial investment during the 1976–80 Plan period were absorbed by phosphate mining, phosphate fertilisers, potash, petroleum refining and cement.[53] The industries which did achieve some import substitution benefited from strong overall protection through government participation in these industries, and monopolistic or quasi-monopolistic status.[54] This applies for example to leather (the Jordanian Tanning Company), petroleum and cement. The shift to export expansion was encouraged by the success of some Jordanian exports in the Middle East partly due to special trading agreements within the region.

One of the main problems of import-substitution in Jordan is the highly liberal policy towards imports. Jordan has not applied a quota system against imports and maintains an import duty system primarily for revenue purposes. The protective function of these duties has been secondary to, and in conflict with, the revenue motive, particularly since they constitute the bulk of domestic fiscal revenue. Although tariffs did afford some effective protection in the early 1970s, they were reduced in 1976 for allegedly anti-inflationary purposes. Moreover, control of imported inflation has not been helped by the failure of import tariffs in Jordan to distinguish explicitly between luxury goods and essentials.

*Exchange rate policy*
Exchange rate policy in Jordan has probably been the most deliberately used tool for limiting the impact of imported inflation. The Jordanian dinar (JD) has been pegged to the SDR since 1973; the government has a strong preference for a stable exchange rate against the major hard currencies.[55] The authorities decided that their highly open economy, heavily dependent on imports, warranted an overvalued JD, although the weakness of productive capacity did not justify it. However, given that aid was available to help the balance of payments problems, e.g. arising out of overpriced Jordanian exports, this was in their view the correct policy.

In fact, Jordan had learned this lesson from its unsuccessful devaluation in 1971. It accelerated inflation in 1972 and did not help close the trade deficit which also increased by 20 per cent in that year. But as a recent study has demonstrated, exports are a casualty of Jordan's exchange rate policy, particularly in the Gulf markets. If one takes 1975 as a base year, the relative price competitiveness of exports (as measured by the real effective exchange rate, i.e. relative to prices) has by 1981 deteriorated 14 per cent in comparison with other leading suppliers to Jordan's most vital markets.[56] There are arguments for modifying this policy.

*Wages*
At the beginning of the 1970s wages in Jordan were so low that Jordan
and Kuwait had the widest wage differentials in the Middle East.[57]
Moreover the availability of a surplus of unemployed labour in the
Palestinian refugee camps put a downward pressure on wages.

With the increasing migration to the Gulf countries in the mid-1970s,
shortages appeared in some occupational groups. Unemployment
declined from 14 per cent in 1970 to 2.1 per cent in 1975, with probably
no more than frictional unemployment in 1976. Average wages
increased by 18.6 per cent per year between 1972 and 1976, higher than
inflation; in industry the rate of wage increases was around 20 per cent
per year between 1972 and 1979, i.e. an improvement of real wages of 7.2
per cent per year.

One factor which restrained the inflationary impact of wage rises was
the import into Jordan of replacement labour, mainly from Egypt. This
labour is underpaid by Jordanian standards, particularly in agriculture.
A highly undesirable effect of replacement migration is the creation of
'negative' status occupations. Jordanians refuse to work in areas now
associated with migrant workers. It also reinforces rural-urban migration
and the abandoning of agriculture by Jordanian labour. Rapid population
growth, the slowing down of net emigration by Jordanian workers, and
the creation of these new 'negative' status occupations, explain the rise
of unemployment to 8 per cent in the early 1980s.

*Aid and borrowing policy*
Ever since its creation, Jordan has depended heavily on aid. Strategic
factors, as in the case of many other aid recipients, influenced the value
of aid that Jordan was able to attract. The country had strategic value to
both Western and Arab countries, particularly in view of the existence
of a major percentage of the Palestinian population in Jordan.[58]

A new characteristic of grants and loans during the 1970s was the
growing share of Arab sources. Several Arab summit conferences had
pledged support to Jordan. The Baghdad summit conference in 1978
gave Jordan a promise of $1.2 billion in grants per year, for five years. In
1979 $1 billion were actually transferred.

Between 1970 and 1976, an average loan contracted would carry an
interest rate of 2.4 per cent per year, a maturity of 29 years with 6 years
grace in addition. Debt service was quite moderate, around 2 per cent of
exports of goods and services in 1976. Commercial loans were a very
small proportion of the total (12 per cent in 1976). During this period 75
per cent of total debt outstanding came from major bilateral creditors
(FRG, USA, UK, Kuwait, Iraq, Iran, Saudi Arabia and Abu Dhabi).

Between 1976 and 1980 the overall situation remained favourable
due to Arab grants, despite slightly stricter lending terms. Debt service

remained manageable at 5 per cent of exports (including remittances). This was helped by transfers which were four times the value of new loans. Moreover, 75% of the loans were again bilateral and concessionary.[59] The same group of countries accounted for the bulk of loans. OPEC countries provided 25 per cent of total disbursed bilateral loans, while the USA, the UK and the FRG gave 38 per cent.

## Subsidies and state trading

As of the mid-1970s the Jordanian state exercised selective direct intervention in pricing and distribution. Subsidies became important in 1974–75 after the sharp rise in the world price of wheat and sugar. These subsidies were meant to allow the sale of essential (politically sensitive) goods at reasonable prices. This was due to the existence of near-monopolistic pricing because of the domination of a few large merchants. Other subsidised goods included flour, bread and meat. Moreover, extra-budgetary (implicit) subsidies exist in the case of petroleum due to sales at prices beneath world levels.

The share of subsidies in the government budget has been growing and taking its toll on revenue. In 1980 the burden was estimated at 14 per cent of current revenues.[60] This is an under-estimate since foreign aid finances oil products.

After the large increase of world oil prices in 1979, the government decided to start closing the gap between domestic and border prices. In 1981 the current expenditure budget registered a 31.2 per cent decrease in fuel support, and the 1982 average weighted price of oil products was 95 per cent of the average border price.[61]

State trading is a recent phenomenon in Jordan. It started with the establishment of the Ministry of Supply in 1974. Control of inflation was a main motive. The Ministry wanted to combat the near-monopoly power of large merchants over basic goods. It had to ensure supplies, prevent contrived or real shortages and secure price-stability. Thus when inflation was high in 1974, the government granted the Ministry monopoly power over the import of sugar, rice, flour, wheat, poultry, fish, garlic, olive oil, onions, potatoes, maize, tomatoes, pasta and powdered milk, in order to bring down prices and ensure availability around the country.[62]

State trading went further as the Ministry opened shops where it sells at special tax free prices a wide variety of consumer products to members of the armed forces and civil service. Access to these shops is via special cards; but it seems to be an open secret in Amman that widespread lending of these cards to friends and relatives is well established. The implications of this policy for political stability should not be underestimated. Despite successive increases in public sector salaries, real wages remain modest. Moreover, given the politically sensitive issue of direct taxation, this seems like an alternative way of forcing prices and profits down. The state becomes a competitor.

## Conclusion and prospects

Imported inflation in Jordan was largely allowed to set the pace and upper limit of domestic inflation. The high growth of the 1970s necessitated a heavy import requirement due to limited domestic production capabilities. This growth was derived from the boom in the Middle East oil countries with which Jordan has a special relationship.

The two main causes of growth and inflation were at one and the same time their main financiers: financial aid and workers' remittances. They reinforced the structural excess demand of the economy over domestic supply. The balance of payments surpluses combined with huge jumps in domestic liquidity, partly undetected due to the non-official transmission of remittances, created a situation which monetary policy could not handle. Neither could fiscal nor wages policies, due to their partial non-existence. Indirect taxes, the chief source of domestic revenue in Jordan, were not meant to restrict imports. However, exchange rate policy helped slightly by cheapening imports via an overvalued JD. The main method of absorbing inflationary pressure was to allow imported supplies to satisfy it with minimal hindrance.

Apart from the conventional policy areas, the state intervened in trading by subsidising and undercutting commercial prices. Government shops helped shield public sector employees from imported inflation. This was also a means of dealing with market structure imperfection and merchant capital through non-fiscal methods.

The 1980s seem to be a tougher decade for Jordan. The political turmoil of the region, and the slowdown of economic activity in the Middle East mean less remittances, and aid. This is reflected in the slowdown of GNP growth in 1982 and the first balance of payments deficit for eleven years.

Even windfall gains have turned sour. The great Iraqi dependence on Jordanian trade routes and services has had to be partly diverted via Turkey for strategic and political reasons. These developments combined are forcing the government to borrow commercially more than before. Hopefully, however, the development of the domestic financial sector will help avoid excess dependence on the Euromarket.

And, finally, the dependence of growth and inflation on external factors has meant that as these slow down, so does inflation. In fact in 1982 the cost of living index registered an increase of 7.6 per cent compared to 11.1 per cent in 1981. Long term prospects of dealing with inflation will depend however on success in expanding production capacity, particularly in agriculture and essential consumer goods.

## Appendix

**Table 13.8 Summary of the balance of payments, 1974–1981**

(millions of SDRs)

| | 1974 | 1975 | 1976 | 1977 | 1978 | 1979 | 1980 | 1981 |
|---|---|---|---|---|---|---|---|---|
| Current account | 2.9 | 36.8 | 31.3 | −12.8 | −226.3 | −3.9 | 286.7 | −32.2 |
| Merchandise exports fob | 128.9 | 126.0 | 179.2 | 213.3 | 236.9 | 311.0 | 441.0 | 631.3 |
| Merchandise imports fob | −359.5 | −534.2 | −786.2 | −1049.2 | −1064.2 | −1347.0 | −1636.6 | −2420.3 |
| Other goods services and income: balance | −44.6 | −34.0 | −15.6 | 33.3 | −39.4 | −178.5 | −33.8 | −116.0 |
| Private unrequited transfers (net) | 68.4 | 141.8 | 348.0 | 360.6 | 373.3 | 393.8 | 511.2 | 793.1 |
| Official unrequited transfers | 209.6 | 337.3 | 306.0 | 429.4 | 267.1 | 816.8 | 1005.0 | 1080.0 |
| | | | | | | | | |
| Direct investment and other long-term capital | 28.5 | 113.4 | −38.3 | 130.2 | 231.2 | 153.2 | 82.1 | 180.3 |
| Direct investment | 2.9 | 16.0 | −8.9 | 9.6 | 45.0 | 20.4 | 23.8 | 121.2 |
| Other long term capital | 25.7 | 97.4 | −29.5 | 120.5 | 186.2 | 132.9 | 58.3 | 59.1 |
| | | | | | | | | |
| Other short term capital | 4.4 | 22.2 | 52.2 | −14.6 | 103.5 | 54.3 | 171.5 | 72.9 |
| | | | | | | | | |
| Net errors and omissions | −14.1 | −29.9 | −21.4 | 57.5 | 91.1 | 44.7 | −197.6 | −81.7 |
| | | | | | | | | |
| Counterpart items | 15.1 | 5.5 | 7.4 | 9.5 | 48.7 | −28.4 | 87.8 | −21.7 |
| | | | | | | | | |
| Total | 36.8 | 148.0 | 31.1 | 169.8 | 248.3 | 219.9 | 430.4 | 117.5 |

*Source:* Adapted from IMF, *Balance of Payments Statistics Yearbook*, vol. 32, part 1, 1982.

**Table 13.9 Consumer price index for selected ECWA countries (1970–1980)**

(1975 = 100; per cent change)

|  | Jordan | | Kuwait[a] | | Saudi Arabia | | Syria[b] | |
|---|---|---|---|---|---|---|---|---|
| 1970 | 59.6 | — | 68.2 | — | 48.2 | — | 58.9 | — |
| 1971 | 62.5 | 4.8 | 72.7 | 6.5 | 50.5 | 4.7 | 61.7 | 4.7 |
| 1972 | 67.3 | 7.6 | 74.8 | 2.8 | 52.7 | 4.3 | 62.2 | 0.8 |
| 1973 | 74.8 | 11.1 | 81.1 | 8.4 | 61.2 | 16.1 | 74.6 | 19.9 |
| 1974 | 89.3 | 19.3 | 91.8 | 13.1 | 74.3 | 21.4 | 86.1 | 15.4 |
| 1975 | 100.0 | 11.9 | 100.0 | 8.9 | 100.0 | 34.5 | 100.0 | 16.2 |
| 1976 | 111.5 | 11.5 | 105.5 | 5.5 | 131.6 | 31.6 | 111.4 | 11.4 |
| 1977 | 127.7 | 14.5 | 114.2 | 8.2 | 146.6 | 11.3 | 124.6 | 11.8 |
| 1978 | 136.6 | 6.9 | 124.5 | 9.0 | 144.2 | −1.6 | 130.9 | 6.0 |
| 1979 | 156.0 | 14.2 | 130.9 | 5.1 | 146.8 | 1.8 | 136.8 | 4.5 |
| 1980 | 172.7 | 10.7 | 138.7 | 5.9 | 149.0 | 1.4 | 163.0 | 19.1 |
| Average yearly increase: | | | | | | | | |
| 1970–80 | 11.2 | | 7.3 | | 12.5 | | 10.9 | |
| 1970–73 | 7.8 | | 5.9 | | 8.3 | | 8.4 | |
| 1974–80 | 12.7 | | 7.9 | | 14.3 | | 11.9 | |

*Source:* UN Economic Commisson for Western Asia (ECWA), *Statistical Abstract of the Region of the Economic Commission for Western Asia 1970–1979*, Beirut 1981; and *Survey of Economic and Social Developments in the ECWA Region 1981* (no date).

*Notes:* (a) 1980 index covers the first five months.
(b) 1980 index covers the first six months.

**Table 13.10  External trade distribution by economic function and by region, 1971–1981**

(per cent)

| | Average 1971–1975 | 1976 | 1977 | 1978 | 1979 | 1980 | 1981 |
|---|---|---|---|---|---|---|---|
| *By economic function:* | | | | | | | |
| Domestic exports | 100 | 100 | 100 | 100 | 100 | 100 | 100 |
| Consumer goods | 42.1 | 51.3 | 53.4 | 50.3 | 50.8 | 45.1 | 45.4 |
| Raw materials | 47.0 | 44.5 | 34.1 | 36.8 | 36.0 | 42.7 | 45.4 |
| Capital goods | 10.8 | 4.2 | 12.5 | 12.9 | 13.2 | 12.2 | 9.2 |
| Miscellaneous | 0.1 | – | – | – | – | – | 0.2 |
| Imports | 100 | 100 | 100 | 100 | 100 | 100 | 100 |
| Consumer goods | 42.0 | 39.3 | 32.4 | 38.3 | 36.5 | 33.5 | 31.0 |
| Raw materials | 21.1 | 26.5 | 26.7 | 25.6 | 30.5 | 31.7 | 29.2 |
| Capital goods | 26.9 | 33.7 | 40.5 | 35.1 | 32.8 | 34.5 | 39.6 |
| Miscellaneous | 10.0 | 0.5 | 0.4 | 1.0 | 0.2 | 0.3 | 0.2 |
| *By region:* | | | | | | | |
| Domestic exports | 100 | 100 | 100 | 100 | 100 | 100 | 100 |
| Arab Common Market[a] | 29.2 | 27.0 | 27.2 | 32.2 | 36.8 | 39.8 | 48.2 |
| Other Arab countries[b] | 24.1 | 21.3 | 32.6 | 34.2 | 30.7 | 20.9 | 19.5 |
| EEC | 1.8 | 5.1 | 1.4 | 2.1 | 1.4 | 1.7 | 1.5 |
| Socialist countries | 8.5 | 14.7 | 6.9 | 10.0 | 6.5 | 12.6 | 11.5 |
| India | 10.5 | 3.4 | 6.4 | 5.6 | 7.4 | 6.7 | 6.1 |
| Japan | 6.3 | 3.9 | 4.4 | 2.8 | 3.5 | 3.3 | 2.3 |
| Other | 19.6 | 24.5 | 21.1 | 13.1 | 13.7 | 15.0 | 10.9 |
| Imports | 100 | 100 | 100 | 100 | 100 | 100 | 100 |
| Arab Common Market[a] | 8.3 | 5.5 | 5.1 | 5.2 | 4.1 | 2.6 | 1.8 |
| Other Arab countries[b] | 10.8 | 12.4 | 10.9 | 13.7 | 14.7 | 18.2 | 18.6 |
| EEC | 29.6 | 37.1 | 34.8 | 36.6 | 35.8 | 36.3 | 30.8 |
| Other European countries | 5.7 | 6.7 | 5.7 | 6.8 | 8.6 | 6.9 | 7.2 |
| USA | 13.1 | 9.2 | 14.8 | 7.3 | 7.5 | 8.6 | 15.9 |
| Socialist countries | 8.1 | 7.4 | 9.3 | 10.9 | 8.7 | 6.9 | 7.8 |
| India | 1.6 | 3.9 | 0.9 | 0.6 | 0.6 | 0.3 | 0.2 |
| Japan | 5.7 | 6.3 | 6.2 | 6.7 | 6.3 | 7.2 | 6.8 |
| Other | 17.1 | 12.1 | 12.3 | 12.8 | 13.7 | 13.0 | 10.9 |

Source:  Central Bank of Jordan, *Annual Report*, 1978 and 1981.

Notes:  (a)  Includes mainly Egypt, Syria and Iraq.
(b)  Includes mainly the oil exporting countries of the Gulf, Saudi Arabia and Maghreb countries.

**Notes and references**

1 The consequences of Israeli occupation of the West Bank necessitates restriction of the discussion to post-1967 territory under Jordanian rule, i.e. the East Bank of the Jordan. This is not to deny that economic ties with the West Bank remain important and are relevant to the subject of this paper as indicated further on.

2 See, for example, Michal Kalecki, *Essays on Developing Economies,* Chapter 5, 'The problem of financing economic development', pp. 41–63, Hassocks, The Harvester Press Ltd., 1976. Referring to the primary inflationary pressure experienced in the course of rapid economic development as the result of basic disproportions in productive relations, Kalecki concludes: 'The solutions of the problem must be based on economic policies embracing the whole process of development', (p. 62).

3 H. Odeh, *Economic Development of Jordan 1954–1971,* Amman, Jordanian Press Foundation, 1972, pp. 36–38.

4 In 1966 Agriculture, Manufacturing, Mining, Electricity and Construction accounted for only 37.5 per cent of GDP.

5 Ian J. Seccombe, 'Manpower and Migration: the effects of international labour migration on agricultural development in the East Jordan Valley 1973–1980', University of Durham, Centre for Middle Eastern and Islamic Studies, Occasional Paper Series No. 11, 1981, p. 30.

6 National Planning Council, *Five Year Plan for Economic and Social Development 1981–1985,* pp. 68–70. The low productivity of rainfed areas is reflected in their constituting 90 per cent of cultivable land while producing less than half of total agricultural output.

7 World Bank sources, 1982.

8 Michael P. Mazur, *Economic Growth and Development in Jordan,* London, Croom Helm Ltd., 1979, p. 94. The figures refer to the East Bank only. See also Seccombe, p. 8. The participation rate refers to Jordanians working in Jordan.

9 *Five Year Plan 1981–1985,* p. 14.

10 Ibid., p. 1. Recent World Bank figures give an average real annual growth of GDP at factor cost of 10 per cent and at market prices of 12 per cent for 1976–80.

11 Yusif A. Sayigh, *The Economics of the Arab World,* London, Croom Helm Ltd., 1978, p. 187.

12 See data in the Jordanian Department of Statistics' *Statistical Yearbook* 1981, tables 1–5.

13 Industrial census of 1974.

14 Sayigh notes that in 1966 Jordan had by far the highest ratio of university students in the Arab World: Sayigh, p. 202.

15 See *World Development Report,* 1982 and earlier years.

16 J.S. Birks and C.A. Sinclair, *Arab Manpower,* London, Croom Helm Ltd., 1980, pp. 292–294.

17 Estimated on the basis of employment in agriculture, mining, manufacturing and electricity, water and gas as a percentage of East Bank residents. The addition of the construction labour force would yield a 12 per cent figure. Calculated from National Planning Council data.

18 Data supplied by the National Planning Council; also available in Department of Statistics publications.

19  Mahmoud Abd Al Fadeel, *The Problem of Inflation in the Arab Economy*, Beirut, Centre for Arab Unity Studies, 1982, pp. 9–10 (Arabic text).

20  The Jordanian Ministry of Labour estimated the number of Jordanians working abroad at the end of 1980 at 305,400. This would amount to 66 per cent of the labour force according to the 1979 Census. See J. Anani and T. Abd Al-Jaber, 'The experience of Jordan and its policies towards the transfer of labour force', in *The Population Culture Project*, The Ministry of Labour and the ILO, Amman, 1982, p. 99 (Arabic text).

21  Central Bank of Jordan, *Monthly Statistical Bulletin*.

22  Mohamed Saad Amerah, 'Import substitution or export expansion as strategies for growth: A case study of Jordan', Ph.D. Thesis, University of Keele, February 1982, p. 48. I am grateful to Dr. Amerah for allowing me to benefit from this very valuable thesis and from discussions with him at the Royal Scientific Society in Jordan.

23  A.A. El-Sherbini, ed., *Food Security Issues in the Near East*, published for UN-ECWA by Pergamon Press, 1979, pp. 1–3. Other countries included in the study are: Iraq, Lebanon, Syria, A.R. Yemen and PDR Yemen.

24  Amerah, pp. 86–89, 116 and 114–5.

25  Ghazi Assaf, *The Size Distribution of Income in Jordan in 1973*, Amman, Royal Scientific Society, 1979; and 'Distribution of income in Jordan', an unpublished study prepared by the research staff of the National Planning Council in Jordan, to whom I am very grateful for allowing me to look at this paper during my visit in May 1983. A recent World Bank report on Jordan confirms the view that income remains quite unequal and has improved very little since 1970.

26  Abd Al-Fadeel, pp. 61–62.

27  Bassam K. Saket, *Economic Uses of Remittances – the Case of Jordan*, Amman, Royal Scientific Society, March 1983, pp. 20–26.

28  Central Bank of Jordan.

29  Amerah, p. 135.

30  International Monetary Fund, 'Jordan: Recent economic development' (unpublished report), Washington D.C., January 1978, p. 7 (Henceforth, IMF).

31  This has been confirmed by several discussions with economists working with the government. One businessman stated frankly that below a 100 per cent mark-up he would not have considered starting his flourishing business.

32  Seccombe, p. 20.

33  This was estimated by a non-Jordanian economist invited by the Government and was reported to me by the research department of the Central Bank.

34  I am grateful to Dr. Adeeb Haddad for allowing me to read his study and discuss it with him. For a summary of this study see Dr. Adeeb Haddad, 'Inflation in Jordan: A reappraisal', *Jordan Times*, Saturday, March 27, 1982.

35  IMF, p. 11. See also Mazur, p. 137.

36  I am very grateful to Charles Harvey for having emphasised this point in our discussions, and shown its relevance to Jordan's case.

37  Postponement here means delaying policies that could restrain imported inflation rather than shielding its full impact.

38  *Middle East Economic Digest*, Jordan, a MEED Special Report, June 1980, p. 6.
39  Mazur, pp. 132–135.
40  CBJ, *Annual Report* 1982, p. 19.
41  Rami G. Khouri, 'The Jordanian banking system and capital market', Peter Field and Alan Moore, eds. *Arab Financial Markets*, London, Euromoney Publications Ltd., 1981, p. 146.
42  Nabeeh Yousef Mousa, *Liquidity Indicators in the Jordanian Economy*, Department of Research and Studies, Central Bank of Jordan, July 1981, pp. 12–13 (Arabic text).
43  World Bank sources.
44  CBJ, *Annual Report* 1982, table 16, p. 31.
45  Haddad, 'Inflation in Jordan'.
46  See for example Harbi Al-Banawi and Salim Abu Al-Sha'r, *Workers' Remittances in the Light of the Migration of Jordanians Abroad*, Department of Research and Studies, the Central Bank of Jordan, May 1982, pp. 24–26, (Arabic text); also Saket, p. 9.
47  Saket, p. 7 and 28, Annex 1. The survey involved a sample of 1800 households in the Amman governorate.
48  Similar approximations are made by Al Banawi and Abu Al-Sha'r, p. 26.
49  Based on econometric evidence in Haddad.
50  World Bank sources, 1982.
51  Amerah, p. 238 and pp. 252–255.
52  For a concise critique of Latin American industrialisation in relation to inflation see Dudley Seers, 'Structuralism vs monetarism in Latin America: A reappraisal of a great debate, with lessons for Europe in the 1980s', Karel Jansen, ed., *Monetarism, Economic Crisis and the Third World*, London, Frank Cass and Co., Ltd., 1983, pp. 110–126.
53  This has been mentioned by a recent (1983) World Bank report on industrial exports in Jordan. The report also mentioned that energy, fuel and water is virtually more expensive in Jordan than any country in the Middle East.
54  Amerah, pp. 252–256.
55  Lloyds Bank Group, *Economic Report 1982 Jordan*, p. 20.
56  World Bank sources, 1983.
57  UN, ECWA, *Survey of Economic and Social Developments in the ECWA Region, 1981*, p. 69. The level was low enough to provoke unrest in the armed forces.
58  Rivier, F., *Croissance industrielle dans une economic assistée: lecas Jordanien*, Beyrouth C.E.R.M.O.C. 1980, pp. 34 and 38–39.
59  World Bank sources, 1982.
60  *Five Year Plan 1981–85*, p. 10.
61  World Bank sources, 1983.
62  Amerah, p. 199.

# 14 Conclusions

*Stephany Griffith-Jones and Charles Harvey*

## Introduction

As noted at the end of Chapter 1, this concluding chapter will attempt to extract and comment upon similarities and differences which emerge from the country case studies. One of the original expectations of the study was that it would be possible to generalise about the different country experiences categorised on the basis of their trade surplus or deficit in energy, food and capital goods. Another expectation was that their success in adapting to a changing international environment would depend, in part, on their policy response to changing international prices, changing that is in both a relative and an absolute sense.

As was to be expected, factors other than trade in energy, food and capital goods also proved important; the severity and length of the post-1979 recession created financial and other forms of crisis for a wide range of countries, making it harder than expected to distinguish between the successful and unsuccessful. Nevertheless, the categorisation did prove useful; and it was possible to draw some general conclusions about policy reactions to changes in international prices. The management of the global economy, or rather its lack of management, points to the need for changes that would make it less difficult for developing countries to adjust and maintain some progress in the future.

## Impact of recession

Two elements in the international economy stand out from the period since 1970. One is the much greater severity and length of the post-1979 recession, as compared with that of post-1973. To a considerable extent this was a result of the different reaction of the OECD governments (as already noted in Chapter 2). In 1974, there was considerable collective concern, for example at the Interim Committee of the IMF, to avoid global deflation. The main priorities at that time were the resumption of growth and the holding-down of unemployment. In the post-1979 period the OECD governments were in general much more concerned to reduce inflation, by means of restrictive monetary policies and in particular by holding down public borrowing. Furthermore, whereas the IMF introduced the Oil Facility and the Trust Fund on the first occasion, there was nothing comparable after 1979; and intensified protectionism, the inadequate response of official development assistance and the international debt crisis all made it harder for developing countries to finance their external deficits in the early 1980s.[1]

Second, the impact of the post-1979 recession was made worse than it would otherwise have been because so many governments expected the experience of the post-1973 period to be repeated, namely that there would be a relatively short setback followed by a rapid recovery. This expectation was strengthened by the comments and public statements of official bodies (such as the OECD, the IMF and the World Bank) which repeatedly forecast that recovery could be expected within a year, despite repeated disappointments as the recovery failed to appear. As a result, many governments pursued policies that might have been successful – avoiding external financial crisis, a worsening of income distribution and falling output and employment as a result of import shortages, and maintaining government services, subsidy programmes, economic growth and broader goals such as national autonomy in policy-making – if the world economy had indeed recovered in 1981. In particular, the use of commercial and, especially, short-term credit to maintain import levels and output growth proved extremely damaging. The effect was worsened as international interest rates moved from having been mainly negative in real terms to the highest positive real values seen since the Second World War. Ironically, this set of developing country policies helped the OECD countries to improve their balance of payments, and delayed the fall in the volume of world trade until 1982.

As a result, by the early 1980s a wide range of developing countries – whether categorised by their trade in oil, food and capital goods or by the different policies they pursued – were in severe economic and financial difficulties. Many were also in political difficulties, as the impact of the recession and of national policies to cope with it reduced the income of different social groups and brought about reductions in welfare programmes. Judgements as to whether particular categories of country or of policy were 'successful' or not have therefore had to be more subjective than if the international economy had not inflicted a degree of failure on both the 'successful' and the 'unsuccessful'. Nor was it clear at the time of writing whether or how quickly the different countries would recover.

The main categories suggested in Chapter 1 were based on whether countries imported, exported or were self-sufficient in energy, food or capital goods, since it was these categories of product whose relative prices changed so violently in the 1970s and early 1980s. In the sample of 11 countries, these categorisations did indeed turn out to be more useful than the simple division of economies into oil-exporting and oil-importing, so widely used.

Equally interesting, however, were the different experiences of countries which were in the same or similar categories. For example, taking maintenance of growth as one measure of relative success, among economies that were net exporters of oil and net importers of capital goods Tunisia continued to grow in 1980 and 1981, whereas Venezuela's economy stagnated from 1977 onwards and the country's external debt had to be rescheduled in 1983. Although Tunisia was in some difficulty by late 1983, there can be little doubt that it got through the period more successfully than Venezuela, despite Venezuela's very much greater gains from the increase in the price of oil. Argentina was nearly self-sufficient in oil and a net food exporter, and so was far less affected by adverse international changes than most countries in this study. Yet it had the worst record as regards growth of output in the 1970s.

Among exporters of manufactured goods with a rapidly increasing proportion of capital goods exports, Korea enjoyed not only rapid but accelerated growth in the mid-1970s, appeared to have managed to resume economic growth in the 1980s after only one year of recession and maintained its capacity to attract large amounts of commercial foreign credit. Brazil, on the other hand, suffered a severe recession and a major foreign debt crisis in the early 1980s – although it must be noted that this occurred after a long period of rapid growth.

Among importers of oil and capital goods, Malawi seemed to have got through much of the post-1979 recession somewhat better than Tanzania. Malawi's economy did deteriorate, including two years of zero growth of output and a very rapid increase in the debt-service ratio leading to a debt rescheduling. But, at least until 1983, Malawi's production was not constrained by import scarcity, as was the case in Tanzania. Malawi's relative immunity to the international problems of the post-1973 period could be explained by its being usually self-sufficient in food. In contrast Tanzania experienced large grain deficits in drought years (1973–74 and 1979–83) and was unable to devise a way to use surpluses from good years (1970–72 and 1975–78); the impact of higher grain imports and prices was most severe in 1974–75 when it 'had a greater impact on external balance than did petroleum prices on the external balance' (Chapter 3, p. 55 above). But the difference in performance requires further explanation, as does the relative success of Sri Lanka in maintaining output growth, at least in 1980 and 1981 (see Table 14.2). However, the relative success of Malawi and Sri Lanka in maintaining growth was accompanied by a falling real wage rate (Malawi) and a reduction in welfare services (Sri Lanka); and all three countries suffered from reduced autonomy in policy making, including having to agree to IMF programmes or to cope with the results of failure to agree.

This chapter looks, then, at the impact of the rise and relative changes in international prices, on each category of country; and looks also at the important differences between countries in the same or closely similar categories. In particular, various policies are compared to see whether there are general conclusions suggested by the experiences of these countries.

### The effect on growth of output

By one means or another, most of the countries in the sample managed to maintain their rates of growth of *output* in the 1970s surprisingly well (as did most developing countries), despite the problems created by the external environment: higher rates of inflation, slower rates of growth in the developed countries, and unprecedentedly large changes in the relative prices of food, energy and capital goods. Further, Table 14.1 shows that in four countries growth of output was actually faster (by a significant amount) in the 1970s than it had been in the 1960s. Only one of those four countries (Tunisia) was a net exporter of oil. It is important to note that the figures are for growth in output, uncorrected for changes in the terms of trade, so that they measure the countries' performance in increasing production, but do not show how real income changed: for example, Sri Lanka suffered so severely from adverse terms of trade changes that consumption per head failed to grow despite the maintenance of output growth, and real income in Kuwait grew rapidly despite deliberate reductions in oil output, as explained below.

Two countries in the table had markedly lower growth of output in the 1970s: Argentina and Kuwait. Interestingly, Argentina was nearly self-sufficient in oil (and a major food exporter) while Kuwait was a major exporter of oil.

**Table 14.1 Growth of real GDP, 1960s and 1970s**

|  | *1960–1970* | *1970–1979* |
|---|---|---|
| Argentina | 4.3 | 2.5 |
| Brazil | 5.4 | 8.7 |
| Ireland | 4.2 | 3.7 |
| Korea | 8.6 | 10.3 |
| Kuwait | 5.7 | 2.0 |
| Malawi | 4.9 | 6.3 |
| Sri Lanka | 4.6 | 3.8 |
| Tanzania | 6.0 | 4.9 |
| Tunisia | 4.7 | 7.6 |
| Venezuela | 6.0 | 5.5 |

*Source: World Development Report, 1981.*

*Note:* Jordan omitted because no real GDP data available. Private consumption in Jordan, deflated by the consumer price index, grew at 5.2 per cent a year from 1970 to 1979.

Figures *not* corrected for changes in the terms of trade.

The case of Kuwait is quickly explained. Kuwait's real *income* grew rapidly. Oil accounted for over 90 per cent of exports, so that the combined effect of the rise in the price of oil and the increase in Kuwait's share of oil company profits more than offset (by a large amount) the deliberate reduction in oil production. Crude oil production was reduced steadily from 1,091 million barrels a day in 1970 to 411 million barrels a day in 1981, while the purchasing power of Kuwait's exports rose nearly sixfold. Meanwhile, Kuwait's non-oil GDP increased rapidly enough to offset (by a relatively small amount) the fall in oil production. Kuwait's case was very much that of an economy having such a large current account surplus that fluctuating revenue was reflected merely in fluctuations in that surplus; the economy was not really required, therefore, to make any significant adjustment – at least not in comparison with almost all other countries. Moreover, by the end of the decade Kuwait's foreign investments were yielding an income almost as great as the income from oil production, making the economy even less vulnerable to changes in the price and volume of oil exports.

The case of Argentina was greatly complicated by drastic political changes and consequently by a series of policy changes which tended to have a greater impact than external forces. Thus Argentina should have been relatively immune from the effect of rising oil prices, benefited from rising food prices, and had an *economic* structure potentially far more flexible that that of the lower-income countries in the sample. Yet growth was extremely erratic (see Table 9.7) and on average lower than in the 1960s; and its foreign debt was one of the most rapidly growing among developing countries. Indeed, 'the effect of external factors is at times difficult to detect and is sometimes neglected in an economy subject to such strong internal forces' (Chapter 9, p. 196; above). Domestic mismanagement culminated in the opening up of the economy from 1976 onwards, to free flows of goods and services on the one hand, and to capital flows on the other. The country then accumulated large amounts of expensive foreign debt, at variable interest rates which subsequently rose sharply; the borrowing was used principally to pay for imported goods (and services) which displaced domestic production, to finance capital outflows, and to maintain an overvalued exchange rate. The result was economic stagnation – GDP in 1982 was still below the level of 1977 – while foreign debt grew from $9.7 billion in 1977 to $35.7 billion in 1981.[2]

For the other countries in the sample, the international upheavals of 1973 to 1975 had a relatively minor effect on growth of output, as can be

**Table 14.2 Growth of output, 1970–1982, by period[a]**

|  | 1970–73 | 1973–75 | 1975–79 | 1980 | 1981 | 1982 |
|---|---|---|---|---|---|---|
| Argentina | +2.9 | +2.7 | +2.3 | +0.6 | −6.0 | −5.4 |
| Brazil | +1.0 | +7.7 | +6.6 | +7.9 | −3.5 | b |
| Ireland | +4.5 | +3.0 | +4.0 | +2.1 | +1.1 | +1.2 |
| Korea | +10.4 | +8.2 | +10.6 | −3.4 | +7.1 | +5.3 |
| Kuwait | +3.5 | −4.3 | +8.2 | −10.2 | −2.8 | c |
| Malawi | +10.2 | +2.4 | +6.0 | +0.4 | −0.8 | +3.0 |
| Sri Lanka | +2.5 | +5.6 | +10.4 | +5.8 | +5.4 | +5.1 |
| Tanzania[d] | +4.6 | +4.2 | +6.3 | +3.6 | −1.8 | −3.5 |
| Tunisia | +9.5 | +9.6 | +6.7 | +6.8 | +6.5 | +1.5 |
| Venezuela | +4.4 | +5.5 | +4.8 | −1.6 | +0.4 | +0.6 |

*Source: International Financial Statistics,* figures for real GDP at constant 1975 prices.

*Notes:* (a) Jordan's real private consumption growth rates were −0.1, −2.4, +13.1, +26.3, +7.2 in the first five periods; real GDP data not available.
(b) Output probably fell again in 1982, as import volume fell 9 per cent.
(c) Oil output fell by over 30 per cent in 1982, as it had in both 1980 and 1981, so real GDP probably also fell, with oil output offsetting growth in the non-oil economy (of 12 per cent in current prices).
(d) Output change for Tanzania in 1981 and 1982 from Budget Speech 1983.

seen when growth rates are broken down by period as in Table 14.2. But after 1979 they nearly all experienced severe difficulties. This is not apparent from the table in all cases, since some countries managed to keep growth going for a year or two. Furthermore, the statistics are not fully up to date; and the effects of the recession were still an ongoing process and not a past event in 1983 and 1984.

As the table shows, with the exception of Kuwait, all the countries maintained growth of output in 1973–75; only Malawi, and to a lesser extent Ireland, faltered somewhat, but both recovered in the 1975–79 period. Indeed, in the four years after the 1975 recession real output in all the countries except Argentina grew rapidly. After 1979, country after country ran into serious trouble. Some managed to keep output growing for longer than others, but that was not necessarily an advantage if it depended on unsustainable short-term borrowing and resulted in a more damaging and disruptive crisis at a later date. In contrast, Korea appeared to have resumed growth in 1981 after only one year of falling output.

Falls in output were not the only indicators of crisis. Of the countries in the sample, Argentina, Brazil, Malawi and Venezuela had to reschedule their external debts, and the first three had to submit to IMF-imposed cutbacks in demand and growth as a result. In the case of Malawi, this occurred despite falling real wages in the 1970s and early 1980s. Tanzania was in such a serious state that 'any assumptions which take present (and reasonably projectable) earned import capacity and resource transfers point to a continuing decline' (Chapter 3, above). Sri Lanka abandoned much of its admirable welfare and income support system. Even Tunisia, one of the countries able to sustain output growth in both 1980 and 1981, was by 1983 in financial difficulty, in particular over maintaining food subsidies.[3]

Only Ireland, Korea, Kuwait and Jordan were not in immediate financial difficulty by the end of 1983, although Ireland (as already mentioned) grew at less than 1.5 per cent a year from 1980 to 1982. As an OECD member and a member of the EEC, Ireland, although having the lowest income per head of all the industrial market economies, appeared to have been able to avoid the sort of economic and financial crisis common to so many developing countries. Ireland was able to increase official external debt to over 50 per cent of GDP without becoming less creditworthy; and gained access to the EEC market at a time when other industrialising countries were facing increased protection (to Ireland's advantage).

Kuwait, as already noted, had such a high income, both from oil and from the foreign investment of past surpluses, as to be able to ride out comfortably all the fluctuations so far occurring in the world economy.

And Jordan was so profitably linked into aid and the remittances of migrant workers in nearby oil exporting countries as to be relatively immune to the effects of the recession – although of course vulnerable to reduction of those sources of income as was beginning to occur in the 1980s (see next section, below).

It is rather more difficult to explain why Korea managed to resume growth so quickly, and sustain its ability to obtain foreign commercial credits, in contrast to Brazil, for example. Some explanations are suggested in the next section, where the differential access of each country to the newly-increased income and assets of oil exporting countries is investigated, as a partial explanation of their success in maintaining output growth after 1973.

## Ability to respond to shifts in global income

An important aspect of adjustment for oil importing countries was their ability to benefit from the increased income of oil exporters. To some extent this was a matter of chance: traditional links with OPEC donors, geographical nearness for some exports and for sending migrant workers (although some very distant countries sent workers to the Middle East, for example). But very important benefits were also secured by those countries able to respond flexibly and fast to these external changes: for example, by supplying manufactured goods in general and by switching into capital goods exports in particular; by bidding successfully for construction contracts; and by borrowing from international banks to finance the structural changes required in order to respond flexibly (some countries borrowed for other purposes, with quite different result as already noted above).

Sri Lanka, Jordan and to a much lesser extent Korea, all received increasing flows of foreign exchange from migrant workers in oil exporting countries. Tunisia and Malawi were also significant labour exporters. But 60 per cent of Tunisia's remittances came from France, with only 17 per cent coming from Libya; these proportions changed little over the 1970s. Malawi's migrant workers went mainly to South Africa, Zimbabwe and other neighbours (the numbers going to South Africa fell during the decade).

As is clear from Table 14.3, Jordan is an extreme case of a country able to benefit from sending a big proportion of its labour force to work abroad; and Sri Lanka, having had almost no earnings from this source in 1970, developed it as a major means of adjustment in the next ten years. Korea, on the other hand, expanded its visible exports so rapidly that workers' remittances declined to being of negligible importance, despite quadrupling in absolute dollar value.

Korea and Brazil were the only countries in the group to take large-

**Table 14.3 Significance of workers' remittances, 1970 and 1981**

| Recipients | Receipts 1970 (US$m) | % of exports | Receipts 1981 (US$m) | % of exports |
|---|---|---|---|---|
| From OPEC sources: | | | | |
| Jordan | 16 | 47 | 1047 | 141 |
| Sri Lanka | 3 | 1 | 230 | 22 |
| Korea | 33 | 4 | 126 | 1 |
| From non-OPEC sources: | | | | |
| Malawi | 10 | 17 | 17 | 6 |
| Tunisia | 29 | 14 | 357 | 16 |

Source: World Development Report, 1983; *International Financial Statistics.*

scale advantage of the growing demand for goods and services, other than labour, in the oil exporting economies. Most developing countries were not in a position to export the manufactured goods, and especially the heavy manufactures, required for the rapidly expanding development and consumption spending of the oil exporters. For example, Korea's exports of heavy industrial products rose from 14 per cent to 43 per cent of total merchandise exports between 1971 and 1981 (Chapter 8, Table 8.4A) enabling Korea to take full advantage of the second oil price rise – Korean exports to oil exporting countries rose by 230 per cent between 1977 and 1981, compared with 126 per cent for total exports. The share of machinery and transport equipment in Brazil's exports rose from less than 0.5 per cent in 1960 to 17 per cent in 1980, not as dramatic a transformation as Korea's, but contributing to the fact that Brazil's exports to oil exporting countries also rose by more than 200 per cent over the same period, compared with a 92 per cent rise in total exports.[4]

In contrast, the share of exports from Argentina and Sri Lanka going to oil exporters actually declined after 1977, and for Venezuela the figures were insignificant (0.1 per cent in 1977 and 0.2 per cent in 1980). Jordan continued to sell a high proportion of its exports to oil exporters, because of geographical nearness, but merchandise exports were a fairly minor source of foreign exchange for Jordan compared to OPEC aid and migrant workers' remittances. Tunisia and Ireland increased their export sales to oil exporters, but not by a significant amount; while Tanzania and Malawi did not export the manufactured goods demanded by the oil exporters. For example, Tanzania's attempts to build up two-way trade with several oil exporters resulted in few exports beyond minor sales of tea and non-quota coffee. The crucial point was that Korea and Brazil were the only countries in the sample to have the flexibility needed to respond to the new opportunities thrown up by changing international prices.

Jordan was the only country in the sample to gain on a large scale from the increase in OPEC's aid flows. Inflows of OPEC aid to Jordan were of the same order of magnitude as migrants' remittances, if not quite as large. Tunisia (consistently) and Sri Lanka and Tanzania (at times) also received some OPEC aid, but only a small fraction of the flows to Jordan. In all cases except Tanzania, OEPC aid fell after 1980 as the total was rapidly reduced (in Tanzania's case the post-1980 flows were mostly disbursements on a single large project committed before 1980). This contrasted with the earlier post-1973 period, when OPEC aid rose very fast (see Table 14.4, note b).

## Table 14.4 Receipts of OPEC bilateral aid

(US$m.)

|  | 1980 | 1981 | 1982 |
|---|---|---|---|
| Jordan[a] | 932 | 911 | 709 |
| Tunisia | 50 | 44 | 37 |
| Sri Lanka | 59 | 1 | — |
| Tanzania | 7 | 15 | 24 |
| Total OPEC bilateral aid[b] | 8732 | 7612 | 5507 |

*Source:* OECD Development Assistance Committee, *Annual Reviews*, 1982 and 1983.

*Notes:* (a) The grant element of Jordan's OPEC aid was over 90 per cent, whereas for the other countries it was between 45 per cent and 55 per cent.
(b) Total OPEC aid grew very rapidly in the early 1970s, from $398m. in 1970 to $6239m. in 1975.
　　Net disbursements of all concessional assistance by OPEC members, including multilateral aid, were $9,690m., $7,612m. and $6,803m. in 1980, 1981 and 1982.

The remaining way of taking advantage of the shift of income to OPEC was to borrow from international banks. OPEC surpluses were by no means the only source of funds in the eurocurrency markets, but did contribute to their more rapid growth after the early 1970s.

   The major borrowers from private banks among developing countries in the group were Brazil (by far the largest borrower), Korea, Argentina and Venezuela. Jordan, Malawi, Sri Lanka, Tanzania and Tunisia borrowed very little from private banks, and Kuwait not at all. Not all the major borrowers had a debt crisis (Korea being the exception); and not all the minor borrowers managed to avoid debt problems, although only Malawi rescheduled (quickly and easily enough to suggest that a 'crisis' was avoided). Tanzania reversed its previous policy over 1979–81, and sought substantial export credits; it was unable to avoid running up massive commercial arrears, an even less satisfactory form of debt (see Chapter 3).

   Of the major borrowers, Argentina managed to borrow large amounts of expensive commercial money without having much to show for it: output stagnated, inflation and unemployment increased. Venezuela also had relatively little to show for its large amount of foreign debt (much of it incurred short-term and at high cost by parastatals because of ineffective regulations). Venezuela's situation was not nearly as serious as that of Argentina, though, and Venezuela managed to maintain a much higher rate of growth of output. Brazil and Korea, in contrast, both grew very fast in the 1970s and, most crucially, increased their exports very fast. The interesting question is why, at the time of writing, Korea appeared to have resumed growth after only one

**Table 14.5 Dependence on foreign finance: Brazil and Korea, 1978–1982**

|  | 1978 | 1979 | 1980 | 1981 | 1982 |
|---|---|---|---|---|---|
| Capital inflow as per cent of imports | | | | | |
| Brazil | 70 | 20 | 33 | 48 | 26 |
| Korea | 14 | 28 | 27 | 19 | 17 |
| Capital inflow as per cent of investment | | | | | |
| Brazil | 22 | 8 | 14 | 19 | .. |
| Korea | 14 | 27 | 32 | 26 | 21 |

*Source: International Financial Statistics.*

*Note:* Capital inflow: net long and short term capital inflow from balance of payments accounts in US$. Imports from same tables.

   Investment: Gross Fixed Capital Formation from national accounts tables in local currencies, converted to US$ at official average annual exchange rates.

recession year and remained creditworthy internationally, while Brazil had suffered a major recession and debt crisis.

One possibility was that Brazil had relied more heavily than Korea on foreign loans to finance imports and investment. But although Table 14.5 shows that Brazil financed rather more of current imports with foreign borrowing (especially in 1978), Korea financed a rather higher proportion of investment in that way, in the period from 1978 to 1982.

International creditworthiness depends to a large extent on rapidly growing export volume and earnings, and on those earnings growing continuously or nearly continuously; Table 14.6 shows those rates of growth, as well as foreign exchange reserves as a percentage of annual imports, since that is also used from time to time as an indicator of creditworthiness.

**Table 14.6 Indicators of creditworthiness: Brazil and Korea, 1978–1982**

(per cent)

|  | 1978 | 1979 | 1980 | 1981 | 1982 |
|---|---|---|---|---|---|
| Growth of export earnings |  |  |  |  |  |
| Brazil | 4 | 20 | 32 | 16 | −13 |
| Korea | 27 | 16 | 17 | 21 | 1 |
| Growth of export volume |  |  |  |  |  |
| Brazil | 13 | 9 | 23 | 20 | −9 |
| Korea | 14 | −1 | 11 | 18 | 8 |
| Reserves as per cent of imports |  |  |  |  |  |
| Brazil | 79 | 49 | 20 | 31 | 19 |
| Korea | 34 | 30 | 30 | 28 | 30 |

*Source: International Financial Statistics.*

There are of course many other factors which affect banks' willingness to lend to developing countries; but the particular strategy pursued by these two countries, namely very rapid growth based to a large extent on foreign borrowing invested in that growth, did depend on being able to demonstrate to outside observers that the 'economic miracle' was continuing. Or in other words, the whole process depended on its own continuation. Table 14.6 shows that Brazil did at least as well as Korea in increasing the country's export volume and earnings (except in 1978), and sometimes better, until 1982. In 1982, Brazil suffered from having redirected so much of its trade to developing countries (50 per cent), and to oil exporters in particular, as these countries cut back their imports. Finally, loss of confidence by the banks in Latin American debtors following the Mexican default broke the circle of causation and pushed Brazil into its own debt crisis and a major recession.

It would also appear that despite the evidence that Brazil was as successful as Korea in export growth and in financing less of investment with foreign credit, nevertheless Brazil's foreign debt did become unmanageably large, both absolutely and in relation to exports. Foreign debt was estimated at $90 billion in 1982, and debt service as a percentage of exports rose above 50 per cent in 1977, reaching the astonishing figure of 86 per cent in 1982 (see Table 6.6, p. 119). On *public sector* foreign debt only, Brazil's debt service rose two and a half times (from 13 per cent to 32 per cent), whereas Korea's actually *fell* in the 1970s (from 19 per cent to 13 per cent).[5]

A final point is that Brazil suffered the greater external shocks, from falling terms of trade and rising international interest rates. Brazil's terms of trade fell by 45 per cent from 1977 to 1981, whereas Korea's fell only marginally (from 121 in 1976–78 to 110 in 1979–81; see Table 8.5). Furthermore, Brazil was more badly hurt by the rise in international interest rates, as already in 1979 Brazil's total variable interest rate debt was four times larger than that of South Korea, even though the value of Brazil's total exports during that year was only about 20 per cent larger than that of Korea.

Reviewing this evidence, it seems nevertheless that there was not such a very big difference between the two countries' strategies, and in their management of those strategies. For both countries the chosen strategy was risky, but paid off in the form of rapid growth over a long period. It would seem that Brazil suffered a major financial crisis and severe recession, whereas Korea did not, partly because Brazil took the greater risk of the two countries and partly because it suffered from a bigger set of external shocks.

Finally, it should be noted that two countries in the group, Malawi and Tanzania, had little or no access to the increased income of oil exporters. They lacked the capacity to sell the goods or services demanded by oil exporters, did not send migrant workers to oil exporting countries, received minimal amounts of OPEC aid and borrowed little from the euromarkets.

## Evaluation of different policies

### Commitment to long term structural change
It would appear from the country case studies that countries attempting long term structural change become very much more vulnerable to

external shock. Such change requires a sustained period of investment during which time it is quite likely that output will not grow quickly from the new investment; indeed output may even fall in the short run. Major changes in existing systems of production, the creation of new institutions, the introduction of new systems of management and of new things to manage are all quite likely to add to output only in the longer term, even if eventually successful. In such circumstances, mistakes are more likely to occur and the vulnerability of the economy to external shocks is greatly increased. Furthermore: 'domestic inefficiency compounds the impact of external shocks but is also a nearly inevitable consequence of such shocks' (Chapter 3, p. 70, above).

Tanzania embarked upon such a transformation of both the social and productive organisation of peasant agriculture, on the one hand, and of the level of industrial capacity and interdependence, under public sector management, on the other. As Green points out, such a strategy requires a large and sustained capacity to import. Moreover, the shift to importing intermediate and capital goods, from importing consumer goods, had a twofold effect on the economy when a balance of payments deficit had to be reduced: the much lower level of (mainly essential) consumer imports limited the possibility of further cutbacks, and cuts in imports of intermediate goods had a multiple effect on output, employment and income. In other words, an economy attempting a structural transformation goes through a stage of being dependent on continued imports of intermediate goods because those goods cannot yet be manufactured locally. Progress is therefore heavily dependent on vulnerable commodity exports unless and until manufactured exports can be developed, and so requires standby lines of credit, or large reserves, or both, in order to avoid damaging cuts in bad years for exports. Tanzania was caught in just such a trap after 1979, compounded by a neglect of the export sector during the 1970s.[6]

The general point illustrated by the case of Tanzania is that long-term structural change requires particularly prudent short term economic and financial management. The changes themselves required *sustained* availability of finance, and made heavy demands on good management, especially in view of the emphasis placed on parastatal institutions. These demands were increased by the external fluctuations affecting the economy, and the crisis management they made necessary.

In a quite different sense, Venezuela also attempted a structural shift. The country had to decide (from a position of comparative wealth and development) how to manage a big increase in export earnings. The strategy chosen was of big, capital and import-intensive projects, with long gestation periods, in such industries as iron ore and steel, petrochemicals and aluminium. The new industries were directly financed and controlled by the state, through state corporations. The argument for this strategy was that it economised on scarce domestic production capacity while making extensive use of plentiful foreign exchange earnings. It was based on the expectation that foreign exchange earnings would continue to be plentiful for a lengthy period; yet at the same time revenues were also committed to subsidies on basic consumer items and to rapidly increasing imports, demanded because of the holding down of domestic prices and rapid wage increases. When oil revenue stagnated in the 1977–79 period, just as the projected large-scale investments began to be implemented, the programme was sustained by large scale external borrowing.

At this point, the admittedly difficult problem of managing enormous fluctuations in external earnings was compounded by inadequate policies. Investment by the government was cut back sharply in 1979, just before the oil price rise, which was not anticipated. But parastatal corporations continued to borrow on their own account from abroad, in an uncontrolled manner and at higher cost. The increased revenues from the second oil price increase were then used to resume rapid growth in public spending; there was a brief experiment with price deregulation, subsidy cuts and tariff reduction, quickly abandoned as inflation tripled in two years; and wages were increased by between 20 per cent and 50 per cent to compensate for higher prices. Ultimately, in 1983, Venezuela of all countries was forced into a debt rescheduling exercise.

Comparing Venezuela and Tunisia, since both were net oil exporters and importers of capital goods, it is striking how much more successfully Tunisia seemed to get through the early part of the post-1979 recession (it is not possible to tell at the time of writing how serious Tunisia's problems were at the beginning of 1984). Tunisia's GDP grew at more than 6 per cent in 1980 and 1981, continuing the strong growth performance of the 1970s (although growth fell to 1.5 per cent in 1982). Tunisia was of course very fortunate in the 1970s: the country's terms of trade increased by an average of 2.5 per cent a year during the decade. But in addition both exports of manufactured goods and earnings from international tourists increased enormously, and migrants' remittances were sustained. Between them, tourism and remittances supplied 27 per cent of current account receipts in 1981, only slightly down from their share in 1972 (33 per cent), despite the big increase in the share of oil in export earnings as the oil price rose.[7] Tunisia's considerable success was not, on the face of it, at all surprising for an economy which was so lucky. But Venezuela was even luckier. For example, Venezuela's terms of trade rose by 136 per cent from 1978 to 1981, compared with 'only' 28 per cent for Tunisia.

Probably the single most important difference in domestic policy was that Tunisia *built up* its non-oil foreign exchange earning sectors. Venezuela, on the other hand, simply allowed oil to rise from 93 per cent to 95 per cent of visible exports, developing almost no manufactured exports nor any other source of foreign earnings; and did less than Tunisia to increase food output (see Table 14.9 below). This noted, one has still to ask *why* the difference was so marked. A partial answer would seem to be that Venezuela acted very much in the way that one might expect of a newly rich economy; Tunisia did so to a lesser extent, perhaps because although Tunisia did quite well out of oil price increases (and favourable shifts in other export prices) the level of oil production and of *net* oil exports was never such as to create a sense of unlimited riches.

Tunisia does remain extremely vulnerable. Tourism is both highly competitive and demanding of a stable and safe image: international tourists could only too easily go to other countries, in the Mediterranean or elsewhere, if for some reason Tunisia's reputation were to be tarnished. Migrant remittances can be equally vulnerable – and indeed 13,700 Tunisian workers were expelled from Libya in 1976. Exports of light manufactures face both fierce competition from other exporters and increased protection in industrial economies. The latter is especially true for textiles, which were 18 per cent of Tunisia's exports in 1980. But although each of these risks is important, taken together they provided Tunisia with more diversified foreign exchange earnings. Put slightly differently, Tunisia seemed to cope with external fluctuations more successfully because it has relatively modest net oil exports; Kuwait coped quite easily because oil exports were so great in relation to population and import capacity that external fluctuations were reflected in a fluctuating surplus rather than in any need to adjust domestically; Venezuela appeared to be somewhere in between – rich enough as a result of oil price rises to have attempted over ambitious structural change, but not rich enough to be able to maintain that policy through periods of oil price fluctuation.

The contrast between Tanzania and Malawi was of a different type. Tanzania clearly had the more ambitious plans to transform its social and economic structure, as already noted. But Malawi also pursued a policy which caused a major structural shift *within* the all-important agricultural sector, away from smallholder production and towards agricultural estates: by buying from smallholders at low prices and investing much of the surplus in estates; by forcing a large increase in the share of bank lending going to estates; and, most remarkably, by forcing smallholder income down (and reducing the outflow of migrant labour) so that estates were able to increase their labour force rapidly at a declining real wage. Clearly there must be a limit to such a process. But the growth of estates did generate agricultural exports, which grew rapidly and (with only occasional setbacks) continuously. That is not to say that agricultural exports might not have grown as fast or faster if smallholders had been favoured rather than estates.

Both Malawi and Tanzania achieved output growth in the 1970s with considerable success; but in both cases there were in-built contradictions that made it unlikely that growth could continue. Tanzania neglected the development of exports, while pursuing a policy that required a sustained growth in export capacity over a long period. Exports from Tanzania actually fell over the 1970s. Malawi drove down real wages and smallholder incomes and then found that all the sources of finance for further investment in estate exports had dried up in 1980. So although it might appear that Malawi's capacity to cope with external circumstances was more soundly based than that of Tanzania (see Table 14.7), the case studies of both countries conclude with considerable pessimism about the prospects for resumed growth and development.

**Table 14.7 Export volume in Malawi and Tanzania, 1960–70 and 1970–80**

|  | *1960–70* | *1970–80* |
|---|---|---|
| Malawi | +11.6% | +5.9% |
| Tanzania | +3.4% | −8.1% |

*Source: World Development Report*, 1983.

*Note:* Annual percentage changes in export volume indices.

In addition, it is worth noting that adjustment to losses in real income from falling terms of trade (much more severe in Tanzania than in Malawi), and to drought and the cost of war, was more difficult in a country such as Tanzania, whose government perceived the groups whose incomes needed protecting most vigorously as the extensive peasant class and the urban poor.

*Subsidies*
Several of the countries studied used subsidies as a way of protecting people from the effects of price increases, including those on imported goods. Their experience suggests a number of generalisations:

(a) Governments found it difficult to raise the price of subsidised goods. Having once taken responsibility for the prices of subsidised goods, and the political *credit* for keeping prices down, governments were unwilling to face the political *blame* for raising prices – especially when the impact would fall most heavily on urban groups well able to voice their protests.

(b) As a result, the cost of subsidies tended to be unsustainable over time, because the gap between market and controlled prices rose with general inflation and governments' unwillingness to increase the prices of subsidised goods.

(c) The greater the gap between controlled prices and *either* import costs *or* the price necessary to extract an adequate domestic supply, the greater was the shock of an attempt to close the gap.

(d) If a government did remove subsidies on basic consumer goods, the resulting upward shift in the rate of inflation was unlikely to be temporary.

Only Kuwait appeared to be an exception to these generalisations. Kuwait was rich enough to subsidise a large number of consumer items, with family entitlements generous enough that not all were used. The government also provided free local telephone, television and water services, zero interest rate loans for housing sold at less than market value, and electricity, and public transport and petrol at very low costs. The impact was mainly on the lower income groups, including the large number of foreign migrant workers (60 per cent of the population in 1981 was non-Kuwaiti); the lack of domestic political influence of the migrant workers may explain to some extent the unusual trend in Kuwaiti subsidies, namely that their total cost fluctuated rather than increasing continually. The total cost of budget subsidies on consumer items peaked in 1975 and 1976, falling well below that level in 1977 and 1978 (see Table 10.7 above).

But in Venezuela, Sri Lanka and Tunisia, for example, the cost of subsidies did grow unmanageable; and in each case the financial impossibility of maintaining the programme led to cuts in subsidies, which in turn caused major problems. In Sri Lanka, the government abandoned much of its subsidy programme after 1979. Although food stamps were introduced to protect the lower income groups, there was a big increase in prices which 'reduced real incomes, especially of the urban poor'.[8] Until 1979, the share of money income going to low income groups had on the whole been maintained (see Chapter 4, Table 4.10), although this statistic did not cover the loss of free rice and so overestimates the maintenance of poor people's income.

In Tunisia, the price support system was funded by specially earmarked taxes, with some income elasticity, giving the programme a greater chance of being sustained. But the cost accelerated, exceeding the ear-marked revenues, so that the government tried to remove them in early 1984. The gap between market and subsidised price had grown so great that the price of bread doubled; a violent popular reaction forced a reversal of the price increase.[9]

Jordan subsidised some prices, mostly food and petrol, although subsidies on petrol were reduced after 1979. Jordan also introduced state trading stores selling at special lower, tax-free prices, as a way of attacking the high prices of merchant trading monopolies and of protecting certain privileged groups. Jordan's special position, by which (because of its close links with oil-exporting states) it participated in their prosperity rather than suffering from its own lack of natural resources (apart from an exceptionally well educated labour force), may have enabled it to maintain its subsidy programme. The facts that lower level jobs were being done by immigrants with little political influence and thus unlikely to demand equal treatment and that so many Jordanians (many with high levels of education) were abroad, kept down the total cost and enabled the programme to continue.

There is clearly much to be said in favour of subsidising the cost of essentials for poor people (particularly as alternative ways of redistributing income, for example through redistribution of assets, may not always be technically or politically feasible). There are however difficulties in sustaining a subsidy programme in practice because of the tendency of the cost to grow to levels unsustainable even by net oil exporters such as Tunisia and Venezuela.

Many of the same arguments apply to the maintenance of overvalued exchange rates, which provide a generalised 'subsidy' to all imported goods and services. Several governments attempted to protect people from rising import prices in this way (Argentina went even further and announced such a policy in advance as a way of trying to reduce inflationary expectations). Maintaining an overvalued exchange rate was frequently easier than introducing explicit subsidies because it did not require budget expenditure. As with subsidies, the longer the policy continued the harder it was to change, because of the increasingly large gap between current and market price, and the increasing size of the shock that would occur if the policy were to be changed.

In the case of Argentina's attempt to change inflationary expectations, the rate of inflation in Argentina was so much greater than in the rest of the world that the impact on the rate of inflation would have had to be total and virtually immediate, because of the speed with which the nominal and purchasing power parity rates were diverging. Furthermore, opening up an economy such as Argentina's, which had previously had extensive controls on current and capital flows into and out of the country, did *not* result in an external equilibrium. An extended period of controls, particularly over the right to buy foreign exchange as an asset but also over the right to buy imports of goods and services generally, created a pent-up demand for foreign exchange. In the case of both Argentina and Venezuela, this demand could only be satisfied by foreign borrowing. Part of the problem in Argentina was probably that a liberal policy, coming after a long period of controls, lacked credibility. So investors preferred foreign assets because of the possibility of the reintroduction of controls, to some extent regardless of whether or not *current* economic and financial conditions made local assets more attractive.

### Sectoral policies: energy

The large relative increase in the price of energy from 1974 onwards posed a policy dilemma for many oil importing countries. Governments had to decide whether to pass on the full increase in the international price of oil into domestic prices, with the likely widespread impact on rates of inflation (energy enters into the cost of almost all goods), or whether to protect consumers and producers. Even in countries where the price of petroleum products was not controlled, there was an important policy choice: petrol was and is taxed quite heavily in nearly all countries, usually on a specific basis (a fixed amount of money per litre), so that passing on the full increase in the import cost would not have resulted in an equal percentage rise in the price to the final user. Governments had therefore to make a positive decision on whether to increase the tax by as much as (or more than) the rise in import cost, as well as whether to allow the import cost to rise. It could even be argued that the inelasticity of demand for energy required a more than proportionate rise in the domestic price of imported oil in order to avoid a worsening in the external balance; it was usual, however, for the overall balance of payments problem to be managed by a wider range of policies than just putting up the price of imported oil (including, of course, borrowing to finance an increased external deficit).

Alternatively, governments could choose to try and increase production of exports and import substitutes to compensate for the increased cost of imports, rather than trying to reduce the demand for imports (including the demand for imported oil); in particular, there was an increase in expenditure on oil exploration and on investment in domestic substitutes for imported oil. The success of this latter option depended to a considerable degree on luck in finding domestic sources of oil or effective substitutes for oil such as natural gas, or in having the potential for producing hydroelectricity and ethanol. Other specific aspects of domestic energy policies included energy conservation measures, such as speed limits, constraints on petrol sales, and the like.

One way of measuring the relative success of such attempts at adjustment is to observe whether, or rather by how much, the ratio of imported oil to export earnings rose after 1974. Success in reducing the demand for imported oil by raising the price and introducing conservation measures, or success in increasing exports, or success in increasing the domestic supply of oil or oil substitutes, would all have the effect of limiting any increase in the ratio. On the other hand, not forcing up the price of imported oil to final users, or failing to discourage oil consumption by other means, or adjusting by general restrictions on all imports, or failing to have any domestic policy to increase domestic energy supply, would all tend to result in an above average increase in the ratio of imported oil to exports.[10]

Some countries in the table had less of a problem than others. Argentina, as an important producer of oil, was not far from being self-sufficient, and was in a relatively strong position to increase production – although it was argued in the case study that Argentina increased

**Table 14.8  Ratio of imported oil to exports, 1970 and 1982, net oil importers**

(per cent)

|  | 1970 | 1982 | Variation in ratio, 1970–82 |
|---|---|---|---|
| Less than 100 per cent increase in ratio | | | |
| Argentina | 18 | 21 | 17 |
| Ireland | 9 | 16 | 78 |
| Jordan[a] | 79 | 73 | −8 |
| Korea | 15 | 28 | 87 |
| Malawi | 11 | 16 | 45 |
| More than 100 per cent increase in ratio | | | |
| Brazil | 12 | 54 | 350 |
| Sri Lanka | 12[b] | 54 | 350 |
| Tanzania | 9 | 43[c] | 378 |

*Source: International Financial Statistics*; Central Bank of Ceylon, *Annual Reports*; *World Development Report*, 1983 (Jordan).

*Notes:*  (a) Figures for Jordan are for imports of energy for 1960 and 1980, as a percentage of exports.
(b) 1973.
(c) 1981; figure for imports of energy (to include petroleum products as well as crude petroleum).

output of oil by too much, and output of other energy sources (notably gas) by too little, in relation to national reserves. Jordan, because of its large inflows of foreign exchange from major exporters of oil, tended to gain more from a rise in the oil price than it lost and vice versa, as was shown when receipts of OPEC aid fell with the oil price in 1981 and 1982. So long as this relationship held, Jordan could afford to pay little attention to the rising cost of oil. The very high ratio of imported energy to exports in Jordan was simply because of the small proportion of foreign exchange inflows earned by exporting as compared to aid and migrant workers' remittances.

The ratios of three other countries in the group also rose by relatively small amounts. Ireland was able to increase exports at the high rate of 8.4 per cent a year between 1970 and 1981, to the EEC as a result of becoming a member, and to a lesser extent to the oil exporting countries. Malawi was also successful in increasing exports throughout the period (although at the expense of smallholders). In addition, Malawi actually *increased* the proportion of tax in the retail price of petrol, so that it rose by a larger percentage than the import cost; and the country was relatively fortunate in having hydroelectric potential, the right conditions for growing sugar for ethanol, and a relatively high density of population which reduced the per capita cost of internal transport. Korea's success, by this measure, was overwhelmingly founded on rapid growth of exports, and occurred despite the fact that manufactured exports were more energy intensive than, for example, the agricultural exports of Argentina. Moreover, Korea earned additional foreign exchange from overseas construction contracts (mainly in the Middle East oil exporting countries); if this source of foreign exchange were to be included in exports, Korea's ratio in 1982 would be even lower.

In contrast, three countries more than doubled the ratio of oil imports to exports. Of these, Sri Lanka's position was not as bad as the table suggests. First, since 1971 oil imports have been partly for refining and re-export: 44 per cent of oil imports in 1981 were for this purpose. Second, Sri Lanka developed both tourism and migrant workers' remittances as major new sources of foreign earnings in the 1970s, amounting in 1982 to an additional 48 per cent of the amount of visible export earnings. All of these factors taken together would reduce Sri Lanka's ratio in 1982 from 54 per cent to 24 per cent. The latter figure is not comparable with the other figures in the second column of Table 14.8, because some of the other countries in the group also had substantial invisible export earnings; nevertheless, Sri Lanka was not nearly so unsuccessful as suggested by the uncorrected figures in the table. Sri Lanka's energy policy changed in fact in the late 1970s: the price of motor fuel was raised sharply in 1977, and the subsidy on kerosene (used mainly for cooking and lighting by the low income groups) was reduced in 1979. Because the price elasticity of demand for oil products increases over time, the full long-term effect of these changes might not have appeared in the statistics by 1982.

Brazil's pattern of growth was very much based on cheap energy. In the mid-1970s energy policy was to encourage oil exploration, nuclear power, alcohol as a substitute for petrol, hydroelectricity and incentives to use coal. Only the alcohol programme was at all effective in the short term, and to some extent sugar for alcohol was grown at the expense of food. Most of the new hydroelectricity capacity was not available until the early 1980s. A new energy plan was launched in 1979: the share of energy in investment was planned to go up from 10 per cent to 20 per cent, there was a big jump in the petrol price in 1980 leading to a more rapid expansion of alcohol-using cars, and there was pressure on industry to substitute wood and electricity for oil. All of these measures were too recent to show up in Table 14.8.

In Tanzania, the petrol price was pushed up faster than other prices, but the share of taxation declined so that the local price grew by a smaller percentage than the import price. The government wanted to limit the impact on inflation and on low-income groups of increases in the cost of rural transport and low-income group lighting. As mentioned before, Tanzania's flexibility was constrained by concern to protect the real income of the poorest people and by the fact that some 55 per cent of imported oil was used for public transport (including lorries) and a further 10 per cent for rural lighting and urban household fuel, for which there were very few if any substitutes (although some hydro-electricity was developed). Unlike Malawi, Tanzania was also handi-capped by its large area and low population density. However, Tanzania's problem was made worse by the country's poor export performance. Future prospects are improved by a substantial discovery of natural gas; however, the main impact of this development will be on exports rather than on domestic energy use because of the inflexible uses of energy in the economy.

So far, the argument has been entirely concerned with the policies of oil-importing countries. But oil exporters also had to decide whether to raise domestic oil prices in line with the international price of oil. Both Kuwait and Venezuela chose a policy of very cheap energy, although Venezuela did modify this slightly in 1982. Such a policy was obviously much more manageable in the short term for oil exporters precisely because of their increased earnings from oil. But the Venezuela study argued strongly that it had major disadvantages in the medium term, because the large scale, energy and capital intensive investments encouraged by cheap domestic energy were not sustainable and caused severe sectoral and macroeconomic disequilibria. Even in Kuwait, where there was not a medium-term foreign exchange constraint to sustain the investment programme, it was nevertheless argued that the very rapid growth of domestic energy consumption could create problems in the long term.

In Tunisia, rather unusually, petrol taxes were used to finance food subsidies. But there was also an overemphasis on capital and energy-intensive investment, for example in the 60 per cent of agricultural investment going to irrigation. Overall, energy consumption grew faster (9.2 per cent) than GDP (8.2 per cent) or than energy production (6.0 per cent) between 1974 and 1981. The economy thus became more energy intensive over the period; while this was to some extent a measure of success both in raising income and in industrialisation, it was also of concern for the future.

*Sectoral policies: food*
The large price rises for basic food in the 1970s forced countries to choose between subsidies to protect consumers, especially poor ones, or maintaining a low price for local farmers at the risk of lowering output, on the one hand, and increasingly expensive food (but with the hope of production increases), on the other hand. Table 14.9 below shows changes in average indices of food production per head from 1969/71 to 1979/81. The table also shows each country's changing dependence on external sources of food from 1974–1981, although as these figures are for individual years they give only a rough indication of trends because of weather variations.

Of the three countries whose food output per head fell, Malawi increased the official price for maize in 1982 by 70 per cent, and as a result official purchases of maize rose by 56 per cent. Given that output for sale was thought to be about 10 per cent of total output before the price increase, it is probable that the index for Malawi in 1982 rose above 100. This occurred, however, at the expense of sales of other smallholder marketed crops, all of which fell. Malawi's earlier failure to increase food output per head was almost certainly caused by the neglect of the smallholder sector in favour of providing the estate sector (which produces little basic food) with cheap labour. Tanzania's performance occurred despite a food price policy from 1974 to 1981 which on average raised officially marketed food prices by more than inflation and wages. This policy resulted in 4 per cent or so annual growth to 1978. Subsequent poor performance was caused mainly by drought, lack of transport and lack of a proper storage policy (600,000 tons of potential surplus from 1975–78 were not available to meet 1979–82 shortfalls). The third country to have falling food output per head,

**Table 14.9 Domestic food output, food imports and food aid**

('000 metric tons)

| | Index of food output per head[a] | Cereal imports + food aid 1974 | 1981 |
|---|---|---|---|
| **Fall in index** | | | |
| Jordan | 74 | 234 | 703 |
| Malawi[b] | 96 | 17 | 130 |
| Tanzania[b] | 91 | 579 | 502 |
| **Index level** | | | |
| Venezuela | 104 | 1270 | 2378 |
| **Rise in index** | | | |
| Argentina | 116 | 0 | 10 |
| Brazil | 125 | 2516 | 5574 |
| Ireland | 115 | 631 | 598 |
| Korea | 126 | 2679 | 7687 |
| Kuwait | — | 101 | 386 |
| Sri Lanka | 148 | 1222 | 895 |
| Tunisia | 124 | 308 | 1059 |

*Source: World Development Report*, 1983.

*Notes:* (a) Average index of food production per head in 1979–81 with 1969–71 as 100.

(b) Malawi and Tanzania had substantial subsistence production of food, statistics for which were extremely poor. Alternative estimates suggest that food output may have been 20 per cent higher in Tanzania in 1978 than shown by the index used above.

Jordan, had very fast population growth, very little agricultural potential, and concentrated on other sources of income.

The other countries all increased food output per head significantly. Both Brazil and Argentina were in this category, despite a bewildering series of policy changes in Argentina and the increasing competition from export crops and sugar for alcohol production in Brazil (in the 1950s Brazil was able to increase both exports and output for the domestic market because of the availability of spare land). In Argentina, the adoption of wheat-soya double cropping and hybrid seeds enabled output to grow, in spite of (it seemed) official policy. In Brazil, the decline of agricultural export prices from 1980 onwards was particularly important in allowing food output to rise. Tunisia and Korea both managed increases in food output per head, even though rapidly increasing export earnings also allowed them to increase their imports by large amounts. In their case, the increase in food imports was more a measure of overall success in increasing real incomes than a sign of failure in food policy. In addition, both countries distributed that growth to lower income groups, via food subsidies in Tunisia and via rapid employment growth in Korea. Sri Lanka also subsidised both consumers and producers of food, which encouraged output much more than the alternative policy of keeping prices down to both consumers and producers; as in Tunisia, though, the policy proved impossibly expensive (given the government's other competing priorities). Sri Lanka limited food subsidies in 1977 to lower income groups, and introduced food stamps in 1979. Tunisia was much more fortunate financially, but by the time the post-1979 recession had lasted for several years, Tunisia was also having great difficulties in maintaining food subsidies.

## The control of imported inflation

Developing countries generally gave a lower priority to reducing inflation than did the developed industrial countries. Developing countries were more concerned with growth and development, the alleviation of poverty and, in the post-1979 period, with the crisis management of external balance. This section shows moreover that the very means used by developed countries to reduce *their* inflation made it difficult if not impossible for developing countries to do the same – since external imbalance forced many countries into policy actions with inflationary consequences (see point (c) below).

The phrase 'imported inflation' is usually used to refer to the increased cost of imported goods and services. Other ways in which inflation can be transmitted into an economy by external events include:

(a) a rise in export prices, which raises domestic income and spending, and so pushes up the prices of domestically produced goods and services (unless the whole increase in income is invested abroad and the corresponding increase in bank liquidity does not result in increased domestic lending)

(b) easy access to foreign finance, which can have the same effect as a rise in export prices

(c) a decline in the terms of trade, if it induces the country *either* to devalue and so increase the price of imports, *or* to control imports (by such means as import licensing or exchange controls) both of which reduce supply without reducing monetary income and so have an inflationary effect[10]

(d) a recession in the rest of the world, which reduces a country's capacity to import and as a result increases the budget deficit, because revenue from import duties and revenue based on domestic output and income both fall, causing an inflationary increase in the budget deficit

(e) externally induced recession, which pushes up industrial unit costs as capacity utilisation falls.

If the above analysis is correct, and the evidence from the case studies suggests that it is, then recession was just as powerful a cause of inflation in developing countries as the reasons more usually given. Put slightly differently, the main benefit to the OECD countries of the post-1979 recession, namely the reduction of their inflation, was not shared by the developing countries – on the contrary, they suffered from worsening inflation on top of all the other hardships inflicted on them by external events.

Whatever the immediate cause, it was clear that nearly all the countries in the sample suffered from increased inflation during the 1970s and early 1980s because of external forces. The only possible exceptions were those countries which already had rates of inflation very much higher than those prevailing in the rest of the world, namely Argentina and Brazil. The primary causes of inflation in those countries were and remained internal; and in any case an acceleration in imported inflation from 2 or 3 per cent to 20 per cent must have had a much smaller relative effect in countries where inflation was already much higher than that (Argentina's inflation was already over 100 per cent in the period 1970–72, for example; see Table 14.10).

For the remaining countries, whatever the mechanisms for transmitting external factors into higher rates of internal inflation, the consequence was frequently that those higher rates were then built into the domestic economy. So a domestic inflationary process which was started or accelerated by external forces became so institutionalised that it could only be reversed with great difficulty. In particular, a subsequent fall in external inflationary pressures did not necessarily result in a reduction in internal inflation; or it only resulted in a reduction in domestic inflation smaller than the reduction in the rate of increase of import prices. This appeared to have happened in the 1970s and early 1980s. Inflation fell in some of the countries when world inflation fell after 1975, but in most cases it did not fall by as much as import prices. In the period after 1980, the process was even more pronounced: some countries that had reduced their rates of inflation after 1975 actually suffered increased inflation after 1980, and none of the countries were able to reduce their inflation rates as low as those in

**Table 14.10  Rates of inflation in selected periods, 1970–1982**

(annual average percentage increases)

|  | *1970–72* | *1973–75* | *1976–78* | *1979–80* | *1981–82* |
|---|---|---|---|---|---|
| *Global averages* | | | | | |
| World export prices | 6 | 23 | 7 | 19 | −2 |
| Import prices for oil importing developing countries | 4 | 25 | 4 | 20 | −1 |
| Export prices of industrial countries | 7 | 18 | 7 | 14 | −4 |
| *Low inflation countries* | | | | | |
| Ireland | 9 | 16 | 13 | 11 | 14 |
| Jordan | 6 | 14 | 11 | 13 | 8 |
| Korea | 14 | 17 | 13 | 28 | 12 |
| Kuwait | — | 10 | 8 | 6 | 8 |
| Malawi | 7 | 12 | 6 | 15 | 10 |
| Sri Lanka | 5 | 10 | 5 | 18 | 14 |
| Tanzania | 5 | 18 | 10 | 22 | 27 |
| Tunisia | 3 | 6 | 6 | 9 | 13 |
| Venezuela | 3 | 8 | 8 | 17 | 12 |
| *High inflation countries* | | | | | |
| Argentina | 141 | 462 | 246 | 337 | 647 |
| Brazil | 20 | 23 | 41 | 41 | 60 |

*Source: International Financial Statistics* (consumer prices used for national inflation rates).

the industrial countries. Still less were they able to reduce prices in line with the level of import prices – which actually *fell* from 1980 to 1982.

Nearly all the 'low inflation countries' managed to reduce their rates of inflation in 1976–78. Malawi and Sri Lanka even managed to reduce their inflation rates to their pre-1973 levels. The only exceptions were Tunisia and Venezuela, which suffered from a much smaller increase in inflation in the 1973–1975 period; both being net oil exporters, they were not directly affected by the increase in the oil price. Kuwait was in the same position although the absence of inflation data before 1972 prevents a precise comparison.

The experience after 1979 was much more mixed. Only Kuwait appeared unaffected by the big swings in international inflation. All the other countries suffered from increased domestic inflation in the 1979–1980 period; but only some of them were able to lower their inflation rates thereafter. Even among those five countries able to lower their inflation rates in the 1981–1982 period, only Jordan and Korea managed to revert to the pre-1979 level. Malawi, Sri Lanka and Venezuela all suffered higher inflation than before 1979, despite the much sharper reduction in external inflation than had occurred after 1975. And three countries – Ireland, Tanzania and Tunisia – actually had *higher* inflation in the 1981–82 period when world prices were falling, than in 1979 and 1980 when world prices were rising quite rapidly.

In the cases of Ireland and Tunisia, the local currencies were devalued – by 15 per cent and 27 per cent against the SDR respectively – in an attempt to restore balance of payments equilibrium, with the inflationary consequences to be expected. Tanzania devalued very little over this period (by 1 per cent against the SDR, although by as much as 14 per cent against the US dollar), but was forced to control imports very severely by other means as a result, which again had inflationary consequences (see the second paragraph of this section). The other countries which failed to reduce their inflation levels to pre-1979 levels also fell into one or other of these categories: Malawi devalued against the SDR by 15 per cent, while Sri Lanka and Venezuela relied on controls (Venezuela actually appreciated against the SDR from 1980 to 1982, because of an unchanged peg to the US dollar).

What this amounted to, therefore, was that developing countries (and Ireland) not only suffered all the obvious consequences of the unexpectedly prolonged and deep recession caused mainly by the policy reactions of the rich and developed countries, but also failed to benefit at all, or only very partially, from the main objective of developed country policy, namely the reduction of inflation. Furthermore it is very difficult to see, in most cases, just how the poorer countries could have reduced their domestic inflation rates in line with those of richer countries, because of the severe balance of payments and external debt problems created for them by the very means used by the rich countries to reduce their own inflation, namely the world recession. This is not to say that domestic policy could not have been different nor that the policies actually pursued did not in some cases add to domestic inflation; but it is hard to see how for example the poorest countries in the group – Malawi, Sri Lanka and Tanzania – could have avoided entirely the need to devalue or curtail imports by other means, with the inevitable inflationary consequences. It was also true that many developing countries put *less* emphasis on reducing inflation in the post-1979 period (in exact contrast to the developed countries), probably because of the even greater problems of external imbalance and financial crisis.

### The international economy

This study has shown the increased difficulties created for developing countries by large and unexpected changes in the international economy. Fluctuations in the rate of increase in international prices as well as fluctuations in their relative values have been one of the main focuses of the study. Inevitably, the study has also focused on the difficulties created by fluctuating exchange rates, capital flows and interest rates. A more stable world internationally would not only make the task of development easier in a direct way; a more stable world would also make it easier for developing countries to maintain consistency between economic policies and strategies and would make the consequences of inconsistency less severe.

While these points were frequently made about the adjustment problems of the 1970s,[11] their importance was even greater in the deeper and longer post-1979 recession. As was already noted at the beginning of this chapter, the second world recession in less than ten years was so much more severe than the first largely because of the reactions of the major economic powers, who paid much less attention to the consequences of their actions than they had done previously. As a result, even the policies most strongly recommended to developing countries by the major powers, and by the international institutions where their influence was strongest, were imperilled by the policies pursued by the developed countries themselves: including high interest rates, protectionism, reduced demand for Third World exports and static or declining real aid.

It would seem that the only event that made the major economic powers react to the plight of developing countries was the international debt crisis, because it threatened the world's major banks and therefore the financial systems of the industrial countries. The reaction of the IMF, the US government and its allies to the debt crisis was to use existing institutions, mainly the IMF itself but including among others the Bank for International Settlements, to force the private banks to maintain some net increases in their lending to a small number of major borrowers, including Brazil and Argentina. Very little was done about any of the immediate causes of the crisis: high real interest rates, protectionism, etc. Nor was anything done to alleviate the extreme shortages of foreign exchange in the poorer developing countries. Many of the poorer countries also faced external debt crises, but because they did not threaten the banks, there was no pressure on the banks to lend them new money. On the contrary, they were forced in all cases to agree to a deflationary programme with the IMF or simply to suffer from ever-decreasing supplies of imported goods and services.

Furthermore, such action as was taken concerning the developing countries in general, and the poorer ones in particular, was harmful rather than helpful – notably the American refusal to contribute an adequate amount to the IDA replenishment in early 1984, the increasing commercialisation and politicisation of bilateral aid, the inadequate increase in IMF quotas, and the static level of aid in real terms. Overall, there seemed to be a complete refusal to take any notice at all of the impact on the third world of economic policy in the developed countries.

In particular, the United States government seemed to be further than ever from taking any account of Third World interests; on the contrary it appeared to be moving in the opposite direction both in its domestic economic decisions and in its still very considerable influence on official international institutions. The result appeared to be that such institutions as the World Bank and the IMF, for example, were forced to fight to defend existing levels of effectiveness rather than being able to press for new initiatives. The contrast with the immediate post-war period was very great; perhaps this was partly because no one country was dominant, so that collective responsibility was so difficult to establish. Indeed, the major economies seemed unable to manage the global economy in their own interest, still less to do so in the interests of all countries.

Among the few positive signs of progress were the increased share of trade between developing countries in the total of world trade, suggesting that there might be some prospect, at least for some developing countries, of a reduction in dependence on economic events and policy decisions in the developed countries. But this was of greatest significance for the middle income countries with rapidly increasing exports of manufactures, and had relatively little to offer the poorer countries.

## Policy implications of the experience of the 1970s and early 1980s

As we have seen, developing countries faced dramatic changes in the international environment in the 1970s and early 1980s. Initially, they faced a problem of imported inflation as the prices of their main imports (such as energy and food) soared, while the recession in the industrial countries added greatly to their problems; in the 1979–82 period, the main problem faced by developing countries was importing recession from the industrial countries, with *both recessionary and inflationary consequences for their own economies.* For example, the rapid increase in international nominal and real interest rates since 1979 had a clearly recessionary effect on developing countries, particularly those which had borrowed extensively from the private banks at variable interest rates, as it reduced sharply net transfers of external financial resources and thus limited their capacity to import and to sustain or increase output.

It is noteworthy that the negative effect of an increase in international rates on the level of developing-country activity operates in the same direction, but basically through rather different mechanisms than those described by the widely accepted Keynesian model. An increase in interest rates affects not only new decisions to spend, as in the Keynesian model, but also has an impact on debts already incurred for past expenditure. Even more importantly, the resulting restraint on developing-country economic activity does not occur mainly via a reduction in investment which is perceived as less profitable under higher interest rates, but mainly because the foreign exchange crucial to carry out the investment (or indeed any other form of spending) is unavailable. The key problem is therefore not caused by the unwillingness of the investor to spend – though this may also occur – but mainly by the inability of the country's balance of payments to sustain existing levels of activity.

At the same time as higher interest costs had a recessionary impact on developing countries, they were also an important element of cost-push inflation, particularly for enterprises using foreign credit directly or indirectly. Similarly the decline in many developing countries' terms of trade, clearly linked in the early 1980s to the recession in industrial countries, had a recessionary impact on developing countries, as it constrained the availability of foreign exchange for imports. Simultaneously, these countries were forced either to devalue and so increase the price of imports *or* to control imports by some sort of rationing, both of which have an inflationary impact. The inevitable decline in government revenue, resulting from reduced taxes on imports and on domestic sectors forced to cut back because of lack of imported inputs, implied an expanding government deficit, which became an important source of demand inflation. Finally, the externally-induced recession created inflationary pressures, particularly in the industrial sector, as fixed costs per unit increased due to declining capacity utilisation.

As indicated throughout this study, it is necessary to proceed cautiously when attempting to draw general conclusions from the experience of policies in specific countries and in a particular period. However, the case studies in this research programme, as well as related work carried out elsewhere,[12] seem to provide enough material for tentative conclusions to be drawn on the effectiveness of particular types of national policies and of their usefulness in adapting certain types of developing countries' economies to large changes in the international environment, of the type that occurred during the 1970s and early 1980s.

At a national level, the experience of the 1970s examined in the country studies, seems to imply that – particularly for middle income countries – certain broad features of policy-making had a greater degree of success, especially in generating growth.[13]

The first feature which emerges is the *importance of taking account of the country's past history and structural features in designing economic policies and strategies*. For example, South Korea seems to provide almost a textbook example of a country which uses its own strengths – such as an increasingly skilled labour force – to expand those sectors of production which could best benefit from this particular advantage.

Second, at a different level, countries like Brazil, South Korea and Tunisia based their relatively more successful growth strategy and adjustment policy on using existing strengths in their state apparatus – e.g. the large investment role of the state sector, selective distribution of credit to the private sector – to achieve particular targets. Such *consistent use of targeted state intervention* was in sharp contrast with the Argentinian experience, which attempted a rapid reduction of the role of the state in investment, accompanied by a drastic decline in the level of protection, thus implying a sharp break with the country's previous development strategy. Furthermore, the speed with which these structural changes were undertaken in Argentina implied that industries which had grown under a more protectionist regime and with the direct as well as indirect support from the state were destroyed without being replaced by other economic activity.

A third related general feature emerges from the cases studied. *Market management worked better than either freeing market forces or ignoring them.* Thus, economic policies seem to have been most effective for sustaining growth and adapting to changes in the international environment in countries (such as South Korea, Brazil and Tunisia) where policy-makers accepted the important role of market forces, but oriented them according to a clear 'vision' of a development strategy; this could be expressed by saying that 'for the policy-maker, the market is a useful servant but a poor master'.[14] Such deliberate and targeted regulation by the state of the private sector occurred for example through price controls (as in the case of Tunisia), through *selectivity* in credit, so as to orient financial resources to specific sectors (as in South Korea and in Tunisia) and through a protectionist policy which is *selective*, being higher for sectors whose growth is being encouraged (as in Brazil) and/or fluctuating according to the balance of payments and foreign exchange situation (as in South Korea). Selectivity in policies – achieved both through direct state action and/or by incentives granted to and taxation of the private sector – seems particularly necessary in developing countries, given the heterogeneity of their economies and the 'gaps' where market forces do not operate or do so inefficiently. Selective policies seem not only to be useful instruments to encourage growth in certain sectors but can be effectively used – if the government wishes to do so – to achieve greater equity (e.g. Kuwait, Tanzania, and Sri Lanka particularly until the late 1970s).

In countries where the government abandoned its attempts to guide the development process and limited itself to freeing the forces of the market (for example through drastic and indiscriminate liberalisation of trade in Argentina after 1976 and in a more gradual way in Venezuela during the late 1970s) the results seemed on the whole negative for growth and employment, particularly for specific sectors. It is interesting to note that these liberalisation policies often produced opposite results to those pursued and to those which orthodox economic theory expected would be achieved. For example, in Venezuela the reduction in tariffs not only provoked sectoral crises, but is reported in the case study to have contributed to price increases, as firms wanted to sustain their level of profits in a shrinking market. A similar relationship can be found in the freeing of interest rates carried out, for example, in Argentina, with the purpose of encouraging national savings and thus sustaining a higher level of productive investment. The resulting very high interest rates encouraged the placing of money in short-term financial assets or speculative investment and discouraged productive investment which could not earn such high rates of return.

It is noteworthy that the middle-income countries in our sample most able to increase the volume and diversity of their exports and respond most effectively to opportunities opening up in the international economy (such as South Korea, Brazil and Tunisia) were those which promoted exports without simultaneously or previously carrying out a generalised liberalisation of imports. Instead they used a wide range of export-promotion instruments, of which tariff reduction in specific sectors was only one policy tool, used only at particular times. On the other hand, countries attempting deliberately to encourage and diversify exports through a more general liberalisation of imports (such as Argentina and, to a lesser degree, Venezuela) were relatively less successful in this aspect. In this sense, our conclusion seems to confirm that of a Report to the Group of 24[15] which concludes that 'countries successful in export diversification have typically employed a wide array of policy instruments, including export subsidies . . . *ad hoc* policy packages aimed at achieving sectoral goals seems to be more effective in securing export diversification than general across-the-board-measures . . . There are few countries indeed where export promotion is left to the market.'

Countries which, like Tanzania in relation to traditional and other agricultural exports until 1980/81, paid very little attention to the impact of its macroeconomic and investment policies on its ability to respond to or take advantage of international market opportunities, achieved poor results in this field (even though it must be stressed that Tanzania's potential for export growth – like that of most other low-income countries – was more limited that that of the countries discussed above). While Tanzania's export growth potential was limited both for traditional exports and as regards diversification, this suggests that *high, not low, priority* should have been assigned to devising policies to encourage increased and diversified exports (see Chapter 3 above, which in its final section deals with tentative generalisations for low-income, small countries).

This leads us to a fourth feature which seems to characterise more successful policies in the 1970s: *flexibility in responding to large and often frequent changes in the international environment* and ability to capitalise on the new opportunities which it offers. South Korea offers an excellent example of such flexibility, as illustrated by its ability to shift rapidly into production of goods and services, for the most rapidly growing markets (e.g. the Middle East after 1973) and into sectors with rapid growth where the country was facing comparative advantage (e.g. electronics in the early 1970s); this was accompanied by less emphasis on production for exports in those sectors (particularly in light industry) where South Korea was rapidly losing its comparative advantage.

Naturally, not all countries have the economic and institutional base which allows such flexibility. A major challenge for policy-makers in low-income countries during the coming years is to attempt to increase their ability to respond somewhat more flexibly to changes in the international economy.

Greater emphasis should be attached in all categories of countries to close monitoring – at a general as well as a specific level, at the Central Bank and in the large enterprises – of developments in the international economy and to designing appropriate and rapid national responses to those changes. Such detailed monitoring of changes in the international economy and the opportunities and constraints it poses for different categories of developing countries, could in some aspects be carried out jointly, either at the level of all developing countries or at a regional level; already existing work in international agencies – for example – could be geared more closely to the needs of developing countries' policy-makers.

A final characteristic of countries relatively more successful at sustaining growth and development are that they seem to *combine pragmatic use of policy instruments* (which may in many cases be quite unorthodox, if this is most functional to achieving the government's targets) *with prudence in financial management*. The latter avoids excessive imbalances in the state budget and excessive monetary expansion, which may lead to high levels of inflation and/or problems in the balance of payments. Undoubtedly, financial and macroeconomic management is not only decided in the Central Bank or the Ministry of Finance, but is heavily influenced by socio-economic and political forces in the society. Having said that, the experiences of South Korea and Tunisia (with relatively prudent financial management) may offer some useful lessons to Latin American countries (such as Brazil and Venezuela) on how to combine unorthodox growth and development policies with relatively prudent financial management, thus diminishing the risk that at a later stage the country's economic growth may become stunted due to severe financial constraints, and its whole unorthodox strategy threatened. As is illustrated by the case of Tanzania, countries attempting profound structural change require particularly prudent short-term economic and financial management. Furthermore, prudence in financial management may paradoxically be especially important in times of 'importing industrial countries' recession'. As the government's revenue base is eroded in such situations (see above), special efforts need to be made to sustain or increase alternative government revenue.

As so many countries faced similar constraints due both to imported inflation and imported recession – and in particular as in so many of the low-income countries these constraints limited very severely the possibilities for sustaining growth and development – we will refer (albeit rather briefly) to desirable international changes and policies which would allow a more favourable environment in the future than the one which took shape in recent years.

Drawing from our previous analysis, such a more favourable international environment would clearly include greater flexibility by international financial institutions (and particularly the IMF) on the type of conditionality which they require countries to accept before granting them credit. Our study seems to confirm the effectiveness of a pragmatic, country-specific and sometimes unorthodox policy approach. For this reason, greater flexibility and humility by international organisations on the policy advice they offer and the conditions they demand for granting credit would be greatly desirable. Naturally, conditionality is the aspect of most legitimate interest to the international financial community – the performance on the current account

– would of necessity be maintained. This would be the international counterpart of what we expressed above within the national context: the acceptance of unorthodox policies combined with financial prudence, where the latter is required. An important caveat must be made here: if deflationary policies are simultaneously pursued by a number of deficit countries, the total impact of such policies may be a major world deflation or a reduction of world economic growth, without necessarily improving the imbalances on the current accounts of individual countries. Focusing only on individual deflationary adjustments, without realising the aggregate impact of those adjustments on world trade, implies a serious 'fallacy of composition'. It could be expected that institutions which look at adjustment from a world perspective would avoid such a fallacy of composition and therefore have a far more expansionary bias than those which examine adjustment from a national perspective. The fact that an international financial institution like the IMF does not in practice have such a bias towards growth may perhaps partly be explained by the fact that it lacks such a truly international perception.

At a broader level, this study confirms the desirability for sustained and high economic growth in the industrial countries, as low and fluctuating growth in them obviously has negative effects on developing countries. In this respect, a greater voice of developing countries in joint world economic management may well imply a greater emphasis on growth as a target for industrial countries.

The case studies also seem to illustrate the damaging effects of very large fluctuations in internationally-determined economic variables (such as prices of internationally-traded goods, international interest rates, levels of international financial flows) because such violent and unexpected fluctuations make clearly defined economic strategies of development difficult to sustain. This confirms the importance of international measures which would attempt to reduce such fluctuations. Amongst them could be measures which would programme in advance official flows (possibly through planned issues of SDRs); measures to encourage a shift towards a greater proportion of lending to LDCs at longer maturities and at fixed interest rates; and measures to sustain private financial flows. Amongst the latter is, for example, a proposal to create an international lender of last resort which would help moderate private lending in times of euphoria and sustain such lending in times of financial distress or crisis,[16] as well as proposals to reduce uncertainty in the rate of interest charged on private loans. To the extent that certain variables – e.g. international commodity prices – are not or cannot be regulated, it may be particularly valuable to implement measures which moderate the negative impact of such fluctuations on developing countries. An example of such measures is the expansion and broadening of compensatory financing so as to fully compensate developing countries for fluctuations in their export earnings or import prices beyond their control; measures of this nature would not only allow developing countries a more gradual – and thus less painful – adjustment to external changes, but would also provide the world economy with an important counter-cyclical element.

Finally, our study illustrates how, particularly during recent years and for lower-income developing countries, negative changes in the international environment (sometimes reinforced by domestic inefficiency and by factors such as bad weather) have led to dramatic declines in import levels which threaten the very viability, both economic and political, of certain countries as well as causing increased human misery. These low levels of imports also erode the capacity to produce, process and transport exports thus building in a continual downward dynamic. In such countries, additional foreign exchange would be particularly valuable to help improve the conditions of the poor and improve the prospects for reversing economic decline and initiating recovery. This strengthens the case for at least sustaining, and hopefully increasing, real levels of ODA towards those low-income countries. Present levels of imports in some of these low-income countries are so depressed that capacity utilisation in many sectors is very low, thus justifying a higher proportion of international aid and finance geared towards programme rather than project finance.

### Notes and references

1 See IMF, 'World economic outlook' 1983 for a summary.
2 A similar and equally peculiar strategy has been tried in Chile and Mexico, namely a reduction in import restrictions, a failure to devalue and a rise in interest rates in order to attract foreign capital. It has had disastrous results in all three cases, in terms of inflation, basic external imbalance and cost of subsequent adjustment. It should also be noted that the relative lack of success of Argentina's policies was not unique to the post-1970 period.
3 No direct causation can of course be proved, but economic difficulties must have contributed to, or made it harder to avoid, the communal violence in Sri Lanka in 1983; and the attempt to remove food subsidies in Tunisia led directly to riots and reversal of the new policy in early 1984.
4 United Nations, *International Trade Statistics Yearbooks;* and World Banks, *World Development Report 1983.* Korea was particularly successful in selling to the 'high income oil exporters' (Libya, Saudi Arabia, Kuwait and United Arab Emirates) who increased their purchases from 0 per cent to 10 per cent of Korea's total merchandise exports between 1960 and 1981 (*World Development Report 1983*).
5 *World Development Reports.* Both Korea and Brazil paid higher interest rates on public sector debt, reflecting greater reliance on floating rate

borrowing as well as the rise in interest rates. Maturities also shortened, more seriously in the case of Brazil, and much more rapidly if short term borrowing could be included in the figures.

6  For a summary of two points of view concerning Tanzania's performance – that Tanzania's position during the 1970s was one of increasing structural deficit, which the coffee price boom of 1976–77 temporarily concealed, or that it overcame the post-1974 crisis relatively successfully – see James H. Weaver and Arne Anderson 'Stabilisation and Development of the Tanzanian economy in the 1970s' in William R. Cline and Sidney Weintraub *Economic Stabilization in Developing Countries* (Brookings Institution, 1981).

7  Petroleum exports from Tunisia rose from 26 per cent to 54 per cent of visible exports from 1972 to 1981; however, in 1981, Tunisia also *imported* 252 million dinars of petroleum, against 657 million dinars of exports, so that net petroleum exports were only 33 per cent of visible exports. The comparable figure in 1972 was 21 per cent.

8  OECD Development Assistance Committee, *Annual Review 1983*, p. 24.

9  It was not clear at the time of writing what the eventual outcome would be of this dispute.

10  For a slightly different categorisation see Surjit S. Bhalla 'The transmission of inflation into developing economies' in William R. Cline and Associates *World Inflation and the Developing Countries* Brookings Institution, 1981. Bhalla concludes that the world wide increase in inflation in 1974 and 1975 was caused more by inflows of capital, in particular eurodollar credits, than by increases in the cost of imports.

11  See for example the analysis and recommendations in Sydney Dell and Roger Lawrence, *The balance of payments adjustment process in developing countries* Pergamon, 1980.

12  See, for example, Cline and Weintraub cited in note 6 above; and, in particular, Dell and Lawrence op. cit.
*Process in Developing Countries,* Pergamon, 1980.

13  It is far more complex to examine the impact of specific policies on other development targets (although we have attempted to do so in the case studies) and particularly it seems more difficult to extrapolate in this aspect experiences from one country to the other, due to the large role played by the socio-political set up; furthermore, although most LDC governments pursue growth as an important policy target, certainly not all of them *de facto* consider a more equal income distribution a desirable target, even though they may say so in their declarations; thus in certain cases, a more unequal income distribution may be the real target of a particular government, even though it is obviously an unstated one.

14  This phrase was used by B. Van Arkadie in his article 'The IMF prescription for structural adjustment in Tanzania' in K. Jansen (ed.) *Monetarism, Economic Crisis and the Third World,* Frank Cass, 1983.

15  *Structural Adjustment Policies,* Report to the Group of 24 by S. Dell, C. Diaz Alejandro, R. Ffrench-Davies, T. Gudac, and C. Ossa, UNCTAD/MFD/TA/, 15 June 1981.

16  See, for example, M. Lipton and S. Griffith-Jones 'International lenders of last resort; are changes required?' *Towards a New Bretton Woods,* Selected background papers, Commonwealth Economic Papers no. 18, Commonwealth Secretariat.

## Appendix to Chapter 3

**Table 3.1 Gross domestic product at factor cost 1969–1982 (Sh. 000,000)**

A. Current Price

| Sector | 1969 | 1972 | 1974 | 1976 | 1977 | 1978 | 1979 | 1980 | 1981 | 1982 |
|---|---|---|---|---|---|---|---|---|---|---|
| Agriculture, fishing, forestry | 3081 | 4020 | 5440 | 9537 | 13343 | 15719 | 16792 | 18458 | 20544 | 21789 |
| Mining | 139 | 95 | 128 | 116 | 123 | 120 | 176 | 207 | 175 | 162 |
| Manufacturing | 752 | 1144 | 1482 | 2047 | 2424 | 2932 | 3340 | 4034 | 3935 | 3924 |
| Electricity, water supply | 74 | 97 | 116 | 206 | 221 | 240 | 278 | 432 | 417 | 515 |
| Construction | 319 | 468 | 682 | 712 | 842 | 922 | 1192 | 1376 | 1776 | 1720 |
| Commerce | 911 | 1248 | 1913 | 2351 | 3044 | 1634 | 1763 | 2075 | 2128 | 2093 |
| Transport, communications | 668 | 860 | 1282 | 1618 | 1705 | 2942 | 3038 | 3386 | 3296 | 3183 |
| Finance, real estate | 804 | 1048 | 1409 | 1788 | 2102 | 2869 | 3309 | 3703 | 4260 | 5032 |
| Public administration, other services | 814 | 1172 | 1786 | 2455 | 2708 | 2796 | 3229 | 3281 | 4260 | 4793 |
| Less imputed bank charges | (92) | (156) | (228) | (224) | (372) | (520) | (721) | (850) | (901) | (954) |
| GDP at factor cost | 7460 | 10032 | 14010 | 20606 | 26140 | 29653 | 32396 | 36102 | 39890 | 42257 |
| Monetary* | 5239 | 7106 | 10205 | 13843 | 17316 | 17798 | 19554 | 21451 | 23110 | 23518 |
| Subsistence* | 2221 | 2926 | 3805 | 6763 | 8824 | 11855 | 12842 | 14651 | 16780 | 18739 |

## B. Constant 1966 Price

| | | | | | | | | | | |
|---|---|---|---|---|---|---|---|---|---|---|
| Agriculture, fishing, forestry | 3086 | 3425 | 3315 | 3988 | 4316 | 4326 | 4356 | 4570 | 4184 | 3819 |
| Mining | 135 | 119 | 88 | 77 | 63 | 70 | 81 | 69 | 74 | 72 |
| Manufacturing | 672 | 850 | 900 | 961 | 1017 | 1104 | 1244 | 1048 | 761 | 568 |
| Electricity, water supply | 82 | 106 | 127 | 142 | 148 | 168 | 193 | 212 | 218 | 232 |
| Construction | 291 | 402 | 413 | 360 | 350 | 347 | 406 | 419 | 504 | 479 |
| Commerce | 914 | 990 | 1068 | 1092 | 1195 | 1217 | 1187 | 1284 | 1317 | 1350 |
| Transport, communications | 644 | 869 | 958 | 1034 | 1088 | 1127 | 1170 | 1166 | 1107 | 989 |
| Finance, real estate | 745 | 831 | 929 | 961 | 1003 | 1034 | 1070 | 1111 | 1148 | 1194 |
| Public administration, other services | 772 | 1071 | 1362 | 1684 | 1794 | 2013 | 2107 | 2313 | 2673 | 2907 |
| Less imputed bank charges | (85) | (124) | (140) | (134) | (146) | (153) | (158) | (168) | (174) | (183) |
| GDP at factor cost | 7259 | 8539 | 9020 | 10165 | 10828 | 11253 | 11656 | 12014 | 11812 | 11427 |
| Monetary* | 5122 | 6138 | 6590 | 7231 | 7656 | 8301 | 8682 | 9019 | 9194 | 9039 |
| Subsistence* | 2137 | 2401 | 2430 | 2934 | 3172 | 2952 | 2974 | 2995 | 2618 | 2388 |

* The monetary/subsistence breakdown increasingly misallocates monetary food to subsistence because commercial food is estimated by an obsolete formula and deducted from the basic physical food production estimate.

Source: Adapted from Annual Economic Surveys.

**Table 3.2 Balance of payments estimates 1969–1982** (Sh. 000,000—end of year)

| | 1969 | 1972 | 1974 | 1976 | 1977 | 1978 | 1979 | 1980 | 1981 | 1982 |
|---|---|---|---|---|---|---|---|---|---|---|
| Visible exports (fob) | 1718 | 2258 | 2851 | 4108 | 4519 | 3688 | 4250 | 4723 | 4806 | 4145 |
| Visible exports (cif) | 1790 | 3006 | 5422 | 5350 | 6200 | 8719 | 9073 | 10262 | 9740 | 10357 |
| Trade balance | -73 | -747 | -2571 | -1242 | -1681 | -5110 | -4553 | -5539 | -4934 | -6212 |
| Balance on services | 177 | 256 | 182 | 466 | 602 | 211 | 306 | 157 | 569 | 364 |
| Balance on transfers[1] | 76 | -30 | 351 | 464 | 962 | 147 | 232 | 159 | 193 | 187 |
| Grant aid | na | na | na | na | na | 1125 | 1215 | 896 | 1694 | 889 |
| Current account balance | 180 | -521 | -2038 | -312 | -117 | -3627 | -2800 | -4327 | -2478 | -4772 |
| Net government borrowing | 138 | 821 | 698 | 831 | 723 | 729 | 1136 | 765 | 1370 | 769 |
| Net parastatal borrowing | 58 | 44 | 160 | 55 | 342 | 378 | 240 | 279 | 397 | 345 |
| Net private borrowing | 17 | -7 | 15 | -1 | 38 | -58 | 3 | 35 | 5 | 7 |
| Suppliers credits | na | na | na | na | na | na | 473 | 536 | 834 | 127 |
| Other capital movements[2] | -62 | 11 | 22 | -349 | -120 | -35 | -76 | -37 | -733 | -314 |
| Special transactions[3] | 7 | 36 | 51 | — | 213 | -97 | 425 | 1162 | 651 | 1761 |
| Errors and omissions | -175 | 124 | 70 | -69 | -106 | -2 | -234 | -380 | -53 | -406 |
| Net reserve changes[4] | 163 | 507 | -1023 | 156 | 993 | -2227 | 437 | 18 | 77 | -473 |
| Arrears | — | — | — | — | — | 481 | 802 | 1224 | -22 | 1198 |

1. Excluding grant aid from 1978 onward.
2. Includes commercial credit.
3. Balance of payments support and IMF transactions.
4. + Indicates reserve *increase*.

*Sources:* Bank of Tanzania, World Bank.

**Table 3.3 Public finance/gross domestic product ratios 1961–1980** (stated as % of GDP)

| | 1960/61 | 1963/64 | 1966/67 | 1969/70 | 1972/73 | 1975/76 | 1977/78 | 1978/79 | 1979/80 | 1980/81 | 1981/82 |
|---|---|---|---|---|---|---|---|---|---|---|---|
| Recurrent revenue | 13.0[3] | 14.2 | 15.5 | 20.1 | 22.8 | 20.9 | 21.7 | 21.6 | 22.6 | 20.3 | 21.6 |
| Recurrent expenditure[1] | 13.6 | 13.7 | 15.5 | 19.5 | 21.1 | 19.8 | 19.8 | 26.0 | 27.5 | 22.1 | 24.5 |
| Capital expenditure[2] | 2.6 | 2.9 | 4.5 | 7.8 | 7.0 | 12.0 | 11.8 | 15.1 | 15.8 | 11.3 | 11.3 |
| Total expenditure | 16.2 | 16.6 | 20.0 | 27.3 | 28.1 | 31.8 | 31.6 | 41.1 | 43.3 | 33.4 | 35.8 |

*Sources:* Adapted from 'Twenty Year Review' Annex Tables on Gross Domestic Product and Trends in Government Finances: *Financial Statement and Revenue Estimates* (various years); World Bank, *The Economic Development of Tanganika.*

*Notes:*   1. Includes debt service in full. Technically debt redemption should not be included.
  2. 'On budget' items only.
  3. Excludes colonial welfare and development payments.

**Table 3.4 Money supply and domestic credit formation, 1975–1982 (Sh. 000,000 at June 30)**

| Year | Currency in circulation | Money supply (M3) | Domestic Bank Lending* Government | Domestic Bank Lending* Enterprise | Total |
|------|------|------|------|------|------|
| 1975 | 1,421 | 4,694 | 1,856 | 2,919 | 4,775 |
| 1976 | 1,760 | 6,027 | 3,016 | 3,322 | 6,338 |
| 1977 | 1,789 | 6,598 | 2,845 | 3,325 | 6,167 |
| 1978 | 2,059 | 7,457 | 3,309 | 4,038 | 7,392 |
| 1979 | 2,677 | 9,590 | 6,222 | 5,619 | 11,841 |
| 1980 | 3,903 | 12,106 | 9,025 | 5,998 | 15,023 |
| 1981 | 4,873 | 14,618 | 11,943 | 6,659 | 18,602 |
| 1982 | 6,335 | 18,716 | 15,333 | 7,414 | 22,747 |

* Bank of Tanzania plus National Bank of Commerce.
*Source:* Bank of Tanzania

# Index

fall in food crop
production, 1970s 136,
137, 140
food output, imports and
aid, 1974 and 1981 335
minimum prices policy
136, 137
slow growth pre-1973
119, 216
spare land 335
sugar cane expansion 132,
133, 136–7, 140
variations in sown areas
and productivity 137
balance of payments
current account and
variation in reserves,
1971–81 118
debt service ratio, 1971–
82 119, 124
effects of oil price rises
124
from 1974 to 1981 142
international impact on
123–4, 138
post-1973 problems 119–
20
Central Bank 136
Electrobras
borrowing by 134
energy
Alcohol National
Programme to replace
petrol 129, 130–3, 135,
140, 333
coal 129, 134–5
electricity 134, 135
fuel oil in steel
production 135
industrialisation based on
cheap energy 127–8,
333
*Modelo Energetico
Brasileiro* 129–30
nuclear 129, 333
oil prospecting 129, 134,
140, 333
policies to deal with crisis
in 128–30

pricing policy 133–4
ratio of imported oil to
export earnings 331
relation between domestic
prices and cost of
imported oil, 1973–81
133
relation between electric
and oil prices, 1973–80
134
road transport's
dependence on oil 128,
130
use of alcohol in road
transport 131–2, 333
wood 135

exports 114, 127, 323, 344
agricultural 135, 137, 140
average annual growth,
1970–82 123, 322
Befiex promotion
programme 123, 124,
138
commodity price falls,
1981–2 116, 137, 138–9
diversification of markets
and 124
manufacturing 34, 116,
123
price increases, 1971–
81 115–16
price indices, 1971–81
117
primary 114
quantum indices, 1971–81
141
to OPEC countries 319,
320, 323
value and composition,
1971 and 1980 114

growth pattern 118–20, 138,
139, 318
debt-sustained' growth
118, 140, 313, 321–2,
343
from 1974 to 1980 126
GDP 114, 126, 127, 134,
325

migrant labour in 302
balance of payments, 1974–81
305
Central Bank of Jordan 294,
296, 297
creation of 285–6
economic position 286–7
concentration round
capital 287
high educational
standards and 288
services bias in 287
problem of excess demand
288–9, 290, 291
shortage of natural
resources 286–7
structural disequilibrium
289
effect of PLO-Israeli conflict
on, 1967–71 286
exchange rate policy 301
devaluation of 1971 301
pegging of dinar to SDR
301, 304
exports
by function and region,
1971–81 307
casualty of exchange rate
policy 301
expansion 300, 301
to OPEC countries 319
fiscal policy 298–300
domestic revenue, 1972,
1975 and 1980 300
growth of government
budget expenditure
299
reduction in expenditure
growth, 1980 299
taxation 299, 300
foreign finance 302–3, 321
Arab aid 302, 319, 320
dependence on aid and
loans 287, 289, 290,
291, 295, 296, 304, 318
sources 302, 303
strategic factors behind
302
growth 287

determinants of, 1970s
288–95
development indicators
288
effect of surrounding
Middle East unrest on
292–3
imports 290, 291
by function and region,
1971–81 307
dependence on 290
import substitution 300–1
investment programme,
1976–80, and 291–2
luxury goods, 1970s 290
partial coverage by
exports 290
price changes, 1972–9
294, 295
incomes
effect of Palestinian
refugees in reducing
302
increases, 1970s 302
maldistribution 290–1
inflation 304, 339
class structure and 293–4
consumer price index,
1970–80 306
during 1970s 294
economic policy and 295–
304
exchange rate policy and
301
imported 285, 294, 295,
304
ineffectiveness of
monetary policy against
297
policy options 295–6
rates, 1970–82 338
taxation and 300
wages and 302
investment
capital expenditure by
economic activity,
1976–80 291, 292
dependence on grants and
loans 291

increased imports through
291–2
limited opportunities for
298
Jordan Valley 286
migrant workers from 287,
288, 329
importance of remittances
from 289, 290, 291,
295, 304, 318, 319, 320
migrant workers in
Egyptian 302
Ministry of Supply 303
monetary policy 298–300
increase in banking
sophistication 296
ineffectiveness against
inflation 297
interest-rate policy 297–8
monetary expansion,
1973–6 296
objectives 297
reduction in lending 296–
7
specialist financial
intermediaries created
298
population 286
high growth rate 287
ratio of imported oil to export
earnings, 1970 and
1982 331, 332
size 286
state trading 303–4
subsidies 303, 329
unemployment rise, 1980s 302
West Bank
added to Jordan, 1947–8
286
economic importance to
Jordan 286
trauma of loss of, 1967
286
Jordanian Tanning Company 301


Kamori, D.J.M. 52
Kenya 56

Kim, H.T. 176
Kim, June 169
Kim, Prof. Kwang S. 172
Korea, Republic of 145, 146, 152,
158, 160, 169–70
authoritarian government
172–3
balance of payments 182, 186
from 1971 to 1981 193
Bank of Korea 175
devaluations 178, 180, 182,
184, 187, 188
economic development policies
170–7
centralised policy
formation 173
demand management
187, 343
encouragement of foreign
capital inflows 170,
172
energy saving 177
export-oriented growth
170, 172, 177, 180, 188,
189, 321–2
first five-year plan, 1962–
6 173
governmental role 170,
172–3, 343
investment 170, 173, 175
labour force and 170,
171, 343
move into capital-
intensive industries
173, 175, 178, 184–5,
189
preference for growth
over income
distribution 173
promotion of
industrialisation 170,
172, 343
protectionism 344
search for oil supplies 177
use of domestic capital
and savings 170, 175–6,
189
economic prescription for 188–
90

ethanol plant 107
exports 93, 96, 98
  diversified structure of
    94–5
  growth, 1971–81 102, 104
  volume, 1960–80 327
GDP 93
  growth of output, 1970–
    82
    82   316, 317
  growth of real, 1960s–70s
    315
  increase in 95, 96, 102
gross foreign exchange
  reserves, 1978–80 102
impact of international events,
  1964–78 95–7
  debt problems, post-1978
    96
  early assistance from
    Britain 95
  steady growth, 1964–78
    95–6
imports 96, 98
  foodstuffs 106
  fuel 93, 94, 106, 109
  growth in, 1972–80 102
  manufactures 94
independence achieved, 1964
  95
inflation 107–9, 339
  imported and domestic
    rates 108
  rates, 1970–82 338
macroeconomic adjustment,
  1979–81 97–104
  borrowing and debt
    servicing 99–102, 104,
    313, 321, 323
  costs to economy of fall in
    growth and investment
    102–3, 109–10, 313
  debt rescheduling 317
  effect of heavy
    government spending
    98
  problem of worsening
    terms of trade 97, 98,
    102, 104

market orientation in
  economy 95, 106
migrant workers from
  reduction in 107
  remittances from 318, 319
net foreign assets, 1977–81
  101, 102
population 93, 94
wage fall, 1970s 107, 314, 327
Manufactures
  world market price index,
    1955–70 18
  post-SWW explosion in 25–6,
    34
Marquez, G. 240
Marshall Plan 17
Mexico 216
Mishalani, Philip 260, 285
Morgan Guaranty
  *World Financial Markets* 42

Nyerere, Press. J.K., of Tanzania
  52

Oil
  cheapness and abundance,
    1950s–60s 17
  decline in production, 1970s
    26
  development of smaller oil
    companies, by 1970 32
  effect of increased prices,
    1970s 23
    on developing countries
      330–4
  industrial countries'
    dependence on, 1970 32
  nationalisation of supplies 33
  'participation agreements' on
    oil industry 33
  post-SWW domination of
    major oil companies 31–2
  price rises, 1970s 29, 33
  quadrupling of production,
    1950–68 26
  reserves change ownership,
    1971–2 33

structural change in market,
late 1960s to 1979 31–4
theories about price 33–4
world market price index,
1955–70 18
*See also* separate countries
Organisation for Economic Cooperation and Development
(OECD) 312
Organisation of Petroleum
Exporting Countries
(OPEC) 223, 231, 242, 247
concessions obtained in
1960s 32
formation 32
growth of financial
institutions controlled
by 45
market interventions 31,
32, 33
official aid and loans 43,
44, 44–5, 278, 303, 318,
319, 320, 323

Park, Pres., of S. Korea
assassinated, 1980 187
Perez, Pres. Carlos Andres, of
Venezuela 250, 253
Peron, Gen.
death 201
Pisani, Commissioner Edgard 52
Porta, F. and Rama, C. 256
Portugal 269
Prebisch-Singer thesis 34

Reboucas, 0. 114

Sadler, Peter 220
São Paulo, Brazil
farming credits in 136
Saudi Arabia
consumer price index, 1970–80
306

Seers, Prof. Dudley 2, 3
Serra, J. 119
Silva Pinto, L.F. da and
Rodrigues, J.A. 134
Simonsen, M. 121
Singapore 145, 158, 159, 160
manufacturing exports 34
Soviet Union
becomes grain importer 30–1
Spain 154, 269
Sri Lanka 69, 71
agriculture
drive for food production
82–3
food output, imports and
aid, 1974 and 1981 335
harvest failure, 1975 87
land reforms, 1972 84, 86
subsidies for producers
336
banking 80
Central Bank 80, 89, 91
off-shore 80
Special Foreign Currency
Banking Units 80
crisis policies 79
energy
consumption 75
Government Oil Refinery
79, 86
price rises, 1970s 86, 90,
332
ratio of imported oil to
export earnings, 1970
and 1982 331, 332
subsidies 79, 332–3
exports 79–80
as % of GNP 78
Export Promotion Zone
88
major commodities, 1952–
81 77
petroleum 79, 86
promotion from 1977 88
rise and fall in, 1960–80
75, 78–9
to OPEC countries 319
volumes and earnings,
1950–80 78

Foreign Exchange Entitlement
  Certificate (FECC) scheme 83,
  88
foreign finance 321
  OPEC aid, 1980–2 320
foreign trade indicators, 1952–81
  76
Freedom Party (SLFP)
  in government 81, 82, 83
GNP 75
  growth of output, 1970–82
    316
  imports plus exports as % of
    78
  rise in growth, from 1967 83,
    84, 86, 91, 314
  Government Food
    Commissioner 82, 83
  high expectation of life 77
  high literacy rate 77
  inflation 75, 91, 339
    rates, 1970–82 338
  Mahaweli River Valley Project
    88
  migrant workers' remittances
    79, 86, 89, 91, 318, 319, 332
  population 75, 81
  responses to external price
    changes, 1960s 81–4
    crisis of 1966–7 82
  deficit financing 82
  devaluation, 1967 81, 82
  domestic credit creation 82
  drive for food production and
    import substitution 82–3
  economic management policies
    81
  economic structure unchanged
    81
  external borrowing 84
  Foreign Exchange Budget,
    1963 82
    Foreign Exchange
      Entitlement Certificate
      (FECC) scheme 83, 88
    growth rate 81, 315
    import controls 82
    movement of selected
      indicators 83

responses to external price
  changes, 1970s 84–92
  debt service ratio 89
  dismantling of controls,
    from 1977 88
  economic indicators of
    change 85
  exchange rates 84, 88, 89
  financing external
    resources gap 86, 87,
    89
  five-day week adopted
    86, 90
  fluctuations in value of
    rupee, 1977 87–8
  foreign assistance, 1977–
    81 90
  growth rate 88, 314, 315
  import liberalisation from
    1977 88
  import reduction 87
  increase in fuel prices 86
  land reforms, 1972 84, 86
  phase I – 1971–3 84, 86
  phase II – 1974–6 86–7
  phase III – 1977 and after
    87–92
  reduction of budget
    deficit, 1981 91
  rise in employment 88, 89
  rise in interest rates 89
  rise in public debt 88–9
  rise in wages and prices
    87, 88, 89–90
  subsidies for food imports
    86, 88, 328, 336
  terms of trade 87
size 75
terms of trade
  decline in 81, 314
  in 1970s 87
tourism 79, 80, 332
  expansion in 1970s 86
United National Party 81
  in government 81, 82, 87,
    91
wages
  control of 79
  income distribution,

1953–78  91, 344
rises, 1970s  87, 88
welfare programmes  79
cuts in  317
Structural features of economies  4
in relation to adjustment
policies  4
Syria
consumer price index, 1970–80
306


Tanzania
agricultural policy  60–1
failure of storage policy
61, 314, 334
grain deficits, 1973–4  314
balance of payments
management  64, 71
effective until 1977  64
failure from 1978  64
bribery in  67
corruption and profiteering
condemned  67
credit budgeting  60
development pattern impact
66
domestic political constraints
71
economic crisis, 1979–81  57–8,
65, 66, 317
moves toward, 1977–8  57
emergence programme, 1975–
6  56–7, 65, 66
advantage of coffee boom
57
bridging finance  57
problem of increased oil
prices and drought  56,
65
'produce/invest' approach
56–7
exchange rate adjustment  64–
5
devaluation of 1982  65,
339
Tanzanian disagreement
with IMF  68–9

exports  53, 54
decline from mid-1960s
54
export–import imbalance
55
limited future for  68, 345
to OPEC countries  320
volume, 1960–80  327
external finance  55, 57, 321,
323
unlikelihood of major aid
increases  68–9
fiscal policy  59–60
annual recurrent
expenditure  59–60
bank borrowing  60
capital expenditure  60
taxation  59
food
fall in output  334
output, imports and aid,
1974 and 1981  335
rise in prices  334
foreign exchange crisis, 1970–2
56
fuel policy  62–3
energy sources  52–3
gas development  63, 66,
333
hydroelectric capacity  62–
3, 66
petroleum  56, 62, 333
ratio of imported oil to
export earnings, 1970
and 1982  331
Giffen (interior) good paradox
in  69
growth
GDP  52
in output, 1970–82  316
in real GDP, 1960s–70
315
rate, 1961–79  52
imports
control of  339
increase of  70
makeup  52, 53, 54–5

Fifth Plan (1977–81) 265,
  266, 278, 281
Sixth Plan (1982–6) 282
political climate 282
  pressure groups 282
  riots of January 1984
  282–3
population 260, 261
  density 260–1
postponement policies 277–80
price support and subsidies
  278–80, 328–9, 336, 343
  decrease in, 1982–3 281,
    317
  financed by petrol taxes
    334
  inflation and 279, 280
  Price Equalisation Fund
    (PEF) 279, 281, 282
  pricing system 281
prudent financial management
  in 346
size 260
Socialist Destourian Party 276
terms of trade
  in 1960s 264
  in 1970s 263, 268–9, 270,
    325
tourism 271, 272, 325, 326
  decline, 1982–3 282
  receipts from 271
  tourist sources 272
trade deficit 282
  rate of growth, 1971–81
    264
trade unions 263, 282
  UGTT 276
unemployment 263
urbanisation 261, 265


Uganda 54, 56
  war with Tanzania 54, 57, 58,
    67
United Kingdom
  decline in growth, 1970–1 22
  economic relations with Irish
    Republic 145, 146, 151, 157
  inflation, 1970–81 152

United Nations Conference on
  Trade and Development
  (UNCTAD) 29
    Integrated Commodities
      Programme 71
    UNCTAD/UNDP study on
      balance of payments
      adjustment 2

United States of America
  balance of payments, 1960–79
    21
  becomes leading economic
    power 19
  decline in economic growth
    rate, 1970s 22, 23
  dollar as main reserve
    currency 20
  dollar devaluation, 1970s 20
  foreign direct investment in
    developing countries, 1950–
    79 37
  foreign direct investment in
    industrial countries, 1950–
    79 37
  grain market, 1947–75 30–1
  increase in domestic
    consumption of oil, 1960s–
    early 70s 32, 33
  political motive in foreign aid,
    1960s 38
  post-SWW foreign aid 17, 37
  post-SWW international
    economic system and 14
  problems of balance of
    payments for 19–20
  reaction to world recession
    340, 341
  terminates assistance to S.
    Korea, 1960s 172
  terms of trade in relation to S.
    Korea, 1971–81 180, 181
  Triffin dilemma on
    international liquidity and
    20
  US–Venezuela Trade Act 248

Uruguay
  manufacturing exports 34

export reduction by 1983
247
nationalisation, 1976 241
price fall, 1983 247
production, 1950–83 243
receipts, 1950–83 243
reversal of oil price trends
242, 243
subsidies 328
unmanageable costs 328
terms of trade
evolution of 245
rise in, 1978–81 325
trends, 1968–81 246
Trade Act 248
world prices' impact on 252–9
imported inflation 256–7
oil prices 252–6
rise in industrial interest
rates 257

Wells, John 117
Wilde, Oscar 1
World Bank 26, 37, 232, 312, 341
and Malawi 100, 106
and Sri Lanka 75, 79, 81

and Tanzania 55, 58, 59, 64,
71
and Tunisia 261, 278
classification of Irish
Republic 145
classification of Irish
Republic 145
classification of Tunisia 260
'distortion index' 106
*World Development Report
1982* 75, 81
World prices
impact on development 13
World trade
growth, 1820–1980 16
growth-stagnation cycle 16
post-SWW growth rates 16
problem of US balance of
payments deficit and 20
*See also* International market
trends
Yugoslavia
manufacturing exports 34

Zambia
borrowing difficulties with
dollar 101